Forced Migrants
in
Nordic Histories

Edited by

**Johanna Leinonen, Miika Tervonen,
Hans Otto Frøland, Christhard Hoffmann, Seija Jalagin,
Heidi Vad Jønsson and Malin Thor Tureby**

**HUP HELSINKI
UNIVERSITY
PRESS**

Published by
Helsinki University Press
www.hup.fi

First published in 2025

Cover design by Ville Karppanen.
Cover photo by TK-Kivi, Finlandia Kuva, 1944. Finnish Her-
itage Agency, Ethnographic Picture Collection.
Print and digital versions typeset by Jukka Lauhalahti.

ISBN (Paperback): 978-952-369-130-8
ISBN (PDF): 978-952-369-131-5
ISBN (EPUB): 978-952-369-132-2

https://doi.org/10.33134/HUP-32

The full text of this book has been peer reviewed to ensure high
academic standards. For full review policies, see http://www.hup.fi/

VERTAISARVIOITU
KOLLEGIALT GRANSKAD
PEER-REVIEWED
www.tsv.fi/tunnus

Suggested citation:
Leinonen, Johanna, Miika Tervonen, Hans Otto Frøland, Christ-
hard Hoffmann, Seija Jalagin, Heidi Vad Jønsson and Malin Thor
Tureby, eds. 2025. *Forced Migrants in Nordic Histories*. Helsinki:
Helsinki University Press. https://doi.org/10.33134/HUP-32.

To read the free, open access version of this book
with your mobile device, scan this QR code:

Contents

Figures and Tables

Every effort has been made to identify copyright holders and obtain their permission for the use of illustrations. Notification of any additions or corrections that should be incorporated in this volume are greatly appreciated.

Figures

Tables

Acknowledgements

This volume is the result of the dedication and collaborative efforts of many individuals. First, we wish to express our sincere gratitude to the Joint Committee for Nordic Research Councils in the Humanities and Social Sciences (NOS-HS) for funding the project *Histories of Refugeedom in the Nordic Countries* (2020–2023), from which this book has emerged.

This volume developed within a broader framework of scholarly collaboration. We extend our gratitude to all those who contributed to and participated in the three workshops organized by the *Histories of Refugeedom* project, which were instrumental in shaping this publication. We offer our deepest thanks to the keynote speakers—Heaven Crawley, Noora Kotilainen, Tony Kushner, Philip Marfleet, Stephen Naron, Saima Nasar, Katarzyna Nowak, Christine Schmidt, Machteld Venken, and Zoë Waxman—for their insightful lectures and generous engagement with the participants' work. We are also grateful to the doctoral students and postdoctoral researchers who presented papers at the workshops, contributing to the scholarly discussions that informed our work as editors.

We are thankful to the two anonymous referees for their thoughtful comments and suggestions. Finally, we warmly thank research assistants Yasemin Murr and Otso Metsola (Centre of Excellence in Law, Identity and the European Narratives, University of Helsinki, Finland) for their valuable help in editing Chapters 2 and 5.

Contributors

Dalia Abdelhady is an associate professor of sociology at Lund University. Her research examines how immigrant communities navigate institutional structures in their new homes. Through numerous publications, she analyzes immigrant experiences across global cities, media representations of refugees, and the complex dynamics of integration. Her scholarship brings crucial postcolonial perspectives to migration sociology, examining both structural constraints and individual agency while contributing to academic and policy discussions on migration and integration.
ORCID: https://orcid.org/0000-0002-9447-0390

Outi Autti, PhD and associate professor (docent), specializes in multidisciplinary research in the fields of environmental sociology, cultural studies, rural studies, and human geography at the University of Oulu. Her research is rooted within communities at the forefront of today's climate, ecosystem, and land rights issues, and she leads the project *Muistin marginaalista*, focusing on the social and cultural history of the Lapland War and postwar reconstruction.
ORCID: https://orcid.org/0000-0002-9624-9585

Tine Brøndum is a postdoctoral researcher at the Danish School of Education, Aarhus University. She earned her PhD in pedagogy in 2017 from the University of Southern Denmark. Brøndum was previously a postdoctoral researcher at the University of Copenhagen, Section for Education, where she conducted research on forced migrants' memories and narratives of arriving in Denmark as refugees. Her research interests focus on forced migrants' experiences with reception and integration policies in Denmark, narrative, and memory, as well as educational pathways, including ethnic, social, and gender segregation in higher education.

ORCID: https://orcid.org/0000-0003-0953-8889

Íris Ellenberger is an associate professor at the Faculty of Subject Teacher Education, University of Iceland. Her scholarship centers on migration and transcultural history, particularly focusing on Danish–Icelandic relations in the nineteenth and twentieth centuries. Her work examines transculturation and contact zones in Iceland from 1890 to 1920, analyzing how newcomers navigated cultural tensions and social transformation in Reykjavík. Beyond migration history, she studies marginalized communities in Iceland, including her research on LGBTQ+ history. Her work provides insights into the historical dynamics of inclusions, exclusions, and social change in modern Iceland.

ORCID: https://orcid.org/0000-0001-7879-4814

Martin Englund is a PhD student in history and teacher educator at Södertörn University. He is in the final stages of his PhD project, "We, the Expelled" ("Vi, de fördrivna"), which is both a public collection at the Nordic Museum (Nordiska museet) and his doctoral research. "We, the Expelled" collects and researches the historical experiences of the Polish Jewish forced migrants who arrived in Sweden between 1967 and 1972 as a result of the antisemitic campaign in Poland. His research interests include oral history, Jewish history, and hermeneutics.

ORCID: https://orcid.org/0000-0001-6543-8765

Hans Otto Frøland is a professor of contemporary history at the Department of Modern History and Society, Norwegian University of Science and Technology, Trondheim. He holds a doctorate in history from the same university (1993). He has been adjunct professor at UiT, the Arctic University of Norway, Tromsø. His current research interest lies within the field of war and society, resource conflicts, and legacies of war and conflict.

ORCID: https://orcid.org/0009-0000-9292-6289

Vendula V. Hingarová is an assistant professor at the Department of Scandinavian Studies at Charles University. She teaches courses in

Scandinavian and Latin American history and Czech–Scandinavian relations. She holds a PhD in Latin American history from Charles University (2011) and a master's degree in Scandinavian and Hispanic studies from the same university (2003). Her research focuses on transnational migration, forced labor, and memory of war.
ORCID: https://orcid.org/0009-0002-8300-0075

Christhard Hoffmann is a professor emeritus of modern European history at the University of Bergen. He completed his PhD in history in 1986 at the Technical University Berlin (Center for Research on Antisemitism), where he also worked as a researcher and assistant professor (1987–1994), followed by positions at UC Berkeley (1994–1998) and the University of Bergen (1998–2022). He has developed special research interests in the history of migration and minorities; antisemitism and Jewish history; and public uses of history and memory.
ORCID: https://orcid.org/0000-0001-5662-0768

Aleksi Huhta is a postdoctoral researcher at the Department of Philosophy, History, and Arts at the University of Helsinki. He completed his PhD history in 2018 at the University of Turku. He holds the title of associate professor (docent) in migration history from the University of Turku (2022). His research interests include migration history, Finnish-American history, labor history, deportation history, and the history of imperialism and colonialism.
ORCID: https://orcid.org/0000-0003-3092-9331

Seija Jalagin, PhD, is a senior lecturer of history at the University of Oulu, Finland, and she holds the title of associate professor (docent) in the history of cultural interaction at the University of Turku. In addition to cultural encounters, Jalagin is specialized in gender history, migration, and integration. Recently her research has focused on refugee policies and practices in twentieth-century Finland as well as familial memories of forced migration.
ORCID: https://orcid.org/0000-0002-4762-0288

Heidi Vad Jønsson, PhD, is an associate professor of political history at the University of Southern Denmark. Her research focuses on welfare-migration dynamics, with a particular emphasis on the historical development of integration policies. Her work has significantly contributed

to advancing scholarly understanding and shaping policy debates in this field. In her current research she explores state responses to refugee crisis in the twentieth century and how immigrant categorizations function as tools of governance in the Nordic countries.
ORCID: https://orcid.org/0000-0003-3640-9345

Johanna Leinonen is a research specialist at the Novia University for Applied Sciences, Finland. She completed her PhD in history in 2011 at the University of Minnesota, US. She holds the title of associate professor (docent) in research on multiculturalism from the University of Turku (2016). Her research interests include migration history, forced migration and family separation, family and marriage migration, memory and migration, transnationalism, and gender and migration.
ORCID: https://orcid.org/0000-0003-1359-8235

Henrik Lundtofte is head of the archives of Danish occupation history at Museum Vest in Esbjerg, Denmark. He completed his PhD in history 2018 at the University of Aarhus. He has published books and articles on radicalization and on propaganda in German-occupied Denmark during and after the Second World War and in 2022–2025 is heading a research project supported by the VELUX Foundation on the political and social handling of convicted collaborators, former resistance members, and German refugees in postwar Danish society.

Philip Marfleet is emeritus professor of migration studies at the University of East London. He has published widely on migration and the state; patterns and dynamics of mass displacement; refugee histories; diaspora; racism and exclusion in Europe; and migration and religion. He is the author of *Refugees in a Global Era* (Palgrave Macmillan), and inter alia of the articles "Displacements of Memory," "Explorations in a Foreign Land: States, Refugees and the Problem of History," "'Hidden'/'Forgotten': Predicaments of the Urban Refugee," and "Refugees and History: Why We Must Address the Past." He is also the author of several books on social and political movements in the modern Middle East, most recently *Egypt – Contested Revolution* (Pluto Press).

Victoria Van Orden Martínez is a researcher in the Department of History at Lund University, where she is affiliated with the North

European Center for Research about Antisemitism and the Holocaust at Lund University (NORAH). Originally from the US, she holds a PhD in history from Linköping University in Sweden. Her research interests include forced migrants in history, women's and gender history, intersections of gender and other differences in relation to forced migration, survivors of Nazi persecution in the aftermath of the Second World War and the Holocaust, and the histories of knowledge and medicine.

ORCID: https://orcid.org/0000-0003-4491-5520

Minja Mårtensson is a researcher whose work examines media representations and migration through postcolonial perspectives. With a master's degree in Middle Eastern Studies from Lund University and a bachelor's from Sciences Po Paris, she brings an interdisciplinary approach to understanding global mobility and sociopolitical narratives. Her research investigates how media shapes public discourse around migration and explores the complex intersections between representation, power, and identity in contemporary society. Through her work, she contributes to critical discussions about the role of media in shaping perceptions of migration and migrants in global contexts.

Trine Øland is a senior researcher at University of Copenhagen. She completed her PhD in educational studies at the University of Copenhagen in 2007, was appointed associate professor in educational studies in 2012, and has headed the Section for Education since 2013 and the research group "The History and Sociology of Welfare Work" since 2014, University of Copenhagen. Her research interests include cultural integrationism, colonial and racial histories, migration governance, and how institutional power and inequality affect what it means to be human.

ORCID: https://orcid.org/0000-0002-1286-9032

Saara Pellander is director of the Migration Institute of Finland. She is a doctor of social sciences and holds the title of associate professor (docent) in political history from the University of Helsinki. She has worked and published on issues related to the regulation of cross-border intimacies and bordering policies and their implementation, as well as media representations of (forced) migration and related activism. One of her recent articles in *Media History* (28:2/2022), coau-

thored with Noora Kotilainen, analyzes media images of refugeeness since the 1930s in Finland, linking them to racialized and global political hierarchies in visual arrangements of picturing refugees.
ORCID: https://orcid.org/0000-0002-0432-4390

Päivi Pirkkalainen is a lecturer of sociology at the Department of Social Sciences and Philosophy in the University of Jyväskylä. She completed her PhD in sociology in 2013 at the University of Jyväskylä and holds the title of associate professor (docent) from the University of Helsinki (2023). Her research interests include migrant participation, transnationalism and diaspora, deportations, and emotions and affect.
ORCID: https://orcid.org/0000-0003-3705-0899

Kristina Stenman is a doctoral candidate in the doctoral program of the Faculty of Law at the University of Helsinki. The theme of her dissertation in the field of comparative legal history is the development of asylum law in the Nordic countries in the 1970s to 1990s. She has a master of laws from the University of Helsinki. Her research interests include human rights, particularly in the field of asylum and migration, and equality law, particularly from the perspective of ethnic minorities and migrants. She is currently the non-discrimination ombudsman in Finland.

Miika Tervonen is a university researcher and an associate professor (docent) at the University of Helsinki. He is a historian interested in migration, minorities, nationalism, coloniality, and borders in the Nordic nation/welfare states. Tervonen received a PhD at the European University Institute, Italy (2010). He leads a Research Council of Finland–funded project Gatekeeping the Nation that deals with contemporary Finnish and Nordic histories of deportation.
ORCID: https://orcid.org/0000-0003-2762-9629

Malin Thor Tureby is a professor of history and head of research at the Department of Society, Culture and Identity, Malmö University. Her research is situated at the intersections of Holocaust studies, migration studies, and cultural heritage studies. Her current research interests lie in the history of survivors' memory work, the archival and digital practices of cultural heritage institutions, and the history and practice of

shared authority and ethics within Holocaust studies, migration studies, and minority studies.
ORCID: https://orcid.org/0000-0001-8232-8664

Sjamme van de Voort is a postdoctoral researcher at Vrije Universiteit Amsterdam, currently working on history and cultural memory in agricultural communities in Brazil and the Netherlands. He earned his PhD in Latin American Studies from the University of Nottingham in 2021. His research interests span cultural memory, migration studies, sustainability history, and human rights, with a focus on Cuban and Chilean diasporas. His interdisciplinary approach integrates memory studies with a wide array of methodologies through oral history.
ORCID: https://orcid.org/0000-0003-0550-9503

Introduction

Johanna Leinonen

Novia University of Applied Sciences

Miika Tervonen

University of Helsinki

This anthology delves into the histories and historiographies of forced migrants in the Nordic countries – Denmark, Finland, Iceland, Norway, and Sweden – during the twentieth and twenty-first centuries. The book's motivation stems from the relative invisibility of forced migrants, broadly defined here as those whose departures are marked by involuntariness (such as refugees, asylum seekers, deportees, and internally displaced people), within Nordic historical writing. We argue that the marginalization of histories of forced migration in narratives of the Nordic past has obscured a constitutive element in the formation and imagining of the Nordic societies from the nineteenth century to the present. Peter Gatrell lamented in 2016 that historians have been slow to wake up to the fact that, while nation-states produce refugees, refugees can also make states. From this perspective, it is not enough to write histories of certain refugee groups; instead, as Gatrell argues, historians need to consider seriously the role that refugees have had in shaping the twentieth century. Population displacements

How to cite this book chapter:
Leinonen, Johanna and Miika Tervonen. 2025. "Introduction." In *Forced Migrants in Nordic Histories*, edited by Johanna Leinonen, Miika Tervonen, Hans Otto Frøland, Christhard Hoffmann, Seija Jalagin, Heidi Vad Jønsson and Malin Thor Tureby, 1–17. Helsinki: Helsinki University Press. https://doi.org/10.33134/HUP-32-1.

and the displaced people themselves have been integral to "to war and peace, statebuilding, economic development, nationalism, and the construction of memory and identity" (Bon Tempo 2014, 1650–51). Furthermore, as Frank and Reinisch (2014, 477) argue, refugees are "barometers of intolerance" in the sense that states' responses to the needs of displaced people tell something about the ideological groundings of the states.

We take inspiration from these scholars to begin exploring the role of displacements and the displaced in the development of the Nordic region. As our overview in Chapter 2 illustrates, early modern and modern Nordic societies have experienced a vast diversity of mobilities among various types of forced migrants. These movements have involved hundreds of thousands of people from different parts of the world, occurring well before the current era of globalization of migration. They have included groups such as Huguenots, slaves sent to Swedish and Danish colonies, refugees of the Russian revolutions, Jews and political refugees from Nazi Germany, Second World War forced laborers and prisoners of war. Later arrivals have included dissidents from the communist Eastern and Central European countries, and refugees with a multitude of backgrounds and histories from all over the World, including migrants identifying with Yazidi, Tamil, Hazara and Roma minority communities, for example. This superdiversity of forced migrants has shaped the Nordic societies in multiple ways, from economy and culture to foreign policy, ideas of "us" and "them," and systems of welfare and border control. Mikael Byström (2014, 620) has pointed out, for example, that Sweden's development into a welfare state took place side by side with its development into a country of immigration, and that the emerging welfare system made use of the methods tried and tested in the handling of Second World War refugees.

The marginalization of such connections has narrowed the understanding of the past and contributed to exclusionary policies and discourses (Gatrell 2013; Horsti 2019). Public memory of forced migration tends to be short and highly selective. Meanwhile, historians have increasingly begun to examine specific movements of forced migrants, including in the Nordic countries. However, research still often focuses on high-profile cases that have already received a lot of attention in their own time, and approaches these as separate cases, unintegrated into broader national, regional, or global frameworks. This conforms to a broader pattern where episodic histories of forced migration are often "packed away in national boxes" (Frank and Reinisch 2014, 479; see also Stone 2018a), rendering them inaccessible to broader analysis or international audiences.

This volume aims to partially address these gaps by presenting the first anthology focused on these movements within, between, to, and from the Nordic countries. While many of the chapters focus on case studies in one of the five Nordic countries, most of them also highlight the fundamentally transnational nature of histories of forced migration. The Nordic countries – consisting of two formerly multinational empires (Sweden and Denmark), three later-emerging nation-states (Norway, Finland, and Iceland), and colonized territories (e.g., Greenland, the Faroe Islands, Sápmi) – have deep historical ties and long traditions of influencing and cooperating with each other in terms of migration policies. In the postwar period, the Nordic countries formed an area of free movement that remains exceptional in the depth of social rights that it allows to Nordic citizens. While internationally famous for the extensive welfare systems developed during this period, the Nordic countries also share a tradition of relatively strict control over their borders and access to social membership (e.g., Brochmann and Hagelund 2011; Tervonen 2022). From this background, we focus on the twentieth and twenty-first centuries, a period characterized by increasing control of migration by nation-states on one hand and mass-scale refugee movements sparked by warfare, revolutions, and decolonization on the other.

Displaced histories

Migration and mobility have overall been marginal topics in Nordic national narratives (see Chapter 2; also Tervonen 2014), and the movements of forced migrants have been particularly absent. This reflects a broader European tendency to imagine the past as "sedentary," and migration to and from nation-states as exceptional. Leo Lucassen (2005, 13–14), for example, notes how historical amnesia regarding past mobilities renders migration a "permanent exception." Yet extensive scholarship makes it clear that mobilities to, from, and within Europe have been characteristic and, indeed, constitutive of European societies (e.g., Page Moch 2003, 1). While historians have started to correct the distorting sedentary lens on the past, the imagery of stable, self-contained nations continues to shape both public and scholarly debates.

Indeed, the marginalization of histories of forced migration has also been evident within the expanding fields of migration studies and forced migration research, where contemporary perspectives from the social sciences and humanities have tended to dominate. Philip Marfleet noted in 2007 that "there is a dual problem of disinterest among historians in refugee matters and an aversion among specialists in forced migration vis-à-vis history" (2007, 136). A 2017 overview of Nordic migration research thus highlighted a need to bring historical and social scientific research into deeper conversation with one another (Pyrhönen, Leinonen, and Martikainen 2017). As a concrete example of this disciplinary gap, major European conferences on migration, such as the biannual Nordic Migration Research conference and the annual IMISCOE[1] conference, frequently feature few (if any) historical panels, which tend to be attended by a handful of highly specialized scholars (an occurrence that the editors of this book have witnessed multiple times over the years). While an increasing number of scholars are working toward bridging this gap between history and social sciences, it still visibly exists.

The tendency to disregard past forced migrations is not only a scholarly issue. Kleist (2017) argues that the ahistorical approach to forced migration leads to a situation where the arrival of refugees is repeatedly treated as a surprise by policymakers, the media, and society at large. Consequently, each "refugee crisis" appears unprecedented and exceptional, and subsequently a threat (Lucassen 2005). This, in turn, may lead to ad hoc policy responses, as witnessed during and after the so-called "refugee crisis" of 2015–2016. By ignoring history, we lack perspective on the root causes of population displacements as well as states' responses to them (Gatrell 2016).

Lucassen attributes the tendency to disregard the past migrations to "the dominant ideology of the nation-state" – the idea of European nation-states as homogeneous nations with stable and static populations (Lucassen 2005, 13–14, 198). This characterization applies to Nordic histories particularly well. Several researchers have pointed out that the Nordic countries have been imagined, and consciously constructed in history writing, as exceptionally homogeneous (e.g., Keskinen, Skaptadóttir, and Toivanen 2019; Ryymin 2019; Tervonen 2014). Mobile people and minorities have fitted poorly with homogenizing national narratives. The myth of homogeneity can be traced back to the latter half of the nineteenth century, to the nation-building processes aiming "to incorporate peripheral domains and to assimilate diverse peoples into the body politic" (Häkkinen and Tervonen 2004, 22; see also Keskinen, Skaptadóttir, and Toivanen 2019). It has influenced various aspects of society, including social policies, media representations, political discourses, and questions of belonging (see, e.g., Leinonen 2012). National identities have been constructed around notions of cultural and racial homogeneity (e.g., Hervik 2019; Keskinen, Skaptadóttir, and Toivanen 2019; Chapter 4 in this volume). The idea of a homogeneous society has further influenced the development of social policies and welfare systems, creating boundaries for social inclusion (Keskinen, Skaptadóttir, and Toivanen 2019).

Our contribution is inspired by the recent scholarship challenging the idea of homogeneity and highlighting the diverse and dynamic historical nature of Nordic societies (see also Schmidt 2021; Tervonen and Leinonen 2021). We are further motivated by an interest in the agency of forced migrants and countering their portrayal as helpless victims (Gatrell 2013, 2019; Malkki 1995). Scholarship on refugee histories tended until recently to focus on the actions of nation-states and nongovernmental organizations (NGOs) during "refugee crises," rather than on the experiences and memories of the forced migrants themselves. This is partially due to a lack of primary sources that capture the personal experiences and voices of forced migrants. However, this also relates to the questions of memory and remembrance. Traditionally, the field of memory studies focused on national history narratives and political uses of the past; migration research and memory studies were two separate fields (see, however, Creet and Kitzmann 2011; Glynn and Kleist 2012; Palmberger and Tošić 2016). Thus, the mnemonic agency of people whose lives have been marked by (forced) migration received only scant attention from scholars. Recently, however, scholars have examined, for example, linkages between state history narratives, migration policies, and discourses of belonging (Glynn and Kleist 2012), displaced people's memories of home (Pineteh 2005), and how the collective memory of injustices can forge a shared identity for people dispersed in different countries (e.g., Tiilikainen 2003). Many chapters in this volume bring out the mnemonic agency of forced migrants (see Chapters 8, 11–14). The acts of remembering (and forgetting) may provide forced migrants with an opportunity to reconstitute themselves in the face of a possibly traumatizing past (Eastmond 2016; Palmberger and Tošić 2016).

The processes of remembering and forgetting are political, as they create and reproduce normative and informal boundaries of inclusion and exclusion. All nations engage in selective remembering of their pasts, but the marginalization or erasure of memories of forced migration can have particularly harmful consequences (Lacroix and Fiddian-Qasmiyeh 2013). Dan Stone (2018b) has argued that Europe's avoidance of publicly remembering its failures when dealing with refugees in the 1930s, and with Holocaust survivors and other displaced people during and after the Second World War, contributes to Europe's current inability to respond to the plight of refugees. Scholars of contemporary forced migrations have observed that, in public and political discourses, forced migrants are often portrayed either as "victims," in need of humanitarian aid and the charity of European benefactors, or as "villains," potential threats to the supposedly peaceful and harmonious European nation-states (e.g., Sirriyeh 2018; see also Chapter 6 in this volume). Against these discourses, it is all the more important to consider how these images of forced migrants have been historically formed, and how forced migrants are historical actors shaped by historical and geopolitical contexts.

Categorizing forced migration

Forced migration can be regarded as a subcategory under the broad umbrella of different types of migratory movements. However, the boundary between forced and voluntary migration is often blurry (Erdal and Oeppen 2018). Forced and voluntary migration are not mutually exclusive categories but operate on a continuum. Despite this categorical blurriness, it is evident that there are migrations where coercion plays a significant role. For example, Marta Erdal (2020, 109) has recently suggested that forced migration is movement where "coercion plays a significant role, or where the decision to leave is in some sense involuntary – not the preferred choice for the individual involved," while underlining the conceptual blurriness of the term. Researchers have pointed out that in accordance with such broader view, also slavery is a form of forced migration (Carpi & Owuso 2022).

In this book, by using the concept of forced migrants, we consider not only refugees and asylum seekers but also internally displaced people, evacuees, deportees, and forced laborers – that is, people who have moved because an element of coercion or involuntariness was involved. We examine different forms and categories of forced migration in order to gain a temporally and geographically more diverse understanding of displacement in Nordic histories. Our exploration focuses not only on wartime forced migrations but also on other, more "mundane" involuntary movements, such as deportations (see Chapters 3 and 10).

We are aware of the critical insights that highlight how labels such as "forced migrants" may not align with people's self-perception or identity. Additionally, labels assigned to individuals, for example through migration governance, can significantly impact their migratory trajectories and, indeed, their life course. As Erdal and Oeppen (2018, 983) observe,

> In migration and refugee studies, the discourse and "labels" (Zetter 1991, 2007) to describe migrants sway the selection of responses – which are "acceptable" and which are even possible – to those migrants. Whether someone is discursively presented as an economic migrant or a refugee, for instance, majorly influences their treatment by immigration authorities and humanitarian actors … In other words, a key part of the discursive significance of identifying people as refugees, vis-à-vis other migrant categories, is how they will be treated.

As this excerpt aptly illustrates, categories used in migration research are embedded in and shaped by political discourses. As Diana Thomaz (2018) notes, the processes of categorizing fundamentally shape migrants' rights, ascribe identities, and even influence their chances of survival. Media also create categories and framings for people moving out of coercion, and wield considerable power in how forced migration and groups of forced migrants are viewed in society at large (see Chapters 7, 9, and 10). Therefore, it is important to consider these categories as constructs, developed in specific historical, societal, and political circumstances and, consequently, intimately tied to states' bordering practices and their exercise of power over who can move and on what terms (see Chapters 4 and 5).

Moreover, the term "forced migrant" is a classification used by academics and international organizations such as the EU for certain types of migration, and it does not necessarily reflect how individuals experiencing migration would define or categorize themselves. Research has shown that migrants may resist or distance themselves from categories such as "refugees" and "asylum seekers," as these labels carry their own, often racialized, meanings and stigmas. For example, Hack-Polay et al. (2021) find that forced migrants often see their refugee identity as a liability and strive to adopt identity categories perceived as advantageous in their new social systems. Despite these shortcomings, we maintain that the category of a forced migrant is useful in an academic context, where the purpose is, for example, to analyze the distinct historical and sociopolitical contexts that coerced people to leave, to unearth people's experiences and agency in these coercive circumstances, to highlight the significant human rights issues forced migrants may face, or to inform more effective policies and programs tailored to their unique circumstances. The key is to remain critical of the categories and concepts used, and recognize the academics' role in creating and maintaining categories related to people on the move (see Crawley and Skleparis 2018; Erdal and Oeppen 2018; Stone 2018b).

The history of the concept of the "refugee" poignantly illustrates the political and historically contingent nature of categories. In the Geneva Refugee Convention of 1951, a "refugee" became defined in international law as a person forced to flee his or her home country because of persecution, war, or violence. The refugee category was "built on a heroic image of mostly male and White individuals persecuted by oppressive regimes" in the Eastern Bloc (Thomaz 2018, 201). The convention's geographical and temporal restrictions were removed in the 1967 Protocol to the Convention, as it was evident that people were escaping conflicts, persecution, and repression globally. However, a large proportion of the world's displaced people – those who did not cross an international border – were excluded from this convention and became invisible to state authorities, policymakers, and scholars (Marfleet 2007).

In the decades following the end of the Cold War, the image of the refugee became racialized, victimized, and increasingly associated with people fleeing from the Global South. Importantly, many categories related to forced migration also carry legacies of European colonialism (Mayblin 2017). For example, these legacies have shaped welfare regimes and influenced the inclusion or exclusion of people placed in certain categories, such as refugees or asylum seekers (Jubany and Mayblin 2024). Currently, these categories are at the center of public and political debates concerning migration in Europe, as noted above.

Simultaneously, access to asylum and refugee status has become ever more restricted for migrants originating from outside Europe, to the point that European states circumvent or directly violate international refugee law. As Chapter 6 shows, colonial legacies also shape the lives of forced migrants in the Nordic countries today.

Framing and outline of the book

This book is the result of the collaboration between the editors in the Nordic networking project "Histories of Refugeedom in the Nordic Countries," funded by the Joint Committee for Nordic Research Councils in the Humanities and Social Sciences (NOS-HS)[2] in 2020–2023. The project organized an exploratory workshop series to take the first steps toward understanding how histories of forced migrations have shaped the Nordic region. Our key goal was to examine gaps and silences in histories of forced migration and how memory politics influence what is memorized (or forgotten) over time with regard to these movements.

The first workshop, "Who Is a Refugee? Shifting Categorizations in Forced Migration," organized on April 22–23, 2021, by the University of Oulu and the Migration Institute of Finland, probed into the negotiations, acts of resistance, and lived experiences connected with the categorizing of forced migrants. The second workshop, "Refugees Remembered or Forgotten? Forced Migration and Public Memory," organized by the University of Bergen on January 20–21, 2022, combined research on forced migration and memory studies to explore how forced migration features in public memory. The third workshop, "Refugees and Survivors in Historiographies and Public History: Archives, Voices and Memories," organized by Malmö University on June 16–17, 2022, brought together forced migration research and Holocaust studies to explore the role that refugees, forced migrants, and genocide survivors have played and continue to play in documenting, remembering, and producing knowledge about genocide, oppression, and forced migration.

The workshops played a crucial role in the forming of the intellectual rationale of this book. Many of the contributors to this anthology also presented their work at one or more of the workshops. Altogether, by discussing the regulation of forced migration, representations of forced migrants in public discourses, and memories of forced migrants, the book brings out how the marginalization of these histories in narratives of the Nordic past has obscured a constitutive element in the formation and imagining of Nordic societies in the twentieth and twenty-first centuries. In what follows, we describe each theme of the book in more detail.

The book begins with a section close to the heart of our project: reflecting on the ways in which forced migrants have been near-systematically omitted from the national narratives that emerged in Europe as part of nation-building processes from the nineteenth century onward. In Chapter 1, Philip Marfleet creates a global overview of a striking paradox: while "the construction of the modern order over the past 400 years" has been achieved through processes involving vast numbers of involuntary migrants, these migrants have been by and far omitted from history. Following this, in Chapter 2, the editors of this volume turn to the Nordic case. We make the first overview of forced migrants in Nordic historiographies, asking to what extent their experiences have been included or excluded in history writing.

The second theme of the book is the regulation of forced migration. Forced migration to, from, and within the region has taken place in the context of welfare/nation-states developing side by side with migration control and a sharpening division between citizens and aliens (Torpey 1998). The countries have adopted policies, legal systems, and practices to regulate the entry, reception, aid, and statuses of forced migrants. The regulation of forced migration in the Nordic countries stems from and has developed according to national and international value systems and conventions but also depends on the contemporaneous political and economic needs.

In Chapter 3, Aleksi Huhta starts the section by forming a novel perspective on the history of Nordic transatlantic migrations through examining deportations from the US and Canada to Finland during the Great Depression of the 1930s. Huhta focuses on deportees' experiences and postdeportation lives. He argues that the study of deportations can add much to our understanding of the history of forced migration in the Nordic region, while pointing also to the oft-ignored role of the receiving states in shaping deportation practices.

In her overview of regulations of forced migration in Iceland in the second half of the twentieth century, Íris Ellenberger (Chapter 4) emphasizes the very restrictive tradition of the country and the lack of an explicit refugee policy. Forced migrants, whom the United

Nations High Commissioner on Refugees (UNHCR) recommended for resettlement, had to undergo a very strict selection process, based on criteria of utilitarianism, assimilability, and whiteness, before they were accepted to Iceland. These selection criteria preferred children, women, families, and industrial workers, often young adults. Refugees from Vietnam, the only non-European group of forced migrants during the twentieth century, were exposed to specific assimilatory measures (a change of name). In addition to refugee groups coming on request by the United Nations, there was the possibility to enter the country as individual asylum seekers. Only one applicant, however, received formal refugee status in Iceland before the year 2000.

In Chapter 5, applying an approach of comparative legal history, Kristina Stenman explores the responses of four Nordic countries to the refugees from the Balkan Wars during the 1990s. Placing Nordic asylum policies into a wider historical perspective, she identifies two opposing trends: attempts at harmonization and coordination on the one hand, and an increasing focus on national self-interest on the other. Both trends also shaped the responses to the Balkan refugees. While the four countries supported the humanitarian efforts of the UN and cooperated with the UNHCR to provide temporary protection to Bosnian refugees, the legal and policy choices vis-a-vis the asylum seekers were made in a strongly national setting. Even though all countries in the end offered permanent residence to the Balkan refugees, Stenman regards their initial reaction as a turning point toward a more national asylum policy.

In Chapter 6, Tine Brøndum and Trine Øland examine the incorporation of refugees in Danish integration and welfare practices, in the context of the contemporary neoliberal shift from welfare to workfare, and the continuing impact of colonial hierarchies on Danish "interior frontiers" (Stoler 2022). Brøndum and Øland juxtapose their interviews with integration workers with those with individuals who have fled to Denmark since the 1990s. The chapter identifies processes through which refugees are cast as unemployed people in need of activation programs, while incorporated into a "sinking ladder" of low-paid work.

Our third theme focuses on forced migrants in public discourses, investigating how forced migrants have been discussed and framed in, for example, political debates and media texts. The purpose is to study discourses and rhetoric related to forced migration as products of temporally and politically specific settings. While public discourses may tell something about their target groups, they typically expose more about the multilayered and contested views evolving in the host society.

Henrik Lundtofte (Chapter 7) elaborates the Danish underground resistance discourse of the anticompassion campaign directed toward the around 200,000 citizens from Prussia and Pomerania whom the Nazi government evacuated to Denmark in spring 1945. He suggests that it was not only a response to Nazi brutalities but served as well to signal support for the Allied course in the context of a former strong state collaboration with Germany during the occupation. The refugee discourse was instrumentalized.

In Chapter 8, by elaborating the life of Polish Ludwika Broel-Plater, who worked to document the history of Polish refugees in postwar Sweden, Victoria van Orden Martínez examines how Broel-Plater was invisible in the contemporary Swedish refugee discourse, despite her continuous efforts at the Polish Research Institute. While suggesting that Broel-Plater was subjected to deliberate silencing, the author also constructs an alternative narrative, showing Broel-Plater's accomplishments in the refugee discourse. By doing this, Martínez reveals that dominating refugee discourses may neglect the existence of refugees' agency.

Since the Second World War, Sweden has cultivated a humanitarian self-image as a refuge for asylum seekers, despite recent restrictive policies. Chapter 9, by Dalia Abdelhady and Minja Mårtensson, examines how mainstream media's portrayal of refugees from former Yugoslavia, Syria, and Ukraine shapes public perception, balancing humanitarian ideals with restrictive measures. Through historical analysis, the study reveals the institutional logic of media representation, which often juxtaposes Sweden's humanitarian image with narratives of refugees as fraudulent or threatening. The chapter underscores the media's role in politicizing refugees and reinforcing national narratives over different contexts and time periods.

In Chapter 10, Päivi Pirkkalainen and Saara Pellander explore the changing Finnish discourse on incoming forced migrants by focusing on justifications applied in the editorials of the country's most influential newspaper, *Helsingin Sanomat*. The study looks for discursive changes as new migration laws have been implemented. They suggest that the justification discourse changed from an emphasis on migrants' rights to one where migrants were represented as a societal threat.

The book concludes with the fourth theme, understanding the totality of the experience of forced migration through personal memories and accounts as well as oral histories. As noted above, state-centered histories typically exclude forced migrants' memories of displacement. Tony Kushner (2006), for example, notes that refugees are almost entirely absent from mainstream history writing, and, if they are included in national narratives, their histories are often instrumentalized in a self-congratulatory fashion, presenting them as helpless victims without agency of their own. The fourth theme thus responds to the repeated call to bring forth forced migrants' personal memories, experiences, and narratives. This enables writing history with forced migrants rather than of them (Banko, Nowak, and Gatrell 2022).

In Chapter 11, Hans Otto Frøland and Vendula V. Hingarová explore how a cohort of Czech forced laborers, whom Nazi Germany brought to Norway during the Second World War, experienced their constraints during the displacement and how this experience was memorialized after the war. The collective experience carried an ambiguity between victimhood on one side and an exciting touristic mood on the other. This ambiguity endured the memorialization processes among the group after their repatriation to Czechoslovakia, as the tropes proved to be resilient throughout the Cold War. Only the discourse of a compensation scheme in the late 1990s seems to have shoved the balance of memory tropes in favor of victimhood.

Outi Autti explores childhood memories of those evacuated to Sweden or Finnish Ostrobothnia during the Lapland War in Finland in 1944–1945 in Chapter 12. Narrated some 70 years after the events in interviews or written recollections, these memories demonstrate that children were exposed to dangers and insecurity, confusion, and chaos, but that they could also find the long evacuation journeys and new environments exciting. Even if the narratives followed the so-called "model stories," formed collectively in families and local communities during the postwar decades, they also contain some individual memories that seem ambivalent or incompatible with the prevailing narratives, thus pointing to the importance of studying childhood experiences and their far-reaching effects in later life.

Chapter 13, by Martin Englund, investigates how one person's historical experiences of forced migration, displacement, survival, and integration during and after the Second World War can be understood in relation to the historical consciousness regarding the Holocaust and forced migration in Sweden. The chapter discusses the story of the Swedish Polish Jewish survivor Maria, explaining how Maria survived the Holocaust in the Soviet Union and came to Sweden due to an antisemitic campaign. Through Maria's story, Englund illuminates that survival in the Soviet Union is not a topic that easily integrates into the normative aims of the public Holocaust memory in Sweden.

The book is concluded by Sjamme Van De Voort's Chapter 14, which employs five life-story interviews with women belonging to the Chilean diaspora in Gothenburg, Sweden, to explore diasporic cultural memory in the context of exile. Chilean migrants are reaching old age in their adopted countries, during a time when the Chilean constitution is being rewritten in a democratic process that involves the heritage of the diasporic community. In this context, the chapter offers an exploration of cultural dynamics among migrants situated at a crossroads of history where interpretations of the past and expectations of the future in Chile are framed by the spatial dimension of migration.

Together, the chapters in this book illuminate the multifaceted dimensions of forced migration in the Nordic context, offering a rich tapestry of scholarly perspectives. They not only enrich research on (forced) migration in the Nordic countries but also highlight the enduring impact of forced migration on both refugees and host societies, thereby contributing to a more comprehensive understanding of these nations' histories.

Notes

1 International Migration, Integration and Social Cohesion.
2 Research Council of Finland (RCF)/NOS-HS decision number 329015. The following research projects have contributed to the publishing of this book, as the editors were working within these projects during the editorial process: Refugee Journeys: Narratives of Forced Mobilities (RCF, decision numbers 344707 and 317751); Mobile Futures: Diversity, Trust, and Two-Way Integration (Strategic Research Council within RCF, decision numbers 364421 and 345401); Centre of Excellence in Law, Identity and the European Narratives (RCF, decision number 353311); Gatekeeping the Nation: Deportation at Finnish Borderscapes from the Cold War to Europeanization (RCF, decision number 347906); The Ethical Dilemmas of Digitalization: Vulnerability and Holocaust Collections (Swedish Research Council (SRC), Dnr. 2021-01428); Memory and Activism: Survivors Remembering, Commemorating and Documenting the Holocaust (SRC, Dnr. 2023-05994).

Bibliography

Banko, Lauren, Katarzyna Nowak, and Peter Gatrell. 2022. "What Is Refugee History, Now?" *Journal of Global History* 17 (1): 1–19. https://doi.org/10.1017/S1740022821000243.

Bon Tempo, Carl. 2014. "Review of the Making of the Modern Refugee". *The American Historical Review* 119 (5): 1650–51. https://doi.org/10.1093/ahr/119.5.1650.

Brochmann, Grete and Anniken Hagelund. 2011. "Migrants in the Scandinavian Welfare State: The Emergence of a Social Policy Problem". *Nordic Journal of Migration Research* 1 (1): 13–24. https://www.jstor.org/stable/48711192.

Byström, Mikael. 2014. "When the State Stepped into the Arena: The Swedish Welfare State, Refugees and Immigrants 1930s–50s". *Journal of Contemporary History* 49 (3): 599–621. https://doi.org/10.1177/0022009414528259.

Carpi, Estella and Portia Owusu. "Slavery, lived realities, and the decolonisation of forced migration histories: An interview with Dr Portia Owusu". *Migration Studies* 10 (1): 87–93. https://doi.org/10.1093/migration/mnac009

Crawley, Heather and Dimitris Skleparis. 2018. "Refugees, Migrants, Neither, Both: Categorical Fetishism and the Politics of Bounding in Europe's 'Migration Crisis'". *Journal of Ethnic and Migration Studies* 44 (1): 48–64. https://doi.org/10.1080/1369183X.2017.1348224.

Creet, Julia and Andreas Kitzmann, eds. 2011. *Memory and Migration: Multidisciplinary Approaches to Memory Studies*. Toronto: University of Toronto Press.

Eastmond, Marita. 2016. "Shifting Sites: Memories of War and Exile across Time and Place". In *Memories on the Move: Experiencing Mobility, Rethinking the Past*, edited by Monika Palmberger and Jelena Tošić, 19–46. London: Palgrave Macmillan. https://doi.org/10.1057/978-1-137-57549-4_2.

Erdal, Marta Bivand and Ceri Oeppen. 2018. "Forced to Leave? The Discursive and Analytical Significance of Describing Migration as Forced and Voluntary". *Journal of Ethnic and Migration Studies* 44 (6): 981–98. https://doi.org/10.1080/1369183X.2017.1384149.

Erdal, Marta Bivand. 2020. "Migration, Forced". In the *International Encyclopedia of Human Geography*. Second edition, edited by Audrey Kobayashi, 105–110. Amsterdam: Elsevier.

Frank, Matthew and Jessica Reinisch. 2014. "Refugees and the Nation-State in Europe, 1919–59". *Journal of Contemporary History* 49 (3): 477–90. https://doi.org/10.1177/0022009414529318.

Gatrell, Peter. 2013. *The Making of the Modern Refugee*. Oxford: Oxford University Press. https://doi.org/10.1093/acprof:oso/9780199674169.001.0001.

Gatrell, Peter. 2016. "Refugees – What's Wrong with History?" *Journal of Refugee Studies* 30 (2): 170–89. https://doi.org/10.1093/jrs/few013.

Gatrell, Peter. 2019. *The Unsettling of Europe: How Migration Reshaped a Continent*. New York: Basic Books.

Glynn, Irial and J. Olaf Kleist, eds. 2012. *History, Memory and Migration: Perceptions of the Past and the Politics of Incorporation*. Basingstoke: Palgrave Macmillan. https://doi.org/10.1057/9781137010230.

Hack-Polay, Dieu, Ali B. Mahmoud, Maria Kordowicz, Roda Madziva, and Charles Kivunja. 2021. "'Let Us Define Ourselves': Forced Migrants' Use of Multiple

Identities as a Tactic for Social Navigation". *BMC Psychology* 9: 125. https://doi.org/10.1186/s40359-021-00630-6.

Hervik, Peter, ed. 2019. *Racialization, Racism, and Anti-Racism in the Nordic Countries*. Cham: Springer International Publishing. https://doi.org/10.1007/978-3-319-74630-2.

Horsti, Karina, ed. 2019. *The Politics of Public Memories of Forced Migration and Bordering in Europe*. Cham: Palgrave Macmillan.

Jubany, Olga and Lucy Mayblin. 2024. "Asylum, Welfare and Colonialism in Europe: Who Belongs, and Who Deserves?" *Social Sciences* 13 (11): 1–6. https://doi.org/10.3390/socsci13110620.

Keskinen, Suvi, Unnur Dís Skaptadóttir, and Mari Toivanen, eds. 2019. *Undoing Homogeneity in the Nordic Region: Migration, Difference and the Politics of Solidarity*. Abingdon: Routledge. https://doi.org/10.4324/9781315122328.

Kleist, J. Olaf. 2017. "The History of Refugee Protection: Conceptual and Methodological Challenges". *Journal of Refugee Studies* 30 (2): 161–69. https://doi.org/10.1093/jrs/fex018.

Kushner, Tony. 2006. *Remembering Refugees: Then and Now*. Manchester: Manchester University Press.

Häkkinen, Antti and Miika Tervonen. 2004. "Ethnicity, Marginalization and Poverty in 20th Century Finland". In *New Challenges for the Welfare Society*, edited by Vesa Puuronen, Antti Häkkinen, Anu Pylkkänen, Tom Sandlund, and Reetta Toivanen, 22–39. Joensuu: University of Joensuu.

Lacroix, Thomas and Elena Fiddian-Qasmiyeh. 2013. "Refugee and Diaspora Memories: The Politics of Remembering and Forgetting". *Journal of Intercultural Studies* 34 (6): 684–96. https://doi.org/10.1080/07256868.2013.846893.

Leinonen, Johanna. 2012. "Invisible Immigrants, Visible Expats? Americans in Finnish discourses on immigration and internationalization". *Nordic Journal of Migration Research* 2 (3): 213–23. https://doi.org/10.2478/v10202-011-0043-8.

Lucassen, Leo. 2005. *The Immigrant Threat: The Integration of Old and New Migrants in Western Europe Since 1850*. Urbana, IL: University of Illinois Press.

Malkki, Liisa H. 1995. "Refugees and Exile: From 'Refugee Studies' to the National Order of Things". *Annual Review of Anthropology* 24 (1): 495–523. https://doi.org/10.1146/annurev.an.24.100195.002431.

Marfleet, Philip. 2007. "Refugees and History: Why We Must Address the Past". *Refugee Survey Quarterly* 26 (3): 136–48. https://doi.org/10.1093/rsq/hdi0248.

Mayblin, Lucy. 2017. *Asylum after Empire: Colonial Legacies in the Politics of Asylum Seeking*. Lanham, MD: Rowman and Littlefield International.

Moch, Leslie Page. 2003. *Moving Europeans: Migration in Western Europe since 1650*. Bloomington: Indiana University Press.

Palmberger, Monika and Jelena Tošić, eds. 2016. *Memories on the Move: Experiencing Mobility, Rethinking the Past*. London: Palgrave Macmillan. https://doi.org/10.1057/978-1-137-57549-4.

Pineteh, Ernest. 2005. "Memories of Home and Exile: Narratives of Cameroonian Asylum Seekers in Johannesburg". *Journal of Intercultural Studies* 26 (4): 379–99. https://doi.org/10.1080/07256860500270221.

Pyrhönen, Niko, Johanna Leinonen, and Tuomas Martikainen. 2017. *Nordic Migration and Integration Research: Overview and Future Prospects*. Oslo: NordForsk.

Ryymin, Teemu. 2019. "Forgetting Diversity? Norwegian Narratives of Ethnic and Cultural Homogeneity". In *Undoing Homogeneity in the Nordic Region: Migration, Difference and the Politics of Solidarity*, edited by Suvi Keskinen, Unnur Dís Skaptadóttir, and Mari Toivanen, 21–34. Abingdon: Routledge. https://doi.org/10.4324/9781315122328.

Schmidt, Garbi. 2021. *Den første ghetto*. Aarhus: Aarhus Universitetsforlag.

Sirriyeh, Ala. 2018. *The Politics of Compassion. Immigration and Asylum Policy*. Bristol: Bristol University Press. https://doi.org/10.46692/9781529200430.

Stone, Dan. 2018a. "Refugees Then and Now: Memory, History and Politics in the Long Twentieth Century: An Introduction". *Patterns of Prejudice* 52 (2–3): 101–6. https://doi.org/10.1080/0031322X.2018.1433004.

Stone, Dan. 2018b. "On Neighbours and Those Knocking at the Door: Holocaust Memory and Europe's Refugee Crisis". *Patterns of Prejudice* 52 (2–3): 231–43. https://doi.org/10.1080/0031322X.2018.1433038.

Stoler, Ann Laura. 2022. *Interior Frontiers: Essays on the Entrails of Inequality*. Oxford: Oxford University Press. https://doi.org/10.1093/oso/9780190076375.001.0001.

Tervonen, Miika. 2014. "Historiankirjoitus ja myytti yhden kulttuurin Suomesta". In *Kotiseutu ja kansakunta: miten suomalaista historiaa on rakennettu*, edited by Pirjo Markkola, Hanna Snellman, and Ann-Catrin Östman, 137–62. Helsinki: Suomalaisen Kirjallisuuden Seura.

Tervonen, Miika. 2022. "Borders of Welfare: Mobility Control and the Nordic Welfare States". In *Nationalism and Democracy in the Welfare State*, edited by Pauli Kettunen, Saara Pellander, and Miika Tervonen, 150–65. Northampton: Edward Elgar.

Tervonen, Miika and Johanna Leinonen, eds. 2021. *Vähemmistöt muuttajina: Näkökulmia suomalaisen muuttoliikehistorian moninaisuuteen*. Turku: Siirtolaisuusinstituutti.

Tiilikainen, Marja. 2003. *Arjen islam. Somalinaisten elämää Suomessa*. Tampere: Vastapaino.

Thomaz, Diana. 2018. "What's in a Category? The Politics of Not Being a Refugee". *Social & Legal Studies* 27 (2): 200–218. https://doi.org/10.1177/0964663917746488.

Torpey, John. 1998. "Coming and Going: On the State Monopolization of the Legitimate 'Means of Movement'". *Sociological Theory* 16 (3): 239–59. https://doi.org/10.1111/0735-2751.00055.

Zetter, Roger. 1991. "Labelling Refugees: Forming and Transforming a Bureaucratic Identity". *Journal of Refugee Studies* 4 (1): 39–62. https://doi.org/10.1093/jrs/4.1.39.

Zetter, Roger. 2007. "More Labels, Fewer Refugees: Remaking the Refugee Label in an Era of Globalization". *Journal of Refugee Studies* 20 (2): 172–92. https://doi.org/10.1093/jrs/fem011.

PART I

National histories and forced migrations

CHAPTER 1

Unheard and forgotten – silencing refugees in modern history

Philip Marfleet

University of East London

Abstract

Forced migration has been integral to the making of the modern state. For almost four centuries nation-states have been constructed through processes of inclusion and exclusion associated with mass movements of population – both within and across state borders. But, with rare exceptions, those affected by displacement do not appear on the historical record – their experiences remain "unheard." Why is forced migration largely absent from the archival record and from mainstream history, and what are the implications for researchers today?

This chapter considers how historians address "national" histories – and the implications for those assumed to stand outside or at the margins of national society. It examines processes that shaped the modern state in Europe and North America, and means by which states emerged across the Global South, producing repeated mass displacements that have often been erased from the historical record.

Why have historians silenced forced migrants? What does this suggest about the agendas of mainstream history and the process of

How to cite this book chapter:
Marfleet, Philip. 2025. "Unheard and forgotten – silencing refugees in modern history." In *Forced Migrants in Nordic Histories*, edited by Johanna Leinonen, Miika Tervonen, Hans Otto Frøland, Christhard Hoffmann, Seija Jalagin, Heidi Vad Jønsson and Malin Thor Tureby, 21–44. Helsinki: Helsinki University Press. https://doi.org/10.33134/HUP-32-2.

state-making – and what can we learn from exceptional cases in which refugees or internally displaced persons have been integrated into official narratives?

Introduction

Refugees are embedded in modern history – as much part of the sociopolitical order as territorial borders, sovereign powers, and ideas about citizenship and national belonging. They have nonetheless been excluded from the literature of mainstream history: with rare exceptions, refugees appear only as shadowy figures, barely visible and apparently silent. The paradox is striking: over the past 400 years, the construction of the modern order has been achieved in part through movements involving vast numbers of involuntary migrants. The circumstances and experiences of forced migrants should be of profound importance to those who explore the past but most have been "forgotten": in effect, they have been excluded from mainstream historical research and writing.

The problem is remarkably persistent. In a pioneering study published in the 1990s in which refugee histories were addressed as matters of intrinsic interest, Tony Kushner and Katherine Knox assessed the record of professional historians, observing a "general silence on refugee questions in the discipline [history]" (Kushner and Knox 1999, 4). Twenty years later, little had changed: Dan Stone could still observe historians' neglect of refugees "in their general national, regional or world histories" (Stone 2018, 101). At the same time, focused research on migrants in general and refugees in particular has largely lacked historical perspective. Academic interest in migration that emerged in North America in the early decades of the twentieth century did not embrace history – and migration studies subsequently developed as a field in which history played a minor role. When refugee studies appeared as a discrete area of research in Britain in the 1980s, the editors of the new journal *Refugee Studies* outlined their main disciplinary concerns: history was absent from the list (Zetter 1998, 2). It was 30 years before a special issue of the journal addressed historical matters.

Aversion to historical perspective is evident equally in the Nordic countries. In 2016, ministers of the Nordic states commissioned Nordforsk to assess global migration trends, to review migration and integration research in the region, and to evaluate research infrastructure in the field. The authors of a subsequent report noted the multidisciplinary character of existing work on migration, embracing researchers in the humanities, social sciences, international relations, law, health sciences, psychology, social work and policy, economics, and geography (Pyrhönen, Leinonen, and Martikainen 2017, 26). History was again absent from the list. Niko Pyrhönen, Johanna Leinonen, and Tuomas Martikainen observe that "global migration is still often framed in research in a rather ahistorical manner," adding that many scholars who participated in the study noted the lack of historical perspective when migration was in focus (Pyrhönen, Leinonen, and Martikainen 2017, 26).

Denial

As Chapter 2 in this volume makes clear, there is a long and complex record of forced migrations in the Nordic region, accompanied by "a general historiographical silence" (p. 73) in relation to those affected. This reflects long-established perspectives worldwide among those who compile records of the past. Catherine Hall and Daniel Pick observe that "the politics of remembering and forgetting have long been explicit concerns of historians" (Hall and Pick 2017, 1). They continue: "Remembrance may consolidate an 'imagined community'; so too, may occlusion and erasure – even major archives, of course, have sometimes been 'misplaced' or 'lost' in the service of national interests" (Hall and Pick 2017, 1).

"Loss" of archives is particularly striking during key periods in the construction or reconstruction of the modern state, often associated with political upheaval, violence, and mass migration. The French republican scholar Ernest Renan observed:

> Forgetting, I would even go so far as to say historical error, is a crucial factor in the creation of a nation, which is why progress in historical studies often constitutes a danger for [the principle of] nationality. Indeed, historical enquiry brings to light deeds of violence which took place at the origin of all political formations … Unity is always effected by means of brutality. (Renan 1882, 8)

Early modern France saw tumultuous changes affecting religious, regional, and linguistic groups. In the case of the Calvinist minority, often called the Huguenots, an increasingly centralized state pursued a policy of repression accompanied by directives to practice *oubliance* – "forgetting" (Trim 2011, 17). Philip Benedict notes sixteenth-century edicts asserting that memories of conflict involving the Calvinists should be "snuffed out and set aside as if they had never happened," together with official efforts to suppress events such as traditional religious processions that might stimulate memories of "the troubles" (Trim 2011, 17). In the following century the monarchy asserted uniformity of religion under the Catholic Church, its *dragonnades* forcing Calvinists to convert or to emigrate, and hundreds of thousands left France, becoming the first involuntary migrants of the early modern era to be identified as *réfugiés*.

The Huguenots were not merely unwanted in France: their exclusion was integral to initiatives undertaken by the state to assert a distinct French identity, with religious affiliation the key means of demarcating subjects of the House of Bourbon. The fate of the Calvinists gave evidence of the authority of the absolutist regime and the implications of national belonging in the modern proto-state. Their exile had a demonstrative purpose – *pour encourager les autres*.[1] It was, suggests Nevzat Soguk, a "symptom of statecraft" practiced by those in authority in a state-in-construction:

> In all, the Huguenot displacement was part and parcel of a larger shift in practices of government by which the absolute state would begin to acquire characteristics of a modern centralizing state. (Soguk 1999, 71)

These developments were significant for processes of state formation that would continue throughout the modern era. Refugees were functional to the modern state: others in relation to a national society bounded socioculturally and territorially. At the same time, Soguk suggests, the Huguenot episode contained signs and symbols of the state as a "political location" patrolled by those in authority motivated to secure external borders *and* to shape the population in order the serve "the felicity of the state" (Soguk 1999, 72–73). Refugees were intrinsic to consolidation of the Bourbon regime. Following their expulsion, however, they were also removed from official records and, so far as was practicable, from popular memory. Trim observes that efforts among Calvinist exiles to recall and celebrate their beliefs and practices were subsequently conducted in the context of official denial in France. Here, he suggests, history was in part "a means of ... dissolution" of Huguenot identity (Trim 2011, 13).

As nation-states "proper" began to emerge over the next 100 years, accompanying the rise of commercial and industrial capitalism, refugees became a more and more common feature of European society – others deemed unwelcome among a host of emerging states and complex new borders. By the nineteenth century, "nationalization" was sweeping Europe, nation-states appearing in territories formerly controlled by imperial blocs and/or by consolidation of regional authorities on the basis of ethno-linguistic principles. The process created vast numbers of forced migrants, as "transfers" or "exchanges" realigned specific population groups across borders defined by principles of national identity. In the case of Eastern Europe, Matthew Frank describes a process animated by "fantasies of ethnic unmixing" (Frank 2011, 81). Populations established widely across the region, notably Jews and Roma, were displaced back and forth across new borders. In the Balkans, national movements seeking states based upon ethnoreligious criteria on the European model focused upon the expulsion of Muslims, even when the latter constituted a majority of the population (Chatty 2010, 79).

Narratives of nation

Who established archives and wrote narratives of new and emerging states, shaping histories of these national ventures? Eric Hobsbawm observes of nineteenth-century practice that specialists – archivists, writers, and professional historians – played a key role:

> [T]he history which became part of the fund of knowledge or the ideology of nation, state or movement is not what has actually been preserved in popular memory, but what has been selected, written, pictured, popularized and institutionalized by those whose function it is to do so. (Hobsbawm 1983, 7)

Official narratives play a key role in shaping records of the past. Although popular memory may never be entirely displaced, ideologues of modern states in construction, or those reshaped in the era of the nation-state, have invariably celebrated specific agendas that include foundational accounts of the national collective and projects of national self-assertion vis-à-vis external enemies and internal others. Those displaced as part of the process of national consolidation have rarely had a significant role: excluded by means of what Renan calls "historical error," their circumstances and experiences have routinely been "forgotten."

For much of the nineteenth century, refugees – often known as "exiles" – could be found in most regions of Europe. Repudiated in places of origin, they largely disappeared from those regions' official records, from mass media, and from educational curricula. In receiving states they might be recognized and in rare cases celebrated as incomers whose presence embellished the status of a "host" society. For several decades refugees in Britain were accommodated by governments prepared to receive migrants they viewed as their "enemies' enemies," notably radical activists from France and nationalist opponents of imperial blocs such as Russia and Austria-Hungary. Bernard Porter comments that the refugees were presented officially as "brave freedom-fighters" against foes who were also enemies of the British state (Porter 1979, 4). Here, refugees were mobilized instrumentally to complement the official British narrative. They were situated positively in national history, notably in Samuel Smiles's account of Huguenot migrations to England almost two centuries earlier. Published in 1867, Smiles's *The Huguenots: Their Settlements, Churches and Industries in England and Ireland* was focused less upon the French refugees than on their reception in England, where, wrote the author, "The people crowded round the remarkable sufferers with indignant and pitying hearts … received them into their dwellings, and hospitably relieved their wants" (Smiles 1867, 222). Bernard Cottret observes that Smiles aimed primarily to present the Huguenots as part of "the positive image of Britannia" and contemporary refugees as beneficiaries of "British liberty" (Cottret 1991, 194).

Amnesia

There have been other exceptions to the pattern of "forgetting" – usually when refugees are made to complement national narratives of the "host" society or play a key role in foundational myths of the nation-state. In general, however, refugees have been silenced by what Tony Kushner calls "a deliberate policy of amnesia" among historians (Kushner 2017a, 197). State-building, "statecraft," and mass displacement accompanied European colonialism and the establishment of colonial polities across the Global South. For centuries European powers engaged in projects of mass displacement and transportation. Colonial

administrators, military officials, settlers, and entrepreneurs under-
took mass clearances and programs of enslavement affecting people
who would be viewed today as internally displaced persons or even
as refugees. The colonial state was a key means of ensuring control
over diverse populations and movements of resistance. Agendas for
state construction brought into being novel entities as vast numbers
of people were moved into alignment with borders that violated all
manner of preexisting economic, sociopolitical, and cultural arrangements. Typically the strategy of *divide et impera* privileged certain ethnoreligious communities at the expense of marginalized or excluded
others, while mobile people were a special target for authorities eager
to assert control. Precedents had been set in Europe, where states oper-
ated forms of surveillance requiring statistics, registers, surveys, and
maps – part of the project to identify and control territorial space, fix-
ing places and people within it. In the Global South, mobile communities including pastoralists, hunter-gatherers, and itinerants were the
object of sustained offensives that sometimes forced large populations
across newly established borders: on the basis of twentieth-century
legal definitions they became "refugees."[2] These mass displacements,
including sustained genocidal offensives, were routinely "forgotten."
In the case of the US, Ali Behdad suggests, amnesia became "denial"
(Behdad 2005, 4), as Native Americans were excised from mainstream
history in "a deliberate attempt to cover up records and memories of
the past" (Behdad 2005, 5).

The first genocide of the twentieth century was undertaken in 1904
by German colonial authorities in Namibia (then South-West Africa),
when some 150,000 members of the Herero, Nama, and San ethnic
groups were shot or driven into the Namib desert, where they died of
starvation and dehydration: survivors were, in effect, refugees from the
slaughter. Henning Melber comments on German historians' continuous failure to address the events: "There are different ways and views
to distort the past," he observes. "One of them is the simple denial of
what had happened" (Melber 2005, 139). It was more than 60 years
before scholars in Germany examined the events in detail, finding
ample materials on which to establish "a solid foundation" for assessing the genocide and its consequences in Namibia and in Germany
(Melber 2005, 139). It was another 40 years before officials of the German government acknowledged responsibility on behalf of the state.
A century of denial had involved the military establishment, colonial

administrators, politicians, journalists, archivists, and professional historians in the production of what Reinhardt Kössler calls "a denialist literature" (Kössler 2008, 334).

"Loyalists" and "aliens"

Intensification of national sentiment during periods of war or social tension may make the process of exclusion more marked. Following the American Revolution of 1776 and prolonged conflict with Britain, some 60,000 "Loyalists" associated with the British Crown departed territories of the independent United States of America. This mass migration, which dispersed refugees to British colonial territories worldwide, was not addressed systematically by historians for over 200 years. Maya Jasanoff writes of "scholarly neglect":

> In the United States, the history of the American Revolution was written by the victors, who were chiefly interested in exploring the revolution's many innovations and achievements. Loyalist refugees simply fell outside the bounds of American nationalist narratives. They received scant attention from British historians in turn, as embarrassing reminders of defeat. (Jasanoff 2011, 10)

The largest refugee movement to Britain took place during another historic conflict, when in 1914 some 250,000 Belgians escaping early offensives of the First World War arrived during the course of a few weeks. A reluctant government was compelled to accept them as "our enemy's enemies." Widely distributed across British towns and cities, they often enjoyed close relations with the local population. By 1919, however, all but a handful had been repatriated by state authorities focused upon the presence of "aliens" and challenged by domestic industrial struggles and a surge in radical political activism. The repatriation, observes Hannah Ewence, "descended into an exercise in hasty, even brutal efficiency to rid the country of any refugee who remained":

> those who lingered found themselves the object of increasingly stringent rhetoric which reframed them as a "problem", and their "option" of repatriation replaced by the prospect of forced deportation. (Ewence 2017, 73)

Physical exclusion of the refugees was paralleled by their ejection from British history. It was more than 60 years before their experiences were addressed by Peter Cahalan, whose pioneer thesis highlighted the absence of research on a significant mass movement (Cahalan 1997). He observed: "The Belgians were an ephemeral part of the English scene: they disappeared as quickly as they had come" (Cahalan 1997, 3). Twenty years later, Pierre Purseigle reexamined the Belgian migration, noting that it had been "surprisingly neglected, as if historiography and collective memory alike concurred in marginalising the Western Front refugees" (Purseigle 2007, 427).

As Belgian refugees were arriving in Britain, a series of mass expulsions took place in the Middle East, where the Ottoman Empire was being dismantled by nationalist forces and interventions by both Britain and France. The Turkish nationalist movement sought to assert control of Anatolia, a region of particular ethnoreligious complexity. Its ideologues and military leaders asserted a specific Turkish identity vis-à-vis others from territories of the Empire, producing multiple displacements – of Arabs, Jews, Kurds, and numerous heterodox Christian and Islamic communities.[3] None, however, reached the scale of mass movements of ethnic Greeks and Armenians. In the case of the latter, a genocidal offensive that began in 1915 cost the lives of a million people, most compelled to march to their deaths in the Syrian desert.[4] Survivors were scattered across the Middle East and more widely across continents, so that refugee communities eventually emerged in Europe, Australia, and the Americas.

For decades Turkish historians produced accounts that sanitized the events, integrating them positively into achievements of the new state. The Turkish revisionist historian Doğan Gürpınar comments that the genocide was "ignored, silenced and trivialized … left to the dustbin of history as if the 'Armenian problem' had in some way been 'resolved' for good" (Gürpınar 2016, 218). Successive generations of academics and public intellectuals engaged in "historiographical apology," he suggests, acting with and on behalf of the state and its agenda of denial, as "a cluster of intellectuals mobilized as apparatchik historians" (Gürpınar 2016, 225). In 2015, a century after the first assaults, "official state policy remained stringently denialist," supported by minor modifications in academic practice as some historians, still within the mainstream of statist discourse, introduced a "flexible denialism" (Gürpınar 2016, 236).

Any historical narrative, observes Michel-Rolph Trouillot, is "a bundle of silences" (Trouillot 1995, 58). In the case of Turkey, says Ayhan Aktar, there were sustained efforts to "homogenise" the nation, both by means of mass expulsion and by excision of those affected from the historical record (Aktar 2003, 79). At the same time, migrants who moved to Anatolia as part of population "exchanges" with Greece – the "Ottoman Muslims" – were marginalized within Turkish society. As refugee incomers to Anatolia – seen as the territorial heartland of the national project – they were deemed insufficiently Turkish and characterized, says Çağlar Keyder, as "'others' … who were not really of us" and whose presence disturbed accounts of a unified national collective (Keyder 2003, 49–50).

Partition

"History is the fruit of power," observes Trouillot (1995, xix). Production of historical narratives, he suggests, involves an uneven contribution of competing groups and individuals who have unequal access to the means of such production. Those affected by mass displacement are among the most disadvantaged in the construction of narratives that embrace their specific experience. Involuntary migration invariably involves separation from resources integral to accustomed life. It may fragment or even atomize sociocultural networks, rendering those affected vulnerable to institutional bodies, notably state forces – armies, police, border patrols, immigration authorities – and to powerful ideological agencies including the mass media. Refugees are not rendered powerless – they do not lose agency or the capacity to shape strategies and to act upon them. At the same time, their range of choices is constrained and they face continuing difficulty in addressing their circumstances and in articulating preferences and aspirations. "Unequal access" is emphasized by the disproportion between their resources and institutional means available to those who work in official archives, research centers, academic institutions, and the mass media.

Critical historiography suggests that disregard for refugees is associated with construction and vitalization of dominant narratives of the nation-state *and* with the unequal relationship of displaced people vis-a-vis those who write these accounts. The impact of the partition of colonial India in 1947 was not confined to episodes of communal conflict, ethnic cleansing, and refugee journeys through regions that had in effect become war zones. Partition was soon embedded in the lives of the displaced *and* in the policies and practices of those who shaped the new polities. In the independent state of India, refugees soon disappeared from view, as historians, writers, and educators "forgot" the experiences of millions of citizens. Ideologues of the new state, says Gyanendra Pandey, together with "the long arm of the publishing houses and modern media and the homogenisation of culture," disseminated accounts of national development that centered on the state itself, to the exclusion of those displaced – notwithstanding their experiences (Pandey 2001, 9). Pandey observes that "historian's history," worked "to produce the 'truth' of the traumatic, genocidal violence of Partition and to elide it at the same time" (Pandey 2001, 45).

Following the events of 1947, suggests Tapan Bose, state-building strategies in India emphasized communalism, "politicising all the ethno-linguistic, ethno-religious and tribal groups" – part of a drama of national self-assertion in which subsequent generations of displaced people were systematically excluded and rendered voiceless (Bose 1997, 57). It was almost 50 years before Indian scholars addressed partition as both a historic episode and an enduring feature of Indian society, uncovering what Urvashi Butalia calls "an archive with a difference" that placed refugees centrally within the contemporary Indian experience (Butalia 2001, 214). She observes that mainstream history in India long asserted that partition was "over, done with, a thing of the past" (Butalia 1998, 7). Everyday life told a different story: "all around us was a different reality: partitions everywhere, communal tension, religious fundamentalism, continuing divisions on the basis of religion" (Butalia 1998, 7).

The work of feminist activists and revisionist historians in India who have collected and assessed oral testimony of mass displacement has changed attitudes to partition and the refugee experience. Voices have emerged to challenge mainstream history written, says Shahid Amin, with the aim of constructing an "uncluttered national past" (Pandey 2001, 4). Jonathan D. Greenberg observes that "partition" can only be understood in the context of detailed, specific memories, images, and stories remembered and transmitted by individuals. Testimony and storytelling, however, are set in the context of collective memory and dominant narratives (Greenberg 2005, 90). In India and in colonial Palestine, Greenberg suggests, the partitions of 1947 and

1948 were not only associated with conflict, displacement, and exclusion but also with continuing attempts to interpret their significance in the national context. These efforts privileged certain versions of the partition story over others, heightening some memories and suppressing others with the purpose of mobilizing communities in the service of the "integrative revolution" necessary to build viable independent states (Greenberg 2005, 94). In both cases a disproportion between the resources of official history – associated with institutions of the new polity – and refugee populations rendered vulnerable and exposed, is very striking.

In Palestine, a state of Israel was established to realize the aims of the Zionist movement; Palestinians, rendered stateless, were dispersed widely across the Arab East and into conditions of marginality that would persist for generations. Practices of narrating partition were strikingly different: while Israeli scholars and educators worked intensively through institutions of the new state, Palestinian communities, fragmented and dispersed, lacked resources to record and disseminate their experiences. Elie Podeh observes that for several decades Israeli academics and educators pursued predominantly a "national" approach, with the aim of developing societal awareness of the state-building project (Podeh 2000). This reached into the school classroom by means of instruction and through official textbooks. Podeh quotes Mihael Ziv, head of Israel's Department for Secondary Education, to the effect that: "the values underlying the official historical narrative, as introduced in the classroom, must accord with society's principal values" (Podeh 2000, 72). Material chosen for this purpose, Ziv insisted, had a specific aim:

> [to] instill love and respect for our most important and cherished values, and encourage the young to identify utterly with [Israeli] society's goals, fight for its continued existence and play an active role in its development and progress. (Podeh 2000, 72)

Issam Nassar observes that dispersion of the urban elite in Palestine profoundly affected means of articulating the Palestinian experience (Nassar 2001, 8). Loss of institutional capacities – including archives, libraries, colleges, schools, and access to mass media – meant that communities of the diaspora lacked resources to develop coherent narratives. Palestinian historian Nur Masalha observes: "Narratives of memory and oral history became a key genre of Palestinian historiography – a genre guarding against the 'disappearance from history' of the Palestinian people" (Masalha 2008, 167). It was only in the 1980s that Palestinian scholars began sustained efforts to mobilize these perspectives, alongside Israeli scholars of the revisionist school who challenged mainstream narratives, notably the "national" account of events in 1948 and their outcomes.

Celebrating refugees

Forgetting is integral to the process of narrating national history. "Once a nation is established," observes Michael Billig, "it depends for its existence upon a collective amnesia" (Billig 1995, 35). Such forgetting is purposeful – a sifting of materials through which stories of nation and state are embellished and most displaced people excluded. Refugees may nonetheless be remembered and even celebrated, notably when they are seen as participants in the foundation or consolidation of the state, as with the "Pilgrim Fathers" of the US; Jewish refugees from Europe and the Middle East to Israel; and Calvinist migrants from France to South Africa, commemorated 300 years after their emigration with celebratory literature, a special monument and a museum (Britz 2006). So too with Huguenot migrants to England in the seventeenth century, long seen in mainstream history as "profitable Strangers" – coreligionists who not only brought capital and skills but also ideological resources vis-à-vis a rival state (Kershen 2004). Huguenots were enthusiastically recruited to English colonies in North America: Lisa Clark Diller observes that "promotion of ... empire and extension of English commerce was exactly what the English were happiest about with regards to the Huguenot immigrants," helping to secure their place in the national/imperial narrative (Diller 2011, 110). In Britain the Huguenots have since remained an archetype of the "genuine" refugee, often mobilized in contemporary political discourse as model immigrants against whom others seeking refugee status should be assessed. Tony Kushner observes that, together with Jewish refugees of the mid-twentieth century, they have been prominent among those chosen for "special, positive consideration" – refugees whose stories and the responses to them have been "shaped, or reshaped, to fit certain narrative conventions and expectations" (Kushner 2017b, 59). Today, he suggests, a belief in "decent and fair treatment" of certain immigrants, notably Huguenots and Jews, is "essential to notions of

Britishness" (Kushner 2006, 20). Here, certain refugees are functional to mainstream ideas of national identity, their place in history defined by processes of inclusion/exclusion through which, says Robin Cohen, "the British … are delineating one or other aspect of themselves" (Cohen 1994, 198).

In an important observation about history, contemporary political discourse and refugee policy, Kushner comments that "genuine" refugees of the past "can be used as a stick to hit the modern-day alleged abusers of the system" (Kushner 2006, 20). History is "instrumentalised," he suggests, in order to support highly charged exclusionary agendas "couched … in a discourse of morality" (Kushner 2003, 257). In the case of Jewish refugees to Britain in the 1930s, repeated claims about government "generosity" must be set against years of denial and official rejection of pleas for asylum. In a detailed history of governmental responses to the Jewish predicament during the rise of fascism in Europe, Louise London observes that politicians and officials assessed requests "primarily in terms of British self-interest," with the result that "exclusion was the fate of the majority" (London 2003, 2, 12). When Jewish children – not adult members of their families and communities – were eventually admitted, they were represented as the "saved" – people rescued by British hospitality and whose presence embellished ideas about the nation and its people. For several decades following the Second World War a national self-image cultivated by historians, politicians, religious leaders, and the mass media saw Britain as a sanctuary for Jews – a refuge in which victims of Nazism could be safe in the arms of an embracing society.[5] This selective history of the Jewish refugees continues play a key role in highly charged contemporary debates about immigration and sanctuary.

Memory and change

What are methodologies and guiding principles that can place refugees appropriately within history, recognizing the meaning of their experiences and their significance for the wider society? For Trouillot, the key measure is "extra labour" at the archives, achieving "retrospective significance" vis-à-vis the past (Trouillot 1995, 26). The proposition seems to assume access to ample archival resources. Maya Jasanoff quotes Lorenzo Sabine, the first American historian to address the fate of Loyalist refugees following the War of Independence, on the problem of locating such material. "Men … who become outlaws, wanderers and exiles," he wrote, "such men leave few memorials behind them. Their papers are scattered and lost, and their very names pass from recollection" (Jasanoff 2011, 10). Here, it seems, archives are absent or cannot be located. But Jasanoff takes a different view: "In fact," she says, "it is remarkable how much *does* survive: personal letters, diaries, memoirs, petitions, muster rolls, diplomatic dispatches, legislative proceedings … The challenge is putting it all together" (Jasanoff 2011, 10).

Jasanoff's assertion is important – detailed records are often available for those who wish to locate and assess them. But researchers within the mainstream of professional history have seldom addressed her "challenge." In 1920 Britain's Ministry of Health produced an account of the mass migration of Belgians six years earlier. *Report on the Work Undertaken by the British Government in the Reception and Care of the Belgian Refugees* ran to over 100 pages, giving detailed information on the migrants and their relations with government and local communities (Ministry of Health 1920). This account, together with many official local documents, was freely available but did not draw the attention of researchers. When Cahalan eventually investigated the Belgians' experiences he noted that although they had been "objects of vast interest in England" in 1914 they had subsequently been ignored by historians: "General histories fail to mention them at all or relegate them to a few brief lines," he observed, "Even specialist works ignore them" (Cahalan 1997, 2). After the Belgian repatriation successive British governments worked for decades to inhibit similar mass movements. Immigrants in general and refugees in particular were unwelcome throughout an "Age of Exclusion" during which the state imposed autarkic control of borders (Marfleet 2006, chap. 6). As people widely accepted by public opinion and accommodated in communities nationwide the Belgians violated official agendas – and historians subsequently neglected them. Hall and Pick observe, "[a]s historians are well aware, archives may be technically open, but nobody bothers to look in them for reasons that might include, amongst others, an unacknowledged discomfort at the thought of what they contain" (Hall and Pick 2017, 1).

It is only under specific circumstances that documents become relevant to researchers, who may be compelled to confront dominant ideas and even powerful institutions in order to pursue their work. David MacDonald examines "history wars" in the US, Australia, and Canada.

Intense debates about key issues in history are typically prompted, he suggests, by "catalytic events" such as anniversaries or commemorations and can also develop when revisionist historians seek to counter hegemonic approaches by highlighting experiences of subaltern populations, "exposing instances of strategic forgetting, or 'chosen amnesia'" (Macdonald 2015, 412). Israeli historian Ilan Pappe observes that reassessment of the partition of Palestine in 1948, and its implications for Israelis and Palestinians, has involved "an ideological stance that has touched the most sensitive nerves of [Israeli] Jewish society" (Pappe 1997, 37). During the 1980s, investigation of Israel's state records by revisionist historians involved a critique of foundational myths and assumptions about the origin of the nation-state. Pappe observes that they "mined the archives," including documents that had been available for decades but had seldom been accessed by scholars likely to criticize narratives of national self-assertion (Pappe 1997, 29). Importantly, he suggests, a new generation of historians also critiqued the role played by the country's academic institutions in shaping dominant interpretations of "the Palestine reality" (Pappe 1997, 29). For the first time, mass displacement of Palestinians and their circumstances as refugees found a place in Israeli scholarship.

"Extra work" at the archives may involve intense disputes about their relevance and take in wider issues of scholarly ethics and public responsibility. Such debates have been focused largely on official archives and how their contents are interpreted: many episodes of mass displacement, however, pose special problems. Those involved may not have formal documentation; records have been lost, destroyed, or seized by hostile forces. It is nonetheless possible to mobilize a wide range of sources and research techniques. Kushner and Knox demonstrate that creative use of "gray" literature, diaries, memoirs, and cultural artifacts can establish a meaningful account of the Belgian migration to Britain in 1914 (Kushner and Knox 1999). So too with Joel Beinin's account of Jewish refugees from Egypt, widely dispersed during the 1960s across Europe, North America, and the Middle East. Using all manner of formal records, together with literary materials, cinema and oral testimony, he creates a holistic account of lives before, during, and after migration (Beinin 2005). Oral testimony has become a key resource for understanding contemporary refugee movements. Urvashi Butalia's "archive with a difference" engages directly with those who have experienced mass displacement and/or its outcomes.

To understand India's partition of 1948 and its consequences, she says, official records must be questioned by "turning the historical lens to a somewhat different angle," giving due attention to oral narrative and engaging with memory (Butalia 1998, 13).

Oral history has its origins in the US in the 1930s, later energized by those who collected and disseminated testimony of survivors of the Holocaust.[6] The focus on testimony and biographical materials remains contentious among professional historians, however. Robert Perks and Alastair Thomson suggest that oral history "has challenged the historical enterprise" (Perks and Thomson 2015, ix) and David Nasaw asserts that "[b]iography remains the profession's unloved stepchild," noting that for scholars in the mainstream of the profession it is widely seen as "a lesser form of history" (Nasaw 2009, 573). In refugee-centered research, oral history is nevertheless well-established.[7] Investigating experiences of Colombian refugees, Pilar Riaño-Alcalá suggests that "the axis of memory [becomes] a vital form of action through which individuals make sense of the past, present and future" (Riaño-Alcalá 2008). In an important observation about the value of testimony in challenging dominant narratives, she observes:

> [M]emories, in the case of Colombia's forced migrants, are not attached to a unified national narrative but rather to dispersed, fragmented, and contested narratives of the past and to the complexities of a conflict with a plurality of agents, causes, local histories and alliances. (Riaño-Alcalá 2008, 1)

In countless forced migrations oral testimony subverts dominant narratives – notably those of institutional bodies and of ideologues of the state or of powerful nonstate actors. Assessing the value of such testimony as part of qualitative research, Valerie J. Janesick notes its special importance when "outsiders and peripheral members of society are included" (Janesick 2007, 116). Here, "knowledge of the past can serve to refute myths, half-truths, fabrications, and faulty perspectives" (Janesick 2007, 116). Such projects are often associated with initiatives for social justice: in the field of transitional justice, Anna Bryson notes, they play a key role in addressing legacies of institutional abuse, racism, colonialism, and other historical wrongs (Bryson 2016, 303).

Oral narrative presents specific challenges for researchers. For Edward Said, "collective memory is not an inert and passive thing, but a field of activity in which past events are selected, reconstructed, maintained, modified, and endowed with political meaning" (Said 2000, 185). Memory is fluid, contingent, and an expression of lives in process. It draws upon personal experience inflected by the passage of time and upon "postmemory" – the influence of recollections passed on by family, community, and wider social networks (Van Alphen 2006). In the case of displaced people, typically vulnerable to those endowed with authority, it may also reflect changing relations with institutional bodies. When Palestinians began to assess experiences of mass displacement they did so in the context of diaspora, notably their lives under regimes of close control in Arab states, and the emergence of embryonic national structures in the form of the Palestine Liberation Organization (PLO), strongly influenced by a new middle class located in states of the Gulf. Stein and Swedenburg identify the emergence of an "'intifada culture' of struggle, sacrifice and austerity," reflecting discourses of national liberation and the agendas of the PLO. This began to change as young Palestinians engaged with global cultural influences (Stein and Swedenburg 2004, 12). The refugee experience became more complex, as "intifada culture" was modified by the impact of "national, regional and global circuits" and "diverse histories" (Stein and Swedenburg 2004, 15).

A similar process can be identified in some regions of South Asia. In the case of Hindu communities displaced from East Bengal to West Bengal as part of mass movements in 1947, autobiographical accounts and local community histories have appeared with increasing regularity. Uditi Sen explores how in the writing of personal and "amateur" accounts some memories "feed into history while others are forgotten" (Sen 2014, 39). Refugee experiences have become increasingly disparate, shaped by differences of class and caste, and by localized struggles over access to resources and clashes with those in authority. Formal scholarship has rarely addressed these issues; rather, it has depicted "a nameless and faceless homogeneity" that largely erases refugee agency (Sen 2014, 76).

The Nordic states

The apparent paucity of historical work on refugees in the Nordic states, including oral narrative, suggests a paradox. Organizing a symposium in 2022, Martin Englund and Malin Thor Tureby observed that oral history had become "a vast and diversified field" in the region

(Thor Tureby 2022). Several national museums maintain dedicated oral history archives and in recent years networks of scholars have emerged in Norway, Finland, Sweden, and Iceland. In the case of Denmark, caution and even skepticism among some professional historians has inhibited such developments: here, Sofie Lene Bak tellingly observes, most contemporary historians "have long had a somewhat problematic relationship with oral testimony" (Bak 2016, 9).

Engagement with oral testimony in relation to refugees varies widely in the region – reflecting varying approaches among scholars and differing national refugee policies. In an important development, mass movements to Sweden in 2015 prompted public reflection on the country's historic relationship with refugees, notably those who had arrived in the 1940s as survivors of Nazi concentration camps. A series of projects, including collections of oral testimony, were initiated to document arrival and reception of the twenty-first-century immigrants. These raised all manner of questions about ethics, methods, and the implications for the refugees involved. Malin Thor Tureby and Kristin Wagrell observe that several initiatives took the form of "crisis collections" in which refugees' life stories and other archival objects "become detached from their social and institutional context":

> [M]any memory institutions did not primarily aim to document the refugees' or migrants' experiences but, rather, they centered their projects on documenting the impact that the crisis had within the countries experiencing an influx of refugees and migrants. (Thor Tureby and Wagrell 2022, 347)

In a nuanced analysis of aims and outcomes of oral history research, including that undertaken by major national institutions in Sweden, Thor Tureby and Wagrell emphasize the importance of refugee participation in the initiation and execution of projects, avoiding "the paternalistic treatment of migrants that has characterized previous collections concerned with marginalized groups" (Thor Tureby and Wagrell 2022, 369). They challenge those who collect and assess oral narrative to ensure that refugees are at the active center of research, complementing advances in the fields of refugee studies and narrative studies in which refugees are viewed as participants and coauthors, with academics as facilitators rather than experts whose interventions shape the project (Andrews, Squire, and Tamboukou 2013). Here, refugee narratives are understood in the light of social and historical phenomena, and in their economic, social, and cultural contexts. As historians who have addressed forced migration over the decades in India, Palestine, and elsewhere have revealed, it is recognition of the complexity of the refugee experience that facilitates understanding of mass displacement and of the agency of those involved.

Notes

1 This phrase, coined by Voltaire in the mid-nineteenth century to capture the intent behind efforts to discipline military leaders, might be applied equally to Bourbon efforts almost two centuries earlier with the purpose of marshaling popular opinion behind the state's vision of France and French identity.

2 See for example British policy in the newly established state of Iraq, where in the 1920s nomadic and seminomadic communities were moved across novel desert borders invisible to those affected (Marfleet 2020).

3 On the scale of mass displacements in and from Anatolia and the Arab East see Marfleet, 2020.

4 Chatty 2010, chap. 4, reviews contending accounts of successive conflicts and massacres, culminating in the events of 1915.

5 As late as 2006, Jonathan Sacks, Britain's chief rabbi, could assert: "The Jews who came here loved Britain. They owed it their freedom to live as Jews without fear. In many cases they owed it their lives. Perhaps it takes an outsider fully to appreciate how remarkable Britain is. Jews loved its tolerance, its courtesy, its understated yet resolute commitment to liberty and civility. They loved Britain because it was British" (Lappin, 2008).

6 Collated most effectively by Israel's Yad Vashem Holocaust Martyrs' and Heroes' Remembrance Authority.

7 See debates about methodology and ethics of oral history as reviewed by Sheftel and Zembrzycki, 2019: "Who's Afraid of Oral History? Fifty Years of Debates and Anxiety about Ethics."

Bibliography

Aktar, Ayhan. 2003. "Homogenising the Nation, Turkifying the Economy: The Turkish Experience of Population Exchange Reconsidered". In *Crossing the Aegean: An Appraisal of the 1923 Compulsory Population Exchange between Greece and Turkey, edited by Renée* Hirschon, 79–96. Oxford: Berghahn. https://doi.org/10.3167/9781571817679.

Andrews, Molly, Corinne Squire, and Maria Tamboukou, eds. 2013. *Doing Narrative Research*. London: Sage. https://doi.org/10.4135/9780857024992.

Bak, Sophie Lene. 2016. "Indledning". In *Oral History i Danmark*. Odense: Syddansk Universitetsforlag.

Behdad, Ali. 2005. *A Forgetful Nation: On Immigration and Cultural Identity in the United States*. Durham, NC: Duke University Press. https://doi.org/10.1215/9780822387039.

Beinin, Joel. 2005. *The Dispersion of Egyptian Jewry: Culture, Politics, and the Formation of a Modern Diaspora*. Cairo: American University in Cairo Press.

Billig, Michael. 1995. *Banal Nationalism*. London: Sage.

Bose, Tapan. 1997. "The Changing Nature of Refugee Crisis". In *States, Citizens and Outsiders: The Uprooted Peoples of South Asia*, edited by Tapan Bose and Rita Manchanda, 40–59. Katmandu: South Asia Forum for Human Rights.

Britz, Dolf. 2006. "The French refugees in 20th century South African Historiography". In *Von Schweden bis Südafrika: Vorträge der Internafionalen Hugenotten-Konferenz in Emden*, edited by Andreas Flick and Walter Schulz. Bad Karlshafen: Verlag der Deutschen Hugenotten-Gesellschaft, 9–33.

Bryson, Anna. 2016. "Victims, Violence, and Voice: Transitional Justice, Oral History, and Dealing with the Past". *Hastings International & Comparative Law Review* 39 (2): 299–354.

Butalia, Urvashi. 1998. *The Other Side of Silence: Voices from the Partition of India*. New Delhi: Penguin Books India.

Butalia, Urvashi. 2001. "'An Archive with a Difference': Partition Letters" in *The Partitions of Memory: The Afterlife of the Division of India*, edited by Suvir Kaul. Delhi: Permanent Black.

Cahalan, Peter. 1997. "The Treatment of Belgian Refugees in England During the Great War". PhD thesis, McMaster University.

Chatty, Dawn. 2010. *Displacement and Dispossession in the Modern Middle East*. Cambridge: Cambridge University Press. https://doi.org/10.1017/CBO9780511844812.

Cohen, Robin. 1994. *Frontiers of Identity: The British and Others*. London: Longman.

Cottret, Bernard. 1991. *The Huguenots in England*. Cambridge: Cambridge University Press.

Diller, Lisa. 2011. "How Dangerous, the Protestant Stranger? Huguenots and the Formation of British Identity C. 1685–1715". In *The Huguenots: History and Memory in Transnational Context*, edited by David Trim, 103–20. Leiden: Brill. https://doi.org/10.1163/ej.9789004207752.i-313.24.

Ewence, Hannah. 2017. "Bridging the Gap between 'War' and 'Peace': The Case of Belgian Refugees in Britain". In *Minorities and the First World War: From War to Peace*, edited by Hannah Ewence and Tim Grady, 89–113. London: Palgrave Macmillan. https://doi.org/10.1057/978-1-137-53975-5.

Frank, Matthew. 2011. "Fantasies of Ethnic Unmixing: 'Population Transfer' and the End of Empire in Europe". In *Refugees and the End of Empire: Imperial Collapse and Forced Migration in the Twentieth Century*, edited by Panikos Panayi and Pippa Virdee, 81–101. Basingstoke: Palgrave Macmillan. https://doi.org/10.1057/9780230305700.

Greenberg, Jonathan. 2005. "Generations of Memory: Remembering Partition in India/Pakistan and Israel/Palestine". *Comparative Studies of South Asia, Africa and the Middle East* 25 (1): 89–110. https://doi.org/10.1215/1089201X-25-1-89.

Gürpınar, Doğan. 2016. "The Manufacturing of Denial: The Making of the Turkish 'Official Thesis' on the Armenian Genocide between 1974 and 1990". *Journal of*

Balkan and Near Eastern Studies 18 (3): 217–40. https://doi.org/10.1080/19448
953.2016.1176397.

Hall, Catherine and Daniel Pick. 2017. "Thinking about Denial". *History Workshop Journal* 84: 1–83. https://doi.org/10.1093/hwj/dbx040.

Hobsbawm, Eric. 1983. "Introduction: Inventing Traditions", in *The Invention of Tradition, edited by* Eric Hobsbawm and Terence Ranger, 1–14. Cambridge: Cambridge University Press.

Janesick, Valerie. 2007. "Oral History as a Social Justice Project: Issues for the Qualitative Researcher". *Qualitative Report* 12 (1): 111–21. https://doi.org/10.46743/2160-3715/2007.1648.

Jasanoff, Maya. 2011. *Liberty's Exiles: The Loss of America and the Remaking of the British Empire*. London: Harper Collins.

Kershen, Anne. 2004. *Strangers, Aliens and Asians: Huguenots, Jews and Bangladeshis in Spitalfields 1666–2000*. London: Routledge.

Keyder, Çağlar. 2003. "The Consequences of the Exchange of Populations for Turkey". In *Crossing the Aegean: An Appraisal of the 1923 Compulsory Population Exchange between Greece and Turkey, edited by Reneé* Hirschon, 39–52. Oxford: Berghahn. https://doi.org/10.3167/9781571817679.

Kössler, Reinhart. 2008. "Entangled History and Politics: Negotiating the Past between Namibia and Germany". *Journal of Contemporary African Studies* 26 (3): 313–39. https://doi.org/10.1080/02589000802332531.

Kushner, Tony. 2003. "Meaning Nothing but Good: Ethics, History and Asylum-Seeker Phobia in Britain". *Patterns of Prejudice* 37 (3): 257–76. https://doi.org/10.1080/00313220307593.

Kushner, Tony. 2006. *Remembering Refugees: Then and Now*. Manchester: Manchester University Press.

Kushner, Tony. 2017a. *Journeys from the Abyss: The Holocaust and Forced Migration from the 1880s to the Present*. Oxford: Oxford University Press.

Kushner, Tony. 2017b. "Writing Refugee History – Or Not". In *Refugees in Europe, 1919–1959: A Forty Years' Crisis? edited by Matthew* Frank and Jessica Reinisch, 51–66. London: Bloomsbury Academic. https://doi.org/10.5040/9781474295734.0008.

Kushner, Tony and Katherine Knox. 1999. *Refugees in an Age of Genocide*. London: Frank Cass.

Lappin, Shalom. 2008. "This Green and Pleasant Land: Britain and the Jews". Working Paper #2, The Yale Initiative for the Interdisciplinary Study of Antisemitism: https://citeseerx.ist.psu.edu/document?repid=rep1&type=pdf&doi=d1d1f4a8c34c1c728a54714e4dd34a9281fd7b85.

London, Louise. 2003. *Whitehall and the Jews 1933–1948: British Immigration Policy, Jewish Refugees and the Holocaust*. Cambridge: Cambridge University Press.

MacDonald, David. 2015 "Canada's History Wars: Indigenous Genocide and Public Memory in the United States, Australia and Canada". *Journal of Genocide Research* 17 (4): 411–31. https://doi.org/10.1080/14623528.2015.1096583.

Marfleet, Philip. 2006. *Refugees in a Global Era*. Basingstoke: Palgrave Macmillan.

Marfleet, Philip. 2020. "Borders, Migration and the State". In *Iraq Since the Invasion, edited by Keiko* Sakai and Philip Marfleet. London: Routledge. https://doi.org/10.4324/9780429201936.

Masalha, Nur. 2008. "Remembering the Palestinian Nakba: Commemoration, Oral History and Narratives of Memory". *Holy Land Studies* 7 (2): 123–56. https://doi.org/10.3366/E147494750800019X.

Melber, Henning. 2005. "How to Come to Terms with the Past: Re-visiting the German Colonial Genocide in Namibia". *Afrika Spectrum* 40 (1): 139–48.

Ministry of Health. 1920. *Report on the Work Undertaken by the British Government in the Reception and Care of the Belgian Refugees.* London: His Majesty's Stationery Office.

Nasaw, David. 2009. "Introduction – Roundtable Historians and Biography". *The American Historical Review* 114 (3): 573–78. https://doi.org/10.1086/ahr.114.3.573.

Nassar, Issam. 2001. "Reflections on Writing the History of Palestinian Identity". *Palestine-Israel Journal* 8 (4): 24–37.

Pandey, Gyanendra. 2001. *Remembering Partition: Violence, Nationalism and History in India.* Cambridge: Cambridge University Press. https://doi.org/10.1017/CBO9780511613173.

Pappe, Ilan. 1997. "Post-Zionist Critique on Israel and the Palestinians: Part I: The Academic Debate". *Journal of Palestine Studies* 26 (2): 29–41.

Perks, Robert and Alastair Thomson, eds. 2015. *The Oral History Reader.* London: Routledge.

Podeh, Eli. 2000. "History and Memory in the Israeli Educational System: The Portrayal of the Arab-Israeli Conflict in History Textbooks (1948–2000)". *History and Memory* 12 (1): 65–100.

Porter, Bernard. 1979. *The Refugee Question in Mid-Victorian Politics.* Cambridge: Cambridge University Press.

Purseigle, Pierre. 2007. "'A Wave on to Our Shores': The Exile and Resettlement of Refugees from the Western Front, 1914–1918". *Contemporary European History* 16 (4): 427–44.

Pyrhönen, Niko, Johanna Leinonen, and Tuomas Martikainen. 2017. "Nordic Migration and Integration Research: Overview and Future Prospects". Nordforsk Policy Paper 3/2017. https://www.diva-portal.org/smash/get/diva2:1085791/FULLTEXT01.pdf.

Renan, Ernest. 1882. *Qu'est-ce Qu'une Nation?* Paris: Michel Levy Freres.

Riaño-Alcalá, Pilar. 2008. "Journeys and Landscapes of Forced Migration: Memorializing Fear among Refugees and Internally Displaced Colombians". *Social Anthropology/Anthropologie Sociale* 16 (1): 1–18. https://doi.org/10.1111/j.1469-8676.2008.00036.x.

Said, Edward. 2000. "Invention, Memory, and Place". *Critical Inquiry* 26 (2): 175–92.

Sen, Uditi. 2014. "The Myths Refugees Live By: Memory and History in the Making of Bengali Refugee Identity". *Modern Asian Studies* 48, 37–76. https://doi.org/10.1017/S0026749X12000613.

Sheftel, Anna and Stacey Zembrzycki. 2019. "Who's Afraid of Oral History? Fifty Years of Debates and Anxiety about Ethics". *The Oral History Review* 43 (2): 338–66. https://doi.org/10.1093/ohr/ohw071.

Smiles, Samuel. 1867. *The Huguenots: Their Settlements, Churches and Industries in England and Ireland.* London: John Murray.

Soguk, Nevzat. 1999. *States and Strangers: Refugees and Displacements of Statecraft.* Minneapolis: University of Minnesota Press.

Stein, Rebecca and Ted Swedenburg. 2004. "Popular Culture, Relational History, and the Question of Power in Palestine and Israel". *Journal of Palestine Studies* 33 (4): 5–20. https://doi.org/10.1525/jps.2004.33.4.005.

Stone, Daniel. 2018. "Refugees Then and Now: Memory, History and Politics in the Long Twentieth Century: An Introduction". *Patterns of Prejudice* 52 (2–3): 101–6. https://doi.org/10.1080/0031322X.2018.1433004.

Thor Tureby, Malin 2022. "Oral History in the Nordic Countries: Past, Present and Future": http://mau.diva-portal.org/smash/record.jsf?pid=diva2%3A1689664 &dswid=-620.

Thor Tureby, Malin and Kristin Wagrell. 2022. "Crisis Documentation and Oral History: Problematizing Collecting and Preserving Practices in a Digital World". *Oral History Review* 49 (2): 346–76. https://doi.org/10.1080/0094079 8.2022.2101933.

Trim, David. 2011 "The Huguenots and the Experience of Exile (Sixteenth to Twentieth Centuries): History, Memory And Transnationalism". In *The Huguenots: History and Memory in Transnational Context*, edited by David Trim, 1–42. Leiden: Brill.

Trouillot, Michel-Rolph. 1995. *Silencing the Past: Power and the Production of History*. Boston, MA: Beacon Press.

Van Alphen, Ernst. 2006. "Second-Generation Testimony, Transmission of Trauma, and Postmemory". *Poetics Today* 27 (2): 473–88.

Zetter, Roger. 1988. "Refugees and Refugee Studies – A Label and an Agenda: Editorial Introduction to the Journal of Refugee Studies". *Journal of Refugee Studies* 1 (1): 1–6.

CHAPTER 2

Forced migrants in Nordic historiographies

Miika Tervonen
University of Helsinki

Hans Otto Frøland
Norwegian University of Science and Technology

Christhard Hoffmann
University of Bergen

Seija Jalagin
University of Oulu

Heidi Vad Jønsson
University of Southern Denmark

Johanna Leinonen
Novia University of Applied Sciences

Malin Thor Tureby
Malmö University

How to cite this book chapter:
Tervonen, Miika, Hans Otto Frøland, Christhard Hoffmann, Seija Jalagin, Heidi Vad
Jønsson, Johanna Leinonen and Malin Thor Tureby. 2025. "Forced migrants in
Nordic historiographies." In *Forced Migrants in Nordic Histories*, edited by Johanna
Leinonen, Miika Tervonen, Hans Otto Frøland, Christhard Hoffmann, Seija
Jalagin, Heidi Vad Jønsson and Malin Thor Tureby, 45–90. Helsinki: Helsinki
University Press. https://doi.org/10.33134/HUP-32-3.

Abstract

The chapter provides the first comparative analysis of forced migrants in the Nordic historiographical traditions. Research outside the Nordic context has pointed to silences and blind spots regarding forced migrants, who have appeared as anomalies in nation-state-centric historiography. To what extent does a hypothesis of silences hold in the case of the Nordic countries? The chapter analyses relevant research in history and related fields in Denmark, Finland, Norway, and Sweden that covers the period from early modern times to the present. While highlighting the scale and complexity of histories of forced migration in the Nordic region, the overview finds highly patchy national research fields well into the 1990s, with forced migrants rarely in the focus and often subsumed into general migration or labor history. After the Second World War, specific groups such as Jewish refugees or Karelian "evacuees" received some scholarly attention, with critical research questioning self-celebratory national narratives particularly from 1970s onward. Yet major publications appeared as exceptions to an overall rule of silence and were often written outside the profession of history. Only from the 1990s onward has there been a sustained historical interest, reflecting contemporary debates on immigration and human rights. Expansion of research has been accompanied with diversifying methodological and theoretical approaches and a shift of focus towards the perspectives, agency, and specific experiences of forced migrants.

Introduction

The Nordic region has a centuries-long history of movements of religious and political dissidents, refugees escaping war and persecution, captives and prisoners of war, forcibly conscripted soldiers, forced laborers, vagrants, slaves, and expellees. In this chapter, we analyze the main phases and narratives of historiographies of forced migrants in the Nordic countries. To what extent have forced migrants and their experiences been included in or excluded from history writing? Which groups have been highlighted and which have been forgotten or silenced? What are the main narratives and ways to conceptualize forced migrants in historiography?

International literature not including the Nordic countries has pointed to patterns described as "silence," "blind spots," or "collective amnesia" with regard to histories of forced migration (e.g., Kushner 2006; Marfleet 2007). Migrants more generally have fitted poorly into the dominant nation-state-centric and homogenizing understanding of society, and seen as exceptions to the rule of territorial confinement (Wimmer and Glick Schiller 2003). With most forced migrants, particularly nonnationals and deportees, this has arguably been doubly so, with even large-scale displacement frequently failing "to show up on the radar of historians" (Gatrell 2017, 175). The "history of refugee history," to paraphrase Peter Gatrell, points to selective inclusions and shifting interpretations, as some histories have been more compatible with the conventional national narratives of the past than others. To what extent does a hypothesis of historiographical silences hold in the case of the Nordic countries?

In this chapter, we provide the first comparative overview of the main patterns of inclusion and exclusion of forced migrants in the Nordic historiographical traditions. We further address the impact of changing public debates and political responses to the scholarship of forced migration. The periodization follows major changes in Nordic refugee histories and historiographical developments. We identify in broad strokes four distinctive periods: the early modern and modern era up to the Second World War, during which the forced migration began taking its modern shape both as a mass-scale phenomenon and as a political "question"; the Second World War, acting as a rupture and a turning point both in the mass movements of forced migrants and in public and scholarly perceptions; the period of Cold War and decolonization; and the contemporary period of globalization and Europeanization of Nordic migration regimes coinciding with a proliferation of academic (if mostly not historical) interest.

Since forced migrations have been frequently absent from popular narratives of Nordic history, we begin each section with a brief historical contextualization. This will provide the reader with a basic overview of the key historical events, structures, and groups involved in the multifaceted flows of forced migrants. The contextualizing sections are in no way meant as comprehensive accounts, and the case of Iceland is in particular mostly not included (see Chapter 4 in this volume, by Íris Ellenberger). Nor do we aim to offer fixed categorizations over the various groups and individuals of refugees, expellees, prisoners of wars, and others. Rather, the main focus of the chapter lies on the development of Nordic historiography. This is the first Nordic overview on this field, and as scholars working in different national contexts we have sought to compile as comprehensive a picture as the state of current knowledge allows. We have aimed to identify the main developments in historical writing and, in some cases, in related arenas such as social sciences, cultural studies, and museology, as well as to compare across the different historiographical traditions. Aside from change, our findings point to long-term continuities and remaining gaps in the Nordic history writing vis-à-vis forced migrants, which we will outline in the concluding section.

Refugeedom before the Second World War and Nordic historiographies

Three major forces shaped the histories of forced migration in the Nordic region in the early modern period. The first was the rise of centrally ruled kingdoms commanding growing military and tax resources and often seeking to extend their territories through warfare. The second was the emergence of religious divisions during the Reformation and the establishment of the Lutheran Church as a basis for social and ideological organization of society. Third were colonial engagements of the kingdoms of Sweden and Denmark, as well as the Russian Empire. Each of these factors – together with periodic famines, for example – produced involuntary migrations and shaped the ways in which those seeking shelter were received and conceived of.

From the sixteenth century onward, the Reformation and Counter-Reformation, wars of religion, and religious persecution brought refugees to the kingdoms of Denmark and Sweden, but also forced some to leave. In the late seventeenth century, persecution in Catholic countries brought small numbers of Protestant refugees, in particular Huguenot émigrés, to the kingdoms of Denmark and Sweden. These refugees did not arrive spontaneously but were invited by the king. In Norway, for example, the municipalities of Kristiansand and Fredrikstad were declared sanctuaries for the Calvinist Frenchmen. Meanwhile, after Sweden conquered and annexed Kexholm county in Karelia in 1617, a large part of the local Orthodox population fled to Russia. Many of them did so in order to avoid forced conversion to the Lutheran faith (Laitila 2020; Salenius 1911).

Centuries of warfare between the Swedish kingdom and its neighbors to the East, particularly Russia, gave rise to periodic westward flows of refugees from Finland and the Baltic provinces when Swedish losses led to invasion and pillaging. From late 16th Century onwards, thousands of peasants moved from Finland to Sweden, with an ongoing emigration likely increased by the wars, famines and rebellions of the period.

Meanwhile, the colonies acquired by the Danish and Swedish kingdoms during this time produced specific forms of involuntary mobilities. Soldiers, vagrants, prisoners, and indentured laborers – Forest Finns among them – were sent to the short-lived colony of "New Sweden" in Delaware (1638–1655). West African slave labor was forced to the Danish West Indies, held by Denmark from 1672 to 1848, to produce sugar, coffee and tobacco. Between the 1660s and the beginning of the 1800s, more than 100,000 slaves were transported under the Danish flag (Gøbel 2016; Olsen 2017). Swedish actors were also engaged in the slave trade (Wilson 2023), and slavery remained legal in the Swedish Caribbean colony of Saint Barthélemy from 1784 until 1847.

During the Great Northern War (1700–1721), an estimated 10,000–30,000 civilians fled from Finland to Sweden, with an additional 10,000–20,000 captured and taken to slavery in Russia. The arrival of tens of thousands of refugees to Sweden led to one of the first institutional attempts – the founding of a refugee commission in Stockholm – to alleviate their situation (Aminoff-Winberg 1995, 2007). The Great Northern War also led to Russia's conquest of the Baltic provinces and to a more long-term movement of Baltic refugees to Sweden and the Finnish Grand Duchy that continued well into the nineteenth century (e.g., Östman 2023; Papp 1988). Diverse refugees and political exiles also arrived in Sweden in the aftermath of Poland's partition and rebellions and the Russian conquest of Finland in 1808–1809. Finland was annexed by Russia and became its administratively separate Grand Duchy. Thousands of convicted criminals and vagrants were subsequently exiled to Siberia as part of penal policy. As attempted Russification of the Grand Duchy from 1889 onward led to strong Finnish resistance, a small number of political dissidents were also sent to Siberia (Juntunen 1983).

Religious affiliation remained a major reason for flight and the basis for either the acceptance or exclusion of refugees throughout the nineteenth century. Jewish westward migrations reached the Nordic region and intensified during 1881–1906 by waves of violent antisemitic pogroms in the so-called Pale of Settlement area (for Jews) in the Russian Empire. At the beginning of the century, the reception of the Jewish migrants in Nordic countries was already ambivalent, with partly diverging directions of development. The Norwegian constitution of 1814, for example, categorically denied Jews – along with Jesuits and monastic orders – from entering the realm, a clause that was only rescinded in 1851. Meanwhile, in Denmark, Jews gained in principle equal rights that same year (1814). In Sweden, Jews were first allowed to settle in the 1770s and were granted general emancipation in the 1870s. As there were few restrictions from 1860 to 1914, 3,000–4,000 Jews immigrated from Russia and Poland (Carlsson 2021). In contrast, the Finnish Grand Duchy not only retained its Swedish-era restrictions but also deported a significant share of its small Jewish population in the 1830s and the 1880s–1890s. Amid heated debates on the so-called Jewish question, a ban on Jewish immigration was upheld until Finland's independence in 1917.[1]

From the turn of the twentieth century onward, nation-state-building, associated ethnic cleansings and denaturalizations, the First World War, and the Russian revolutions produced an era of mass refugee movements in Europe. The First World War also heralded an era of unprecedented policing of borders. These developments were reflected in the Nordic region. It underwent a transition to constitutional democracy, and from multinational empires or conglomerate states to sovereign nation-states. Norway's union with Sweden was dissolved in 1905 and Finland became independent from Russia in 1917. Denmark lost a substantial part of its territory to Germany in 1864, while regaining parts of Schleswig in the peace settlement after the First World War.[2] Both Denmark and Sweden lost most of their overseas colonies by the early twentieth century.[3] Iceland became a fully sovereign kingdom in 1918 that remained in personal union with Denmark until 1944.

The reshaped Nordic nation-states immediately faced inflows of forced migrants. Revolutionary and separatist currents in the Russian Empire brought anarchists, socialists, nationalists, and other political dissidents to Scandinavia from the 1860s onward. These flows were greatly intensified by the 1905 First Russian Revolution, the outbreak of the First World War, and particularly the Bolshevik Revolution in Russia in 1917. The refugees fleeing the October Revolution and the

Russian civil war constituted a first large-scale refugee "question" in most Nordic countries, particularly in 1918–1922 (e.g., Engman 2007; Nevalainen 1999; Tevlina 2020), with the arrival of tens of thousands of ethnically, politically, and socially heterogeneous displaced people who often transited further to Western Europe or the US. In Finland, tens of thousands of Russian soldiers were posted between 1914 and 1918, as well as thousands of Chinese and other Asian forced laborers brought in to fortify Helsinki (Halén 2004). Following the Finnish Civil War, an estimated 18,000 to 80,000 Russian and Russian-speaking civilians and soldiers were deported from the country (Engman 2007; Leitzinger 2008). This mass deportation was paralleled and followed by the arrival of around 44,000 refugees from Russia. Among them were "white" Russian refugees or *emigres*, refugees of the Kronstadt rebellion, Ingrians and East Karelians fleeing Bolsheviks after their failed Finnish-supported uprisings, and even some Muslim Tatars, who added to the small already-existing community in Finland (Elmgren 2021).[4] Additionally, Finnish civil war led to the fleeing of around 10,000 "reds" to Soviet Russia in 1918, with hundreds (if not thousands) also seeking shelter from Sweden between 1917 and 1924.[5] An internment camp was set up for the initial arrivals in Morvjärv, close to the Finnish border. While most revolutionary refugees from Finland were ultimately given residence permits in Sweden, authorities sought to control particularly communist and anarchist refugees – also arriving from Russia – with many red refugees either denied entry or deported back to Finland during the 1920s and 1930s (Hammar 1964, 72–74, 115, 261–88, 390–96; Svanberg and Tydén 1992, 249–54).

The mass displacements following the First World War gave rise to the first serious attempts to form internationally negotiated refugee agreements, with the active involvement of some of the Nordic countries. Norway in particular advocated a humanitarian refugee policy in its international stance, and the Nansen passport formed a major attempt to create a framework for protection of stateless migrants and refugees. On its own borders, however, Norway, as much as other Nordic countries, had taken a security-oriented and restrictive turn, and sought above all to limit and control incoming forced migrants (Kjeldstadli 2003, 466–73).

This was evident especially from 1933 to 1939, when each Nordic country was confronted with the exodus of Germans, Austrians, and Czechoslovakians who had fled Nazi persecution. Around half a million people sought refuge from Germany and its annexed areas. These included political refugees such as social democrats and communists, Jews, and artists and academics (Kjeldstadli 2003, 404–8). Compared to other German neighboring countries such as Belgium and the Netherlands, few refugees came to the Nordic countries, which also actively sought to limit the number of incomers.[6] The restrictive border control with its underlying racial character targeted in particular at Jewish refugees, who were initially labeled as pure economic migrants and therefore not seen as much in need of help as the social democratic or communist political opponents of the Nazi regime. In Denmark, protection was offered for Jews for a very limited time and, from 1934 to 1938, the Danish immigration policy became continuously more restrictive. By 1938, the Danish minister of justice decided that Jews could not receive asylum as refugees in Denmark (Rünitz 2005). After the annexation of Austria and Czechoslovakia and the November pogroms in 1938, more Jewish refugees arrived. Several humanitarian and political NGOs provided relief work for the refugees, but the Nordic countries simultaneously maintained and reinforced the restrictions that had been introduced in the early 1930s (Kirchhoff 2005; Kirchhoff and Rünitz 2007). Jewish refugees thus continued to be excluded from asylum based on a narrow definition of a political refugee. Many were turned back or deported into mortal danger, such as the group of 60 Jewish refugees who were turned back from Finland to Germany in 1938 (Torvinen 1984, 93).

Historiography

Professional historiographical traditions emerged in the Nordic countries during the nineteenth century in close connection with the nation-building efforts (see e.g., Haapala, Jalava, and Larsson 2017). These traditions aligned very much with the wider European pattern that mostly omitted histories of forced migration along with most migration more generally. Before the Second World War – and, in fact, mostly before the late 1980s – refugees, displaced people, and deportees were by and large not written into mainstream national historiographies. Moreover, when interest in forced migrants gradually emerged from the 1990s onward, the focus of research was strongly on either 1933–1945 or the Cold War period.

The Finnish government further evacuated around 104,000 people from northern Finland during the Lapland War in autumn 1944, when the Wehrmacht retreated into northern Norway (see Chapter 12). Half of them were given refuge in Sweden, while the rest were internally displaced in Finland. For the Sami population especially, evacuations to Ostrobothnia signified a total transformation of environment and lifestyle.[12]

After the Wehrmacht Lapland Army entered Norway in the autumn of 1944, German authorities and the Quisling government forcibly evacuated 50,000 Norwegians further south in Norway, including around 10,000 Sami (Elstad 2020). In the winter of 1945, when Soviet troops advanced into East Germany, the Nazi government in Germany organized the evacuation of around 250,000 Germans to Denmark. Above 9,000 Norwegians (Ottosen 2004) and 6,500 Danes were deported to penitentiaries or concentration camps in the Reich.

As a consequence of Nazi policies of genocide of the European Jews, thousands of Jewish citizens and refugees residing in the Nordic countries were either deported or forced to flee. Between November 1942 and February 1943, 773 of the around 2,200 Jews in Norway (roughly one-quarter of whom were refugees) were arrested and deported, most of them sent to Auschwitz–Birkenau; the rest fled to Sweden (Bruland 2017). Almost simultaneously in October 1942, eight Jewish refugees were deported from Finland to Nazi Germany on board the German transport vessel *Hohenhörn*. After Hitler declared in October 1943 that the Jews in Denmark should be arrested and deported, 6,500 managed to flee to Sweden, but 470 were caught by the Gestapo and sent from Denmark to Theresienstadt concentration camp.[13]

In numerical terms, an even larger group than the evacuated or deported civilians was formed by "institutional" forced migrants (Lucassen and Lucassen 2017). These included drafted Wehrmacht troops (of whom were many thousands of non-Germans from areas annexed by Germany), prisoners of war (POWs), and civilian forced laborers drafted from all over Europe and deployed by Nazi Germany, which occupied Norway and Denmark 1940–1945 and maintained a military alliance with Finland 1941–1944. While conventionally not understood as "forced" migrants (or, for that matter, as *migrants*), this category possibly included more than 800,000 people dislodged more or less involuntarily from their home countries for extended periods of time. German troops, by autumn 1944 accounting for more than

350,000 in Norway (Korsnes and Dybvig 2018), around 200,000 in Finland (Fagertun et al. 2022), and 186,000 in Denmark (Christensen et al. 2005), were moved over state borders, until 1943 also through neutral Sweden. More than 300,000 were deployed in Denmark as the war ended, more than a third of them in transit after having retreated from Finland through Norway. The POWs and civilian forced laborers belonged to Wehrmacht auxiliary forces and followed the Wehrmacht. They added to around 130,000 people in Norway (Hatlehol 2020) and around 20,000 in Finland (Westerlund 2008). Denmark, meanwhile, was not supplied with foreign POWs or foreign forced laborers; in 1943, around 25 percent of Wehrmacht troops in Denmark had been recruited in Soviet POW camps (Christensen et al. 2005).

Finland held almost 80,000 Soviet soldiers as POWs; 19,000 of them died, 2,400 were transferred to the Germans, and 48,000 were repatriated to the Soviet Union by 1955 (Pohjonen 2008, 186). In the Soviet areas occupied by the Finnish army in 1941–1944, around 24,000 civilians were categorized as "nonnationals" and interned in camps, as opposed to 36,000 Karelians and other "kinfolk" people who were allowed to stay in their occupied home villages (Westerlund 2009, 70–71, 85, 91, 143–45, 149–50).

Almost 60,000 Norwegians (Hansson 2019, 131; Ulstein 1965; 1967; 1974; 1975) and around 20,000 Danes fled their country individually or in small groups to become refugees, with Sweden being by far the largest receiver. Sweden had had about 5,000 refugees and evacuees at the beginning of the war, and ended it with close to 200,000. They originated in multiple countries, the bulk coming from Finland, Norway, Denmark, Germany, Poland, Estonia, and Latvia. For example, more than 30,000 Baltic refugees fled Soviet recapture of the region to Sweden, including whole communities (around 6,500) of Swedish speakers from the Estonian coast (Olsson 1995; Svanberg and Tydén 1992, 285). In addition, Sweden received non-Nordic "institutional" forced migrants who deserted from the Wehrmacht or its auxiliary forces, roughly estimated at around 5,000 people. In 1945, Sweden further welcomed 31,000 survivors from the Nazi concentration camps via two operations, the first initiated by the Red Cross, the next by the United Nations Relief and Rehabilitation Administration (UNRRA).

Historiography

After the Second World War, historiography and different national narratives developed in the Nordic countries depending on the countries' different experiences but tended to highlight patriotic narratives of national heroism or at least innocence, at the face of overwhelming evil and might of Nazi Germany – or, in the case of Finland, Stalin's Soviet Union (Åmark 2011; Corell 2010; Kinnunen and Kivimäki 2012; Kirchhoff 2001). Most of the displacements during the Second World War were long not acknowledged (Stenius, Österberg, and Östling 2011).

In Norway, the first postwar accounts of war experience fully ignored the foreign forced migration and their repatriation. A structural backdrop was the fact that the Allies had decided during the war that war crimes must be brought before courts in the domicile countries of the victims. Hence the public eye focused on crimes against Norwegians, not on potential crimes against foreign forced migrants brought to Norway (Frøland 2017). Additional focus was on Norwegians forced to flee the country and dispatches of them returning home. Ragnar Ulstein subsequently published histories of the about 4,000 people who fled the sea route to Britain (Ulstein 1965, 1967) and the around 50,000 who fled across the Swedish border, including about 1,200 Jews (Ulstein 1974, 1975). The Norwegian diaspora in Sweden was addressed as well (Grimnes 1969). Kristian Ottosen published histories of political prisoners who were sent to various other concentration camps. He also published a list of Norwegian prisoners, showing that among the around 44,000 imprisoned for political, religious, or ethnic reasons about 10,000 were deported to camps in the Reich (Ottosen 2004).

Historiography tended to understand the refuge and deportations in the combined framework of resistance to and victimhood from the Nazi Germany. The history of the southward deportation of civilians in the northernmost part of Norway in the winter of 1945 fits into this framework (Eriksen and Halvorsen 1987). Whereas the forced Jewish migration to Sweden and the horrible destiny of those who were deported for extermination was acknowledged, the Norwegian contribution to the Holocaust was neglected until the 1990s (Bruland 2017).

Sweden was not occupied during the Second World War, like Norway and Denmark were, and did not fight in the war, like Finland

did. The Swedish Second World War historiography was first dominated by the narrative of neutrality or small-state realism, legitimating
Sweden's actions during the war and maintaining that as a small and
militarily weak state it had had no real choice but to make conces-
sions to Nazi Germany. Sweden's relations with other countries and
the Swedish government's political decisions during the war were the
focus of a major research project, "Sweden during the Second World
War" (SUAV, 1971–1986), which resulted in 20 doctoral dissertations
(Ekman 1980). Only one examined forced migration or Swedish refugee policy during the war, however (Lindberg 1973).

In Swedish historiography, a distinction is sometimes made
between research about the Second World War and the more sensitive
issue of Sweden's response to the Holocaust. The historian Paul A. Levine (1996) argued in the mid-1990s that, although an extensive historical literature on the former existed, only one study, Steven Koblik's *The
Stones Cry out: Sweden's Response to the Persecution of Jews 1933–1945*
(1987), addressed the latter. According to this logic, Levine's own dissertation about Swedish diplomacy during the Holocaust was only the
second to deal with Swedish response to the Holocaust. A critical view
and questions regarding Sweden's actions and nonactions during the
war was also raised outside academia in Maria-Pia Boëthius's *På Heder
och Samvete* (1991). Subsequent research (e.g., Andersson and Tydén
2007; Byström 2006; Kvist Geverts 2008) partly responded to Koblik's
and Levine's initiatives but also to the fierce public reactions to Boëthius's critical view on Swedish neutrality.

While Koblik, Levine, and Boëthius initiated critical research on
Sweden's response to the Second World War and the crimes of the
Nazi regime, they also followed previous research in focusing mainly
on the Swedish state's perspectives and political history. However, two
dissertations based on oral history and with Jewish refugee/survivor-
centered perspectives were also published in 1990s (Lomfors 1996;
Sterner Carlberg 1994), as well as a book on the Polish refugees and
survivors in Sweden during the Second World War (Uggla 1997). Refugee and survivor testimonies and stories had in fact been collected
and Holocaust and refugee archives created even before the end of the
war. These collecting, documenting, writing and research activities
continued in Sweden with the arrival of survivors. Most of the collected materials were intended to be used as evidence in trials against
the Nazi perpetrators or for future scientific or historical studies. In

a recently published report on scholarship about Holocaust testimonies and survivor stories in Sweden it was concluded that little research exists on the situatedness of Swedish collection efforts in a greater European and international context (Thor Tureby and Wagrell 2020). Although some efforts have been recently made to highlight that the refugees and survivors themselves were some of the most ardent collectors of testimonies and creators of survivor and refugee (his)stories (see for example Martínez 2023; Thor Tureby 2020; Chapter 8), these aspects of Holocaust and/or refugee historiography in Sweden and the Nordic countries need to be further explored.[14]

Finnish historiography initially largely ignored or only mentioned in passing forced migrants from areas ceded to the Soviet Union and from Lapland. The theme dominating historiography was why and how the country drifted into the *Waffenbrüderschaft* with Nazi Germany during the Continuation War (Hentilä 2010; Kivimäki 2012, 13–14). A critical turn took place at the turn of the 1970s–1980s, at least partly influenced by international Holocaust debates (although antisemitism never became a major topic in Finnish historiography). In 1982 Antti Laine published a thorough investigation of the Finnish occupation policy in Soviet Karelia and its relation to the German policies, and focused particularly on the social history of occupation. The fate and deportations of Ingrian Finns in 1943–1944 were investigated by Pekka Nevalainen in 1990, and have subsequently received gradually growing scholarly and public attention (e.g., Flink 2010; Pakkanen and Pakkanen 2020; Rautajoki 2017; Reuter 2023). In general, Finnish historiography (and popular writing) has been dominated by "classic military history, the battlefields and soldiers" (Kivimäki 2012), for which five years of constant warfare gave plenty of material. Following the collapse of the Soviet Union and questions about Finland's relationship to the genocidal policies of Nazi Germany, in the early 2000s the National Archives headed a project on wartime deportations and handling of the interned and POWs[15] (Westerlund 2008; earlier works include Kujala 2008; Roiko-Jokela 2004). Pioneering studies of the Wehrmacht troops' relation to the Finnish civilian population were also published at the turn of the century by Marianne Junila (2000).

Internally displaced people, in particular the 420,000 Karelian refugees – who gradually came to be known as 'evacuees' – were initially studied by scholars other than historians and largely in a national framework of sacrifice for survival. The social political researcher

Heikki Waris (1952) depicted the resettlement and social integration of Karelian evacuees as a governmentally organized success story. His interpretation prevailed for a long time and also affected the displaced Karelians' self-image. Over time, the evacuees became an important part of the national narrative of Finland's development through hardship to prosperity. After the Cold War years, the perspectives of research on Karelian refugees have diversified, but research has still often taken place outside the field of history. Folklorists and other cultural studies scholars focused on the individual, intergenerational and transnational memories of loss and displacement among the evacuees and war children (e.g., Kanervo, Kivistö and Kleemola 2018; Korppi-Tommola 1996; Leinonen 2020; Neuvonen-Seppänen 2020; Raninen-Siiskonen 1999; Savolainen 2015; Savolainen and Fingerroos 2018). Economists have drawn on the exceptionally accurate demographic databases on Karelian refugees to study the cross-generational trends generated by their displacement (e.g. Sarvimäki, Uusitalo, and Jäntti 2022). Meanwhile, doctoral dissertations by Heli Kananen (2010) on the integration of and discrimination against displaced Karelian Orthodox people in 1946–1959 and by Tiina Harjumaa (2021) on the displaced population of Petchenga represent the relatively sparse historical scholarship. Increasing interest in the effects of war also led to the opening of MUISTI Centre of War and Peace in 2021 in Mikkeli in the premises of the Finnish military headquarters during the Second World War.

Danish Second World War history writing follows the Nordic pattern as early histories focused on the Danish resistance and national opposition to the German occupation forces. This has been the case especially with accounts of how and why 95 percent of all Jews in Denmark made it to safety in Sweden in 1943. In 2001, Sofie Lene Bak published a systematic analysis of the dominant narratives in both public imagination and in research with her book *Jødeaktionen oktober 1943 – forestillinger i offentlighed og forskning*. The events of 1943 have led to extensive research emphasizing the importance of several variables. This research highlights that the escape represented not only a demonstration of national solidarity in a crisis situation but also involved elements of human trafficking. Aside from this so-called rescuing of Danish Jews, the arrival of 250,000 East Prussian (German) refugees has also been extensively researched. The Danish reaction to these refugees was included in local history books that sought to provide accounts of the situation in the Oxbøl camp, the biggest refugee camp that Denmark has ever had. The question of living conditions for the German refugees and the responsibilities of Danish doctors became a heated debate among historians when Kirsten Lylloff defended her dissertation *Barn eller fjende?* (2006). As a medical doctor she aimed to explore and explain the high rates of child mortality in the Danish refugee camp and argued that Danish doctors had not provided the necessary medical treatment and help for the German refugees as they were seen as enemies in the years immediately following the Second World War. Lylloff was subsequently criticized in the Danish journal *Historisk Tidsskrift* for insufficient understanding of the context. The debate showed that, even in the 2000s, the Second World War was still giving rise to emotional debates over responsibilities and national self-understanding.

Research in the Danish reaction to and the conditions for German refugees in Denmark continues to draw attention of historians and the public. In 2020, Thomas Harder published *De uønskede*, in which he narrates causes and effects of German refugees in Denmark. The same year John V. Jensen published a book titled *Tyskere på flugt* in the national history series "100 Histories of Denmark" as part of a large research project on the effects of the end of the war on welfare state development. In both these cases, emphasis has been on the role of the Danish state and civil society as well as the experiences of those who fled either from Denmark because they were Jews or to Denmark because the Nazi regime ordered them to flee (evacuate).

As later research has challenged patriotic memories (Fure 1999; Lagrou 1999), the histories of displacements have also begun to attract more attention. The process has been slow, however. In Norway in the 1980s, an eight-volume work on the war experience still largely ignored the large-scale influx of "institutional migrants" (Hatlehol 2020). A first scholarly account of the horrendous conditions in the Yugoslav prisoner camps in northern Norway in 1952 was only published decades later (Christie 1972). The first efforts to investigate the fate of the foreign prisoners brought to Norway were student works in the late 1980s (Koch 1988), while the first doctoral dissertation was produced by a Polish scholar (Denkiewicz-Szczepaniak 1999). The former addressed Soviet, Polish, and Yugoslav prisoners of war, whereas the latter investigated the civilian Poles who were drafted for forced labor in Norway and Finland. The pioneering study of forced immigration to Norway during the war was Hallvard Tjelmeland's (2003, 11–39) chapter, titled "Immigrants of War" (*Krigens innvandrere*), in the three-volume series of Norwegian migration history. However short, it observes a wide specter of forced migration, including Wehrmacht troops. Historians have since developed extensive knowledge about the many categories of forced labor migrants and to some extent about their repatriation. While the fluctuating presence of the Wehrmacht was established in 2018, a study of its transnational Nordic movements is pending. Lately, it has been argued that Norway and Finland must be treated as one functional unit regarding institutional migrants (Frøland and Lundemo 2022).

Marianne Neerland Soleim (2009) provided in-depth knowledge about the around 95,000 Soviet POWs brought to Norway and Lars Westerlund (2008) for the 20,000 in Finland.[16] Around 500 camps were set up in Norway alone. The significantly smaller number of camps in Finnish Lapland were supplied by the Stalag camp at Elvenes in Norway. The POWs were often sick and in bad conditions when they arrived, and they worked under harsh conditions that worsened when resources became increasingly scarce from autumn 1944 (Hatlehol and Soleim 2022). About 17,000 did not survive (Soleim 2009). Among the civilian forced laborers the Yugoslavs, mainly Serbs accused of partisan activity, faced extremely harsh condition and death rates (Stokke 2024). Hatlehol (2015), meanwhile, has examined the composition and various conditions of the workforce in Norway. His inquiry included probably close to 20,000 foreign civilian forced laborers working for Organization Todt (OT) in Norway, who originated in 21 countries. Additionally, Mari O. Lundemo suggests there might have been around 6,000 non-German civilian forced laborers working for OT in Finland winter 1943 (Lundemo 2020), with a nationality ratio approximately equal to the civilian forced laborers in Norway. Repatriation has been addressed for the Soviet POWs in Norway (Panikar 2021; Soleim 2009, 2016;), as well as for the Czech civilian workers (Hingarová and Maršálek 2022). They show that nationalities were gathered in joint camps irrespective of the person's former function. The around 1,000 remaining Czech civilian forced laborers and the 13,000 Czechs who had been drafted to serve for the Wehrmacht were treated as a group.

In all Nordic countries, recent decades have seen a gradual expansion of research on forced migrants of the Second World War and broadening of methodological and theoretical approaches. The opening of the Danish museum FLUGT, the plans for a Museum of Movements, and the establishment of the Swedish Holocaust Museum have further sparked new debates about refugee policies during and immediately after the Second World War, as well as their contemporary relevance. These developments highlight the importance of engaging with refugee-centered research and exhibitions (Zabalueva 2023).

Cold War (1948–1990)

The chaotic situation for different groups of forced migrants at the end of the Second World War made it clear that new initiatives and policies were necessary. In 1950, a new policy platform was established with the foundation of the UN Refugee Agency (later the United Nations High Commissioner on Refugees (UNHCR)). The agency followed in the footsteps of the Nansen office, but with the establishment of the UN Refugee Agency/UNHCR and the passing of the first UN Refugee Convention (1951) a new framework for global refugee governance had seen the light of day. Denmark was the first country to sign the convention, and by 1968 all the Nordic countries had signed and ratified it. This early globalization of policies for refugees and forced migrants came to shape Nordic refugee histories in the rest of the twentieth century and to the present day (Salomon 1991).

International organizations and conventions were important factors in refugee reception in the postwar years and in the following four decades of the Cold War between East and West. During the Cold War, international relations, especially toward the Soviet Union and the Eastern bloc, and security considerations had a fundamental influence on refugee policies in Europe, including in the Nordic countries (Notini Burch 2014).

The Nordic countries received the first significant group of Cold War refugees after the communist takeover in Czechoslovakia in February 1948. About 60,000 Czechs and Slovaks left the country in the years after the takeover and were first settled in displaced people's camps in Allied occupied Germany and Austria. From there, they were slowly resettled with the mediation of the International Refugee Organization. Scandinavian countries received a quota that in Sweden and Norway included a number of handicapped people and tuberculosis patients (Thor 2007; 2008). When the Soviet Union violently suppressed the uprising in Hungary in November 1956, almost 200,000

Hungarians fled to neighboring countries (Austria and Yugoslavia). Many were subsequently resettled in Western countries (Kecskés 2022), including Denmark (1,390), Sweden (7,290), Norway (1,590), and Iceland (50). Norway had initially followed a policy to assist the refugees "where they were" (in Austria) and agreed later to resettle some of them (Tjelmeland 2003, 49–56).

During the Cold War, help for refugees from the communist countries was essential to the self-concept of the liberal-democratic West and was frequently used as a propaganda tool, comparable with the positive reception of religious refugees, such as the Huguenots, in the age of Protestant–Catholic antagonism. A decade after the Hungarians, several thousand Polish Jews fled from an antisemitic campaign initiated by the Communist Party in Poland. Many of these forced migrants received asylum in Denmark and Sweden. At the same time, the violent end of the "Prague Spring" forced between 100,000 and 130,000 Czechoslovaks to leave the country and seek refuge elsewhere. In the context of the Cold War, refugees from communist countries were generally warmly welcomed and their histories were reported by the press.

Finland formed an exception to this. Following the Finnish–Soviet Agreement of Friendship, Cooperation and Mutual Assistance of 1948, Finland was highly cautious in its handling of political refugees from communist Eastern Europe. Human rights considerations were trumped by foreign policy, and 114 of the 153 dissidents fleeing from the Soviet Union between 1945 and 1981 were handed over to the Soviet authorities (Pekkarinen and Pohjonen 2005, 343; see also Roiko-Jokela 1999). Asylum applications were rejected to such an extent that serious doubts were raised about Finnish neutrality abroad. Only after the first Aliens Act (1983) did the possibilities for Soviet defectors to gain asylum begin to improve.

During the Cold War period, non-European refugees began arriving in the Nordic countries. All Nordic countries began receiving the so-called quota refugees through the United Nations Refugee Agency's (UNHCR) resettlement program. Sweden in particular also began receiving independently arriving refugees, such as the Assyrians who from the late 1960s onward fled ethnic and religious persecution in their homeland areas in Turkey, Iraq, Iran, and Syria (e.g., Lundgren 2019). Other non-European refugees often fled from conflicts caused by violent (and frequently incomplete) processes of decolonization and the global Cold War. The numerically largest groups included the Chileans leaving their country after the right-wing military coup against the Allende government in 1973 (see Chapter 14) and Vietnamese refugees (often called the "boat people") who came to the West and the Nordic countries in the late 1970s after the long war in Vietnam ended in the victory of the Communists. After the Islamic Revolution in Iran in 1979 and the subsequent period of war and instability, many thousand Iranian refugees came to the Nordic countries during the 1980s. The eruption of a civil conflict in Sri Lanka in 1983 caused the mass emigration of Tamils, first of whom arrived in the Nordic countries in the mid-1980s. In Norway, most of them settled in Finnmark, where they found employment in the fishing industry (Brochmann 2003, 224–26). Owing to the conflict of the Kurdish independence movement and intensified persecution of Kurdish separatism in Turkey, Iraq, and Iran, the number of Kurdish refugees coming to the Nordic countries, particularly Sweden, began to grow in the 1980s and continued to increase in the following decades.

While most of the Cold War era refugees were received in the Nordic countries until the 1980s according to quota agreements with international agencies such as the UNHCR, individual asylum seekers subsequently became more frequent. The arrival of higher numbers of migrants sparked debates about who should be granted refugee status and given protection according to the Refugee Convention and who should be seen primarily as "economic migrants" and therefore sent back. In reality, the interpretative openness of these categorizations resulted in mixed policy outcomes. Rejected asylum seekers could, in many cases, remain in the country, for example with a humanitarian visa (Brochmann 2003, 183–85).

Historiography

Much of postwar Nordic historiography continued to perceive migration primarily in terms of emigration or internal migration connected to urbanization. In terms of *immigration*, the relatively strong position of economic and labor history was reflected on the prominence of social history approaches, influenced from the 1970s onward by a growing international research field and journals such as *Immigrants & Minorities* (1981–). Social history research rarely focused on forced migrants, however. Historical research dealing more specifically with

Cold War refugees in the Nordic countries emerged largely only after the Cold War had already ended. It tended at least initially to focus on state policies and has shown that these were not only shaped by humanitarian, security, and foreign policy considerations but to a large extent by the primacy of labor market orientation.

This has been particularly evident in the case of Sweden. At the end of the Second World War, when Sweden had already received more than 185,000 forced migrants, refugee policy became an integral part of general labor market policy. In his pioneering study on the resettlement of Baltic refugees and the liberated Polish concentration camp prisoners in Sweden, Lars Olsson (1995, 1997) demonstrated that refugees were treated primarily as a workforce to fill labor shortages (Byström and Frohnert 2013, 167–223). The dominance of labor market orientation, manifested in the central role of the Labor Market Board (*Arbeidsmarknadsstyrelse* – AMS) in the reception and distribution of refugees in Sweden, is also significant with respect to the Cold War refugees, as Anders Svensson (Wigerfelt) (1992) and Łukasz Górniok (2016) have shown in their respective studies on Swedish policies toward the Hungarian, Czechoslovakian, and Polish-Jewish refugees. The primacy of labor market concerns is also evident in the fact that refugees were placed into work where they were needed with little regard to previous education or experience.

The relatively few historical studies on Cold War refugee groups have often focused on integration into work life. Johan Svanberg has, for example, studied the integration of Estonian refugees (1945–1952) from a labor perspective and on a local level in Sweden (Svanberg 2010). Another example is the study of Anders Svensson Wigerfelt (2010) that compares the Hungarian refugees of 1956, the Iranian refugees of the 1980s, and the Bosnian refugees of the 1990s by focusing on the changing conditions of labor market integration in Sweden. It can be argued that the histories of Cold War refugee groups have in fact often not been understood in the context of *refugee* history as much as in the context of general *labor* and *migration* history, with an emphasis on resettlement and integration (housing, labor market, education) (e.g., Lundh and Ohlsson 1994).

Meanwhile, pioneering works such as Haci Akman's study (1993) on Vietnamese refugees or Line Alice Ytrehus's thesis (2004) on refugee intellectuals in Norway originated in cultural studies and social sciences rather than in history. New perspectives on the experiences, memories, and identity formations of Cold War period refugees also came from the works of – and literary studies on – individual exile writers in Scandinavia, such as Rubén Palma, Michael Konupek, Fateme Behros, Azar Mahloujian, and Maciej Zaremba (Bonsager 2014, 53–67; Humpál 2016, 224–32; see also Kongslien 2007, 197–226; Lane, Kjelsvik, and Bøstein Myhr 2022; Zaremba 2018). These personal narratives revealed lived experiences often bypassed in sociohistorical integration research. Yet, in contrast to the US and Great Britain, there were only a few "community histories" written by representatives of a particular refugee groups themselves. Some refugee groups have had their history written by scholars, such as Latin American refugees who came to Sweden and other Western European countries in the 1970s (Lundberg 1989).

Meanwhile, synthesizing works on national histories of migration, such as the three-volume *Norsk innvandringshistorie*, aimed at integrating political, social, and cultural aspects of migrant and refugee experiences, and also referring – to some extent – to subjective experiences of individual migrants. Same is true of some broader-scale research combining social history and a national perspective on the development of the welfare state and migration policy (e.g., Byström 2012; Byström and Frohnert 2013; Byström and Frohnert 2017). Shorter studies, typically in the form of master's theses at universities, have further addressed aspects of integration and acculturation of individual Cold War refugee groups or subgroups (e.g., Eidem 2010; Korsvold 2020). In Finland, there has also been detailed research on the POWs, internees and refugees extradited to the Soviet Union (Roiko-Jokela 1999; Pekkarinen and Pohjonen 2005).

Forced migration of the Cold War period has also been studied in the broader context of international history. For example, a pioneering historical project on the emergence of the international refugee regime after the Second World War was carried out at Lund University in the late 1980s and early 1990s, producing a number of critical studies on the topic (Ruthström-Ruin 1993; Rystad 1990; Salomon 1991; Sjöberg 1991), introducing new concepts and perspectives into the historiography of forced migration in the Nordic countries.

End of the Cold War? Globalization and Europeanization

The end of the Cold War marked the beginning of a new global order. The political geography of Europe changed dramatically after the fall of the Berlin Wall, with borders redrawn and regimes reshaped. Refugees from the Middle East and Somalia and the war in Yugoslavia in the early 1990s made it clear that the end of the Cold War did not mark the end of wars and forced migration. On the contrary, the post–Cold War period turned out to be an era of mass displacement, with the arrival of refugees from the so-called Global South becoming a contentious political issue.

At the same time, national refugee policies were increasingly shaped by an international sphere of policymaking. European integration formed a new layer between national and international migration politics. Denmark had been a member of the European Economic Community since 1973, and as the iron curtain fell the two neutral Nordic countries, Sweden and Finland, joined the EU in 1995. Norway became a part of the European Single Market and joined the Schengen Agreement in 2001. Subsequently, the EU became an important factor shaping international migration policies.

The complex interplay between national, regional, and international levels was evident when refugees from former Yugoslavia arrived in the Nordic countries in large numbers. A new system of temporary protection was introduced, developed in cooperation with the UNHCR, as a means of providing protection for refugees on a collective basis without individual examination but also without providing a permanent residence. While intended as a temporary solution, by the mid-1990s all Scandinavian countries had introduced special legislation that gave residence permits to refugees from Yugoslavia (Brochmann 1997; see also Chapter 5).

Also, intra-Nordic cooperation on social policy issues remained relevant. Even though the Nordic welfare states provided somewhat different answers to similar questions, the tendency from the late 1990s was toward welfare reforms and integration policies shaped by the idea of an active labor market (Brochmann and Hagelund 2010; Jønsson 2018a; 2018b; Nielsen Breidahl 2012; see also Chapter 6). At the same time, the refugee issue moved to the top of the political agenda. New political parties were established with restrictive migration and refugee policy as their main election issue. The tremendous political weight of refugee questions also forced established parties to develop detailed migration policy platforms, with sharp value-based cleavages between the older political parties too (Green-Pedersen 2012; Välimäki 2019).

By the turn of the millennium, all Nordic countries had introduced new integration policies and reformed migration policies. In the aftermath of the 9/11 terrorist attacks, there was an increase in securitization and restrictions, with Denmark in particular introducing successive restrictions to the Aliens Act. Sweden, meanwhile, retained broadly a humanitarian-oriented and liberal approach at least until 2015. However, this contrast has been described as partly one of "discursive divergence and practical convergence" (Hedetoft 2006). In the long term, Sweden, Norway, and Finland have shifted toward more restrictive refugee policies and a focus on returning unwanted migrants, converging with the broader "deportation turn" (Gibney 2008) in the Global North. Returning hundreds of thousands of people into their countries of departure has subsequently amounted to a large-scale state-induced form of forced mobility (e.g., Lindberg 2022; Tervonen 2022a).

Despite this, forced migration has continued to grow in the twenty-first century. The wars following 9/11 caused a mass displacement of people in the Middle East (particularly Iraq) and Afghanistan. Tens of thousands of Syrians, Iraqis, and refugees of other nationalities applied for asylum in the Nordic countries during the so-called "refugee crisis" in 2015. However, European countries – Nordic countries included – did not introduce collective protection for the Syrian refugees as a group as they did in the 1990s with the Bosnian refugees but insisted on individual asylum applications (see Lucassen 2018, 383–410; Sandanger 2021; Chapter 5). The 2001 EU Temporary Protection Directive was only launched for the first time in March 2022 in response to the refugee crisis caused by the Russian invasion of Ukraine, with numbers of refugees exceeding those of 2015 in most Nordic countries.

Historiography

The post–Cold War period has been marked by increased migration, restrictive policy reforms, and internationalization and Europeanization of spaces for policymaking. Yet the study of these developments has been dominated by social and political sciences. These disciplines have produced a huge body of literature dealing with forced migration

-related issues, from electoral politics to social trust in welfare states, and from questions of identity to the insecurities and inequalities produced by restrictive migration policies.

The highly visible and politicized role of migration and diversity in present-day Nordic societies has been reflected also on the field of history, however, and produced in each country a steadily growing literature related to forced migrations in the post–Cold War era. In the 1990s, the history of migrants and refugees became a topic at universities, with numerous master's theses and doctoral dissertations written on it. In Norway, Knut Kjeldstadli and Jan Eivind Myhre directed one of the first large-scale migration histories with the "Norwegian Immigration History" project. While not specific to the post–Cold War period, the works published within this project explored also contemporaneous histories of migration and diversity in Norway and conveyed the basic insight that these were neither new nor exceptional but connected to a continuum that is fundamental also in Nordic history. This argument was also prominent in the Danish historian Bent Østergaard's (2007) *Indvandrerne i Danmarks Historie*, which triggered public debates over the place of migrants within the national history.[17]

In more specialized publications dealing with contemporary forced migration, several key themes have been prominent. First, the cultural turn of the 1980s was reflected in history writing from the early 1990s onward, with several studies on language, concepts, and discourses. Regarding the last of these, research on media and parliamentary debates about migration and refugees was published in all Nordic countries (see Boréus 2005; Holm 2005; Hvennegaard-Lassen 2002; Johansson 2005; Jørgensen 2006; Kotilainen and Laine 2021; Lepola 2000; Välimäki 2019). This literature has provided insights into the dramatic shifts in discourses within each country and across the Nordic countries. Most of these studies have analyzed discourses vis-a-vis both labor migrants and forced migrants, showing both similarities and significant divergences.

From the early 2000s onward, another approach came to the fore, as several studies of institutions, societal change, and welfare bordering were published. While drawing on insights from discourse analysis, these studies analyzed the institutional development of migration and refugee policies, focusing on how the Nordic welfare states and policy-makers reacted to the arrival of labor migrants as well as refugees and other forced migrants (e.g., Brochmann and Hagelund 2010; Jønsson 2018b; Nielsen Breidahl 2012; Tervonen 2022b).

While research in policies and politics (including debates and discourses) has been a growing part of histories within this area, it has been complemented by a similarly growing interest in memory history (e.g., Huttunen 2002; Pentikäinen 2005). In Finland, there has been growing research and community interest in the return migration of Ingrian Finns, and the intergenerational memories and traumas connected to it (e.g. Kähäri 2024; Kähäri, Turjanmaa, and Leinonen 2023; Pakkanen and Pakkanen 2020). More broadly, new museums and research centers were established to include migrants and refugees in national histories, and in recent years the process of giving voice and space to refugees has gained increased attention (Johansson 2015; Johansson and Bevelander 2017; Thor Tureby and Johansson 2020). Use of oral history and ethnographic methods has been harnessed to researching the experiences and histories of different refugee groups (Adjam 2017; Hall 2023; Lindholm 2016; Strollo 2013).

The so-called refugee crisis was the subject of documentation and research from the very beginning, often with a focus on the reception and help provided to the refugees more than on the refugees themselves (see for example Lilja et al. 2019; Lyytinen 2019; Sjöberg 2018; Thor Tureby and Wagrell 2022). As an example of how the contemporary migration "crisis" has shaped the historical research agenda, the increasing numbers of returns, citizenship deprivation, and deportations of noncitizens has been reflected in historical interest in forced removals (e.g., Tervonen 2022a; Välimäki 2022; see also Birkvad 2023). Additionally, historians have pointed to the diversity and prominent roles of ethnic and racialized minority groups in the histories of forced migration (e.g., Tervonen and Leinonen 2021). Moreover, a postcolonial turn and rise of critical migration studies has prompted collaboration between social scientists and historians in studying the connection between present-day racializing migration policies and the historical legacies of colonialism in the Nordic countries (e.g., Keskinen, Skaptadóttir, and Toivanen 2019).

Conclusion: from silence to inclusion?

If migration is still often understood in the Nordic countries as something "new," this is even more so with regard to forced migration, which in contemporary public discourse is frequently understood exclusively as a post–Second World War phenomenon. In this chapter, we have highlighted the centuries-long depth and the immense scale and complexity of histories of forced migration in the Nordic region. These histories have touched upon the lives of hundreds of thousands of people (or, if counting POWs, forced laborers, and other "institutional migrants," several millions) from the sixteenth century to the present. At the same time, our initial hypothesis about a general historiographical silence regarding forced migrants appears to be largely confirmed in the context of Nordic historiography. Well into the 1990s, and in many cases long after this, we find distinctively patchy – if not outright missing – national research fields with a highly selective focus.[18] Before the end of the Cold War, the most important relevant publications have formed exceptions to an overall rule of silence (e.g., Hammar 1964; Torvinen 1984) and have often been written outside the profession of history (e.g., Sana 1979).

During a formative period of professional historiographic traditions in the Nordic countries from the nineteenth century to the early twentieth, the perception of migration was largely dominated by overseas migrants leaving for North America. Yet, from the turn of the twentieth century onward, each Nordic country also received successive incoming groups of refugees, from "Pogrom" Jews to Russian revolutionaries and "White emigres" to Central Europeans fleeing Nazi persecution. These migrants received scant scholarly attention at the time and were by and far excluded from the emerging national narratives. Only in rare cases was a particular group of forced migrants fitted into such narratives. This was the case with the eighteenth-century Finnish refugees of the Great Northern War, who had already received an exceptional amount of public attention in their own time and were "re-discovered" several times as a trope of nationalist historiography.

In the decades immediately following the Second World War, interest in the occupation years in Norway and Denmark and in narratives of national resistance brought some attention to groups such as Norwegian deportees to North Norway or Nazi Germany and Norwegian and Danish refugees, among them Jews, fleeing to Sweden. From the 1970s onward, critical historians gradually began to probe issues previously bypassed in dominant Nordic national narratives, including the treatment of refugees. In Sweden and Norway, a number of historians pointed to prewar traditions of exclusion and restrictionism toward especially Jews and Roma, both of whom were victims of deportations to German death camps during the war. Finnish researchers similarly posed questions about the country's de facto alliance with Nazi Germany in 1941–1944, which also brought attention to the deportation of a small number of Jewish refugees to Nazi Germany in 1942.

Meanwhile, postwar Scandinavia and Sweden in particular had become the destination areas for a wide diversity of forced migrants from Europe and beyond. These new movements were by and large not reflected in history writing before the 1980s, however. A gap appears to have opened between history and social sciences, the latter of which could address immediate questions related to newly arrived refugees while making few connections with comparable situations in the past (see also Marfleet 2007, 137).

From the 1990s onward, there has been a slow recognition of wider histories of refugeedom in the Nordic countries. Expansion of research has been accompanied by diversifying methodologies and theoretical approaches and a shift from the focus on political events and statistical analysis to social history and migrants' experiences and personal memories. Debates on multiculturalism, human rights, transnationalism, and later on gender, intersectionality, critical race theory, and postcolonial perspectives have significantly shaped the research agenda. More recent research has dealt, for example, with the cases of Russian Jews and German postwar refugees in Denmark; refugees and survivors of the Holocaust and Nazi persecution; forced migrants and slave laborers in occupied Norway; and Ingrian evacuees and refugees of the Lapland War (1944–1945) in Finland.

Tony Kushner has argued in the context of British historiography and heritage that "[o]nly a few and carefully selected groups, and especially the help that was given to them, have been recognized and celebrated, especially in relation to those who escaped Nazism" (Kushner 2006, 223). Kushner's critique, aimed particularly at the self-gratulatory public narratives of the Kindertransport in Britain, appears to bear some relevance in the Nordic case, particularly before the 1970s. However, our chapter has also pointed to a subsequently expanding research field often posing questions critical to nationalist narratives of the past. On some level, it would seem that the picture is one of a transition from predominant silences to an increasing inclusion of forced migration in historiography. However, persistent blind spots remain evident, along with gaps between history and social sciences, the latter frequently operating from a presentist perspective. One example is the study of forced migrants *rejected* rather than accepted by the nation-states, i.e., deportees, a theme that is only gradually emerging as a historical rather than merely legal and political science subject. There is also room for more research and public acknowledgement on the extensive forced mobilities of indentured laborers and slaves connected to Swedish and Danish colonial histories

More generally – and with some notable exceptions – histories of forced migration and refugeedom have tended to be particularized as something separate from the broader frame of national or even migration history. There has further been a tendency to equate refugees and other forced migrants with the broader category of migrants, or, at times, to selectively present particular refugee experiences as success stories of "model minorities." Our chapter thus points toward a challenging balancing act of holistic yet analytically rigorous research on forced migration, which neither exceptionalizes the object of its study nor obscures it merely as a subsidiary part of "migration" in general.

Notes

1 In Norway, the exclusionary clause in the constitution was rescinded with respect to Jews in 1851, to monastic orders in 1897, and to Jesuits in 1956. Since the sixteenth century, there had existed a tradition of exclusion vis-à-vis "Gypsies" (*tatere*), who often were denied access or expelled (Sogner 2003). In Denmark, a royal charter in 1814 granted the Jews the same rights as other Danish citizens, but with the Jewish society (*Mosaisk Trossamfund*) obligated to adjust their practices, for example to adopt a "Jewish version" of the Protestant confirmation rite (Blüdnikow, 2019). By the beginning of the twentieth century nearly 3,000 Russian Jews had settled in Copenhagen (Thing 2008). In Finland, the Jewish population before 1918 consisted mostly of retired soldiers from the Russian army and their families. Their civil rights were heavily debated in the Finnish diet.
2 In 1864, the Kingdom of Denmark lost Schleswig Holstein, sparking migration of Danish bureaucrats to Denmark and to the US.
3 The Danish West Indies were sold to the US in 1917, while Greenland, Iceland, and the Faroe Islands remained Danish colonies.
4 Those fleeing from Russia to Finland were generally recognized as refugees regardless of their nationality. While thousands returned home during the 1920s, some 19,000 stayed in Finland (Nevalainen 1999, 35, 56–57).
5 Swedish police compiled lists of 583 Red refugees 1917–1924, but it can be assumed that many more came to the country but chose to hide their status as political refugees (Hammar 1964, 273).

6 The numbers of German-speaking refugees present in Denmark are: 1933: 800; 1938: 1,300; 1939: 1,772; 1940: 2,198; in Norway 1933: 40; 1938: 1,000; 1939: 800; 1940: 840; in Sweden: 1933: 200; 1938: 2,000; 1939: 1,800; 19340: 3,200 (Meyer 2001, 47). Finland, meanwhile, has been estimated to have received around 900 refugees before the outbreak of the war (Leitzinger 2008, 181–82).

7 One exception was the history of the expulsion and reception of religious refugees in the early modern period, in particular of the French Protestant *réfugiés*. The Huguenot Refuge established the term "refugee" in Europe and formed a reference point in the memory culture of Protestant countries (Lachenicht 2010; Kushner 2006). Since the number of Huguenots who settled in Scandinavia was relatively small, this was, however, less the case in the Nordic countries.

8 After Finnish independence, the deporting of Finnish activists to Siberia gained some scholarly and popular historical attention (e.g., Räikkönen 1928).

9 For an overview about the historiography in the Scandinavian countries, see Hoffmann 2016. For Denmark, see Thing 2008; for Finland, Torvinen 1989; for Sweden, see Carlsson 2004.

10 The same is true of the around 15,000 Finns who left illegally for the Soviet Union during the Great Depression and were caught in Stalin's purges (Kostiainen 1988; Lähteenmäki 2022).

11 At the time of Ingrian repatriations, around 2 800 Soviet citizens from occupied Karelia fled to Finland with the retreating Finnish army. Some returned after 1944, some stayed in Finland, and a few hundred fled to Sweden to avoid deportation to the Soviet Union (Hyytiä 2008, 313; Jalagin 2021a).

12 The Skolt Sami lost their homeplaces as their lands were ceded to the Soviet Union and had to wait until 1949 before resettlement in new municipalities. Other Sami groups, like much of the population of Lapland, faced reconstruction of the built environment from scratch (Lehtola 2019).

13 Most Norwegian Jews who had been deported were killed in Auschwitz–Birkenau, with only 34 survivors (Bruland 2017). Fifty-two of the deported Danish Jews died at the Theresienstadt concentration camp, while the majority survived.

14 This was also the focus of the third workshop organized by our network, "Refugees and Survivors in National Historiographies and Public History. Archives, Voices and Memories," at Malmö University, June 16–17, 2022.

15 The project website contains a database on prisoner-of-war and civilian deaths on both Finnish prisoner-of-war-camps and camps for civilian internees in Eastern Karelia: https://kronos.narc.fi/frontpage.html.

16 The bulk of the prisoners had been captured on the southern sections of the Eastern front and transported through Ukraine, Poland, Stettin, and Tallinn. They were subsequently moved from Stalag camps to labor camps set up at construction sites (Soleim 2009).

17 For example, a recent general account of Danish history (Lind and Roslyng-Jensen 2019) received criticism for only including very limited mentions of immigrants and refugees in Danish history. Similar debates have also taken place in Finland, where a project led by Mats Wikström (Åbo Akademi, 2025–2028) aims to provide an overview of history of migration between 1809 and 2024.

18 This was of course not a unique situation, and much the same applies for groups such as women, minorities, and migrants more generally.

Bibliography

Aaltonen, Jouko and Seppo Sivonen. 2019. *Orjia ja isäntiä: ruotsalais-suomalainen siirtomaaherruus Karibialla*. Helsinki: Into.

Adjam, Maryam. 2017. *Minnesspår: hågkomstens rum och rörelse i skuggan av flykt*. Höör: Brutus Östlings bokförlag Symposion.

Akman, Haci. 1993. *Landflyktighet. En etnologisk undersøkelse av vietnamesiske flyktninger i eksil*. Bergen: Etno-folkloristisk institutt.

Åmark, Klas. 2011. *Att bo granne med ondskan. Sveriges förhållande till nazismen, Nazi-Tyskland och Förintelsen*. Stockholm: Bonnier.

Aminoff-Winberg, Johanna. 1995. *Finska flyktingar i Sverige under stora ofreden: Flyktingförteckningar*. Helsinki: Sukutietotekniikka.

Aminoff-Winberg, Johanna. 2007. *På flykt i eget land: internflyktingar i Sverige under stora nordiska kriget*. Åbo: Åbo Akademis förlag.

Andersson, Lars M. and Mattias Tydén, eds. 2007. *Sverige och Nazityskland: Skuldfrågor och moraldebatt*. Stockholm: Dialogos.

Andersson, Lars M. and Karin Kvist Geverts, eds. 2008. *En problematisk relation? Flyktingpolitik och judiska flyktingar i Sverige 1920–1950*. Uppsala: Uppsala universitet.

Andersson, Martin. 2018. *Migration i 1600-talets Sverige. Älvsborgs lösen 1613–1618*. Lund: Universus Academic Press.

Arnesen, Thomas. 2000. *Norsk flyktningpolitikk i internasjonale fora 1930–1940. Humanitære ideal versus statlig suverenitet*. Unpublished MA thesis, University of Bergen.

Banke, Cecilie F. S. 2005. *Demokratiets skyggeside. Flygtninge og menneskerettigheder i Danmark før Holocaust*. Odense: Syddansk Universitetsforlag.

Berger, Stefan and Christoph Conrad. 2015. *The Past as History: National Identity and Historical Consciousness in Modern Europe*. Basingstoke: Palgrave Macmillan.

Birkvad, Simon R. 2023. *Alien Citizens. A Sociological Thesis on the Re-emergence of Citizenship Deprivation in Norway*. Oslo: University of Oslo.

Blüdnikow, Bent. 2019. *Jødefejden: 1819*. Aarhus: Aarhus University Press.

Boëthius, Maria-Pia. 1991. *Heder och samvete: Sverige och andra världskriget*. Stockholm: Norstedt.

Bonsager, Kristina. 2014. "Identity and Integration in Danish Exile: Language, Culture, and Memory in Rubén Palma's The Trail We Leave". *Latin American Literary Review* 42 (84): 53–67.

Boréus, Kristina. 2005. *Diskriminering med ord*. Stockholm: Stockholms universitet.

Brochmann, Grete. 1997. "Bosnian Refugees in the Scandinavian Countries: A Comparative Perspective on Immigration Control in the 1990s". *Journal of Ethnic and Migration Studies* 23 (4): 459–510. https://doi.org/10.1080/1369183X.1997.9976608.

Brochmann, Grete. 2003. "Del II. 1975–2000". In *Norsk innvandringshistorie, vol. 3: I globaliseringens tid 1940–2000*, edited by Knut Kjeldstadli, 137–387. Oslo: Pax.

Brochmann, Grete and Anniken Hagelund, eds. 2010. *Velferdens grenser. Innvandringspolitikk og velferdsstat i Skandinavia 1945–2010*. Oslo: Universitetsforlaget.

Brochmann, Grete and Knut Kjeldstadli. 2008. *A History of Immigration: The Case of Norway 900–2000*. Oslo: Universitetsforlaget.

Bruland, Bjarte. 2017. *Holocaust i Norge: Registrering, Deportasjon, Tilintetgjørelse*. Oslo: Dreyers Forlag.

Brustad, Jan A. S. 2018. "Norwegian Roma and the Authorities, 1915–1956: Exclusion, Persecution and Extermination". *Bulletin Muzea romské kultury* 27: 46–67.

Brustad, Jan A. S. 2023. *I limbo. Norge og de jødiske flyktningene 1933–1945*. Oslo: Cappelen Damm.

Byström, Mikael. 2006. *En broder, gäst och parasit: uppfattningar och föreställningar om utlänningar, flyktingar och flyktingpolitik i svensk offentlig debatt 1942–1947*. Stockholm: Stockholms universitet.

Byström, Mikael. 2012. *Utmaningen: den svenska välfärdsstatens möte med flyktingar i andra världskrigets tid*. Lund: Nordic Academic Press.

Byström, Mikael and Pär Frohnert, eds. 2013. *Reaching a State of Hope: Refugees, Immigrants and the Swedish Welfare State, 1933–2000*. Lund: Nordic Academic Press.

Byström, Mikael and Pär Frohnert. 2017. *Invandringens historia: från "folkhemmet" till dagens Sverige*. Stockholm: Delmi.

Carlsson, Carl-Henrik. 2004. *Medborgarskap och diskriminering: östjudar och andra invandrare i Sverige 1860–1920*. Uppsala: Uppsala universitet.

Carlsson, Carl-Henrik. 2021. *Judarnas historia i Sverige*. Stockholm: Natur & Kultur.

Castrén, K. U. 1865. *Lähteitä ison vihan historiaan: Handlingar till upplysande af Finlands öden under det Stora nordiska kriget*. Helsinki: Suomalaisen Kirjallisuuden Seura.

Christensen, Claus B, Joachim Lund, Niels Wium Olesen, and Jakob Sørensen. 2005. *Danmark besat. Krig og hverdag*. Copenhagen: Informations Forlag.

Christie, Nils. 1972. *Fangevoktere i konsentrasjonsleire: En sosiologisk undersøkelse av norske fangevoktere i "serberleirene" i Nord-Norge i 1942–43*. Oslo: Pax Forlag.

Corell, Synne. 2010. *Krigens ettertid. Okkupasjonshistorien i norske historiebøker*. Oslo: Scandinavian Academic Press.

Denkiewicz-Szczepaniak, Emilia. 1999. *Polska siła robocza w Organizacji Todta w Norwegii i Finlandii w latach 1941–1945*. Toruń: Wydawnictwo UMK.

Eidem, Grid Haraldsdotter. 2010. "'Altså, Ungarn er som min mor, og Norge er som min kjæreste'. Den ungarske migrasjonen til Norge 1956/57". MA thesis, University of Oslo.

Ekman, Stig. 1980. "The Research Project Sweden during the Second World War (SUAV)", *Meddelande från Arbetarrörelsens arkiv och bibliotek* 16 (4): 16–22.

Elmgren, Ainur. 2021. "Tampere, Berliini, Istanbul: Suomen ensimmäisen muslimiyhteisön ylirajaisuus". In *Vähemmistöt muuttajina. Näkökulmia suomalaisten muuttoliikkeiden monimuotoisuuteen*, edited by Miika Tervonen and Johanna Leinonen, 71–96. Turku: Siirtolaisuusinstituutti.

Elstad, Ingunn. 2020. *Tvangsevakueringa: Finnmark og Nord-Troms 1944 – bakgrunn, gjennomføring og overleving*. Stamsund: Orkana akademisk.

Engman, Max. 2007. *Raja: Karjalankannas 1918–1920*. Helsinki: WSOY.

Eriksen, Knut E. and Terje Halvorsen. 1987. *Frigjøring. Norge i krig vol. 8*. Oslo: Aschehaug.

Fagertun, Fredrik, Palle Ydstebø, Hans Otto Frøland, and Mari Olafson Lundemo. 2022. "Frigjøringens militære forutsetninger". In *Andre verdenskrig i nord Bind 3: Kampen om frihet*, edited by Stian Bones, 37–83. Stamsund: Orkana Akademisk.

Flink, Toivo. 2010. *Kotiin karkotettavaksi: Inkeriläisen siirtoväen palautukset Suomesta Neuvostoliittoon vuosina 1944–1955*. Helsinki: Suomalaisen Kirjallisuuden Seura.

Frohnert, Pär. 2019. "Swedish Refugee Relief NGOs in the Shadow of Nazi Germany: Possibilities and Restraints in 'the People's Home'". *Journal of Migration History* 5: 277–303. https://doi.org/10.1163/23519924-00502004

Frohnert, Pär. 2024. *"Hjälp våra flyktingar!" Politisk och ideell hjelpvirksamhet i Sverige 1933–1939*. Lund: Nordic Academic Press.

Frøland, Hans Otto. 2017. "Forced Labour and Norwegian War Profiteers in the Legal Purges after Second World War". In *The International Criminal Responsibility of War's Funders and Profiteers*, edited by Nina Jorgensen, 37–60. Cambridge: Cambridge University Press. https://doi.org/10.1017/9781108692991.003.

Frøland, Hans Otto and Mari O. Lundemo. 2022. "Tysk bygging av militær og sivil infrastruktur Nord-Norge og Nord-Finland". In *Andre verdenskrig i nord Bind 1: Overfall og okkupasjon*, edited by Fredrik Fagertun, 192–241. Stamsund: Orkana Akademisk.

Fure, Odd-Bjørn. 1999. "Norsk okkupasjonshistorie: konsensus, berøringsangst og tabuisering". In *I krigens kjølvann: nye sider ved norsk krigshistorie og etterkrigstid*, edited by Stein Ugelvik Larsen, 31–46. Oslo: Universitetsforlaget.

Gatrell, Peter. 2017. "Refugees—What's Wrong with History?" *Journal of Refugee Studies* 30 (2): 170–89. https://doi.org/10.1093/jrs/few013.

Gibney, Matthew J. 2008. "Asylum and the Expansion of Deportation in the United Kingdom". *Government and Opposition* 43 (2): 146–67. https://doi.org/10.1111/j.1477-7053.2007.00249.x.

Gøbel, Erik. 2016. *The Danish Slave Trade and Its Abolition*. Leiden and Boston, MA: Brill.

Górniok, Łukasz. 2016. "Swedish Refugee Policymaking in Transition? Czechoslovaks and Polish Jews in Sweden, 1968–1972". PhD diss., Umeå: Umeå University.

Green-Pedersen, Christoffer. 2012. *Partier i nye tider*. Aarhus: Aarhus University Press.

Grimnes Ole Kristian. 1969. *Et flyktningesamfunn vokser fram. Nordmenn i Sverige 1940–45*. Oslo: Aschehoug.

Günther, Dieter. 1982. *Gewerkschafter im Exil. Die Landesgruppe deutscher Gewerkschafter in Schweden von 1938–1945*. Marburg: Verlag Arbeiterbewegung und Gesellschaftswissenschaft.

Haapala, Pertti, Marja Jalava, and Simon Larsson. 2017. *Making Nordic Historiography: Connections, Tensions and Methodology (1850–1970)*. New York: Berghahn. https://doi.org/10.3167/9781785336263.

Häkkinen, Antti, Panu Pulma, and Miika Tervonen, eds. 2005. *Vieraat kulkijat – tutut talot: Näkökulmia etnisyyden ja köyhyyden historiaan Suomessa*. Helsinki: Suomalaisen Kirjallisuuden Seura.

Halén, Harry. 2004. "Kiinalaiset linnoitustyöläiset vuosina 1916–17". In *Venäläis-surmat Suomessa 1914–22. Osa 1*, edited by Lars Westerlund, 107–113. Helsinki: Valtioneuvoston kanslia.

Hall, Emma. 2023. *Mellan rörelse och stillhet: minne och flykt i unga människors berättande 2009–2021*. Malmö: Malmö University.

Hammar, Tomas. 1964. *Sverige åt svenskarna: invandringspolitik, utlänningskontroll och asylrätt 1900–1932*. Stockholm: Statsvetenskapliga institutionen.

Hansson, Svante. 2004. *Flykt och överlevnad. Flyktingverksamhet i Mosaiska försam-lingen i Stockholm 1933–1950*. Stockholm: Hillelförlaget.

Hansson, Lars. 2019. *Vid gränsen. Mottagningar av flyktingar från Norge 1940–1945*. Gothenburg: Göteborgs Universitet.

Harder, Thomas. 2020. *De Uønskede*. Copenhagen: Gyldendal.

Harjumaa, Tiina. 2021. *Menetetty ja läsnäoleva Petsamo. Menneisyyden tulkitsem-inen ja historian rakentuminen petsamolaisessa muistiyhteisössä*. Rovaniemi: Lapin yliopisto.

Hatlehol, Gunnar D. 2015. "'Norwegeneinsatz' 1940–1945. Organisation Todts arbeidere og gradene av tvang". Unpublished PhD diss., NTNU.

Hatlehol, Gunnar D. 2020. "Fangenskap og tvangsarbeid i det tyskokkuperte Norge". *Arbeiderhistorie* 34 (1): 61–83. https://doi.org/10.18261/issn.2387-5879-2020-01-05

Hatlehol, Gunnar D. and Marianne N. Soleim. 2022. "Krigsfanger i krigens slutt-fase". In *Andre verdenskrig i nord, vol. 3: Kampen om frihet*, edited by Stian Bones, 221–43. Stamsund: Orkana akademisk.

Hedetoft, Ulf. 2006. "Divergens eller konvergens? Perspektiver i den dansk-svenske sammenstilling". In *Invandrare och integration i Danmark och Sverige*, edited by Ulf Hedetoft, Bo Petersson, and Lina Sturfelt. Halmstad: Makadam Förlag & Centrum för Danmarksstudier.

Hentilä, Seppo. 2010. "Auf der Schattenseite der Waffenbrüderschaft. Zur neuen Fortsetzungskriegsdebatte in Finnland". In *Vom alten Norden zum neuen Europa: Politische Kultur im Ostseeraum, Festschrift für Bernd Henningsen*, edited by Norbert Götz, Jan Hecker-Stampehl, and Stephan Michael Schröder. 235–50. Berlin: Berliner Wissenschaftsverlag.

Hingarová, Vendula and Zdenko Maršálek. 2022. *Posláni na sever. Češi nucené práci v Norsku*. Červený Kostelec: Nakladatelství Pavel Mervart.

Hoffmann, Christhard. 2016. "Jewish History as a History of Immigration: An Over-view of Current Historiography in the Scandinavian Countries". *Scripta Instituti Donneriani Aboensis*, 27: 203–22. https://doi.org/10.30674/scripta.66576.

Holm, Lærke Klitgaard. 2005. "Diskurser om naturaliserede, flygtninge og indvan-drere". Unpublished PhD diss., Aalborg University.

Humpál, Martin. 2016. "Frihet og Rotsløshet: Michael Konupek's Rutenia". *Transit – "Norden" och "Europa": International Association of Scandinavian Studies* (IASS) 31: 224–32.

Huttunen, Laura. 2002. *Kotona, maanpaossa, matkalla. Kodin merkitykset maahan-muuttajien omaelämäkerroissa*. Helsinki: Suomalaisen Kirjallisuuden Seura.

Hvennegaard-Lassen, Kirsten. 2002. "På lige fod: samfundet, ligheden og folketin-gets debatter om udlændingepolitik 1973–2000". PhD diss., Copenhagen University.

Hyry, Katja. 2011. *Meistä jäi taas jälki: Miten Vienan pakolaiset etsivät paikkaansa, kertoivat kokemastaan ja tulivat kuulluiksi 1900-luvun Suomessa.* Rovaniemi: Lapin yliopistokustannus.

Hyytiä, Osmo. 2008. *"Helmi Suomen maakuntien joukossa". Suomalainen Itä-Karjala 1941–1944.* Helsinki: Edita.

Jalagin, Seija. 2021a. "Pelon ja toivon rajalla: Itäkarjalaisten pakolaisuus Suomesta Ruotsiin toisen maailmansodan jälkeen". *Historiallinen aikakauskirja* 119 (1): 22–35. https://doi.org/10.54331/haik.140776.

Jalagin, Seija. 2021b. "Venäjänkarjalaisesta ruotsinsuomalaiseksi: Toimijuus, hallinta ja pakolaisuuden muistot". In *Vähemmistöt muuttajina. Näkökulmia suomalaisen muuttoliiketutkimuksen moninaisuuteen*, edited by Miika Tervonen and Johanna Leinonen, 149–74. Turku: Siirtolaisuusinstituutti.

Jalagin, Seija. 2021c. "Nimble Nationalism: Transgenerational Experiences of East Karelian Refugees in Finland and Sweden". In *Lived Nation. The Case of Finland as the History of Experiences and Emotions*, edited by Ville Kivimäki, Sami Suodenjoki, and Tanja Vahtikari, 267–93. Basingstoke: Palgrave Macmillan. https://doi.org/10.1007/978-3-030-69882-9_11

Jensen, John V. 2020. *Tyskere på flugt.* Aarhus: Aarhus Universitetsforlag.

Johansen, Per Ole. 1984. *Oss selv nærmest. Norge og jødene 1914–1943.* Oslo: Gyldendal.

Johansson, Christina. 2005. *Välkomna till Sverige? Svenska migrationspolitiska diskurser under 1900-talets andra hälft.* Malmö: Bokbox Förlag.

Johansson, Christina. 2015. *Museums, Migration and Cultural Diversity: Swedish Museums in Tune with the Times.* Innsbruck: Studienverlag.

Johansson, Christina and Pieter Bevelander. 2017. *Museums in a Time of Migration: Rethinking Museums' Roles, Representations, Collections, and Collaborations.* Lund: Nordic Academic Press.

Jønsson, Heidi Vad. 2018a. *Fra lige muligheder til ret og pligt. Socialdemokratiets integrationspolitik 1960'erne til 2000'erne.* Odense: Syddansk Universitetsforlag.

Jønsson, Heidi Vad. 2018b. *Indvandring i velfærdsstaten.* Århus: Århus Universitetsforlag.

Jørgensen, Lars. 2006. "Hvad sagde vi… om de andre? Den udlændingepolitiske debat i Folketinget 1961-1999". PhD diss., RUC.

Junila, Marianne. 2000. *Kotirintaman aseveljeyttä: Suomalaisen siviiliväestön ja saksalaisen sotaväen rinnakkainelo Pohjois-Suomessa 1941–1944.* Helsinki: Suomalaisen Kirjallisuuden Seura.

Juntunen, Alpo. 1983. *Suomalaisten karkottaminen Siperiaan autonomian aikana ja karkotetut Siperiassa.* Helsinki: Valtion painatuskeskus/Arvi A. Karisto OY.

Kähäri, Outi. 2024. "Postmemorial Work of Moral Valence: A Study of the Resistance Practices of Ingrian Descendants". *Memory Studies* 18 (1): 1–17. https://doi.org/10.1177/17506980241255068.

Kähäri, Outi, Elina Turjanmaa, and Johanna Leinonen. 2023. *Vaalimista, vaikenemista ja vastustusta: inkeriläisten perhehistoriat jälkeläisten muistelemana.* Oulu: Oulun yliopisto. https://urn.fi/URN:ISBN:9789526237220.

Kananen, Heli. 2010. *Kontrolloitu sopeutuminen: ortodoksinen siirtoväki sotien jälkeisessä Ylä-Savossa (1946–1959).* Jyväskylä: University of Jyväskylä.

Kanervo, Pirkko, Terhi Kivistö, and Olli Kleemola, eds. 2018. *Karjalani, Karjalani, maani ja maailmani: Kirjoituksia Karjalan menetyksestä ja muistamisesta, evakoiden asuttamisesta ja selviytymisestä*. Turku: Siirtolaisuusinstituutti.

Kecskés, Gustáv D. 2022. "A Cold War Humanitarian Action: The Western Admission of 1956 Hungarian Refugees". *Hungarian Historical Review* 11 (4): 913–35. https://doi.org/10.38145/2022.4.913.

Keskinen Suvi, Unnur Dís Skaptadóttir, and Mari Toivanen, eds. 2019. *Undoing Homogeneity in the Nordic Region: Migration, Difference and the Politics of Solidarity*. Studies in Migration and Diaspora. New York: Routledge. https://doi.org/10.4324/9781315122328.

Kilpi, O. K. 1917. *Suomen siirtolaisuus ja 19. vuosisadan kansantalous*. Helsinki: Sana.

Kinnunen, Tiina and Ville Kivimäki, eds. 2012. *Finland in World War II: History, Memory, Interpretations*. Leiden: Brill. https://doi.org/10.1163/9789004214330.

Kivimäki, Ville. 2012. "Three Wars and Their Epitaphs: The Finnish History and Scholarship of Second World War". In *Finland in World War II: History, Memory, Interpretations*, edited by Tiina Kinnunen and Ville Kivimäki, 1–46. Leiden: Brill. https://doi.org/10.1163/9789004214330_002.

Kirchhoff, Hans. 2001. *Samarbeid og motstand under besættelsen: en politisk historie*. Odense: Odense Universitetsforlag.

Kirchhoff, Hans. 2005. *Et menneske uden pas er ikke noget menneske. Danmark i den internationale flygtningepolitik 1933–1939*. Odense: Syddansk Universitetsforlag.

Kirchhoff, Hans and Lone Rünitz. 2007. *Udsendt til Tyskland. Dansk flygtningepolitik under besættelsen*. Odense: Syddansk Universitetsforlag.

Kjeldstadli, Knut. 2003. "Del III. 1901–1940". In *Norsk innvandringshistorie, vol. 2: I nasjonalstatens tid 1814–1940*, edited by Knut Kjeldstadli, 317–478. Oslo: Pax.

Koblik, Steven. 1988. *The Stones Cry Out: Sweden's Response to the Persecution of Jews 1933–1945*. New York: Holocaust Libr. cop.

Koch, Birgit. 1988. *De sovjetiske, polske og jugoslaviske krigsfanger i tysk fangenskap i Norge 1941–1945*. Unpublished master's thesis, University of Oslo.

Kongslien, Ingeborg. 2007. "New Voices, New Themes, New Perspectives. Contemporary Scandinavian Multicultural Literature". *Scandinavian Studies* 79 (2): 197–226.

Korppi-Tommola, Aura, ed. 1996. *Sotalapset: Tutkimusraportti*. Helsinki: Mannerheimin Lastensuojeluliitto.

Korsnes, Kjetil and Olve Dybvig. 2018. *Wehrmacht i Norge. Antall tysk personell fra april 1940 til mai 1945*. Tromsø/Narvik: Universitetet i Tromsø/Narviksenteret.

Korsvold, Tora. 2020. "'Hungarian Boys' Immigration to Norway, 1956–1957: The Complex Economic, Political and Humanitarian Motives of Minors on the Move". *The Journal of Childhood and Youth* 13 (3): 407–25. https://doi.org/10.1353/hcy.2020.0063.

Kostiainen, Auvo. 1988. *Loikkarit: suuren lamakauden laiton siirtolaisuus Neuvostoliittoon*. Helsinki: Otava.

Kotilainen, Noora and Jussi Laine, eds. 2021. *Muuttoliike murroksessa: metaforat, mielikuvat, merkitykset*. Helsinki: Into.

Kujala, Antti. 2008. *Vankisurmat: Neuvostovankien laittomat ampumiset jatkosodassa*. Helsinki: WSOY.

Kushner, Tony. 2006. *Remembering Refugees: Then and Now*. Manchester: Manchester University Press.

Kvist Geverts, Karin. 2008. *Ett främmande element i nationen: svensk flyktingpolitik och de judiska flyktingarna 1938–1944*. Uppsala: Uppsala universitet.

Lachenicht, Susanne. 2010. *Hugenotten in Europa und Nordamerika: Migration und Integration in der Frühen Neuzeit*. Frankfurt/New York: Campus Verlag.

Lagrou, Pieter. 1999. *The Legacy of Nazi Occupation: Patriotic Memory and National Recovery in Western Europe 1945–1955*. Cambridge: Cambridge University Press. https://doi.org/10.1017/CBO9780511497087

Lähteenmäki, Maria. 2022. *Punapakolaiset: Suomalaisnaisten elämä ja kohtalo Neuvosto-Karjalassa*. Helsinki: Gaudeamus.

Laitila, Teuvo. 2020. "Coercion, Cooperation, Conflicts and Contempt: Orthodox-Lutheran Relations in Swedish-Occupied Kexholm County, Karelia, in the Seventeenth Century". *Entangled Religions* 11 (1): 1–28. https://doi.org/10.46586/er.11.2020.8646.

Lane, Pia, Bjørghild Kjelsvik, and Annika Bøstein Myhr, eds. 2022. *Negotiating Identities in Nordic Migrant Narratives. Crossing Borders and Telling Lives*. London: Palgrave Macmillan. https://doi.org/10.1007/978-3-030-89109-1.

Lehtola, Veli-Pekka. 2019. *Surviving the Upheaval of Arctic War: Evacuation and Return of the Sámi People in Sápmi and Finland During and After the Second World War*, translated by Lina Weber Müller-Wille. Inari: Kustannus Puntsi.

Leinonen, Johanna. 2020. "'The Journey Made Us': Exploring Journey Memories of Karelian Evacuees and Iraqi Refugees". In *Mihin suuntaan Suomi kehittyy? Liikkuvuuden ja muuttoliikkeen dynamiikka. Which Direction is Finland Evolving? The Dynamics of Mobility and Migration*, edited by Elli Heikkilä, 61–76. Turku: Siirtolaisuusinstituutti.

Leitzinger, Antero. 2008. *Ulkomaalaispolitiikka Suomessa 1812–1972*. Helsinki: East-West Books.

Lepola, Outi. 2000. *Ulkomaalaisesta suomenmaalaiseksi: Monikulttuurisuus, kansalaisuus ja suomalaisuus 1990-luvun maahanmuuttopoliittisessa keskustelussa*. Helsinki: Suomalaisen Kirjallisuuden Seura.

Levine, Paul A. 1996. *From Indifference to Activism: Swedish Diplomacy and the Holocaust, 1938–1944*. Uppsala: Uppsala universitet.

Lilja, Märtha, Holger Nilén, Ingrid Sillén, and Ingrid Sjökvist. 2019. *Vi gör vad vi kan: volontärer om flyktingmottagandet i Sverige från 2015*. Södertälje: Liv i Sverige.

Lind, Gunner and Palle Roslyng-Jensen, eds. 2019. *Danmarkshistorien. Samfund, livsformer og politik*. Copenhagen: Gads Forlag.

Lindholm, Susan. 2016. *Remembering Chile: An Entangled History of Hip-Hop In-Between Sweden and Chile*. Malmö: Malmö högskola.

Lindberg, Annika. 2022. *Deportation Limbo: State Violence and Contestations in the Nordics*. Manchester: Manchester University Press.

Lindberg, Hans. 1973. *Svensk flyktingpolitik under internationellt tryck 1936–1941*. Stockholm: Allmänna Förlaget.

Lindeqvist, Karl Olof. 1886. *Suomen olot ison vihan aikana*. Helsinki.

Lindeqvist, Karl Olof. 1919. *Isonvihan aika Suomessa*. Porvoo: WSOY.

Lomfors, Ingrid. 1996. *Förlorad barndom – återvunnet liv. De judiska flyktingbarnen från Nazityskland*. Gothenburg: Göteborgs universitet.

Lorenz, Einhart.1992. *Exil in Norwegen: Lebensbedingungen und Arbeit deutsch-sprachiger Flüchtlinge 1933–1943*. Baden-Baden: Nomos.

Lorenz, Einhart, Klaus Misgeld, Helmut Müssener, and Hans Uwe Petersen, eds. 1998: *Ein sehr trübes Kapitel? Hitlerflüchtlinge im nordeuropäischen Exil 1933 bis 1950*. Hamburg: Ergebnisse-Verlag.

Lucassen, Jan and Leo Lucassen. 2017. "Theorizing Cross-Cultural Migrations". *Social Science History* 41 (3): 445–75. https://doi.org/10.1017/ssh.2017.19.

Lucassen, Leo. 2018. "Peeling an Onion: The 'Refugee Crisis' from an Historical Perspective". *Ethnic and Racial Studies* 41 (3): 383–410. https://doi.org/10.1080/01419870.2017.1355975.

Lundberg, Svante. 1989. *Flyktingskap: latinamerikansk exil i Sverige och Västeuropa*. Lund: Arkiv.

Lundgren, Svante. 2019. *The Assyrians: Fifty Years in Sweden*. Enschede: Nineveh Press.

Lundh, Christer and Rolf Ohlsson. 1994. *Från arbetskraftsimport till flyktinginvandring*. Stockholm: SNS.

Lundemo, Mari O. 2020. "Engineering, Resources and Nature: Organisation Todt in Finland 1941–1944". Unpublished PhD diss., European University Institute.

Lylloff, Kirsten. 2006. *Barn eller fjende: Uledsagede flygtningebørn i Danmark 1945–1949*. Copenhagen: Danmarks Pædagogiske Universitet.

Lyytinen, Eveliina, ed. 2019. *Turvapaikanhaku ja pakolaisuus Suomessa*. Turku: Siirtolaisuusinstituutti.

Maier-Wolthausen, Clemens. 2018. *Zuflucht im Norden: Die schwedischen Juden und die Flüchtlinge 1933–1941*. Göttingen: Wallstein.

Marfleet, Philip. 2007. "Refugees and History: Why We Must Address the Past". *Refugee Survey Quarterly* 26 (3): 136–48. https://doi.org/10.1093/rsq/hdi0248.

Martínez, Victoria Van Orden. 2023. *Afterlives: Jewish and Non-Jewish Polish Survivors of Nazi Persecution in Sweden Documenting Nazi Atrocities, 1945–1946*. Linköping: Linköping University Press.

Meyer, Frank. 2001. *Dansken, svensken og nordmannen. Skandinaviske habitusforskjeller sett i lys av kulturmøtet med tyske flyktninger. En komparativ studie*. Oslo: Unipub forlag.

Miettinen, Samuli. 2021. *Paapeli 1944: Jatkosodan unohdettu internointileiri*. Jyväskylä: Docendo.

Misgeld, Klaus. 1976. *Die "Internationale Gruppe demokratischer Sozialisten" in Stockholm 1942–1945: zur sozialistischen Friedensdiskussion während des Zweiten Weltkrieges*. Uppsala: Uppsala universitet.

Müssener, Helmut. 1974. *Exil in Schweden: politische und kulturelle Emigration nach 1933*. Munich: Hanser.

Neuvonen-Seppänen, Hellä. 2020. *Menetetyn Karjalan valot ja varjot: Siirtokarjalaisuus evakon lapsen elämässä ja muistoissa*. Kuopio: University of Eastern Finland.

Nevalainen, Pekka. 1990. *Inkeriläinen siirtoväki Suomessa 1940-luvulla*. Helsinki: Otava.

Nevalainen, Pekka. 1999. *Viskoi kuin luoja kerjäläistä: Venäjän pakolaiset Suomessa 1917–1939*. Helsinki: Suomalaisen Kirjallisuuden Seura.

Nevalainen, Pekka. 2002. *Punaisen myrskyn suomalaiset: suomalaisten paot ja paluumuutot idästä 1917–1939*. Helsinki: Suomalaisen Kirjallisuuden Seura.

Nevalainen, Pekka. 2006. *Karjalan kansaa valistamassa: Itä-Karjalan pakolaiset opinteillä Suomessa.* Helsinki: Suomalaisen Kirjallisuuden Seura.

Nielsen Breidahl, Karen. 2012. *Når staten lærer: En historisk og komparativ analyse af statslig policy læring og betydningen heraf for udviklingen i den arbejdsmarkedsrettede del af indvandrerpolitikken i Sverige, Norge og Danmark fra 1970 til 2011.* Aalborg: Aalborg Universitet.

Notini Burch, Cecilia. 2014. *A Cold War Pursuit: Soviet Refugees in Sweden 1945–54.* Stockholm: Santérus Academic.

Nygård, Toivo. 1980. *Itä-Karjalan pakolaiset 1917–1922.* Jyväskylä: Jyväskylän yliopisto.

Olesen, Poul Erik, ed. 2017. *Danmark og kolonierne. St. Croix, St Thomas og St. Jan.* Copenhagen: GAD.

Olsson, Lars. 1995. *På tröskeln till folkhemmet: baltiska flyktingar och polska koncentrationslägerfångar som reservarbetskraft i skånskt jordbruk kring slutet av andra världskriget.* Lund: Morgonrodnad.

Olsson, Lars. 1997. *On the Threshold of the People's Home of Sweden: A Labor Perspective of Baltic Refugees and Relieved Polish Concentration Camp Prisoners in Sweden at the End of World War II.* New York: Center for Migration Studies.

Östman, Ann-Catrin. 2023. "Estniska överlöpare i Finland på 1810-talet – krav på förvisningar under en ny gränsregim". *Historisk tidskrift för Finland* 108 (3): 201–33.

Østergaard, Bent. 2007. *Indvandrerne i Danmarks historie. Kultur- og religionsmøder.* Odense: University of Southern Denmark.

Ottosen, Kristian. 2004. *Nordmenn i fangenskap 1940–1945.* Oslo: Universitetsforlaget.

Panikar, Marina. 2021. "Repatriering av sovjetiske krigsfanger fra Nord-Norge". In *Blodige Spor. Sovjetiske krigsfanger i byggingen av Nordlandsbanen 1943–1945*, edited by Joakim A. Markussen, Michael Stokke, and Marina Panikar, 40–52. Narvik: Narviksenteret.

Pakkanen, Lea and Santeri Pakkanen. 2020. *Se tapahtui meille: isän ja tyttären matka inkerinsuomalaisuuteen.* Helsinki: Gummerus.

Papp, David. 1988. "'Livländska rymlingar': Estländsk allmoges flykt till Sverige under 1700- och 1800-talen". In *Estländare i Sverige: Historia, språk, kultur*, edited by Raimo Raag and Harald Runblom, 21–35. Uppsala: Uppsala universitet.

Pekkarinen, Jussi and Juha Pohjonen. 2005. *Ei armoa Suomen selkänahasta: Ihmisluovutukset Neuvostoliittoon 1944–1981.* Helsinki: Otava.

Pentikäinen, Marja. 2005. *Loputon matka. Vietnamilaisten ja somalialaisten kertomuksia pakolaisuudesta.* Helsinki: Työministeriö.

Peters, Jan. 1984. *Exilland Schweden: Deutsche und schwedische Antifaschisten 1933–1945.* Berlin: Akademie-Verlag.

Petersen, Hans Uwe, ed. 1991. *Hitlerflüchtlinge im Norden: Asyl und Politisches Exil 1933–1945.* Kiel: Neuer Malik Verlag.

Pohjonen, Juha. 2008. "Soviet Demands for Repatriations from Finland between 1944 and 1955". In *POW Deaths and People Handed over to Germany and the Soviet Union in 1939–55. A research report by the Finnish National Archives*, edited by Lars Westerlund, 180–211. Helsinki: National Archives of Finland.

Räikkönen, Erkki. 1928. *Svinhufvudin kertomukset Siperiasta.* Helsinki: Otava.

Raninen-Siiskonen, Tarja. 1999. *Vieraana omalla maalla: Tutkimus karjalaisen siir-toväen muistelukerronnasta.* Helsinki: Suomalaisen Kirjallisuuden Seura.

Rautajoki, Reijo. 2017. *Vaiettu sotapakolaisuus: Inkeriläiset kansakoulunopettajat jatkosodan aikana.* Joensuu: Itä-Suomen yliopisto.

Reuter, Anni. 2023. *Inkerinsuomalaisten karkotus, hajaannus ja vastarinta Stalinin ajan Neuvostoliitossa aikalaiskirjeiden ja muistitiedon valossa.* Helsinki: University of Helsinki.

Roiko-Jokela, Heikki. 1999. *Oikeutta moraalin kustannuksella?: Neuvostoliiton kansalaisten luovutukset Suomesta 1944–1955.* Jyväskylä: Jyväskylän yliopisto.

Roiko-Jokela, Heikki, ed. 2004. *Vihollisen armoilla. Neuvostosotavankien kohtaloita Suomessa 1941–1948.* Jyväskylä: Minerva.

Rosvoll, Maria, Lars Lien, and Jan Alexander Brustad. 2015. *Å bli dem kvit: Utviklingen av en "sigøynerpolitikk" og utryddelsen av norske rom.* Oslo: HL-senteret.

Rudberg, Pontus. 2017. *The Swedish Jews and the Holocaust.* Abingdon: Routledge. https://doi.org/10.4324/9781315171746.

Rünitz, Lone. 2005. *Af hensyn til konsekvenserne. Danmark og flygtningespørgsmålet 1933–1940.* Syddansk Universitetsforlag.

Ruthström-Ruin, Cecilia. 1993. *Beyond Europe: The Globalization of Refugee Aid.* Lund: Lund University Press.

Rystad, Göran, ed. 1990. *The Uprooted: Forced Migration as an International Problem in the Post-war Era.* Lund: Lund University Press.

Salenius, J. M. 1911. "Käkisalmen läänin oloista kuudennentoista sataluvun loppupuolella". *Historiallinen arkisto* 22. Helsinki: Suomen Historiallinen Seura.

Salomon, Kim. 1991. *Refugees in the Cold War: Toward a New International Refugee Regime in the Early Postwar Era.* Lund: Lund University Press.

Sandanger, Linn Cecilie S. 2021. "Internasjonale forpliktelser versus nasjonal selvbestemmelse? Offentlige debatter om den norske asyl- og flyktningpolitikken i periodene 1993-1996 og 2015–2016". MA thesis, University of Bergen.

Sana, Elina. 1979. *Kuoleman laiva S/S Hohenhörn: juutalaispakolaisten kohtalo Suomessa.* Helsinki: WSOY.

Sane, Henrik Zip. 2000. *Billige og villige?: fremmedarbejdere i fædrelandet ca. 1800–1970.* Farum: Farums Arkiver & Museer.

Sarvimäki, Matti, Roope Uusitalo and Markus Jäntti. 2022. "Habit Formation and the Misallocation of Labor: Evidence from Forced Migrations". *Journal of the European Economic Association* 20 (6): 2497–539. https://doi.org/10.1093/jeea/jvac037.

Savolainen, Ulla. 2015. *Muisteltu ja kirjoitettu evakkomatka: Tutkimus evakkolapsuuden muistelukerronnan poetiikasta.* Joensuu: Suomen Kansantietouden Tutkijain Seura.

Savolainen, Ulla and Outi Fingerroos. 2018. "Luovutetun Karjalan ylirajainen muisti". In *Karjala, Karjalani, maani ja maailmani: Kirjoituksia Karjalan menetyksestä ja muistamisesta, evakkojen asuttamisesta ja selviytymisestä*, edited by Pirkko Kanervo, Terhi Kivistö, and Olli Kleemola, 149–66. Turku: Siirtolaisuusinstituutti.Sjöberg, Karin. 2018. *Ankomst Malmö: röster om flyktingmottagandet hösten 2015.* Malmö: Malmö Stadsarkiv.

Sjöberg, Tommie. 1991. *The Powers and the Persecuted: The Refugee Problem and the Intergovernmental Committee on Refugees (IGCR), 1938–1947.* Lund: Lund University Press.

Skjønsberg, Harald. 1981. *En flyktningepolitikk utvikles: Norges politikk overfor tyske flyktninger 1933–1940*. Oslo: University of Oslo.

Sogner, Sølvi. 2003. "Taterne eller romanifolket". In *Norsk innvandringshistorie 1*, edited by Knut Kjeldstadli, 356–71. Oslo: Pax forlag.

Soleim, Marianne Neerland. 2009. *Sovjetiske krigsfanger i Norge 1941–1945: Antall, organisering og repatriering*. Oslo: Spartacus.

Soleim, Marianne Neerland. 2016. *"Operasjon Asfalt": Kald krig om krigsgraver*. Stamsund: Orkana akademisk.

Stenius, Henrik, Maria Österberg, and Johan Östling, eds. 2011. *Nordic Narratives of the Second World War: National Historiographies Revisited*. Lund: Nordic Academy Press.

Sterner Carlberg, Mirjam. 1994. *Gemenskap och överlevnad: Om den judiska gruppen i Borås och dess historia*. Gothenburg: Göteborgs universitet.

Stokke, Michael. 2024. "Jugoslaviske fanger i Norge 1942–1945: Fra SS' dødsarbeidsleirer til Wehrmachts krigsfangeleirer". Unpublished doctoral diss., University of Tromsø.

Strollo, Emma. 2013. *Det städade folkhemmet: tyskfödda hembiträden i efterkrigstidens Sverige*. Gothenburg: Makadam Förlag.

Suolahti, Gunnar ed. 1936. *Suomen kulttuurihistoria. 4, Industrialismin ja kansallisen nousun aika*. Jyväskylä: Gummerus.

Svanberg, Ingvar and Mattias Tydén. 1992. *Tusen år av invandring: en svensk kulturhistoria*. Stockholm: Gidlund.

Svanberg, Johan. 2010. *Arbetets relationer och etniska dimensioner: Verkstadsföreningen, Metall och esterna vid Svenska stålpressnings AB i Olofström 1945–1952*. Växjö: Linnaeus University Press.

Svensson, Anders. 1992. *Ungrare i folkhemmet. Svensk flyktingpolitik i det kalla krigets skugga*. Lund: Lund University Press.

Tempsch, Rudolf. 1997. *Från Centraleuropa till folkhemmet. Den sudettyska invandringen till Sverige 1938–1955*. Gothenburg: Göteborgs universitet.

Tervonen, Miika. 2014. "Historiankirjoitus ja myytti yhden kulttuurin Suomesta". In *Kotiseutu ja kansakunta: miten suomalaista historiaa on rakennettu*, edited by Pirjo Markkola, Hanna Snellman, and Ann-Catrin Östman, 137–62. Helsinki: Suomalaisen Kirjallisuuden Seura.

Tervonen, Miika. 2022a. "Näkökulmia karkotuksiin historiallisena tutkimuskohteena". In *Suomesta poistetut: näkökulmia karkotuksiin ja käännytyksiin*, edited by Päivi Pirkkalainen, Eveliina Lyytinen, and Saara Pellander, 31–50. Tampere: Vastapaino.

Tervonen, Miika. 2022b. "Borders of Welfare: Mobility Control and the Nordic Welfare States". In *Nationalism and Democracy in the Welfare State*, edited by Pauli Kettunen, Saara Pellander, and Miika Tervonen, 150–65. Cheltenham: Edward Elgar. https://doi.org/10.4337/9781788976589.00017.

Tervonen, Miika and Johanna Leinonen. 2021. "Johdanto: muuttoliikehistorian kätketty monimuotoisuus". In *Vähemmistöt muuttajina. Näkökulmia suomalaisten muuttoliikkeiden monimuotoisuuteen*, edited by Miika Tervonen and Johanna Leinonen, 11–25. Turku: Siirtolaisuusinstituutti.

Tevlina, Victoria. 2020. "Russian Emigration to Norway after the Russian Revolution and Civil War". In *The Russian Revolutions of 1917: The Northern Impact and Beyond*, edited by Kari Aga Myklebost, Jens Petter Nielsen, and Andrei Rogatchevski, 69–78. Boston, MA: Academic Studies Press.

Thing, Morten. 2008. *De russiske jøder i København 1882–1943.* Copenhagen: Gyldendal.

Thor, Malin. 2005. *Hechaluz – en rörelse i tid och rum: Tysk-judiska ungdomars exil i Sverige 1933–1943.* Växjö: Växjö University Press.

Thor, Malin. 2007. "'Det är billigare att bota ett TBC-fall än att uppfostra en svensk.' Den svenska kvotuttagningen av icke-arbetsföra flyktingar ca 1950–1956". In *Sveriges mottagning av flyktingar – några exempel*, edited by Jan Ekberg. Växjö: Växjö University Press, 9–34.

Thor, Malin. 2008. "Arbetsmarknadsstyrelsen och kvotflyktingarna. Föreställningar om kön, nationalitet, (o)hälsa, yrkeserfarenhet och ålder vid kvotuttagningarna av flyktingar under 1950-talet och 1960-talets första hälft". In *Efterfrågad arbetskraft? Amers årsbok 2008*, edited by Ellinor Platzer and Svante Lundberg. Växjö: Växjö University Press, 5–32.

Thor Tureby, Malin. 2020. "Memories, Testimonies and Oral History. On Collections and Research about and with Holocaust Survivors in Sweden". In *Utredningen om ett museum om Förintelsen: Sveriges museum om Förintelsen. Del 2*, 67–92. SOU 2020:21. Stockholm: Norstedts juridik.

Thor Tureby, Malin and Jesper Johansson. 2020. *Migration och kulturarv: insamlingsprocesser och berättelser om och med de invandrade ca 1970–2019.* Lund: Nordic Academic Press.

Thor Tureby, Malin and Kristin Wagrell. 2020. *Vittnesmål från Förintelsen och de överlevandes berättelser: definitioner, insamlingar och användningar, 1939–2020.* Stockholm: Forum för levande historia.

Thor Tureby, Malin and Kristin Wagrell. 2022. "Crisis Documentation and Oral History: Problematizing Collecting and Preserving Practices in a Digital World". *Oral History Review* 49 (2): 346–76. https://doi.org/10.1080/0094079 8.2022.2101933

Tjelmeland, Hallvard. 2003. "Del I. 1940–1975". In *Norsk innvandringshistorie vol. 3: I globaliseringens tid 1940–2000*, edited by Knut Kjeldstadli, 11–134. Oslo: Pax.

Torvinen, Taimi. 1984. *Pakolaiset Suomessa Hitlerin valtakaudella.* Helsinki: Otava.

Torvinen, Taimi. 1989. *Kadimah: Suomen Juutalaisten Historia.* Helsinki: Otava.

Uggla, Andrzej Nils. 1997. *I nordlig hamn: Polacker i Sverige under andra världskriget.* Uppsala: Uppsala universitet.

Ulstein, Ragnar. 1965. *Englandsfarten I: Alarm i Ålesund.* Oslo: Samlaget.

Ulstein, Ragnar. 1967. *Englandsfarten II: Søkelys mot Bergen.* Oslo: Samlaget.

Ulstein, Ragnar. 1974. *Svensketrafikken: 1. Flyktninger til Sverige 1940–1943.* Oslo: Samlaget.

Ulstein, Ragnar. 1974. *Svensketrafikken: 3. Flyktninger fra Trøndelag og Nord-Norge til Sverige 1940–1945.* Oslo: Samlaget.

Ulstein, Ragnar. 1975. *Svensketrafikken: 2. Flyktninger til Sverige 1943–45.* Oslo: Samlaget.

Välimäki, Matti. 2019. *Politiikkaa kansallisten, kansainvälisten ja ideologisten reunaehtojen puitteissa: Suomalaiset puolueet ja maahanmuutto 1973–2015.* Turku: Turun yliopisto.

Välimäki, Matti. 2022. "Kylmän sodan maastapoistamisen käytäntöjen murros ja nykyperiaatteiden synty". In *Suomesta poistetut: näkökulmia karkotuksiin ja käännytyksiin*, edited by Päivi Pirkkalainen, Eveliina Lyytinen, and Saara Pellander, 101–25. Tampere: Vastapaino.

Vilkuna, Kustaa H. J. 2005. *Viha: perikato, katkeruus ja kertomus isostavihasta*. Helsinki: Suomalaisen Kirjallisuuden Seura.

Waris, Heikki. 1936. "Yleinen väestökehitys 1800-luvun puolivälin jälkeen". In *Suomen kulttuurihistoria. 4, Industrialismin ja kansallisen nousun aika*, edited by Gunnar Suolahti, 11–44. Jyväskylä: Gummerus.

Waris, Heikki. 1952. *Siirtoväen sopeutuminen. Tutkimus Suomen karjalaisen siirtoväen sosiaalisesta sopeutumisesta*. Helsinki: Otava.

Westerlund, Lars, ed. 2008. *The German Strategic Use of POW Labor in the Far North, in Prisoners of War Deaths and People Handed Over to Germany and the Soviet Union 1939–1955. A Research Report by the Finnish National Archives*. Helsinki: The National Archives of Finland.

Westerlund, Lars. 2009. *Sotavankien ja siviili-internoitujen sodanaikainen kuolleisuus. Muonahuolto, tautisuus ja Punaisen Ristin toimettomuus 1939–44*. Helsinki: Suomalaisen Kirjallisuuden Seura.

Wickström, Mats and Charlotta Wolff, eds. 2016. *Mångkulturalitet, Migration och Minoriteter i Finland Under Tre Sekel*. Helsinki: Svenska litteratursällskapet i Finland.

Wigerfelt, Anders S. 2010. *Migration och arbetsliv i förändring*. MIM Working Paper Series 10:1. Malmö: Malmö Institute for Studies of Migration, Diversity and Welfare (MIM).

Wilson, Victor. 2023. "The Swedish Slave Trade Efforts at the Turn of the Nineteenth Century: Case Studies in Nordic Transimperial History". *The Journal of Imperial and Commonwealth History* 51 (3): 555–75. https://doi.org/10.1080/0 3086534.2023.2205698.

Wimmer, Andreas and Nina Glick Schiller. 2003. "Methodological Nationalism, the Social Sciences, and the Study of Migration: An Essay in Historical Epistemology". *The International Migration Review* 37 (3): 576–610. https://doi. org/10.1111/j.1747-7379.2003.tb00151.x.

Ytrehus, Line Alice. 2004. *Intellektuelle i eksil. Inkludering og ekskludering i et livsverdenperspektiv*. Doctoral thesis, University of Bergen.

Zabalueva, Olga. 2023. *"Not All Museums": Memory, Politics, and Museum Activism on the Move*. Linköping: Linköping University Press.

Zaremba, Maciej. 2018. *Huset med de två tornen*. Stockholm: Weylers.

PART II

Regulation and control of forced migration

CHAPTER 3

Undesirable returnees

Deportees from North America in Finland during the Great Depression[1]

Aleksi Huhta

University of Helsinki

Abstract

This chapter examines the return and reception of deported migrants from North America to Finland during the Great Depression of the 1930s. Its main sources compose of case files on deportations held at Finnish diplomatic archives. By using these sources, the chapter looks into the process of deporting migrants from the perspective of the receiving state. It probes the attitudes of Finnish authorities to the deported migrants but also sheds light on the experiences of the deportees themselves. It traces the return journeys of the deportees and their reception in Finland. The chapter illustrates how deportations relied on transnational bureaucratic work. It argues that the reception of deportees was an important yet oft-overlooked venue for state- and nation-building where the deportees, too, had real if circumscribed agency.

How to cite this book chapter:
Huhta, Aleksi. 2025. "Undesirable returnees: Deportees from North America in Finland during the Great Depression." In *Forced Migrants in Nordic Histories*, edited by Johanna Leinonen, Miika Tervonen, Hans Otto Frøland, Christhard Hoffmann, Seija Jalagin, Heidi Vad Jønsson and Malin Thor Tureby, 93–109. Helsinki: Helsinki University Press. https://doi.org/10.33134/HUP-32-4.

Introduction

In June 1936, the Swedish American Line steamer SS *Gripsholm* docked in Helsinki harbor and brought ashore some 500 passengers. Most were Finnish-American tourists on a short visit (*Uusi Aura*, July 13, 1936), but some Finnish returnees from America came for good. One of the latter was Kaisa S., who had emigrated to the US and there married another Finnish immigrant. Kaisa S. was met in Helsinki by her sister, who was shocked by her sibling's appearance. The sister later recounted the encounter in a distraught letter to local authorities. In it she asked how the sister she thought was in New York, happily married to a US citizen, could be sent back from America ailing and penniless, possessing only the clothes on her back. The sickly sister could not herself explain why she had returned; the only clue was her passport, issued by a Finnish consul, which stated that she had been deported for mental sickness. But how could a woman married to a US citizen be deported? And why was she allowed to travel alone in such derelict state? Where were her belongings?[2]

This chapter explores the experiences of migrants like Kaisa S.: Finnish citizens deported from the US or Canada during the Great Depression and its aftermath (*c*.1929–1939). These forcibly removed migrants have received little attention in traditional historiography on Finnish migration to North America. The historiography has been more concentrated on broad social and demographic trends and, more recently, on questions of identity among established Finnish-American groups (for an overview, see Kostiainen 2014b). Also, more generally, migration historiography has until recently paid relatively little attention to experiences of "failed" migration, that is, to stories of people who stayed put involuntarily, whose journeys were interrupted, or who returned against their will. As historian Tara Zahra has noted, histories of "failed" migration and immobility complicate the neatly teleological narratives of the nineteenth and twentieth centuries as a period of ever-advancing globalization and increasing mobility (Zahra 2022, 153; see also Green 2019). The recent turn in migration historiography toward histories of deportation presents one effort to shed light on the diversity of migration experiences beyond the stale models of immigration, integration and assimilation (see, e.g., Hester 2017; Goodman 2020; Tervonen 2022). Deportations from North America to Finland have also attracted limited attention (Kostiainen 2014b; Huhta 2021a).

This chapter draws on and contributes to this emerging body of deportation historiography.

Most studies on deportation regimes concentrate on their workings within a nation-state context. These studies probe the state's power to deport noncitizens, as well as the strategies deportees deploy when navigating the deportation regime (for an overview, see Lemberg-Pedersen 2022). The experiences of deported people after their forced removal have received less attention. This dearth of scholarship can be partly attributed to methodological and source-related challenges. Since the act of removal tends to end the deporting state's interest in the deportee, the deporting state bureaucracies have generated little documentary evidence about postdeportation lives of the expelled migrants. As Shahram Khosravi (2018, 2) has noted, the tendency to ignore post-removal experiences risks "naturalis[ing] and reenforc[ing] the idea of nation-states." It also blurs our understanding of how deportees have experienced their removals: not as one-off events but as multiphased processes with prolonged afterlives. As historian Hidetaka Hirota notes, the "expelled people's lives as migrants obviously did not cease at the point of expulsion; they endured a return journey to their countries of origin and perhaps even further internal migration within that country when they returned" (Hirota 2017, 12). By extending our interest beyond the act of expulsion to the return journeys and arrivals "home," we gain a better appreciation of the emotional toll that forced removal exacted – and of course continues to exact (Gutiérrez 2020, 14–15).

Sources for the historical study of deportations can be notoriously difficult to locate and access (Tervonen 2022, 33–34). The problems are compounded when exploring deportee experiences after deportation, particularly when the deportees can no longer be interviewed. Yet the archives kept by the receiving state's foreign ministry and its embassies and consulates provide some information about deportee lives postremoval. Communications between the foreign ministry and its staff abroad about deportees' citizenship, for example, provide clues about deportees' return journeys and (more limitedly) their postdeportation lives. Archives of local authorities can also offer insight into deportees' settlement in their "home" countries. In this chapter, I examine the Vaasa provincial government's deportee-related correspondence with the Foreign Ministry of Finland. Vaasa Province in western Finland was the Finnish province that witnessed most emigration from the late nineteenth century to the mid-twentieth (Kero 1974, 227–30). To trace individual deportees' life events after their forcible removal from North America, I have also searched the National Library of Finland's online database of digitized newspapers.

Studying deportees' postremoval lives also involves ethical quandaries, especially in cases involving medical conditions. All names of the deportees I use in this chapter are pseudonyms, with the exception of those Finnish-American communists whose deportations from the US were widely publicized. In what follows, I will first briefly recount how the US and Canadian immigration authorities deployed deportation during the Great Depression. I will then examine the deportees' return journeys to Finland. I illustrate how the return trip's multiphased itinerary and the lack of oversight exposed vulnerable returnees to varied troubles but provided opportunities to those deportees, like Communist Party members, who wanted to evade government surveillance. I then probe the lives of the deportees in Finland (and, to a lesser degree, in Soviet Karelia) during the Great Depression and beyond. I highlight how the deportees' postremoval experiences reflected their age, ability, and past immigration experiences.

This chapter can provide only a tentative analysis of the subject but it hopefully charts ground for more detailed and expansive studies in the future. It should be noted, for instance, that Swedish authorities also deported Finnish migrants during these years. A more thorough exploration of postdeportation lives in Finland should thus expand its vision from North American deportees to also look at deportees from other countries.

Deportation nations during the Great Depression

The years of the Great Depression witnessed a sea change in flows of global labor migration. A 1937 International Labour Organization report surmised that the worldwide crisis had in effect reversed migration currents: "Countries that have traditionally been lands of immigration have been transformed into lands of emigration, and the typical countries of emigration have taken on the form of countries of immigration" (quoted in Zahra 2017, 138). As the US and other countries of immigration restricted immigration and enforced stringent deportation regimes, millions of Eastern and Southern European, Indian, Chinese, Caribbean, and other migrants left for their countries of birth or perceived nativity (Zahra 2017, 137–42; Matera & Kent 2017, 117–24). Finland, too, registered more returnees than emigrants in the early 1930s. (CBSF 1933, 7, 11). Not all Finnish returnees from North America "returned" to Finland, however. Between 1930 and 1935, around 6,500 North American Finns migrated to Soviet Karelia, drawn there by an active recruiting campaign by the republic's Finnish communist leadership (Golubev and Takala 2014).

Unemployment, material scarcity, and outright hunger pressured Depression-era migrants to return, but some immigrants faced more than just economic coercion. In the early 1930s, both the US and Canadian immigration authorities used mass deportations – and threats of deportations – as tools to rid their countries of unemployed and other purportedly burdensome foreigners. In addition to formal deportation by federal immigration bureaus, local authorities in both countries pressured foreign-born residents to depart in what were effectively informal deportations. In the US, the federal immigration authorities also coerced undesired foreigners from the country through so-called voluntary departure, a bureaucratically lighter form of expulsion that was employed especially at the US–Mexico and US–Canada borders (Goodman 2020, 37–46).

Since the forms of banishment were many, the responsible authorities diverse, and the documentation on removals often deficient, it has proved difficult to establish exact figures on Depression-era deportations. Still, even the statistics on formal deportations, though deficient, indicate a clear upward trend. Between fiscal years 1930 and 1934, the US immigration authorities carried out 83,000 deportations, compared to 57,000 cases during the preceding five-year period (*ARSL*, 1925–1934). For Canada, the corresponding figures are 27,000 deportations in 1930–1934 compared to 8,700 cases in 1925–1929 (Roberts 1988, 38). These official figures indicate a trend but they conceal the mass removal campaign's true magnitude. Most foreigners (or putative foreigners) who were removed from Depression-era North America did not depart as formal deportees but were coerced to leave through other mechanisms. Especially as public criticism and international pressure forced the US and Canadian authorities to scale down formal deportations from the mid-1930s onward, the authorities increasingly turned to more informal and less bureaucratic forms of removal. As Adam Goodman has shown, the 1930s witnessed a marked shift in American deportation practices from formal removals to less conventional methods of expulsion. The voluntary departure mechanism and public fear campaigns that became the dominant removal mechanisms in post–Second World War America were largely honed during the Depression era (Goodman 2020, 37–46; see also Garland 2014).

Deportations to Finland from the US and Canada also ballooned during the Great Depression. Estimating definite figures is again difficult but official statistics indicate the trend. Between fiscal years 1929 and 1932, the US immigration authorities carried out 450 formal deportations to Finland, up from 266 during the preceding three-year period (Huhta 2021a, 211). During the fiscal year 1934 alone, the Canadian Department of Immigration and Colonization deported 196 people to Finland, three-fourths of whom – including nine children – were deported due to having been considered as "public charges" (DICC 1934, 74). The forced departure of an unknown number of presumed Finnish citizens was orchestrated by not just federal but also county, state, and provincial authorities in the US and Canada. Others "self-deported," with the gnawing fear of detention and deportation persuading many to leave on their own while they still could (on self-deportation as a consciously cultivated removal mechanism in the US, see Goodman 2020, 11–20).

Dereliction after departure: Travel and arrival

In May 1937, Tuomas S. sent a letter to the Foreign Ministry in Helsinki, protesting his recent deportation from the US after 27 years in America. The process of his removal had begun in October 1935, when the immigration authorities detained him at his Maine workplace after he had taken a brief excursion to Canada. Recommended for deportation for unlawful entry, Tuomas S. had to wait a year for the final decision in his case. When the deportation order came in late 1936, he was again detained and spent almost six months in detention as the US and Finnish authorities sought to establish whether he had acquired Canadian citizenship during his 1910–1913 residence in the Dominion. When, in April 1937, his Finnish citizenship was finally ascertained and he was issued a Finnish passport, Tuomas S. was taken from Maine to Boston and put on a ship to Europe. In May, with the journey to Helsinki still fresh in his mind, he recounted to foreign ministry officials his disorienting experiences:

On April 16, I was brought to Boston and put on a ship to Finland …
Already during my journey, they asked me who will pay for my travel,
and they asked this also in Helsinki. Well I did not know what to reply
… I would have never believed that I could get lost in such a terrible
way. First I languished in jail for months without interrogations and
then I was put on a ship in my most terrible condition. I was not given
the time to organize my affairs, I had to leave in bad clothes and without
any money like a great criminal, without knowing if I would meet any
acquaintances here in Finland. (FMFA, 21VA, file S. 1937)

Tuomas S.'s account of his deportation journey gives a good impression of the disorientation that many deportees felt during their long
sea journey that involved at least one change of ship. Since there was
no direct passenger line connecting North America with Finland,
all travelers from the US and Canada to Finland had to first take a
transatlantic liner to a port in Britain, Germany, Sweden, Norway, or
Denmark, and then continue to Finland by a smaller steamer or by
a combination of trains and ships. When, for example, Emma P. was
deported from the US to Finland in July 1938, her itinerary to Finland
– after having been transferred from a Connecticut mental hospital
to New York Harbor – took 12 days and involved two sea voyages and
one rail journey. She left New York on July 5 on a Polish steamer and
disembarked nine days later in Copenhagen, where she transferred
the same day to a train to Stockholm. After a night in the Swedish
capital, she took a steamer to Helsinki, where she arrived on July 16 at
noon (LFWA, Fr:4, file P. 1937). Other deportees took similar journeys
through Gothenburg, Liverpool, Hamburg, or Bremen.

Like all travelers, Finnish deportees experienced their return journey differently depending on their gender, age, and health. Most Finnish deportees of the late 1920s and early 1930s were young men and
women who had arrived in America only recently and were being
deported for unlawful entry to the US (Kostiainen 2014a; Huhta 2021a;
on illegal migration from Europe to the US after 1921, see Garland
2014). They most likely had little practical difficulties in taking the
journey back to Finland, but for the older, the frailer, and the disabled
the long sea journey and the subsequent ship or train transfers must
have been much harder to navigate. Indeed, as Gemma Blok (2015) has
shown, mental hospitals in major transmigration hubs like Rotterdam
frequently hospitalized mentally disoriented migrants who had been

debarred or deported from America. Although governmental and shipping lines' oversight improved in the interwar period, deportees' transfers in transmigration port cities did not always proceed flawlessly. In late 1926, for instance, 42-year-old Oliver S. was deported from Canada only months after his arrival in the country; he had "become insane," the Finnish vice-consul in Montreal reported, and was institutionalized in British Columbia. The Canadian immigration authorities put Oliver S. on a ship to Oslo, from where he was supposed to continue his journey to Finland. Oliver S. was apparently unable to make the transfer himself, however, as he was detained by the Norwegian police in Oslo and taken to a municipal emergency clinic. The Norwegian authorities then sent Oliver S. through Sweden to Finland, protesting to the Finnish Foreign Ministry that Norway had no obligation to treat mentally ill foreigners traveling through its port cities (FMFA, 21VA, case file S. 1926).

Forced return could be particularly harrowing for those deportees who had lived in America for years or even decades. Older deportees who had to leave behind their friends and families most likely experienced the looming return to Finland with profound anxiety. In his May 1937 letter to the Foreign Ministry, the recently deported Tuomas S., who had lived in North America for almost four decades and who had two children in New York, recounted how thoughts of alienation preoccupied him during his journey from Boston to Helsinki. He was unsure if he knew anyone in Finland after decades of absence (FMFA, 21VA, case file S. 1937). Deportees who suffered from psychiatric complications were especially vulnerable during their return travel, as the aforementioned experiences of Kaisa S vividly illustrate.

The lack of oversight exposed vulnerable deportees to diverse risks during their journey, but for other deportees it could present opportunities to evade unwanted government surveillance. In the early 1930s, the US and Canada deported a number of foreign-born communists in an effort to clamp down on the swelling militancy among workers and the unemployed (Buff 2018; Roberts 1988, 125–58). In February 1931, for instance, the immigration authorities in Oregon moved to deport the staff of the Finnish-language communist daily *Toveri* ("Comrade") in Astoria, Oregon. During their detention, the men requested that they be allowed to depart for the Soviet Union instead of being deported to "fascist" Finland. The US immigration authorities rejected this plea, insisting that deportations proceed to their country of citizenship. In early 1932, five of the six men were put on a ship to Germany with passports to Finland (the sixth, Oscar Mannisto, fought his case into 1935, when he, too, was deported). When the five deportees were supposed to transfer ships in Germany, they digressed from their Finland-bound itinerary and defected to the USSR, where they joined the growing community of North American Finns in Soviet Karelia (Hummasti 1995/1996, 386–87). Similarly, August Jokinen, a Communist Party member from Harlem ordered to be deported in 1931, changed his deportation itinerary en route to Finland in early 1933. Jokinen and his wife and daughter instead went to Soviet Karelia (Huhta 2021b, 302). Another Finnish communist, who in 1934 received a deportation order from the Canadian authorities for being a "public charge," evaded the enforcement of the decision until 1937, when he left Canada to fight for the International Brigades in the Spanish Civil War. He was able to return to Canada in 1939 and lived there for the rest of his life. Still another communist deportee sought and received asylum in Sweden during his deportation journey from California through Texas, Germany and Sweden to Finland in 1936 (*Työkansan Sanomat*, June 21, 1946). For these communist deportees, then, expulsion was not a one-off experience but a prolonged process of fits and starts; deportations from America could be but legs in much longer refugee journeys.

Lives after removal

As the diverse journeys of removal suggest, the deportees had no singular, shared experience of deportation. The way they experienced their deportation – and how that deportation came to define their subsequent lives – was very much dependent on their broader life situation and social standing. A healthy 19-year-old man deported for unlawful entry soon after his arrival in North America felt the reverberations of removal differently than did a 40-year-old woman with two underage children and an established social life in America. The abilities of a card-carrying communist deportee to "reintegrate" into the Finnish society of the 1930s – where the Communist Party was illegal and suspected communists were under strict surveillance – were certainly distinct from those without such political baggage. Moreover, a middle-aged deportee who had left Finland as a toddler, spoke no Finnish or Swedish, and knew no one in Finland, came across challenges that deportees with at least tangential connections to Finland did not have to encounter. These differences related to age, gender, political beliefs, and other social categories in many ways shaped the deportees' lives after their removal. Scattered and varied sources – letters penned by deportees or their relatives to the Finnish authorities, the Finnish authorities' correspondence on deported migrants, local newspapers' references to people we know were deported – can shed some light on deportees' postremoval lives in Finland and elsewhere.

Those deportees who had lost most in their forced removal – and who had the social resources to assert that these losses be restituted – are responsible for majority of the paper trail that exists in the Foreign Ministry and embassy archives about deportees' postdeportation experiences. These were usually men who had lived for years in North America, had family there, and wanted to get back. Tuomas S., for instance, visited the Foreign Ministry in Helsinki soon after his deportation to Finland in May 1937 and then wrote the ministry a series of letters protesting his unjust removal from the US, accusing (rather implausibly) his estranged wife of orchestrating his deportation. Having lived in North America since 1910, Tuomas S. had few social connections in Finland and was adamant that he did not want to stay in the country. But because Tuomas S. had been formally deported – no matter how unjust the decision may have been – there was little the Finnish authorities could or were willing to do on his behalf. The Foreign Ministry did consult the Washington embassy, but when the embassy informed them that Tuomas S. had been deported for unlawful entry the Foreign Ministry refused any help to allow him to return.

Those de facto deportees from the US who had not received a formal deportation order but had opted for "voluntary deportation" had at least theoretically better reemigration opportunities. Being a voluntary departee instead of a deportee had certain advantages, as the former designation involved no bar on future entry (Kanstroom 2007, 216). To be sure, emigration to the US was extremely difficult in the 1930s even without formal bars to entry, but a few cleared the hurdles. Peter N., a former seaman, was detained for unlawful residence in the US in 1932 and coerced to "voluntarily depart." He left behind a wife to maintain their small farm alone in New Jersey. When Peter N. arrived in Helsinki, he immediately visited the US consul and applied for an immigration visa. The US consul then consulted the State Department about Peter N.'s past immigration history and issued him a visa five months later. Peter N. was back in New Jersey in early December 1932, seven months after his "voluntary departure," now as a legal immigrant. Even though some voluntary deportees could thus return to their lives in the US, voluntary departures, too, could of course cause distress to immigrant families. In Peter N.'s case, the desperate letters his wife penned to the Finnish Embassy in Washington vividly testify to this sense of distress. Deploring her lonely and deprived existence and fearful that her husband would not be allowed back, Peter N.'s wife castigated the American government for banishing a "decent man" and wrecking her home (LFWA, Fr:3, case file N. 1932).[3]

For the overwhelming majority of deportees, however, return to the US or Canada was not a realistic option, at least for the foreseeable future. Thus, like other returnees, they relocated to the places where they had lived before their emigration or moved to the cities and towns of southern and western Finland that offered better employment opportunities than the Depression-ridden countryside. Some who were deported as psychiatric hospital patients were again hospitalized in Finland (on mental asylums' central role in immigration incarceration in the early to mid-1900s US, see Young 2021, 64–70). When a mental hospital patient was deported, the Finnish legation in Washington sometimes requested that the US authorities send details of deportees' itineraries. This was apparently done so that the deportee could be rehospitalized or at least examined upon arrival. In such cases local authorities could also be alerted to the deportee's arrival. When Jaakko A. was deported from the US in 1937, for example, the Finnish foreign ministry informed the provincial government in Vaasa about the arrival of this "insane" person. The provincial government then alerted the welfare board of the deportee's former home municipality (VPGA, Eab:264, file 122/29).

Although the Foreign Ministry sometimes informed provincial governors about the arrival of deportees to their provinces, there was no systematic attempt to surveil or otherwise control the lives of deported migrants. The most sustained effort at control came in 1933, when Aaro Jalkanen assumed the post of Finland's consul-general in Montreal. In the late 1920s, Jalkanen had been Finland's vice-consul in Duluth, Minnesota, and had then sought to actively curb the American authorities' increasingly arbitrary deportation practices. His motives were a mix of humanitarian concern, economic frugality, and eugenic anxiety for the nation. He felt empathy for the frail and disabled immigrants the

US authorities wanted to wantonly deport, but he also feared that these purportedly defective deportees would burden Finland's economy and adversely influence Finnish racial hygiene (Huhta 2021a). After taking office in Montreal, Jalkanen began to insist that the Finnish provincial authorities deny passports to people who had been deported from Canada. From late 1933 onward, Jalkanen accompanied all reports on deportations to the Foreign Ministry with requests that the ministry inform provincial governments about the deported people's ineligibility for a passport to Canada. For example, in November 1933, when the Canadian authorities deported a family of four – two unemployed parents and two Canadian-born minors – Jalkanen requested that the Foreign Ministry inform the governor of Vaasa Province "that the deportees would not be issued a passport to Canada" (FMF to VPG, Dec. 9, 1933, VPGA, Eab:251, 1933). In those cases where a person was deported for mental illness, Jalkanen requested that the person would not be issued a passport anywhere (FMF to VPG, Jan. 2 and Mar. 14, 1934, VPGA, Eab:255). Based on these requests by Jalkanen, the Vaasa provincial government compiled a list of "persons who have been deported from Canada and who should not be issued a passport to Canada." The list came to include 43 names, including seven small children, some born in Canada (VPGA, Bda:1).

But the local authorities had little incentive to limit the mobility of returning deportees, particularly if they were seen to burden the welfare authorities. Indeed, the practical significance of the list on deportees from Canada was probably small. Emigration to Canada was in any case extremely difficult in the 1930s and 1940s. It also appears that the list was discarded after the war. At least two Canadian-born women whose names were included on the list when they were small children emigrated to Canada in the 1950s. Their parents, deported from Canada in 1933 and also included on the no-passport list, received passports and visas to visit their daughters in Canada in 1957 (NPDA 1952–1971, Ba:1; *Kaskö Tidning*, April 4, 1959).

The two women who had accompanied their deported parents from Canada to Finland in 1933 and then returned to Canada in the 1950s were not the only deportees (or "deportees by proxy," i.e., people who had accompanied deported family members) who remigrated after their deportation. Shahram Khosravi, who has studied contemporary postdeportation lives in Afghanistan, has noted that desires to remigrate are common among deportees (Khosravi 2018, 8–9; see also

Gadd, Al-Jouranj, and Pirjatanniemi 2022, 264). The Finnish deportees of the 1930s did not experience the kind of persecution that com-
pels the deported Afghans or Iraqis today to remigrate, but the priva-
tion of the Depression years, convulsions of the Second World War,
and the postwar shortages and political uncertainty did prompt many
to emigrate anew. While immigration to the US and Canada remained
difficult in the postwar years, the removal of passport controls between
Finland and Sweden in the 1950s made emigration to Sweden simpler.
Searches in digitized newspaper databases produce many articles from
local newspapers in Ostrobothnia, for instance, which indicate that
people deported from North America in the late 1920s or 1930s emigrated to Sweden in the late 1940s or 1950s. For example, Karl L., who
was deported from the US in 1932 for using another person's passport
to enter the country, later emigrated with his family to Sweden, where
he worked in a quarry (*Kaskö Tidning*, October 1, 1955). Gabriel B.,
who had crossed the US–Canadian border illicitly in 1926 and was
deported from the US for unlawful entry in 1932, moved to Sweden at
some point after his deportation and naturalized as a Swedish citizen
in 1950 (*Kaskö Tidning*, April 19, 1950). Of course, not everyone left
their home towns or villages after having been deported from North
America. Samuel S., from a small municipality in Central Ostrobothnia, for example, was deported from Canada in early 1934, and died in
that same municipality four decades later (*Jakobstads Tidning*, October
14, 1976).

Not all deportees to Finland arrived in Finland; some opted for the
Soviet Union. Sadly for them, their eastward removal over the Atlantic
was not the last time they were forcibly uprooted. Like tens of thousands of other Finns in the Soviet Union, they bore the terrible brunt
of the Stalinist terror of the late 1930s. At least four of the five *Toveri*
workers who fled their Finland-bound deportation to Soviet Karelia in
1932 were arrested during the Great Terror of 1937–1938. Väinö Fin-
berg was shot in 1938, Eemeli Parras died in a Gulag in 1939, Theodor
Sausso was sentenced to ten years in a Gulag in 1938, and Matti Lak-
kila received a five-year prison sentence in 1939 (Lahti-Argutina 2001,
87, 393, 478, 279).

In the latter half of the 1930s, deportations from the US to Finland became much more infrequent than they had been during the
early years of the decade. The reforms of the Roosevelt administration,
with its Department of Labor headed by the proimmigration reformist

Frances Perkins, accounted for much of this change. Perkins and other administration reformists insisted, for instance, that the immigration authorities begin to use administrative discretion to avoid deporting aliens whose expulsion would cause undue "hardship" (Ngai 2004, 84). With the onset of the Second World War in September 1939, deportations of Finns and other Europeans from the US were brought to a standstill. During the early Cold War, several Finnish-American communists came under the threat of deportation, as the Internal Security Act of 1950 authorized the exclusion and deportation of noncitizen communists (Tichenor 2002, 189; Buff 2018, 169–78). Taken together, however, deportations from the US to Finland decreased considerably after the Second World War. Between the fiscal years 1946 and 1956, the US Immigration and Naturalization Service (INS) made only 415 formal deportations to Finland, with the yearly toll varying between a low of 16 (1946) and a high of 74 cases (1952) (INS 1946–1956, tables 24). To be sure, this decrease in deportations was small comfort for the many noncitizen Finnish Americans with past or present association with the Communist Party or its front organizations. They continued to live in fear of forced expulsion well into the postwar period (Kostiainen 2014a, 278–80). But, for the vast majority of Finland-born residents of the US, the threat of deportation had ceased to be a serious consideration. Deportations of European immigrants became all the rarer as the INS's efforts centered ever more firmly on the southern border and the mass deportation of Mexicans (Ngai 2004; Kang 2017).

Conclusions

The experiences of Finnish deportees from North America during the Great Depression remind us that Finland, like other Nordic nation-states, has a long history with the politics of deportation. This is easily forgotten as the contemporary media discourse on nondocumented (or "illegal") migrants and deportations in Finland paints a picture of an altogether novel, unprecedented phenomenon (Tervonen 2022). At the same time, as this chapter suggests, Finland has also been a major *receiver* of deportees. From the late nineteenth century to the late twentieth, Finland was characteristically a country of emigration, from where hundreds of thousands of people left for North America, Sweden, Russia (and later the Soviet Union), Australia, South Africa, and other parts of the globe. Not all were accepted in their countries of transit or destination. The deportations from North America to Finland during the Great Depression are but one part of this much larger story that includes not only postentry deportations but also other forms of rejection and expulsion. In the twenty-first century, in connection with Finland transferring from a country of net emigration to one of net immigration in the 1990s, Finland has ramped up its deportation regime and become a net deporter – between 2011 and 2020, the Finnish authorities ordered over 27,000 noncitizen removals (Könönen 2022, 138). Deportations of Finnish citizens, on the other hand, have become quite rare in comparison. For example, of the almost 1.6 million noncitizen removals registered by the US Department of Homeland Security between 2012 and 2021, only 611 concerned citizens of Finland (DHS 2022, 107). The current media focus on and political struggle over Finland's deportation regime has encouraged historians to look at the historical genealogies of Finland's policies on removing foreigners. These genealogies certainly warrant introspection but historians should also remain cognizant of those parts of Finnish deportation experiences that appear less recognizable from today's perspective.

Notes

1 This study was funded by a grant from the Society of Swedish Literature in Finland.
2 Governor of Turku and Pori Province to Foreign Ministry of Finland, September 5, 1936, and the enclosed letter. Case file S., series 21 V a, Foreign Ministry of Finland's Archive, Helsinki (FMFA).
3 The date of Peter N.'s visa issuance and arrival have been procured from Ancestry.com.

Archival sources

Foreign Ministry of Finland Archives, Helsinki (FMFA).
National Archive of Finland, Mikkeli Branch.
   Legation of Finland in Washington DC Archives (LFWA).
National Archive of Finland, Vaasa Branch.
   Vaasa Provincial Government Archive (VPGA).
   Närpes Police District Archive (NPDA).

Bibliography

Blok, Gemma. 2015. "'Insane Emigrants' in Transit: Psychiatric Patients' Files as a Source for the History of Return Migration, c. 1910". *Social History of Medicine* 28 (4): 889–901. https://doi.org/10.1093/shm/hkv023.

Buff, Rachel Ida. 2018. *Against the Deportation Terror: Organizing for Immigrant Rights in the Twentieth Century*. Philadelphia, PA: Temple University Press.

Central Bureau of Statistics, Finland (CBSF). 1933. *Siirtolaisuustilasto. Siirtolaisuus vuosina 1931 ja 1932*. Helsinki: Valtioneuvoston kirjapaino.

Gadd, Katri, Hayder Al-Jouranj, and Elina Pirjatanniemi. 2022. "Maasta poistamisen oikeudelliset edellytykset ja irakilaisten kokemukset paluusta Irakiin". In *Suomesta poistetut. Näkökulmia karkotuksiin ja käännytyksiin*, edited by Päivi Pirkkalainen, Eveliina Lyytinen, and Saara Pellander, 247–70. Tampere: Vastapaino.

Garland, Libby. 2014. *After They Closed the Gates: Jewish Illegal Immigration to the United States, 1921–1965*. Urbana, IL: University of Illinois Press.

Golubev, Alex and Irina Takala. 2014. *The Search for a Socialist El Dorado: Finnish Immigration to Soviet Karelia from the United States and Canada in the 1930s*. East Lansing, MI: Michigan State University Press.

Goodman, Adam. 2020. *The Deportation Machine: America's Long History of Expelling Immigrants*. Princeton, NJ: Princeton University Press.

Green, Nancy. 2019. *The Limits of Transnationalism*. Chicago, IL: University of Chicago Press.

Gutiérrez, Laura D. 2020. "'Trains of Misery': Repatriate Voices and Responses in Northern Mexico during the Great Depression". *Journal of American Ethnic History* 39 (4): 13–26. https://doi.org/10.5406/jamerethnhist.39.4.0013

Hester, Torrie. 2017. *Deportation: The Origins of US Policy*. Philadelphia: University of Pennsylvania Press.

Hirota, Hidetaka. 2017. *Expelling the Poor: Atlantic Seaboard States and the 19th-Century Origins of American Immigration Policy*. Oxford: Oxford University Press.

Huhta, Aleksi. 2021a. "'Joutuisi kykenemättömyytensä tähden yhteiskunnan rasitukseksi' – neuvottelu kyvyllisyydestä ja kansalaisuudesta Yhdysvalloista Suomeen tehdyissä karkotuksissa vuosina 1924–1939". *Historiallinen Aikakauskirja* 119 (2): 208–22. https://doi.org/10.54331/haik.140807.

Huhta, Aleksi. 2021b. *Toward a Red Melting Pot: Racial Thinking of Finnish-American Radicals, 1900–1938*. Helsinki: Työväen historian ja perinteen tutkimuksen seura.

Hummasti, Paul. 1995/1996. "Ethnicity and Radicalism: The Finns of Astoria and the Toveri, 1890–1930". *Oregon Historical Quarterly* 96 (4): 362–93.

Immigration Bureau at the Department of Labor, United States (IBDL). 1932. *Annual Report of the Commissioner General of Immigration to the Secretary of Labor: Fiscal Year Ended June 30, 1932*. Washington, DC: Government Printing Office.

Immigration and Naturalization Service, United States (INS). 1946–1956. *Annual Report of the Immigration and Naturalization Service*. Washington, DC: Government Printing Office.

Kang, S. Deborah. 2017. *The INS on the Line: Making Immigration Law on the US–Mexico Border, 1917–1954*. Oxford: Oxford University Press.

Kanstroom, Daniel. 2007. *Deportation Nation: Outsiders in American History*. Cambridge, MA: Harvard University Press.

Kero, Reino. 1974. *Migration from Finland to North America in the Years between the United States Civil War and the First World War*. Turku: Institute for Migration.

Khosravi, Shahram. 2018. "Introduction". In *After Deportation: Ethnographical Perspectives*, edited by Shahram Khosravi, 1–14. Cham: Palgrave Macmillan. https://doi.org/10.1007/978-3-319-57267-3_1.

Kostiainen, Auvo. 2014a. "Deported Finns". In *Finns in the United States: A History of Settlement, Dissent and Integration*, edited by Auvo Kostiainen, 273–82. East Lansing: Michigan State University Press.

Kostiainen, Auvo. 2014b. "Interest in the History of Finnish Americans". In *Finns in the United States: A History of Settlement, Dissent and Integration*, edited by Auvo Kostiainen, 13–25. East Lansing: Michigan State University Press.

Könönen, Jukka. "Maastapoistamisen aika". In *Suomesta poistetut. Näkökulmia karkotuksiin ja käännytyksiin*, edited by Päivi Pirkkalainen, Eveliina Lyytinen, and Saara Pellander, 131–56. Tampere: Vastapaino.

Lahti-Argutina, Eila. 2001. *Olimme joukko vieras vaan. Venäjänsuomalaiset vainouhrit Neuvostoliitossa 1930-luvun alusta 1950-luvun alkuun*. Turku: Siirtolaisuusinstituutti.

Lemberg-Pedersen, Martin. 2022. "The Contours of Deportation Studies". In *Handbook of Return Migration*, edited by Russell King and Katie Kuschminder, 122–36. Cheltenham: Edward Elgar Publishing. https://doi.org/10.4337/9781839100055.00018.

Matera, Marc and Susan Kingsley Kent. 2017. *The Global 1930s: The International Decade*. Abingdon: Routledge.

Ngai, Mae. 2004. *Impossible Subjects: Illegal Aliens and the Making of Modern America*. Princeton, NJ: Princeton University Press.

Roberts, Barbara. 1988. *Whence They Came: Deportation from Canada, 1900–1935*. Ottawa: University of Ottawa Press.

Tervonen, Miika. 2022. "Näkökulmia karkotuksiin historiallisena tutkimuskohteena". In *Suomesta poistetut. Näkökulmia karkotuksiin ja käännytyksiin*, edited by Päivi Pirkkalainen, Eveliina Lyytinen, and Saara Pellander, 31–49. Tampere: Vastapaino. https://doi.org/10.58181/VP9789517689960.

Tichenor, Daniel. 2002. *Dividing Lines: The Politics of Immigration Control in America*. Princeton, NJ: Princeton University Press.

Young, Elliott. 2021. *Forever Prisoners: How the United States Made the World's Largest Immigrant Detention System*. Oxford: Oxford University Press.

Zahra, Tara. 2017. *The Great Departure: Mass Migration from Eastern Europe and the Making of the Free World*. New York, NY: W. W. Norton.

Zahra, Tara. 2022. "Migration, Mobility, and the Making of a Global Europe". *Contemporary European History* 31 (1): 142–54. https://doi.org/10.1017/S0960777321000758.

CHAPTER 4

Women, children, and hard workers only

The regulation of forced migration in Iceland 1940–2000

Íris Ellenberger
University of Iceland

Abstract

This article examines Iceland's regulation of forced migration and refugee policy from 1940 to 2000, highlighting how the government's approach was highly controlled and selective. During this period, Iceland granted only 374 individuals international protection, despite being a party to the UN Refugee Convention from 1956. The study identifies two distinct categories of refugees: UNHCR-resettled groups, carefully selected based on criteria emphasizing utility, potential for assimilation, and often whiteness, and individual asylum seekers, who were systematically denied formal refugee status.

The research reveals that Iceland's refugee policy prioritized women, children, and workers considered beneficial to the economy to maintain strong control over immigration. Even late-twentieth-century

How to cite this book chapter:
Ellenberger, Íris. 2025. "Women, children, and hard workers only: the regulation of forced migration in Iceland 1940–2000." In *Forced Migrants in Nordic Histories*, edited by Johanna Leinonen, Miika Tervonen, Hans Otto Frøland, Christhard Hoffmann, Seija Jalagin, Heidi Vad Jønsson and Malin Thor Tureby, 111–134. Helsinki: Helsinki University Press. https://doi.org/10.33134/HUP-32-5.

efforts to integrate refugee resettlement with regional development policies reflected this utilitarian mindset. The findings illustrate how Iceland's geographical isolation allowed for particularly restrictive refugee policies, which were driven by economic self-interests and assimilationist perspectives rather than humanitarian considerations.

Introduction

Iceland's experience with forced migration was quite limited until the turn of the twenty-first century. Even after the number of refugees worldwide increased beginning in the late 1970s (UNHCR 2022), Iceland remained largely out of reach. This was partly due to the country's location in the North Atlantic, a good distance from both Europe and North America, which restricted migration to the country. Iceland's remoteness meant that the Icelandic authorities could regulate forced migration with relative ease. They chose to do so in a way that excluded the vast majority of those seeking international protection in the country, with the exception of those who were hand-selected by government officials according to strict criteria.

In this chapter, I explore the regulation of forced migration to Iceland and the nation's refugee policy during the second half of the twentieth century. Compared to other Nordic countries, regulation was intensive, with only 374 people gaining formal refugee status from 1956 (when Iceland became a party to the United Nations Refugee Convention) to 2000. To understand these restrictive measures, I first analyze the laws, regulations, and international treaties that underpinned the policy. I then introduce the two main categories of forced migration, which were constructed based on the Icelandic authorities' drastically different reactions to the groups involved: (a) refugee groups resettled in Iceland by the office of the United Nations High Commissioner on Refugees (UNHCR) and (b) applicants for international protection who reached Iceland of their own accord. Analyzing the Icelandic authorities' different reactions to these categories of refugees will provide insight into how forced migration to Iceland was constructed and regulated, as well as the legal, ideological, and social premises upon which the regulation rested.

Laws and regulations on immigration and forced migration in the twentieth century

In Iceland's history, the twentieth century is marked by the country's struggle for independence. As a part of the Danish state at the beginning of the century, Iceland lacked its own laws and policies but followed the example of Denmark by imposing only minor restrictions on the activities of immigrants, such as land ownership and participation in important industries like fishing and agriculture (Jónsson 1995). In 1918, Iceland became a sovereign nation within the Danish state, which enabled the Icelandic government to shape the country's own policy on foreigners and immigrants. In 1920, the Surveillance of Foreigners Act (Alþingi 1920) was passed in Parliament. The law was the first in Icelandic history to systematically restrict immigration by requiring permission for foreign citizens to enter and reside in the country.[1] The legislation was influenced by recently passed laws on foreigners and migration in other Nordic countries. There was no mention of refugees in the Surveillance of Foreigners Act, but in 1921 that piece of legislation was cited in the deportation of the Russian teenage refugee Nathan Friedman, who resided in Reykjavík under the protection of Iceland's most prominent communist leaders. The act stated that a foreigner could be prohibited from settling in the country if he had a contagious disease (Alþingi 1920). Friedman had an eye infection, which became the official reason for his deportation, although an underlying fear of Bolshevism also influenced the decision to have him deported (Bergsson 2011; Ottósson 1980; Pétursson 2005).

In 1936, a new Surveillance of Foreigners Act was passed by the parliament, this time specifying in greater detail the conditions under which foreign citizens could and should be deported. It included an open provision for the minister of justice to deport a foreigner if "his behavior and circumstances … warrant deportation"[2] (Bergsson 2017, 132). In 1937, the minister introduced a regulation on the surveillance of foreigners, which, together with the new act, placed all decisions on immigration in the hands of the Icelandic authorities. Until then, the Danish authorities had been the primary issuer of residence permits for Iceland, which they had often handed out without much regard for Icelandic laws and immigration policies. The 1937 regulation de facto banned the immigration of people from countries outside the Nordic zone without a special exemption from the minister of justice himself.

The police were required to keep foreign citizens in Iceland under surveillance, and the Alien Office (Útlendingaeftirlit), headed by the Reykjavík police chief, was established to respond to the increased surveillance duties of law enforcement (Bergsson 2017).

The act and regulation on the surveillance of foreigners implemented in 1936–1937 determined how Icelandic authorities would react to the forced migration of Central European Jews in the years leading up to the Second World War, mainly by prohibiting all immigration of Jews to Iceland and deporting those who already resided in the country. The policy was implicit at first, resulting in a flat rejection of almost all applications concerning the employment and business activities of Jews in Iceland. Even those who possessed special skills that were lacking in the country were turned away despite provisions in Icelandic laws for foreign specialists who were deemed necessary or beneficial for Iceland. In 1938–1939, the Icelandic government made two announcements explicitly stating that German, Austrian, and Czech Jews need not apply for a residence permit in Iceland, as their requests would be systematically declined. Conversely, the Icelandic authorities do not seem to have been as thorough in preventing Germans with direct ties to the German Nazi party or affiliated organizations from immigrating to Iceland both during and after the war (Bergsson 2017; Ingimundarson 2013).

The Icelandic government's regulation of forced migration in the period leading up to the Second World War was by no means unique in the Nordic context. The other Nordic countries also sought to limit Jews' access to residency (Frandsen 2013). Despite such restrictions, 1,500 German Jews gained residence permits in Denmark (Boberg-Fazlic and Sharp 2020), so the fact remains that Iceland was among the European nations that sheltered the fewest Jewish refugees during the Second World War, even on a per capita basis. Around 400 Jews applied for a residence permit in Iceland between 1935 and 1940; the vast majority were rejected, except a handful of specialists with influential Icelandic patrons (Bergsson 2017). A group of Icelanders was even denied the opportunity to adopt orphaned Jewish children in early 1939 (Ástgeirsdóttir 2007; see Figure 4.1). By then, at least 16 Jews had been deported, and deportation orders had been handed down for 11 others. The government's reasoning behind its extreme stance toward Jewish refugees was antisemitic, as it was motivated by a desire to safeguard the nation's supposed racial purity against mixing

Mannúð bönnuð á Íslandi

Hermann Jónasson meinar íslenzku fólki að forða munaðarlausum gyðingabörnum undan ofsóknar-æði nazista í Austurríki

Katrín Thoroddsen læknir segir frá

Enn á ný hefur Hermann Jónasson sýnt hvern mann hann hefur að geyma, hversu djúpt drengskapur hans ristir, hve mannúð hans er mikil, hver skilningur hans er á því trúnaðarstarfi, sem honum var upphaflega falið af frjálslyndum flokkum, en sem hann 'nú hefur vegna bandalagsins við afturhaldsklíkur landsins.

Einnig hér úti á Íslandi hafa menn hugmynd um þær þjáningar, sem saklaust fólk verður fyrir í löndum fasismans. Fjölskyldum er sundrað, konur rifnar frá börnum sínum og heimilum og settar í fangabúðir — fyrir það eitt að fæðast af Gyð-

Laust fyrir miðjan desember s.l. það austurísk kona mig um að taka af sér þriggja ára gamla dóttur sína um óákveðinn tíma. Kona þessi er af gyðingaættum og maður hennar er einnig Gyðingur. Annars er það af honum að segja, að hann er starfsmaður við gasstöð í Wienarborg, afskiptalítill meinleysismaður, sem aldrei hafði tekið neinn þátt í stjórnmálum. En þegar Hitler komst til valda í Austur-

írin mundi vilja fá dóttur sína aftur jafnskjótt og hún sæi þess nokkurn kost að sjá henni farborða. Nú er það á allra vitorði, að áðursögð saga er ekkert einsdæmi, því til Friðarvinafélagsins, og spurðist fyrir um það, hvort félagið hefði í hyggju að taka hingað nokkuð af hrakhólabörnum, og ef svo væri, hvort mín stelpa gæti þá ekki fylgt þeim hóp. Jú, Friðarvinafélag-

Katrín Thoroddsen.

Figure 4.1: A well-known article written by Katrín Thoroddsen who attempted to gain permission for Jewish orphans to migrate to Iceland in 1939. The headline reads: "Humanity banned in Iceland. Hermann Jónasson [Minister of Justice] prevents Icelandic people from rescuing orphaned Jewish children from Nazi persecution in Austria." Source: *Þjóðviljinn*, 28 April 1939.

with "impure" Jewish blood. Nationalism and eugenics were the main factors influencing the government's refugee policy before and during the Second World War. Even though the authorities did become more inclined to let Jews into the country as the war tore on in the early 1940s, very few were actually allowed entry, so the end result remained the near-total exclusion of Jews before and during the war (Bergsson 2017; Vilhjálmsson 2019).

In 1944, Iceland gained full independence from Denmark, joining the United Nations in 1946 as an independent nation four years before the office of the UNHCR was established in 1950. The Icelandic Parliament granted permission to ratify the 1951 Refugee Convention in 1955, and it came into effect in Iceland in 1956 (Icelandic Human Rights Centre n.d.). That very first year, Iceland participated directly in UNHCR resettlement efforts by receiving its first group of refugees, who arrived from Hungary.

Although Iceland was bound by the Refugee Convention, it would not be implemented into Icelandic law until 2002 (Alþingi 2002). A new Surveillance of Foreigners Act came into effect in 1965; it was the first Icelandic law to address the presence of refugees (Alþingi 1965). It remained the primary legal grounds for the processing of applications for international protection until the passing of the Foreigners Act in 2002 (Alþingi 2002).

Interestingly, the 1965 Surveillance of Foreigners Act only provided provisions for political refugees, while the Refugee Convention clearly defined refugees as those fleeing because of a fear of being persecuted for "reasons of race, religion, nationality, membership of a particular social group or political opinion" (UNHCR 2010, 14). Furthermore, the act contained no nonrefoulement provisions comparable to Article 33 of the UN Refugee Convention. This discrepancy between Icelandic legislation and the Refugee Convention created uncertainty regarding how to process applications for international protection, as will be examined later in this chapter (Alþingi 1965; Þorsteinsdóttir 1992).

There were few marked changes in the legal basis of Iceland's regulation of forced migration to the country from 1965 until the early twenty-first century.[3] The main exception was the establishment of the permanent Icelandic Refugee Council in 1995, with the participation of five different ministries and an observer from the Icelandic Red Cross. These amendments were only implemented after considerable criticism from left-wing politicians and newspapers (e.g., *Þjóðviljinn* and *Vikublaðið*), as well as Amnesty International and other NGOs. They mainly criticized the lack of a strong legal framework around forced migration and the Icelandic authorities' reluctance to grant forced migrants, especially individuals seeking protection on their own, formal refugee status in Iceland (Guðmundsson 1993; Guðmundsson and Hannesson 1993; Hannibalsson 1993; "Með virkri þátttöku getur almenningur haft áhrif" 1993). Additionally, the UNHCR had been encouraging Iceland to receive a fixed annual quota of refugees since the 1980s (Þorvarðardóttir 1986). As it turned out, the Icelandic Refugee Council's first project was to prepare for an annual reception of refugees through UNHCR resettlement and to decide how many refugees would be invited to Iceland each year (Guðmundsdóttir 2000; "Kvóti flóttafólks brátt ákveðinn" 1995; Tran and Ragnarsdóttir 2022).

The decision to grant refugee groups asylum on a regular basis marked a change in policy regarding the regulation of forced migration to Iceland. Until then, such regulation had been characterized by attempts to close the country off, with only sporadic agreements to receive refugee groups, usually at the request of the UNHCR.

In the following sections, I examine Iceland's refugee policy during the second half of the twentieth century through the lens of two different categories of forced migration to which the Icelandic authorities responded in drastically different ways: refugee groups resettled in Iceland through the UNHCR and applicants for international protection who arrived in Iceland independently. First, however, I address the large group of Germans, partly made up of forced migrants from eastern Germany, who arrived in Iceland in 1949. Although they were usually categorized as "agricultural workers" by the state and the press, the circumstances of their arrival warrant attention, as they set a precedent for how refugees would be received in Iceland from 1956 until the end of the twentieth century.

German postwar forced migrants

Iceland's first encounter with the United Nations' refugee resettlement efforts occurred in 1946, when the United Nations Relief and Rehabilitation Administration (UNRRA) contacted the Icelandic Foreign Ministry, requesting that Iceland accept (presumably Jewish) refugees who did not want to return to Germany after the Second World War. The minister of justice, Finnur Jónsson, politely refused, stating that Iceland had received "a good many" refugees of Jewish descent. Additionally, many German citizens had settled in Iceland after the war, and it could therefore be said, according to Jónsson, that Iceland had received its fair share of refugees. These claims were exaggerated, as only a handful of Jews lived in Iceland in 1946, and most of the German citizens were of Icelandic origin. It can only be assumed that the minister's reaction reflects the continuation of eugenicist and antisemitic policies after the war (Bergsson 2017).

A group partly comprised of forced migrants did, however, migrate to Iceland in the summer of 1949, when 314 Germans – 238 women and 76 men – were employed as workers on Icelandic farms, which were dealing with a constant labor shortage and found it increasingly difficult to find female employees. A sizable part of the group consisted of forced migrants from eastern Germany, who were living in their thousands in and around the city of Lübeck after the war. Their

situation was dire, leading representatives of the Agricultural Association of Iceland to think that they might be easily convinced to
seek employment in Iceland for as little as half the pay that Icelanders
demanded (Eiríksson 2008; Ísberg 2010).

The hiring and selection process was marked by several factors
that would characterize the resettlement of refugee groups in Iceland
throughout the second half of the twentieth century. These included
the preeminence of forced migrants as a labor force and an emphasis on the compatibility of these migrants with the Icelandic genetic
pool and whiteness, as the contract signed by the German agricultural
laborers stated that they should be 20 to 35 years of age and of Northern German origin. As Eiríksson (2008) has pointed out, the project
raised concerns about the mixing of foreign and Icelandic "blood," but
its supporters claimed that there was no cause for alarm since people
from Northern Germany and the Nordic countries were considered to
have the same (superior) racial origins. These concerns suggest that
the workers were intended to stay indefinitely in Iceland, and eventually around half of them made it their permanent home (Ísberg 2010).

Although the group that arrived in Iceland in 1949 was more
diverse in origin than initially intended, the Agricultural Association's
emphasis reflects the desirability of "useful" white refugees of (Northern) European origin. The emphasis on selecting women was partly
due to the need for female labor in a highly gender-segregated labor
market; however, it was also present in subsequent resettlement processes, indicating that women were generally thought to be more suitable as refugees. Ísberg (2010) suggests that this gendered emphasis
was underpinned by women being considered more easily assimilated
into their host nation, which is further reflected in popular discourses
that constructed the true Icelander as exclusively male (Matthíasdóttir 2004; Yuval-Davis 1997). These desirable attributes of the "good"
refugee were to be ensured through careful selection by Icelandic officials, or, in the case of the German agricultural workers, by Árni Siem-
sen, the Icelandic vice-consul in Lübeck, and two Icelandic journalists
hired by the Icelandic Ministry of Employment (Eiríksson 2008).

Refugee groups resettled in Iceland

During the second half of the twentieth century, Icelanders experienced forced migration primarily in the form of the reception of small

Table 4.1: Refugees resettled in Iceland by the UNHCR (by arrival year, origin and number)

Arrival year	Origin	Number
1956	Hungary	52
1959	Yugoslavia	32
1979	Vietnam	34
1982	Poland	26
1990	Vietnam	30
1991	Vietnam	30
1996	Krajina (Croatia)	30
1997	Krajina (Croatia)	17
1998	Krajina (Croatia)	23
1999	Kosovo	75
2000	Krajina (Croatia)	24

Source: Harðardóttir, Jónsdóttir, and Jónsson 2005.

groups of refugees through UNHCR resettlement efforts. In this manner, 373 refugees gained international protection in Iceland between 1940 and 2000, the first group arriving from Hungary in 1956 and the last in 2000 from the Krajina district of Croatia (see Table 4.1). Other groups included refugees from Poland, Yugoslavia, Kosovo, and Vietnam. The latter represented the only non-European refugee group to be resettled in Iceland until 2005, when 24 refugees from Colombia arrived in Reykjavík under the auspices of the UNHCR. The origins of the refugee groups indicate that the Cold War played a significant role in Iceland's participation in UNHCR resettlement projects until the mid-1990s. Those who arrived from 1956 to 1991 were all fleeing nations under communist rule, whereas Iceland, which is a founding member of NATO, has aligned itself politically with the US since the end of the Second World War.

When the first group arrived from Hungary in 1956, the political situation in that country had been frequently discussed in the Icelandic media. During the summer, Gunnlaugur Þórðarson, a lawyer and

a board member of the Icelandic Red Cross, had encouraged Icelanders to receive a small and select group of "vigorous men and women"
(Guðmundsdóttir 2000, 196). In November, when the Icelandic government decided to invite refugees from Hungary, the Red Cross
offered its assistance.

The implementation followed a process similar to the selection
of German agricultural workers in 1949. Þórðarson was tasked with
traveling abroad to interview the Hungarian refugees and select those
who would be invited to Iceland. Announcements about resettlement
opportunities in Iceland were posted in Austrian camps housing Hungarian refugees. Those interested wrote their names on a list, eventually numbering 170 people in total. Þórðarson then interviewed the
refugees and decided which would be invited (Guðmundsdóttir 2000).

The selection process reveals which refugees were considered the
most desirable. First, Þórðarson attempted to gain permission to select
only children, since 111 Icelandic families and individuals had already
volunteered to adopt Hungarian children. When the International Red
Cross refused to let children leave the country, Þórðarson prioritized
young women, but so did other receiving nations, presumably because
women were perceived as less threatening and more likely to be
assimilated into the nation than men, while also ensuring its survival
by giving birth to future citizens (Yuval-Davis 1997). Þórðarson then
decided to select families with young children, but when they showed
little interest in migrating to Iceland he settled upon young people
capable of hard work (Guðmundsdóttir 2000; Þorvarðardóttir 1986).

The selection process was criticized harshly by the socialist newspapers *Austurland* and *Þjóðviljinn*, the latter of which was owned by
the Socialist Party (Alþýðublandalagið). The papers objected to the
utilitarian approach, which privileged young workers over "those who
were in the most need of help" (J. S. 1956, 1). The journalist from *Austurland*, most likely the editor Bjarni Þórðarson, went as far as to claim
that Gunnlaugur Þórðarson sounded like he had "come from a slave
market" and stated that the selection of Hungarian refugees had not
been based on humanitarian considerations but "cold-blooded specu-
lation" ("Íslendingar svívirtir í nafni mannúðar" 1957, 2).

The criticism seemed to have no far-reaching effects and soon
died down, according to Þorvarðardóttir (1986). The same process
was employed during the following years whenever the Icelandic
government decided to take part in refugee resettlement through the

UNHCR, and it became an integral part of the regulation of forced migration to Iceland. Icelandic officials carefully selected each refugee according to predetermined criteria, an approach intended to ensure that those who resettled would either serve the Icelandic economy as labor or be easily assimilated into Icelandic society because of their gender, youth, origin, or perceived compatibility with the Icelandic gene pool. The hierarchy of selection, as in the case of the Hungarians, typically followed this order of priority: children, women, families, and industrious workers, often young adults.

The Icelandic government was not alone in prioritizing refugees in this manner (Østergaard 2007). As Korsvold (2020) explains, Nordic schemes for relocating children and youth were common during the twentieth century and can be traced back to the 1920s. Of the 1,455 Hungarian refugees resettled in Norway in 1956–1957, 355 were unaccompanied teenagers, including minors aged ten to 19 (Korsvold 2020). As in Iceland, humanitarianism was not the sole motivation behind these efforts, which were also heavily influenced by political, social, and economic motives. In Norway, the need for unskilled labor played a significant role in the selection of Hungarian refugees (Korsvold 2020), while the Icelandic selection committee was further preoccupied with the perceived ease with which the refugees could be assimilated into Icelandic society, as already described.

Economic reasons took precedence in 1959, when 32 people from Yugoslavia were selected to relocate to Iceland at the request of the UNHCR (see Figure 4.2). The High Commissioner's representative, C. Brouwer, recommended Yugoslavian fishermen who resided in Italy, as he believed that they would adapt well to another maritime society and become productive participants in the Icelandic fishing industry. Employees of the Ministry of Social Affairs traveled to Italy to select 20 refugees for relocation to Iceland, all men who had been employed in the fishing industry, along with their families. Of 32 refugees in total, 16 were single; the rest were married men and their families ("Flóttamenn frá Júgóslavíu eignast nýtt föðurland hér" 1959; Guðmundsdóttir 2000).

With the exception of the Yugoslavian group, the Icelandic authorities prioritized the invitation of women, children, or families to settle in Iceland. In 1979, the Icelandic government decided to receive refugees from Vietnam. After the foreign minister of Iceland, Benedikt Gröndal, had inquired whether it would be possible to receive children only,

Á efri myndinni sést nokkur hluti júgóslavneska flóttamanna-
hópsins, sem kom til Reykjavíkur í gær. Fremst á myndinni
er Vaggio fjölskyldan. Á neðri myndinni eru tvö börn þeirra
hjónanna. Börnin eru fædd í flóttamannabúðum og fá nú loks
tækifæri til þess að eignast föðurland.

27 júgóslavneskir flóttamenn komnir

TIL Reykjavíkur komu í gær fljúgandi frá Kaupmannahöfn 27 júgóslavneskir flóttamenn, sem ríkisstjórnin hefur tekið á móti að tilhlutan flóttamannastofnunar Sameinuðu þjóðanna. Komu í gær 19 karlmenn, þrjár konur og fimm börn. Meðal þessa fólks er Vaggio-fjölskyldan, sem hefur dvalið um 11 ár í flóttamannabúðum. Eiga þau Vaggiohjónin 4 börn, sem öll eru fædd í flóttamannabúðum og er Ísland fyrsta landið, sem þau geta kallað föðurland.

Þessir júgóslavnesku flóttamenn komu hingað í sambandi við hið alþjóðlega flóttamanna ár Sameinuðu þjóðanna. Fór Flóttamannastofnunin þess á leit við ríkisstjórnina, að hún veitti flóttamönnum viðtöku.

Ríkisstjórnin samþykkti að taka á móti 20 flóttamönnum og skylduliði þeirra. Fór Hallgrímur Dalberg, fulltrúi í félagsmálaráðuneytinu, til Genf snemma í aprílmánuði til þess að semja um flutning flóttamannanna hingað. Lét hann gera pésa með upplýsingum um land og þjóð, sem dreift var meðal Júgóslava í flóttamannabúðunum á Ítalíu.

50 VILDU FARA TIL ÍSLANDS.
50 júgóslavneskir flóttamenn vildu fara til Íslands eftir að hafa lesið pésann. Voru valdir

Framhald á 3. síðu.

Figure 4.2: 27 refugees from Yugoslavia arrived in Iceland on 30 April 1959. On 1 May the left-wing *Alþýðublaðið* ran a story about them on the front page. In caption the author writes about the Vaggio children (front and center on the photo) who, according to the paper, "were born in a refugee camp and finally have the opportunity to find a new homeland." Source: *Alþýðublaðið*, 1 May 1959.

it was agreed that Iceland would invite five to six families to resettle, which were then hand-selected by two members of the Icelandic Red Cross (Guðmundsdóttir 2000). The emphasis on families was partly based on the advice of members of the Danish Refugee Council, who served as advisers on the project. They stated that single individuals were more likely to cause trouble (Guðmundsson 1981). This advice must have aligned with the preferences of the Icelandic authorities, who had previously prioritized children and women in their selection processes.

A similar approach was used in 1982, when a group of 26 Polish refugees was invited to Iceland, and again in 1991 and 1992, when two groups of refugees from Vietnam, each 30-strong, resettled in the country. Only five unmarried adults were among these 86 individuals; the rest belonged to resettled family units (Guðmundsdóttir 2000).

As previously mentioned, refugees from Vietnam were the first non-European forced migrants to resettle in Iceland (see Figure 4.3). The public debate on their resettlement reflects that there were concerns about their ability to adapt to a different climate and way of living, but also about the effects of Vietnamese-Icelandic intimate relationships on the perceived purity of the Icelandic "race" (*kynstofn*) (e.g., "Flestir vilja taka vel á móti þessu fólki" 1979; Geirsson 1979; "Raddir lesenda" 1979). Concerns about these differences were also reflected in the conditions of their resettlement. They were the only refugees to be assigned Icelandic first names upon their arrival.[4] They received free day care, paid for by the Red Cross through 1993, in order to "ensure that the children were not pulled from kindergarten in order to reduce the families' expenses" (Guðmundsdóttir 2000, 219). It was believed that the children would become fluent in Icelandic if they were surrounded by Icelandic culture for a large part of the day. Children of school age also received supplementary education in Icelandic, with "good results" (Guðmundsdóttir 2000). Tran and Ragnarsdóttir (2022) suggest that the main intention behind such efforts was to assimilate the refugees from Vietnam into Icelandic society. The extra efforts to keep the children in kindergarten and hide their unfamiliar names support this interpretation.

During the last decade of the twentieth century, there was a marked change in government policies regarding the continued reception of refugee groups through the UNHCR. As previously mentioned, these changes were partly due to pressure from international human rights

Ekki lengur flóttamenn

Koma vietnamska flóttafólksins hingað til lands hlýtur að vekja okkur Íslendinga til umhugsunar um margt, sem við leiðum ekki hugann að í erli hins daglega lífs. Þeir grimmúðlegu stjórnarhættir, sem hröktu þetta fólk á flótta upp á líf og dauða, minna okkur á, hversu okkur er dýrmætt það frelsi, sem við sjálf njótum, og brýnir okkur til þess að berjast á móti öllum skerðingum á frelsi okkar, smáum sem stórum.

Vitundin um árásirnar, hungrið, klæðaskortinn, vosbúðina og óvissuna, sem flóttafólkið hefur mátt þola undanfarna mánuði, ætti að opna augu okkar fyrir allri þeirri velmegun, sem við búum við, þrátt fyrir okkar sífelldu barlóm. Örlög flóttafólksins frá Vietnam og flutningur þess út um svo til alla heimsbyggðina færa okkur enn eina sönnunina um það, hve heimur okkar er í raun og veru orðinn lítill, þar sem jafnvel ekki her norður á Íslandi verður víkist undan vandamálum fólks lengt suður í Asíu.

Vísir lét á sínum tíma í ljósi efasemdir um það, að rétt væri

Vísir býður flóttafólkið frá Vietnam velkomið til Íslands. Vonandi vegnar því vel hér á landi og finnur það af móttökum okkar, að hinum langa flótta þess sé lokið.

af okkur Íslendingum að flytja sérstaklega hingað til lands hóp fólks af allt öðrum kynstofni en Íslendingar almennt eru og búið hefur við allt aðrar aðstæður en það verður að venjast hér á landi.

Þau vandamál, sem komið hafa upp m.a. hjá mörgum nágrannaþjóða okkar, í sambúð heimamanna og innflytjenda af ólíkum kynstofni, eru vissulega víti til varnaðar. Því er ekki að leyna, að þessir sambúðarerfiðleikar eru a.m.k. að jafnmiklu

leyti sök heimamanna enda hið innflutta fólk í mjög mörgum tilvikum aðlaðandi, nægjusamt og harðduglegt. Við Íslendingar höfum ekki kynnst kynþáttavandamálum nema af afspurn, og höfum því trútt getað talað um þau vandamál hjá öðrum þjóðum. Fyrirfram skulum við þó ekki reikna með meira umburðarlyndi í þessum efnum hjá mörgum meðal okkar heldur en annarra þjóða fólki. Einmitt með því að gera okkur strax grein

fyrir árekstramöguleikunum, þegar fram í sækir, verðum við betur fær um að forðast árekstra, þegar á reynir.

Vísir býður flóttafólkið frá Vietnam velkomið til Íslands. Við skulum vona, að með komu þess hingað sé flótta þess lokið. Við skulum öll reyna að taka þannig á móti því fólki, sem hingað er komið, að því finnist það ekki vera flóttafólk lengur. Hér verður það að byrja nýtt líf í framandi umhverfi. Það kemur hingað með tvær hendur tómar, en sem betur fer eru enn möguleikar hér á landi fyrir duglegt fólk til þess að vinna sig upp, þótt það hafi lítið handa í milli. Vísir vonar, að þessum nýju heimamönnum hér á Íslandi vegni sem allra best og þeir megi verða nýtir borgarar hér á landi. Jafnframt lætur Vísir í ljós þá von, að sambúð þeirra og okkar, sem fyrir erum í landinu, verði farsæl og Íslendingar hafi þroska til að bera, til þess að sætta sig við veru þeirra einstaklinga, sem hingað eru komnir, í landinu, ekki bara þessa dagana meðan sambúðin með þeim er mest, heldur einnig í framtíðinni.

Figure 4.3: The newspaper *Vísir* greeted the group in an editorial titled "Refugees no longer" where the editors wrote "Vísir welcomes the refugees from Vietnam to Iceland. Hopefully, they will do well here in the country and feel from our reception that their long journey has come to an end." Source: *Vísir*, 21 September 1979.

associations, such as Amnesty International, left-wing newspapers, and socialist and social democratic politicians, as well as the UNHCR itself. Although a fair share of the criticism revolved around individuals who applied for international protection in Iceland, the authorities continued to refrain from granting formal refugee status to individuals, as addressed later in the chapter. The government did, however, agree to receive small groups through the UNHCR every one or two years. Interestingly, the Nordic countries developed a common Nordic refugee policy in 1990, which was intended to strengthen their cooperation, for example by increasing the number of refugees that the countries received through the UNHCR every year. However, the countries also agreed that the policy had limited implications for Iceland, which could choose whether and when to participate (Þorsteinsdóttir 1992).

Despite such provisions, five groups of refugees arrived in Iceland during the final five years of the twentieth century: one group of

75 people from Kosovo and four groups, 94 individuals in total, from the Krajina district (the former Serb Republic of Krajina) of Croatia on the Serbian border. The Icelandic authorities followed processes similar to those they had previously employed. Icelandic officials were sent abroad to select applicants, who were then invited to join the group to be resettled in Iceland. As before, emphasis was placed on inviting families rather than individuals to relocate to Iceland (Guðmundsdóttir 2000; "Sendinefnd velur hópinn eftir helgi" 1998).

Previously, refugees had been given a place to live in the capital area; however, in 1996, the town authorities of Ísafjörður in the Northwestern Region of Iceland offered to host the first group from Krajina, which numbered 30 individuals. Subsequently, it was decided to advertise for municipalities willing to receive refugees (Guðmundsdóttir 2000). As a result, 144 of the 169 refugees from Krajina and Kosovo who arrived between 1996 and 2000 were settled in remote villages and towns with 1,000 to 2,800 inhabitants (Statistics Iceland n.d.-c; Hinriksson 2008).[5]

The town authorities in Ísafjörður stated that the main reason behind their offer was to demonstrate that the town could handle such a large project. However, it did not go unnoticed that towns like Ísafjörður were, at the time, dealing with depopulation and increasing difficulties in finding people to work in fish processing, and the fish industry was the most prominent economic sector in the Northwestern Region of Iceland (Directorate of Labor 1999; Þorsteinsson 1997).

Similar considerations were evident in the discourse of the representatives of municipalities such as Snæfellsbær in the Western Region and Hornafjörður in the Eastern Region, which followed Ísafjörður's lead and offered to host subsequent groups from Krajina and Kosovo. As the mayor of Snæfellsbær noted, "of course, the arrival of the refugees will increase the number of families in town and counterbalance those who leave," but, more importantly, the main benefits for the municipality were "new blood, ideas, and currents" (Þorsteinsson 1997, 22). The Minister of Social Affairs pointed out that Icelandic towns did not need refugees to solve their workforce problems, but said, "Of course, it is more secure and better to get people who intend to settle [in the country,] and there is no doubt in my mind that these groups of Yugoslavians are going to be good citizens here. They will probably also strengthen their districts" (Þorsteinsson 1997, 24). The minister then added that the refugees were not serfs and would be able to relocate to other parts of the country. Nevertheless, he anticipated that they would "settle and be happy" where they had been placed (Þorsteinsson 1997, 24).

Contrary to the minister's expectations, this attempt to integrate forced migration policy and regional development policy failed. By 2008, only one family and one individual of the 144 refugees from Kosovo and Krajina remained in the rural towns. In contrast, the majority of the 25 Kosovo Albanians hosted in 1999 by Hafnarfjörður, located just south of the capital Reykjavík, were still residing in the town in 2005 (Harðardóttir, Jónsdóttir, and Jónsson 2005). These were the only individuals of the 169 people from Krajina and Kosovo who were resettled in a mid-sized municipality in the metropolitan area, although Hafnarfjörður had a population of only 20,000.

Those who had relocated from rural Iceland to the capital area did so for various reasons (Hinriksson 2008), among them the lack of long-term employment and infrastructure, such as upper secondary schools for teenage children (Guðmundsdóttir 2000; Harðardóttir, Jónsdóttir, and Jónsson 2005). The development of the Icelandic refugee policy toward the end of the twentieth century thus reflects the long-standing utilitarian policy of the Icelandic government toward refugees, which prioritized the interests of the Icelandic economy and various domestic actors over those of individuals granted international protection (Þorsteinsson 1997). These emphases were most pronounced in the regulation of individual applicants for international protection in Iceland who decided to migrate to the country on their own.

Individual applicants for international protection in Iceland

In the latter half of the twentieth century, forced migration to Iceland was rare, apart from UNHCR resettlement efforts. As a small nation distant from the mainlands of both Europe and North America, Iceland was neither an accessible nor a desirable place for people seeking international protection. There are no statistics available for the number of applications for international protection in Iceland before the mid-1980s. Between 1984 and 1989, only 13 applications were submitted to the Icelandic authorities; during the same period, 35,000 people applied for protection in Denmark and 100,000 in Sweden (Þorsteinsdóttir 1992). The number of annual applications remained very low throughout the twentieth century but rose to 20–30 during its last few years. From 1997–2000, 82 people in total applied for international protection in Iceland: 12 women and 70 men. Most national groups were represented by fewer than seven members each, except Ukraine (15 applicants) and Kosovo (13 applicants) (Statistics Iceland n.d.-a).

The numbers show that very few people applied for international protection in Iceland during the period under study, and even fewer were granted formal refugee status. During the twentieth century, only one applicant – an unaccompanied minor arriving in 1999 – received international protection (in 2000), although several other applicants were given residence permits "for humanitarian reasons." The precise number of these permits granted during the twentieth century is unclear, but from 1997 to 2000 only eight applicants received residence permits (Statistics Iceland n.d.-b). In the year 2000 alone, 1,136 people were granted refugee status in Denmark, and 2,738 were issued de facto and humanitarian protection status (United States Committee for Refugees and Immigrants 2000).

In the general discourse in Iceland, little distinction was made between individual applicants for international protection and refugees who arrived in groups through the UNHCR. Both were usually called "refugees" or *flóttamenn*, or sometimes "political refugees" (*pólitískir flóttamenn*). However, they were treated in distinctly different ways by the Icelandic authorities. On the one hand, the UNHCR-facilitated groups were welcomed to Iceland as formally recognized refugees, having gained the approval of Icelandic officials during the previously discussed selection process. On the other hand, those who sought international protection of their own accord found it impossible to obtain official refugee status in Iceland.

In 1992, Ragnheiður Þorsteinsdóttir remarked that Iceland's reluctance to grant international protection was probably due to fear of setting a precedent that would lead to an increase in applications. During parliamentary debates in October 1991, the minister of justice stated that the government's policy was to assist those applicants who fulfilled the conditions of the Refugee Convention while following the principle that refugees should turn to authorities in their first country of asylum (Þorsteinsdóttir 1992). Iceland is extremely rarely, if ever, the first country of asylum owing to its geographical location. As a result, the government policy of the 1980s and the early 1990s was de facto not to grant international protection at all but rather to turn most applicants away. Some were granted a residence permit "for humanitarian reasons," and the rest were deported. This policy, again, enabled the authorities to pick and choose individual applicants. By substituting residence permits for formal refugee status, the Icelandic authorities were not obliged to provide the applicants with the social and economic support to which only formally recognized refugees had a right according to international treaties. The authorities thus ensured that the applicants would be forced to provide labor for the Icelandic economy in order to make a living.

As previously mentioned, the Surveillance of Foreigners Act of 1965 was the first to mention the word "refugee" (*flóttamaður*) and include provisions for applicants for international protection. The act defines a refugee as a person who flees their country of origin for political reasons only and does not contain provisions for nonrefoulement comparable with Article 33 of the UN Refugee Convention. As the twentieth century drew to a close, legal specialists thought it imperative to amend the Surveillance of Foreigners Act, as it was considered to grant the Icelandic authorities extensive powers to deport and deny foreigners entry into the country without ensuring legal recourse or a right to advocacy or legal assistance for applicants. It was also suspected that refugees were being turned away at points of entry, despite the act explicitly stating that refugees could not be denied entry into the country and that their cases should immediately be submitted to the minister of justice. It was therefore "debatable" whether Iceland was fulfilling its obligations under the Refugee Convention (Þorsteinsdóttir 1992).

This lack of clear provisions in Icelandic law became evident in 1980 when a French citizen, Patrick Gervasoni, applied for international protection in Iceland. Gervasoni had spent a decade incognito in France as a wanted army deserter. He finally fled to Denmark, where he met a group of radical students, among them an Icelander, who was probably the main reason for the group suggesting that Gervasoni should apply for international protection in Iceland (Halldórsson 2016). The "Gervasoni case," as it was called in Iceland, revealed that legal provisions for refugees were unclear and that the Icelandic authorities were unsure of how to process his application. The minister of justice, Friðjón Þórðarson of the right-wing Independence Party, denied his application on the grounds that military service was mandatory in France (see Figure 4.4). The authorities were keen on deporting him back to Denmark, even if he could be sent back to France,

Figure 4.4: Patrick Gervasoni wrote an open letter to the minister of justice, asking him to make a decision about his case. There he wrote: "Though I owe my temporary freedom to the reactions of a large part of the Icelandic nation, you must agree that it is both difficult and terrifying to live and work without knowing whether in the near future one faces imprisonment or freedom. Mr. Minister, what is your decision: imprisonment or freedom?" Source: *Dagblaðið*, 12 November 1980.

putting him at risk of becoming a prisoner of conscience, according to Amnesty International (Halldórsson 2016). Even though Gervasoni was supported by Icelandic socialists and radical students who advocated on his behalf (Jónasson et al. 1980), he was eventually deported. The official reason was that he had broken Icelandic law by entering the country without valid identity documents, despite the Refugee Convention clearly stating that applicants for international protection should not be punished for such offenses. In reality, Iceland's partnership with France within NATO and Gervasoni's left-wing political opinions carried a lot of weight (Halldórsson 2016).

The Gervasoni case also reflects Iceland's fear that granting refugees international protection outside the confines of the UNHCR would provide other prospective applicants with a precedent that might lead to a drastic increase in the number of applications (Halldórsson 2016; Þorsteinsdóttir 1992). The Icelandic authorities were quite committed to preventing that from happening during the twentieth century, as it would undermine their extensive regulation of forced migration to Iceland.

Conclusion

In this chapter, I have traced the history of Iceland's regulation of forced migration in the second half of the twentieth century and reflected upon Iceland's refugee policy, which was implicit during most of the research period. The Surveillance of Foreigners Act, first passed in 1920, did not include explicit references to refugees but was cited nonetheless in the deportation of refugees from Iceland. In the years leading up to the Second World War, the new Surveillance of Foreigners Act and regulations of 1936–1937 provided the minister of justice with an open provision to deport any foreigner in Iceland if "their behavior and circumstances … warrant[ed] deportation" (Bergsson 2017, 132). This legal clause was used to justify the deportation of Jewish refugees from 1936 to 1939, which was in full accordance with Iceland's policy of enacting a near-complete ban on the settlement of Jews in Iceland for antisemitic and eugenicist reasons.

Iceland remains one of the European countries that welcomed only very few Jewish refugees before and during the Second World War. Conversely, the country opened its doors to non-Jewish forced migrants after the war, when the Icelandic Agricultural Association facilitated the migration of 314 Germans, mostly women and some of them forced migrants, who were hired as agricultural workers on Icelandic farms in 1949. This project created a selection process that would be employed in subsequent refugee resettlement programs. Refugees were to be carefully hand-selected by Icelandic officials according to criteria that emphasized (a) utilitarianism, through the emphasis on young families and hard workers, and (b) assimilation, by privileging white women and children, who were considered more easily assimilated into the dominant culture than men. Although the government's utilitarian stance was criticized by the Icelandic socialist media, this selection process seems to have been widely accepted, as it was in use throughout the twentieth century.

The only nonwhite, non-European refugees resettled in Iceland in the twentieth century were three groups of Vietnamese refugees arriving in 1979 and 1990–1991. In their case, extra efforts were made to ensure their proximity to Icelandic culture. Icelandic first names were imposed upon them, and steps were taken to ensure that their young children were immersed in Icelandic culture for a large part of the day. These measures have since been found to be assimilationist (Tran and Ragnarsdóttir 2022).

The reigning utilitarian and assimilationist policy was reflected in the twofold categorization of forced migrants after Iceland became a party to the UN Refugee Convention in 1956. The term "refugees" (flóttamenn) was used to refer to both those who arrived in national groups under the auspices of the UNHCR and those who reached Iceland independently to apply for international protection. The reactions of the Icelandic authorities to their arrival in Iceland, however, reflect that the migrants were placed into two radically different categories. One consisted of refugees who had been carefully selected based on their usefulness (and often whiteness) and were therefore welcome in Iceland. The other was comprised of individuals who had managed to reach Iceland on their own and circumvent the selection process. The latter were systematically denied formal refugee status, although they were sometimes granted residence permits for humanitarian reasons which stripped them of their rights as refugees.

Toward the end of the century, the Icelandic authorities were increasingly criticized for the lack of a clear legal framework concerning forced migration, the low number of refugees received by Iceland through the UNHCR, and their tendency to withhold formal refugee status from individual applicants for international protection. As a result, there was a slight policy shift as Iceland started to receive refugee groups on an annual or biennial basis. The first of these arrived from Kosovo and Krajina and were settled in small and remote municipalities, linking forced migration policy with Icelandic regional development policy. This attempt to utilize refugees to boost local economies failed; however, it stands as a testimony to Iceland's forced migration policy throughout the twentieth century, which was first and foremost marked by Icelandic self-interest and the desire to regulate in minute detail forced migration to Iceland by maintaining strong control over who would be allowed to settle in the country.

Notes

1 Danish citizens, including people from Greenland and the Faroe Islands, did not need permission to immigrate to Iceland.
2 All direct quotations originally in Icelandic have been translated into English by the author.
3 The Surveillance of Foreigners Act was amended in 1996 and 1999; however, no substantial changes to the articles on refugees were implemented.
4 A large part of the group from 1979 received an Icelandic citizenship in 1984. Their Vietnamese names are listed in documents about new citizens from that year, which suggests that the name change from 1979 was informal but still significant as the Vietnamese group was the only one to be assigned Icelandic names upon arrival (Alþingi 1984).
5 The towns and municipalities were Ísafjörður, Siglufjörður, Blönduós, Dalvík, Fjarðabyggð, and Hornafjörður.

Bibliography

Alþingi. 1920. "Lög um eftirlit með útlendingum". In *Stjónartíðindi fyrir Ísland árið 1920 A-deild*, 22–24. Reykjavík: Ísafoldarprentsmiðja.
Alþingi. 1965. "Lög um eftirlit með útlendingum". In *Stjónartíðindi 1965 A-deild*, 101–3. Reykjavík: Ministry of Justice.
Alþingi. 1984. "Lög um veitingu ríkisborgararéttar". In *Stjónartíðindi 1984 A-deild*, 174–76. Reykjavík: Ministry of Justice.
Alþingi. 2002. "Lög um atvinnuréttindi útlendinga". In *Stjórnartíðindi 2002 A-deild*, 276–83. Reykjavík: Ministry of Justice.
Ástgeirsdóttir, Kristín. 2007. "Katrín Thoroddsen". *Andvari* 132 (1): 11–68.
Bergsson, Snorri G. 2011. *Roðinn í austri. Alþýðuflokkurinn, Komintern og kommúnistahreyfingin á Íslandi 1919–1924*. Reykjavík: Ugla. https://doi.org/10.13177/irpa.c.2011.7.2.7.
Bergsson, Snorri G. 2017. *Erlendur landshornalýður? Flóttamenn og framandi útlendingar á Íslandi, 1853–1940*. Reykjavík: Almenna bókafélagið.
Boberg-Fazlic, Nina and Paul Sharp. 2020. "Is There a Refugee Gap? Evidence from over a Century of Danish Naturalizations". CAGE Working Paper no. 506. Warwick: University of Warwick.
Directorate of Labor. 1999. *Annual Report 1999*. Reykjavík: Directorate of Labor.
Eiríksson, Pétur. 2008. *Þýska landnámið*, edited by Ólafur Rastrick. Reykjavík: Sögufélag.
"Flestir vilja taka vel á móti þessu fólki". 1979. *Fjarðarfréttir*, September 1979.
"Flóttamenn frá Júgóslavíu eignast nýtt föðurland hér". 1959. *Morgunblaðið*, May 1, 1959.
Frandsen, Per. 2013. "De ønskede og de uønskede. Indfødsretten og opgøret efter besættelsen". *Historisk Tidsskrift* 112 (1): 92–129. https://tidsskrift.dk/historisk-tidsskrift/article/view/56552.
Geirsson, Ólafur. 1979. "Hvernig lízt þér á þá hugmynd að Ísland taki á móti 50 flóttamönnum frá Víetnam?" *Dagblaðið*, June 22, 1979.

Guðmundsdóttir, Margrét. 2000. *Í þágu mannúðar. Saga Rauða kross Íslands 1924–1999.* Reykjavík: Mál og mynd.

Guðmundsson, Friðrik and Páll Hannesson. 1993. "Geðþótti og hræðsla við fordæmi". *Vikublaðið*, September 3, 1993.

Guðmundsson, Friðrik. 1993. "Endurskoðun laga um flóttamenn ekki á kortinu". *Vikublaðið*, September 10, 1993.

Guðmundsson, Sigurður H. 1981. *Flóttamenn. Verkefni RKÍ 1. júlí 79 - 30. júní 80.* Reykjavík: Red Cross Iceland.

Halldórsson, Björn Reynir. 2016. "Gervasoni-málið. Viðhorf stjórnvalda og almennings til hælisleitanda". *Sagnir* 31: 201–14.

Hannibalsson, Jón Baldvin. 1993. "Griðland?" *Alþýðublaðið*, December 21, 1993.

Harðardóttir, Kristín Erla, Heiður Hrund Jónsdóttir, and Friðrik H. Jónsson. 2005. *Reynsla og viðhorf flóttamanna á Íslandi.* Reykjavík: Flóttamannaráð Íslands.

Hinriksson, Benedikt Bóas. 2008. "Flóttamenn hafa flúið landsbyggðina". *DV*, May 30, 2008.

Icelandic Human Rights Centre. n.d. "Samningur um réttarstöðu flóttamanna". https://www.humanrights.is/is/mannrettindi-og-island/helstu-samningar-og-yfirlysingar/sameinudu-thjodirnar/samningur-um-rettarstodu-flottamanna.

Ingimundarson, Valur. 2013. "Mikson málið sem 'fortíðarvandi'". *Saga* 51 (1): 9–51.

Ísberg, Nína Rós. 2010. "Migration and Cultural Transmission: Making a Home in Iceland". PhD thesis, University of London.

"Íslendingar svívirtir í nafni mannúðar". 1957. *Austurland*, January 4, 1957.

J. S. 1956. "Ungverska flóttafólkið valið eftir afkastagetu". *Þjóðviljinn*, December 28, 1956.

Jónasson, Björn, Pétur Gunnarsson, Torfi Túliníus, and Örnólfur Thors. 1980. "Réttlæti en ekki hefnd: Greinargerð". *Morgunblaðið*, December 13, 1980.

Jónsson, Guðmundur. 1995. "Þjóðernisstefna, hagþróun og sjálfstæðisbarátta". *Skírnir* 169 (Spring): 65–93.

Korsvold, Tora. 2020. "'Hungarian Boys' Immigration to Norway, 1956–1957: The Complex Economic, Political, and Humanitarian Motives of Minors on the Move". *Journal of the History of Childhood and Youth* 13 (3): 407–25. https://doi.org/10.1353/hcy.2020.0063.

"Kvóti flóttafólks brátt ákveðinn". 1995. *Alþýðublaðið*, August 16, 1995.

Matthíasdóttir, Sigríður. 2004. *Hinn sanni Íslendingur. Þjóðerni, kyngervi og vald á Íslandi 1900–1930.* Reykjavík: University of Iceland Press.

"Með virkri þátttöku getur almenningur haft áhrif". 1993. *Vikublaðið*, October 22, 1993.

Østergaard, Bent. 2007. *Indvandrerne i Danmarks historie. Kultur- og religionsmøder.* Odense: Syddansk Universitetsforlag.

Ottósson, Hendrik. 1980. *Hvíta stríðið.* Hafnarfjörður: Skuggsjá.

Pétursson, Pétur. 2005. "'Drengsmálið' og eftirmál". *Morgunblaðið*, February 21, 2005.

"Raddir lesenda". 1979. *Dagblaðið*, June 26, 1979.

"Sendinefnd velur hópinn eftir helgi". 1998. *Morgunblaðið*, April 3, 1998.

Statistics Iceland. n.d.-a. "Asylum Applications by Citizenship, Sex and Age 1997–2019". http://px.hagstofa.is/pxen/pxweb/en/Ibuar/Ibuar__mannfjoldi__3_bakgrunnur__Vernd_dvalarleyfi/MAN45001.px.

Statistics Iceland. n.d.-b. "International Protection Grants by Citizenship, Type, Age and Sex 1997–2019". https://px.hagstofa.is/pxen/pxweb/en/Ibuar/Ibuar__man-nfjoldi__3_bakgrunnur__Vernd_dvalarleyfi/MAN45002.px.

Statistics Iceland. n.d.-c. "Population by Municipality, Age and Sex 1998–2023 – Division into Municipalities as of 1 January 2024". https://px.hagstofa.is/pxen/pxweb/en/Ibuar/Ibuar__mannfjoldi__2_byggdir__sveitarfelog/MAN02005.px.

Þorsteinsdóttir, Ragnheiður. 1992. "Flóttamenn og réttarstaða þeirra á Íslandi". *Úlfljótur* 45 (4): 315–37.

Þorsteinsson, Helgi. 1997. "Flóttamenn sem vinnuafl". *Morgunblaðið*, September 14, 1997.

Þorvarðardóttir, Ólína. 1986. "Flóttamenn". *Heimsmynd* 1 (6): 30–39.

Tran, Anh-Dao and Hanna Ragnarsdóttir. 2022. "Vietnamese and Syrian Refugees in Iceland: Acculturation and Integration in Society and Schools, 1979–2016". *Tertium Comparationis* 28 (2): 159–76.

UNHCR. 2010. *Convention and Protocol Relating to the Status of Refugees*. Geneva: UNHCR.

UNHCR. 2022. "Refugee Data Finder". https://www.unhcr.org/refugee-statistics.

United States Committee for Refugees and Immigrants. 2000. "U.S. Committee for Refugees World Refugee Survey 2000 – Denmark". https://www.refworld.org/docid/3ae6a8d28.html.

Vilhjálmsson, Vilhjálmur Örn. 2019. "Iceland: A Study of Antisemitism in a Country without Jews". In *Antisemitism in the North. History and State of Research*, edited by Jonathan Adams and Cordelia Heß, 69–105. Berlin: De Gruyter.

Yuval-Davis, Nira. 1997. *Gender and Nation*. London and Thousand Oaks, CA: Sage Publications.

CHAPTER 5

At the crossroads between humanitarianism and restrictions

The Nordic countries' response to refugees from the Yugoslav Wars

Kristina Stenman
University of Helsinki

Abstract

The chapter deals with the responses in Denmark, Finland, Norway, and Sweden to the refugee situation due to the wars in former Yugoslavia 1991–2001. The Nordic countries had achieved a common labor market and a joint Passport Control Area in the 1950s. Legislation projects on migration and asylum in the 1980s demonstrated common features. The Nordic countries also coordinated their responses to the conflict resolution efforts in former Yugoslavia. In the responses to refugees arriving from the wars, the Nordic countries, however, chose clearly national paths on visas, residence permit regimes, and the rights that residence permits entailed. By 1997, all countries still had opted for permanent residence for refugees from the Balkans, along the lines of other European countries. Yet there appears initially

How to cite this book chapter:
Stenman, Kristina. 2025. "At the crossroads between humanitarianism and restrictions: the Nordic countries' response to refugees from the Yugoslav Wars." In *Forced Migrants in Nordic Histories*, edited by Johanna Leinonen, Miika Tervonen, Hans Otto Frøland, Christhard Hoffmann, Seija Jalagin, Heidi Vad Jønsson and Malin Thor Tureby, 135–154. Helsinki: Helsinki University Press. https://doi.org/10.33134/HUP-32-6.

to have been a strong political pressure to develop responses from a national perspective, while responses converged over time. The question of temporariness of protection for refugees emerged as a more long-term consequence for refugee law from this situation, including in the Nordic countries.

The setting: from the end of the Cold War toward the start of the Yugoslav Wars

In the 1990s, the dominating refugee issue for Europe was the response to the situation of forced displacement caused by the Yugoslav Wars in 1991–2001. The wars entailed both the internal displacement of some two million people and the flight across borders of some 2.4 million refugees. The disintegration of Yugoslavia and the ensuing wars coincided with, and were partly prompted by, the end of the Cold War and the dissolution of the Soviet Union. Some years earlier, European states had already begun responding to growing numbers of asylum seekers with restrictions such as sanctions for airlines carrying undocumented passengers. Replacing permanent residence with temporary solutions and return also became part of the asylum debate as of the 1980s.

This chapter compares the developments in asylum law and policy during this period in four Nordic countries – Denmark, Finland, Norway, and Sweden – against the setting of the United Nations and European responses.[1] The focus is on the war in Bosnia–Herzegovina and the response to the refugees who arrived in 1991–1995. Given the close political cooperation, joint passport area, and common labor market between the Nordic countries, my question is: to what extent were the political and legal entanglements between the Nordic countries reflected in the countries' responses to the movements of refugees generated by the Yugoslav Wars?

I use the term *refugee* to refer to all those fleeing the Yugoslav Wars outside the region and being granted protection of some kind, regardless of whether they were formally recognized as refugees. It can be argued that, had they been granted an individual asylum procedure, most of them would have fulfilled the criteria for refugee status, having fled not just the general hardship of war but targeted violations against the civilian population on ethnic or religious grounds. My perspective is primarily that of comparative legal history. Legal history seeks to trace the underlying reasons for change in the legal domain.

Comparative legal history examines meaningful points of comparison between developments on an international level (Pihlajamäki 2014, 130–32). I will deal with *law* broadly, as the contents of formal legislation, jurisprudence, and administrative practice. Legislative choices are, however, guided by policy choices, and policy influences the application of the law.

Nordic cooperation has long traditions, with a strong legal component ever since the 1870s. The political cooperation within the Nordic Council since 1960, and the common Nordic labor market and the passport union since 1954 bind the Nordic countries together to form relationships, or *entanglements* (Duve 2014, 6–8).

The response to the displacement caused by the Yugoslav Wars took place within the United Nations framework. In 1992, the United Nations High Commissioner for Refugees (UNHCR) called for open borders and temporary protection for those fleeing (UNHCR 1992). There was no settled international definition for temporary protection, but states generally suspended the processing of asylum applications and granted temporary residence permits on a collective basis for periods of one to three years. Housing, minimum social benefits, access to the labor market, and the right to family reunification were the central components of temporary protection (for the regimes in individual countries, see Humanitarian Issues Working Group 1995). European Union Member States responded based on their national laws, as the EU only took on the creation of common asylum legislation with the Amsterdam Treaty in 1997.

In this chapter, I argue that, while the Nordic countries gave strong support to the humanitarian and peacekeeping efforts of the UN, the responses to the arrival of refugees from the Balkans to the Nordic countries were anchored in national settings and debates, and thus varied. The refugee policies of governments are shaped by many elements: policy on developing international law and rules on refugee protection, humanitarian assistance, possible participation in UNHCR resettlement programs, and, finally, policy and law on asylum, which is often anchored in more general migration policy issues. Nationally, these different elements may play out in varied ways, as they did in the Nordic countries. They each had their own history of and ongoing debate about migration, although the Nordic Passport Union and the common labor market influenced their policy and law. Thus, each country initially chose nationally distinct responses to the entry and residence of the refugees. However, by 1997, the responses had converged toward granting permanent residence to the refugees.

The second question that I will briefly address is: what long-term effects did the temporary protection regime for refugees from the Yugoslav Wars have on refugee protection in the Nordic countries and the European Union? This question relates both to the specific arrangements for the large-scale influx of refugees and to the regular asylum procedure.

Evolving refugee law as a framework for asylum in the Nordic countries

From an exilic bias toward a return bias in Western countries' asylum policy

The evolving refugee situation in the Balkan region emerged at a time when Western European states had for some years introduced measures to curb the arrival of asylum seekers, mainly from the Global South. Chimni (1998, 351–52) argues that the restrictive tendencies in the asylum field from the end of the 1970s onward were legitimized through what he describes as the *myth of difference*: the view that the refugee movements outside Europe were fundamentally different than those within Europe of the Cold War period. This, he argues, was the justification for the general policy of keeping people from the Global South out of the Global North. For asylum policy and legislation, this meant a move from an *exilic bias*, which entailed permanent settlement in the asylum country of refuge toward a focus on repatriation – a *return bias* as the preferred solution to the refugee's situation (ibid.).

The restrictive tendencies in the asylum field were reflected in difficulties in developing a convention obliging states to grant asylum. The United Nations Conference on Territorial Asylum (A/CONF. 78) was arranged in Geneva from January 10 to February 4, 1977. Grahl-Madsen (1982, 64–70) sums up the meager result of a draft text that states that contracting states "shall endeavour" to grant asylum to refugees, concluding that "it was a rude awakening to a harsher international climate." The preparations for a convention on territorial asylum have subsequently never been completed.

The dissolution of the Soviet Union and the independence of the Baltic states profoundly influenced geopolitics in Europe and the

Baltic Sea Region, bringing about the next wave of restrictive tendencies. In the Nordic countries, concerns emerged about mass migration, including asylum seekers. The Nordic countries together with UNHCR engaged in promoting accession to the Refugee Convention and setting up of asylum procedures in the Baltic states. According to Vedsted-Hansen (2002), this was part of a more general ambition to create a "buffer zone" around Western Europe. For the Nordic countries, these efforts were geared toward all asylum seekers, not specifically refugees from the Global South. The Russian Federation acceded to the Refugee Convention in 1993, Estonia, Latvia, and Lithuania in 1997 (UNHCR States Parties).

Asylum policy, including in the Nordic countries, was tied more broadly to general foreign and humanitarian policy, and development aid. Efforts to address the root causes of forced migration and promote voluntary repatriation became a more clearly stated part of UNHCR's agenda, partly in response to Western governments' increasing reluctance to receive refugees (see Jessen-Petersen 1987). Promoting a comprehensive approach in refugee policies and engaging the whole humanitarian and human rights community was a key element in Thorvald Stoltenberg's term as UN High Commissioner for refugees (UN Human Rights Commission/Stoltenberg 1990).

The Nordic countries move toward a similar legal and administrative framework for asylum

The Nordic countries have strongly interlinking histories. Nordic cooperation in the field of law emerged with the first Nordic Lawyers' Meeting in 1872. The cooperation has resulted in common legislation, however, mostly in the field of private and commercial law (Letto-Vanamo and Tamm 2019, 14–16). Still, administration and administrative law, which are of relevance for the study of migration and asylum law, have also developed along similar paths (Mäenpää and Fenger 2019). Regional and formal political cooperation gained momentum after the Second World War, with the Nordic Council, established in 1960, emerging as the framework for cooperation between the Nordic parliaments. The Nordic Ministerial Council, the framework between governments, was established in 1971 (Nordic Council 2019).

The economies of the Nordic countries experienced significant growth in the 1950s and 1960s. Many of the key elements of the Nordic welfare state developed simultaneously. These include universal social security and healthcare, free education, strong local government, rule of law, and equality. By many standards, the Nordic countries are often considered highly successful. "Nordic exceptionalism" entailed viewing the Nordic societies and peoples as the top tier of human development (Hervik 2019, 17–23). This view involved a sense of the Nordic countries being a good place for immigrants and refugees. Byström (2014, 620–21) argues that much of the evolving service structure in the Swedish *folkhem* (welfare state) was built upon experiences of receiving refugees during the Second World War. "Nordic exceptionalism" also contains an understanding of Nordic decision-making as rational and evidence-based, which is reflected in the somewhat technocratic approach to asylum policy and temporary protection among Nordic governments, officials, academics, and NGO representatives.

Denmark, Norway, and Sweden each experienced labor shortage since the 1950s, which incentivized them to establish a common labor market in 1954 and to encourage immigration from countries both in and outside Europe. Sweden had an active policy, with an office of the employment authority (AMS) in Belgrade for the recruitment of immigrants from Yugoslavia established in 1965 (SOU 2006:87, 87). All three countries also received refugees soon after their accession to the Refugee Convention, including refugees of the 1956 Hungarian uprising.

Finland was an exception, with virtually no labor-related immigration or asylum seekers. Finland remained a country of emigration, had less needs for additional workforce, and could meet the needs it had by hiring returnees from Sweden (Välimäki 2019, 68–81; Korkiasaari 2001, 13). Finland, in 1968, signed the Refugee Convention as the last of the Nordic countries, and took part with the other Nordic countries in resettling refugees from Chile in 1973, and Vietnamese refugees in the 1980s.

Postwar migration, including refugee reception, paved the way for the establishment of increasingly elaborate migration legislation, administrative procedures, and specialized administration. Although the development of binding international refugee law had come to a halt in the 1970s, the UNHCR Executive Committee assumed the role of offering guidance to governments on the application of the Refugee Convention through conclusions. Conclusion no. 8 on Determining Refugee Status (UNHCR 1977) offers key elements for asylum procedures with the appropriate legal safeguards. Along the lines of the UNHCR conclusion, the Committee of Ministers of the Council of Europe agreed in 1981 on a recommendation on the harmonization of national procedures relating to asylum (Council of Europe 1981). These recommendations were reflected in reforms in migration legislation in Denmark, Finland, Norway, and Sweden in 1983–1991.

When refugee arrivals from the Balkan area gained pace, all four countries had put in place nationally specific asylum legislation and procedures, and designated specialized authorities for the asylum procedure. There were discernible common minimum standards emanating from the recommendations of UNHCR and the Council of Europe: a personal asylum hearing, interpretation, legal advice, decision by a central administrative authority, and access to a legal remedy. The procedures allowed for both the granting of asylum based upon the refugee definition in Article 1A(2) of the Refugee Convention, and of asylum or residence permits to people in a refugee-like situation. For Denmark, the Aliens Act, Udlændingelov, entered into force in July 1983 (Lov no. 226 af 8.6.1983), was amended in 1985 by two acts, Lov no. 574 10.12.1985 on an accelerated asylum procedure and Lov no. 686 17.10.1986 denying access to the asylum procedure for people entering Denmark via a safe third country. Finland passed a new Aliens Act in 1991 (ulkomaalaislaki – utlänningslagen FFS 378/1991), reflecting Finland's accession to the European Convention on Human Rights in 1989. In Norway, Utlendingsloven (the Aliens Act, LOV-1988-06-24-64) was passed in the Parliament in 1988 after years of preparation and entered into force in 1991. In Sweden, utlänningslagen was reformed in 1989 (SFS 1989:529).

Despite moves toward similar legal and institutional approaches to asylum, asylum trends in the four countries were different, with Sweden receiving by far the largest numbers, followed by Denmark and Norway, while Finland and Iceland received very few arrivals. The figures for 1986 are illustrative (Table 5.1). Still, the structure of the asylum systems was similar, despite the remarkable differences in scale.

Table 5.1: Number of asylum seekers and people granted protection: refugees, de facto protection, humanitarian grounds. The numbers under "Protection granted" may include backlogs, with applications from previous years being handled in 1986.

Asylum seekers, 1986		Protection granted
Sweden	~14,500	~16,000
Denmark	9,299	6,902
Norway	2,700	602
Finland	22	2
Iceland	1	—

Source: Nordic Council 1987a, 80.

A common Nordic asylum policy?

By 1991, the Nordic labor market and passport union had been in place for some 40 years. While regular cooperation and legal harmonization had been established in many areas, this had not happened for migration and asylum, despite some attempts in the Nordic Council. During the council's first sessions in 1961 and 1962, proposals were made but did not gain sufficient support. In 1965, members of the Nordic Council across different political parties took the initiative in the Parliamentary Assembly for a common Nordic procedure in immigration matters. They proposed that the council should recommend to governments to study the possibility for a harmonized immigration legislation and a common Nordic immigration policy (Nordiska Rådet, A 75 j/1966).

A Committee of Experts on a common immigration policy was set up by the Nordic Council on February 1, 1966, and started its work in October 1968. The Committee, consisting of experts from Denmark, Finland, Norway, and Sweden, gave its report on June 16, 1970 (Nordiska rådet 1970). It concluded that there was no basis for a common Nordic immigration policy, as each country's starting points differed. It recommended common guidelines for the harmonization of rules regarding the labor market, housing, and family reunification. International protection was only discussed briefly. The experts noted the extensive reception of refugees since the Second World War, including through resettlement from Southern and Central Europe. They concluded, rather formalistically, that, since all the Nordic countries had acceded to the 1951 Refugee Convention, the countries had a similar refugee policy, and hence a similar policy was likely in the future (Nordiska rådet 1970, 27). Although the report did not lead to any strong common Nordic initiatives, its central suggestions were referred to in the legislation projects described above.

Later, harmonization initiatives were occasionally raised nationally or in the Nordic Council. At the Nordic Council's session in Copenhagen in 1986, a six-point joint program on immigration was approved, followed by a seminar in April 1987 on refugee and migration policy (Nordic Council 1987a). As a background to the seminar, the Ministerial Council commissioned a study on migration and integration policies including expert articles and a legal and statistical overview of the Nordic countries' migration and asylum situation (Nordic Council 1987a). The articles illustrate the political qualms and contradictions surrounding asylum and migration. While the Nordic welfare state was generally understood as welcoming and equal for immigrants, some articles harbored concerns about exclusion and racism (e.g., Hansen 1987, 22–29). There were even echoes of the worries emerging in Western Europe over the economic burdens of assisting refugees, as evidenced by Tomas Hammar's article, titled "När är livbåten full?" ("When Is the Lifeboat Full?"; Hammar 1987, 15–21). Hammar (1987) further raised the issue of whether protection should be seen as a temporary solution.

The seminar, however, did not result in any concrete common Nordic action. In Sweden, Carl Bildt and his Conservative Party (Moderaterna) made an initiative in Parliament in 1989, which included a demand for Nordic initiatives by Sweden (Motion till riksdagen 1989/90: Sf605). Yet, while the common Nordic labor market and passport area were seen as central common elements of all Nordic countries, the asylum regime was generally seen as a markedly national prerogative linked to sovereignty. The decision on whom should be allowed to enter and stay was thus seen by governments not as an issue of collective Nordic harmonization but as one of national politics.

The Yugoslav Wars, temporary protection and the Nordic response

The UN response to the Yugoslav Wars

The Yugoslav Wars of 1991–2001, the extensive war crimes, and the ensuing large-scale displacement came to dominate politics in Europe, and the UN, in the 1990s. The first of the Yugoslav Wars in Slovenia erupted and ended quickly, after Slovenia and Croatia declared independence in 1991. The war in Bosnia–Herzegovina started in April 1992 and went on until December 1995. The Dayton Accords, signed in December 1995, set out the course for peace in Bosnia–Herzegovina. However, warfare continued in Kosovo in 1998–1999, in the Presevo Valley in 1999–2001, and in Macedonia (today Northern Macedonia) in 2001.

The Yugoslav Wars resulted in the large-scale international flight of 2,400,000 refugees and some 2,000,000 internally displaced people, with half of the population of Bosnia–Herzegovina being displaced. Refugee movements from Yugoslavia had already started before the wars but escalated in 1991 and throughout the spring of 1992. In response to the wars and the large-scale displacement, the UN launched a massive humanitarian intervention effort. The deployment of the United Nations Protection Force (UNPROFOR) was approved by Security Council Resolutions 743 (1992) and 749 (1992) in February and April 1992. During the early stages of the wars, UNPROFOR's primary task was to ensure access to humanitarian assistance in certain besieged areas. Later in the war, UNPROFOR was also assigned responsibility to protect people within designated "safe areas" (UNHCR 1999). Denmark, Finland, Norway, and Sweden all deployed police and military staff to UNPROFOR (UN Division of Information). They all actively participated in the diplomatic, peacekeeping, humanitarian, and monitoring efforts, with Nordic diplomats and politicians such as Carl Bildt, Jan Eliasson, Elisabeth Rehn, and Thorvald Stoltenberg holding various positions in the UN and EU frameworks.

During the Yugoslav Wars, the UNHCR was mandated for the first time as the lead UN agency for humanitarian assistance in a country at war (UNHCR 1994, 2). The framework for humanitarian assistance and the UNHCR's tasks as the lead agency were outlined in the "Comprehensive Response to the Humanitarian Crisis in the F Yugoslavia" that had been proposed by the UNHCR at the International Meeting on Humanitarian Aid for Victims of the Conflict in the Former Yugoslavia on July 29, 1992. In roundabout terms, the UNHCR urged governments "to ensure the spirit of solidarity and burden-sharing which underlies international action on behalf of refugees," to keep borders open, and to offer temporary protection (UNHCR 1992).

Despite the High Commissioner's plea, most states still introduced visa requirements, hampering access to international protection. The UN operation was, in essence, one of containment against a large-scale exodus toward Western Europe. In the words of a UNHCR evaluation report, "it was the only response which the international community was prepared to contemplate at that moment" (UNHCR 1994, paras. 107–9). It is estimated that 580,000 Bosnians fled to Western Europe in 1992–1993. Germany, with approximately 345,000 arrivals, hosted 60 percent of the Bosnian refugees (Koser and Black 1999, 533). All Western European countries, as well as Croatia and Slovenia, accepted those who arrived, usually with some type of arrangement of temporary protection (ibid., 523–27). Yet approximately one million displaced people remained within the borders of Bosnia–Herzegovina. The outcomes for many of those who remained were fatal, such as the massacre of some 8000 Bosnian men in Srebrenica on July 8–9, 1995, shows (Human Rights Watch 1995).

The Nordic countries' response to the refugees from the Balkan area

The responses of the Nordic countries to the flows of refugees from former Yugoslavia caused by the wars were informed by a backdrop of an increasing focus on temporariness and an emerging return bias in the Nordic asylum debates and policies, with this focus and bias particularly evident in debates in Norway and Sweden (Brekke 1999, 66–70).

UNHCR's appeal to governments in 1992 had two main elements: open borders, and temporary protection. Concerning the first component, the Nordic countries formulated nationally specific responses, and gradually suspended their visa waiver agreements with Yugoslavia (Kjaer 1999, 31–32). Yet discussion and some degree of coordination took place on a diplomatic level. For example, a memorandum in the archives of the Finnish Ministry for Foreign Affairs (FINMFA) gives an account of a meeting that took place between the Ambassador of Norway to Finland and the Finnish Ministry for Foreign Affairs staff in April 1991 on concerns over growing numbers of asylum seekers from former Yugoslavia and the possibility of introducing visa requirements (FINMFA 1991).

Finland introduced visa requirements for citizens of former Yugoslavia, including citizens of Bosnia–Herzegovina, on July 21, 1992, by stating that the waiver of visa requirements for the Federal Republic of Yugoslavia was no longer in force for the newly independent republics. By that time, some 1,800 asylum seekers had arrived. Sweden had recognized the independence of Bosnia–Herzegovina in May 1992 and considered the visa agreement with Yugoslavia not to apply to independent Bosnia–Herzegovina. A separate visa requirement decision for citizens of Bosnia–Herzegovina was made in June 1993. Sweden had also introduced visa requirements for citizens of the Federal Republic of Yugoslavia (Serbia, Montenegro, and Kosovo) slightly earlier, in October 1992. Denmark introduced visa requirements for citizens of Bosnia–Herzegovina on June 26, 1993. Norway was last to introduce visa requirements for people from former Yugoslavia in October 1993, after some 7,000 arrivals by September 1993. The four countries differed in defining thresholds for introducing visa requirements. In Finland, 1,800 people triggered the imposition of visas; in Sweden, tens of thousands arrived before visa requirements were set up.

For the second element in UNHCR's appeal concerning procedures and rights, the Nordic countries adopted approaches similar to many other Western European countries. Instead of using the regular asylum procedures, a collective basis for decision-making for asylum seekers from former Yugoslavia was introduced (Kjaer 1999, 19–46). Asylum adjudication was suspended for the duration of temporary residence permits. Vedsted-Hansen (1999, 117–67) points out that the suspension of asylum adjudication may have curtailed the rights otherwise granted to refugees, such as access to the labor market and family reunification. In addition, all Nordic countries also resettled medical evacuees and other people in a vulnerable situation. Despite the common emphasis on collective decision-making, the Nordic governments chose different legal pathways to offer temporary protection, and the rights conferred varied, with the greatest divergences appearing between Denmark's and Sweden's conservative-led governments.

The Danish government, headed by Prime Minister Poul Schlüter, initially chose the most restrictive temporary protection scheme of the Nordic countries. This reflected the extremely polarized debate on migration and asylum that had taken place in the Danish Parliament ever since the enactment of the 1983 law. The Danish temporary protection scheme was introduced through a special law (Jugoslaverloven), granting the holders of protection a six-month, renewable residence permit, which depended upon the situation in the country of origin of the holder (Lov no. 933 28.11.1992). The temporary protection scheme granted the holders of protection the possibility of housing and social welfare, but not the right to work or family reunification. It also saw asylum adjudication being suspended for a maximum of two years. In 1993 (Lov no. 459 30.6.1993), the special law was amended to allow for prolonged residence permits, the possibility of resettlement to be expanded, and the establishment of a special office for the processing of applications in Zagreb. The amendments also set in place a limited possibility for family reunification for special humanitarian reasons. In 1994, the special law and the Aliens Act were amended, so that the minister of interior would be able to issue guidelines for asylum decisions, in practice allowing for permanent residence (Lov no. 34 af 18.1.1995). Approximately 17,000 people from former Yugoslavia had been granted protection in Denmark by 1995.

In Finland, an act was passed in November 1992, entailing all people from former Yugoslavia who had arrived before July 22, 1992, to have their asylum procedure suspended and be granted a residence permit on humanitarian grounds for one year (FFS 14/1993). The procedure was expedited, with the local police issuing and renewing the permits. The residence permits were issued in early 1993 and granted the same rights as those granted to people granted asylum. In 1994, all residence permits were extended for another year, and after this permanent residence permits were issued based upon the regular rules of the Aliens Act. Some 2,200 people were issued permanent residence permits under this regime (Humanitarian Issues Work Group 1995).

Norway introduced temporary protection and suspended the treatment of asylum applications for people from Bosnia–Herzegovina in August 1992 for up to three years. This entailed a work and residence permit that did not constitute a basis for permanent residence. By 1993, some 13,000 people from Bosnia–Herzegovina received protection in Norway (Brochmann and Kjeldstadli 2008, 262–66). Temporary protection was initially granted based on administrative decisions and introduced in law (Bosnierlova) in 1995 (Kjaer 1999, 22). Later, the Norwegian government turned to granting permanent residence to those who had come to Norway and wished to stay (Brekke 2001, 8).

Carl Bildt's government in Sweden made a guidance decision in June 1993 to Statens invandrarverk (the State Immigration Authority) for the granting of permanent residence permits to people from Bosnia–Herzegovina (Regeringens proposition 1993/94:51, 2). By 1995, the decision covered some 48,500 people. For people from other areas of former Yugoslavia, temporary residence permits were issued for six months at a time. Sweden also resettled some 10,000 people from former Yugoslavia, mainly Bosnia–Herzegovina, during 1992–1995. Altogether, with the residence permit decisions, family reunification, positive asylum decisions, and resettlement, some 100,000 people from former Yugoslavia settled in Sweden.

Initially, there were differences in the residence permit regimes of each individual country. Over time, however, all countries regularized the stay of Balkan refugees on a permanent basis (Brochmann 1997, 500–502). Brekke (2001, 11–13) attributes this development in Norway to public opinion, where after some years it was difficult to gain acceptance for nonvoluntary repatriation of the refugees. This reflects a common Nordic feature in refugee reception: with strong local government, refugee reception and integration have a decentralized foundation in the local communities, which at best provide strong networks and support for refugees.

The Yugoslav Wars along with the large-scale refugee movements they gave rise to had significant, lasting effects on Nordic temporary protection regimes. Throughout the Yugoslav Wars, the Nordic countries did not yet approach temporary protection as a longer-term alternative to the ordinary asylum procedure in their legislation. However, when the EU began to formulate its asylum legislation after the European Summit in Tampere in 1999, the EU Council Directive on temporary protection 2001/55/EC of July 20, 2001, came to be the first piece of EU asylum legislation to be approved. On a European level, temporary protection was seen as a viable and pragmatic solution for large-scale refugee movements. By then, Finland and Sweden had become members of the EU in 1995, and Denmark had opted out from the common asylum legislation in 1993, after the referendum on the Maastricht Treaty.

Despite this, at the time of the arrival of more than one million Syrian asylum seekers in Europe in 2009–2015, activation of the Temporary Protection Directive was not considered politically feasible (Karci, Dogan, and Berument 2022, 202–3). Instead, the turn toward a return bias in asylum law, the signs of which Chimni (1998) had identified from the 1970s onward, materialized in many Western European countries in the years following the 2015 record year, with 1.2 million asylum applications registered in the EU (EUROSTAT 2016). Temporary residence permits for refugees became an element in the regular asylum legislation in the Nordic countries as well (Brekke, Vedsted-Hansen, and Thorburn Stern 2020).

It took more than 20 years after its approval for the Temporary Protection Directive to be activated, in the context of a war seen, again, as European. After the Russian Federation's invasion of Ukraine on February 24, 2022, the European Council made a rapid decision in March 2022 to apply the Temporary Protection Directive to refugees from Ukraine (Council Implementing Decision (EU) 2022/382). Denmark and Norway applied temporary protection for people fleeing Ukraine.

Discussion: international and Nordic response, but with national traits

At the beginning of this chapter, I raised the question of to which degree the responses to the flows of refugees generated by the Yugoslav Wars reflected a common Nordic approach. Generally, the reforms in immigration and asylum legislation in 1983–1991 reflected a degree of Nordic harmonization and a move toward rights-based legislation, while maintaining a margin for governments to accommodate national interest.

Concerning more specifically the response to the influx of refugees generated by the Yugoslav Wars, the Nordic countries were supportive of the humanitarian operation and of UNHCR, resettled refugees from the region, and responded to calls for medical evacuations. When faced with the arrival of refugees from former Yugoslavia, the Nordic countries did not, however, take a harmonized approach to visa policies. Each country initially took its own path, with the Finnish visa restrictions introduced in July 1992 standing out most clearly. This is perhaps one of the most striking features in the Nordic response, since the common passport area implies a high level of coordination of visa policies.

The legal frameworks and the rights that a temporary protection residence permit granted in the Nordic countries had similarities, but also clear national differences, with Denmark initially establishing the most restrictive regime. As the paths of Denmark and Sweden illustrate, traditional political bloc lines (Conservative vs. Social Democrat) did not appear to be of crucial importance in the formulation of national responses. Overall, there was a recognition of the Yugoslav Wars and the refugee movements as a regional, European matter, and as a common responsibility. Temporary protection was seen as a pragmatic tool in situations of mass displacement, which also unburdened the regular asylum procedure. As the conflict in the Balkans drew on, all four countries turned to permanent residence rights for the refugees, with public opinion strongly rejecting involuntary return. From a technocratic perspective, this local mobilization can be seen as having hampered restrictive, centralized policy moves, as Brekke (2001) suggests. As Brochmann (1997) points out, while the starting point for the responses were different in Denmark, Norway, and Sweden, by 1997 the solutions had converged toward offering permanent residence to the Balkan refugees. The situation was the same also in Finland, with a turn toward permanent residence permits in 1994 (see above).

The solutions developed for the Balkan refugees had long-term effects on EU and Nordic asylum law. They paved the way for the EU Directive on Temporary Protection in 2001, which Finland and Sweden are bound by as EU Member States. The invasion by the Russian Federation of the Ukraine entailed a mass flight to European countries, and a decision by the European Council to activate the directive in 2022. So far, the rapid, group-based decision-making, entailing temporary protection, has been reserved in the EU and the Nordic countries for intra-European refugee movements. For refugees coming from outside Europe, both EU and Nordic countries have moved toward a harsher political climate and emphasis on return rather than protection after the rise in asylum applications in 2015. Instead of safeguarding the humanitarian needs of refugees, securing Europe's borders and focusing on returns emerged to become the common European agenda on refugee mobilities.

Notes

1 I have not included Iceland mostly for practical reasons: I am able to use original texts in the other Nordic languages, but not Icelandic.

Bibliography

Legislation and parliamentary documents– digital sources (a. legislation, b. parliamentary records)

Denmark – a. www.retsinformation.dk; b. www.folketinget.dk.
Finland – a. www.finlex.fi; b. www.riksdagen.fi.
Norway – a. www.lovdata.no; b. www.nasjonalbibiliotekket.no.
Sweden – a. https://lagen.nu; b. www.riksdagen.se.

European Union

Council Directive 2001/55/EC of 20 July 2001 on minimum standards for giving
temporary protection in the event of a mass influx of displaced persons and on
measures promoting a balance of efforts between Member States in receiving
such persons and bearing the consequences thereof https://eur-lex.europa.eu/
legal-content/EN/TXT/PDF/?uri=CELEX:32001L0055.
Council Implementing Decision (EU) 2022/382 of 4 March 2022 establishing the
existence of a mass influx of displaced persons from Ukraine within the meaning of Article 5 of Directive 2001/55/EC, and having the effect of introducing temporary protection https://eur-lex.europa.eu/legal-content/EN/TXT/
PDF/?uri=CELEX:32022D0382.

Archive sources

Ministry for Foreign Affairs Archives, Finland, File on refugees from
Yugoslavia 1991. Memorandum no. 224, August 1991 on visit by the
Ambassador of Norway Kjell Rasmussen to Deputy Head of Depart-
ment Pertti Harvola.

International treaties

1951 Refugee Convention.
Convention Relating to the Status of Refugees 28.4.1951, UNTS Vol. 189 (1954),
No. 2545.
1967 Refugee Protocol.
Protocol Relating to the Status of Refugees, 4.10.1967, UNTS Vol. 606 (1967),
No.8791.

International organizations

Council of Europe

1981. Recommendation No. R (1981) 16 on the Harmonisation of National Procedures Relating to Asylum. https://www.refworld.org/legal/resolution/coe/1981/en/57389.

Nordic Council

1970. *Utlänningspolitik och Utlänningslagstiftning i Norden. Betänkande avgivet av särskilda sakkunniga som i Danmark, Finland, Norge och Sverige tillkallats för att utreda förutsättningarna för en enhetlig nordisk utlänningslagstiftning och en samstämmig utlänningspolitik.* Nordisk utredningsserie, 16/70.

1987a. *Flygtninge- og invandrerpolitik i Norden.* Nordisk Råds Præsidiesekretariat. Edited by Eszter Körmendi. Copenhagen: Bagges kgl. Hofbogtrykkeri.

1987b. *Flygtninge- og invandrerpolitik i Norden.* Seminarierapport.NORD 1987:31.

United Nations

1950. Statute of the Office of the United Nations High Commissioner for Refugees, GA Res 428(V), 14.12.1950.

1990. Thorvald Stoltenberg, Address to the Human Rights Commission 22.2.1990. https://www.refworld.org/policy/statements/unhcr/1990/en/68653.

1995. Humanitarian Issues Working Group. *Survey on the Implementation of Temporary Protection*, 8 March 1995. https://www.refworld.org/docid/3ae6b3300.html.

1996. Department of Public Information. *Former Yugoslavia and UNPROFOR* (not an official UN document). https://peacekeeping.un.org/mission/past/unprof_b.htm.

United Nations High Commissioner for Refugees

1977. Executive Committee Conclusion No. 8 (XXVIII). Determination of Refugee Status. https://www.unhcr.org/sites/default/files/legacy-pdf/578371524.pdf.

1992. *A Comprehensive Response to the Humanitarian Crisis in the Former Yugoslavia*, 24 July 1992, HCR/IMFY/1992/2. https://www.refworld.org/docid/438ec8aa2.html.

1994. Central Evaluation Section. *Working in a War Zone. A Review of UNHCR's Operations in Former Yugoslavia.* EVAL/YUG/14. 01 April 1994.
https://www.unhcr.org/research/evalreports/3bd41feb4/working-war-zone-review-unhcrs-operations-former-yugoslavia.html.

Websites

Århus Universitet. 2019. "Dansk invandrings- och udlaendingepolitik 1970–1992". Danmarkshistorien.   https://danmarkshistorien.dk/vis/materiale/dansk-ind-vandrings-og-udlaendingepolitik-1970-1992/.

EUROSTAT. 2016. "Asylum in the EU Member States. Record number of over 1.2 million first time asylum seekers registered in 2015". News release 44/2016, March 4, 2016. https://ec.europa.eu/eurostat/documents/2995521/7203832/3-04032016-AP-EN.pdf/790eba01-381c-4163-bcd2-a54959b99ed6.

Nordic Council. 2019. "The History of the Nordic Council". https://www.norden.org/en/information/history-nordic-council.

UNHCR/Media. 2024. "States parties, Including Declarations and Reservations, to the 1951 Refugee Convention". https://www.unhcr.org/media/states-parties-including-reservations-and-declarations-1951-refugee-convention.

Literature

Brekke, Jean-Paul. 1999. "Kapitel 2. Midlertidig beskyttelse i nordisk flyktning-politikk". In *Midlertidig beskyttelse og tillbakevendning. Bosniske flygtninger i Norden*, edited by Eva Haagensen, 45–81. Nordisk Ministerråd, NORD 1999:4. Århus: AKA-Print.

Brekke, Jean-Paul. 2001. "The Dilemmas of Temporary Protection – the Norwegian Experience". *Policy Studies* 22 (1): 5–18.

Brekke, Jean-Paul, Jens Vedsted-Hansen, and Rebecca Thorburn Stern. 2020. "Temporary Asylum and Cessation of Refugee Status in Scandinavia: Policies, Practices and Dilemmas". *European Migration Network Norway Occasional Papers*. https://www.udi.no/globalassets/global/european-migration-network_i/emn-norway-papers/emn-occasional-paper-temporary-asylum-and-cessation-of-refugee-status-in-scandinavia-2020.pdf.

Brochmann, Grete. 1997. "Bosnian Refugees in the Scandinavian Countries: A Comparative Perspective on Immigration Control in the 1990s". *new community* 23 (4): 495–510. https://doi.org/10.1080/1369183x.1997.9976608.

Brochmann, Grete and Knut Kjeldstadli. 2008. *A History of Immigration – the Case of Norway 900-2000*. Oslo: Universitetsforlaget.

Byström, Mikael. 2014. "When the State Stepped into the Arena: The Swedish Welfare State, Refugees and Immigrants 1930s–50s". *Journal of Contemporary History* 49 (3): 599–621. https://doi.org/10.1177/0022009414528259.

Chimni, B. S. 1998. "The Geopolitics of Refugee Studies: A View from the South". *Journal of Refugee Studies* 11 (4): 350–74. https://doi.org/10.1093/jrs/11.4.350-a.

Duve, Thomas. 2014. "Entanglements in Legal History. Introductory Remarks". In *Entanglements in Legal History. Conceptual Approaches*, edited by Thomas Duve. Global Perspectives on Legal History, vol. 1, 1–28. Frankfurt am Main: Max Planck Institute.

Grahl-Madsen, Atle. 1982. "Regulating the Refugees: U.N. Convention/Protocol on Territorial Asylum, Legal Developments in Various Countries". *Defense of the Alien* 5: 64–70.

Hammar, Tomas. 1987. "När är livbåten full?" In *Flygtninge- og indvandrerpolitik i Norden*, edited by Eszter Körmendi, 15–21. Copenhagen: Nordic Council.

Hansen, Henny Harald. 1987. "Kan kulturer forenes?" In *Flygtninge- og invandrerpolitik i Norden*, edited by Eszter Körmendi, 22–29. Copenhagen: Nordic Council.

Hervik, Peter. 2019. "Chapter 1: Racialization in the Nordic Countries: An Introduction". In *Racialization, Racism, and Anti-Racism in the Nordic Countries*, edited by Peter Hervik, 3–33. Cham: Springer. https://doi.org/10.1007/978-3-319-74630-2.

Human Rights Watch. 1995. *The Fall of Srebrenica and the Failure of UN Peacekeeping. Bosnia and Herzegovina* by Ivan Lupis and Laura Pitter. https://www.hrw.org/report/1995/10/15/fall-srebrenica-and-failure-un-peacekeeping/bosnia-and-herzegovina

Jessen-Petersen, Søren. 1987. "Hvordan hjælper vi flygtninge tilbage til deres fæderneland?" In Nordic Council 1987b, 66–71.

Karci, Ruya, Nukhet Dogan, and M. Hakan Berument. 2022. "Syrian Refugees to Europe: Are They Different from the Non-Syrians?" *Middle East Development Journal* 14 (2): 199–218. https://doi.org/10.1080/17938120.2022.2138614.

Kjaer, Kim U. 1999. "Kapitel 2. Komparativ landeanalyse". In *Midlertidigt asyl i Norden*, edited by Jens Vedsted-Hansen, Kim U. Kjaer, Terje Einarsen, and Janina W. Dacyl, 19–46. Nordisk Ministerråd. Århus: Aka-print A/S. NORD 1999:3

Korkiasaari, Jouni. 2001. "Suomalaiset Ruotsissa II maailmansodan jälkeen". *Siirtolaisuus – Migration* 28 (1): 13–21.

Koser, Khalid and Richard Black. 1999. "Limits to Harmonization: The 'Temporary Protection' of Refugees in the European Union". *International Migration* 37 (3): 521–43. https://doi.org/10.1111/1468-2435.00082.

Letto-Vanamo, Pia and Ditlev Tamm. 2019. "Nordic Legal Mind". In *Nordic Law in European Context*, edited by Pia Letto-Vanamo, Ditlev Tamm, and Bent Ole Gram Mortensen, 1–19. Ius Gentium: Comparative Perspectives on Law and Justice, vol 73. Cham: Springer. https://doi.org/10.1007/978-3-030-03006-3_1.

Mäenpää, Olli and Niels Fenger. 2019. "Public Administration and Good Governance". In *Nordic Law in European Context*, edited by Pia Letto-Vanamo, Ditlev Tamm, and Bent Ole Gram Mortensen, 163–78. Ius Gentium: Comparative Perspectives on Law and Justice, vol 73. Cham: Springer. https://doi.org/10.1007/978-3-030-03006-3_10.

Pihlajamäki, Heikki. 2014."Comparative Contexts in Legal History: Are We All Comparatists Now?" In *The Method and Culture of Comparative Law: Essays in Honour of Mark van Hoecke*, edited by Maurice Adams and Dirk Heirbaut, 121–32. Oxford: Hart Publishing.

SOU 2006:87. Arbetskraftsinvandring till Sverige. Förslag och konsekvenser. https://lagen.nu/sou/2006:87#S3.

Välimäki, Matti. 2019. *Politiikkaa kansallisten, kansainvälisten ja ideologisten reunaehtojen puitteissa: Suomalaiset puolueet ja maahanmuutto 1973–2015*. Turku: Turun yliopisto.

Vedsted-Hansen, Jens. 1999. "Kapitel 4. TP-ordningens forenlighed med internationale normer". In *Midlertidigt asyl i Norden*, edited by Jens Vedsted-Hansen, Kim U. Kjaer, Terje Einarsen, and Janina W. Dacyl, 117–66. Nordisk Ministerråd. Århus: Aka-print A/S. NORD 1999:3.

Vedsted-Hansen, Jens. 2002. "Nordic Policy Responses to the Baltic Asylum Challenge". In *New Asylum Countries?* edited by Rosemary Byrne, Gregor Noll, and Jens Vedsted-Hansen, 203–303. The Hague: Kluwer Law International.

CHAPTER 6

Refugeedom and its bordering practices

Humanity divided and potentialized within Danish integration[1]

Tine Brøndum

Aarhus University

Trine Øland

University of Copenhagen

Abstract

This chapter portrays the incorporation processes of refugees in Danish integration and welfare practices by including colonial divisions of humanity within Nordic histories. The chapter is based on narrative interviews with forced migrants and local integration workers in Denmark. It identifies four key processes across the narratives as a way of conceptualizing refugeedom and its bordering practices: *Becoming part of a new flock* describes an incorporation where subcategories activate hierarchies of protection, care, and employment, increasingly emphasizing the latter. *Dreaming and becoming rational* testifies to how dreams are instrumentalized in integration processes, creating

How to cite this book chapter:
Brøndum, Tine and Trine Øland. 2025. "Refugeedom and its bordering practices: humanity divided and potentialized within Danish integration." In *Forced Migrants in Nordic Histories*, edited by Johanna Leinonen, Miika Tervonen, Hans Otto Frøland, Christhard Hoffmann, Seija Jalagin, Heidi Vad Jønsson and Malin Thor Tureby, 155–177. Helsinki: Helsinki University Press. https://doi.org/10.33134/HUP-32-7.

hierarchies between citizens and noncitizens. *Work and becoming self-sufficient* describes how refugees are cast as unemployed and in need of activation. Finally, *Rebuilt but kept down* illustrates the paradoxical obligations and expectations that refugees are met with. In conclusion, the chapter identifies refugeedom as a social category inscribed within the multiple economic and sociopolitical workings of global capitalism.

Introduction

From once being one of the most liberal states in the world with respect to immigration, Denmark is today known for having the most restrictive immigration policies of the Nordic countries (Gammeltoft-Hansen 2021; Vedsted-Hansen 2022). In the same period, Danish welfare and integration policies have been reframed into a governmental rather than a humanitarian matter. Integration policies are today thus marked by an employment or activation regime, launched by the social democratic rationale of the 1990s that stressed that "the unemployed should not be supported economically and socially, unless they are prepared to work at any opportunity" (Jønsson 2018, 68, our translation).

A recent press release from the Danish Ministry of Immigration and Integration testifies to this focus. Minister Kaare Dybvad Bek states (Udlændinge- & Integrationsministeriet 2023):

> At a time of very low unemployment, it is hugely positive that so many foreigners choose Denmark and contribute to our labor market. This is a huge gain for Denmark and the Danish economy. Presently we lack hands in both the public and private sectors, and the many who come here on business schemes contribute to growth and better services. I am very pleased that we are succeeding in attracting labor from the outside, while we at the same time have rules that take good care of Danish employees. In addition, we still have low asylum numbers. As a minister, I am very pleased.

In this quote, the minister assures the public that it is a desired kind of foreigner that enters Denmark, that is, those who help "us" fill "our" gaps so "we" can prosper and grow. At the same time, it is emphasized that "asylum numbers" are low, signaling that the intake of undesired kinds of foreigners must remain low. As this chapter shows, there is, however, a spillover between the two tiers, which affects how forced migrants are incorporated into Danish society. The lives of those who seek refuge in Denmark have been regulated by shifting administrative practices, but common to all is that their lives are to be transformed and incorporated into a new social structure, which presents itself as caring and benevolent but is full of complex hierarchies and inequalities.

In this chapter, we ask how this incorporation takes place within Danish welfare and integration provisions. How does the incorporation proceed within a hierarchical social structure? And how does such incorporation make room for the life projects of the displaced? We focus on how this is reported on and given meaning both by individuals who have fled to Denmark within the last 30 years, and by municipal integration workers currently working in local municipal refugee reception and integration. This chapter looks at how transformations are retold by individuals with former and current refugee status and by municipal refugee reception and integration workers. We are interested in the social workings and relations of how life is restored and configured within a new society, and in conclusion we ask how knowledge of these workings can contribute to renarrating Danish histories.

Given the above, our approach may be termed critical integration research in which we seek lenses for research beyond migration, integration, and policy issues. This includes addressing how processes of bordering citizens and noncitizens, and giving rights and freedoms to different groups, work along gradients of racial and colonial divisions of humanity and are a function of democratic and capitalist societies (Lowe 2015). In this way, our contribution to the writing of Nordic histories does not (only) follow the linear narrative of modernity with a clearcut binary of the "now" and "then," something that tends to seal off our relationship with the past, including our colonial past (Benjamin 1998; El-Tayeb 2020).[2] Rather, we aim to present a critical analysis of Danish integration that taps into an emerging research field that dismantle the myths of exceptionalism and innocence and expose complex racial and colonial trajectories and structures within the Nordic countries (Brøndum 2023; Øland 2024; Toivanen, Skaptadottir, and Keskinen 2019).

Theoretical underpinning

Our theoretical approach consists of the concepts refugeedom and interior frontiers. "Refugeedom" is Peter Gatrell's rewording of the Russian phrase *bezhenstvo*, used during the First World War to designate a "new social category that did not correspond to existing categories of status or class in the death throes of the Russian Empire" and point to "a distinctive domain or sphere of practice in relation to a specific category of humanity" (Gatrell 2016, 178). It relates to a broad matrix of relations and practices that include "administrative practices, legal norms, social relations and refugees' experiences, and how these have been represented in cultural terms" (Gatrell 2016, 170). The concept thus stresses that refugees contribute to the shifting matrices of relations and practices, and it calls for the writing of refugee histories in a way that "incorporates a social and cultural history of refugees within shifting systems of power" (ibid., 179).

"Interior frontiers" is a concept we borrow from Ann Laura Stoler (2022) to shed light on how the incorporation process can be seen as shaped by inequality through a "politicality of the senses" (Stoler 2022, 36–37). Thus, we focus on how incorporation takes place within interior frontiers that demarcate some as those who belong and others as those who do not, hence reproducing relations of superiority and subordination, privileged insiders as opposed to dehumanized outsiders (Øland 2019, 164–75). Stoler points to how interior frontiers operate to legitimize and reproduce racial inequities within democratic policies, stressing that a frontier is not simply a line separating people; it can also consist of corridors or border areas with no fixed lines to cross (Stoler 2022, 21). It points to processes in which inequalities (re)emerge and take shape in evaluative and affective spaces tracing differences between social kinds, separated by taste, intuition, remorse and forgetting. In this way, we point to how "the refugee" is drawn in and incorporated, and at the same time distanced and deprived of being perceived as an insider through submetrics of worth. Stoler summarizes interior frontiers as:

> a political concept with imperial features and being affectively charged
> it works through multiple sensibilities recruited to produce hardening
> distinctions between who is "us" and who is construed as (irrevocably)
> "them", across the intimacies of personhood and wider sliding scales.
> (ibid., 6)

Bringing the concepts of refugeedom and interior frontiers together, we illuminate refugeedom as processes of internal frontiers within the gray zones of a political rationality that evokes and makes racial distinctions, demands attention, and animate affective responses. These processes are racializing in the sense that people labeled as refugees are racialized *through* "benevolent" integration work within the capitalist welfare society. The concepts thus help us point to relations within capitalism and racial inequality.

Methods, materials, and analytical reading strategy

The chapter is based on two clusters of empirical material generated from narrative interviews conducted within the research project RESTORE.[3] One cluster consists of biographical narrative interviews with individuals who have fled to Denmark within the last 30 years (Jackson 2002) and another cluster comprises narrative interviews with integration workers, who work in the fields of refugee reception, integration, schooling, employment, and adult education (e.g., Phillips 1995).

The selection of interviewees includes some of the major national groups that have entered Denmark as refugees during the last 30 years, that is, Bosnian, Iraqi, Somali, Afghan, and Syrian refugees. The three municipalities included for this chapter's analysis have varied political leaderships and sociogeographical locations and can be characterized as: X, an isolated rural municipality; Z, a city; and Y, a rural municipality.[4] We conducted 15 interviews with individuals with refugee backgrounds and 30 interviews with municipal integration workers[5] between November 2021 and September 2022.[6]

First, each cluster of material was *described analytically*. The interviews with individuals who had fled to Denmark were described narratively and thematically by summarizing stories about homeland and childhood, the flight, self-understanding, and the encounter with Danish welfare. The interviews with municipal integration workers were described by summarizing the notions they used to describe the refugees, and the stories they told about interventions activated to integrate refugees, the driving actors in the integration processes, and the municipality's development in relation to receiving refugees. The results of these first descriptive analyses were noted and exemplified with quotes from the original transcripts to produce 304 pages of tables. These are the documents we refer to when citing from our material.

Against this backdrop, we constructed a second *analytical reading strategy*, teasing out mediated connections across refugees' stories and municipal integration workers' stories about refugees. In this reading strategy, we read through our tables looking for instances where aspirations and willpower are in focus, formed or challenged by the integration workers, and where understandings of "the refugee" and "the human" are in play. These readings resulted in our drafting of four key processes that we unfold in the analysis, and which help us sketch out a concept development regarding refugeedom and its bordering practices as part of Danish integration and the renarration of Danish histories.

We include accounts of both former and current refugees as background material from where a renarration of Danish social and cultural histories can transpire. This is a renarration that includes multifaceted layers of prior experiences and memories of refugeedom throughout the last 30 years, due to the different arrival points of the various interview participants. In this way, we include affective memories and stories of the participants as examples of what Michelinos Zembylas and others have called "minor feelings" (Zembylas 2022, 345–46), which are minoritized people's affects, oppositions, and responses to demands and situations that are often not heard and therefore excluded from history. While this chapter primarily concerns the contemporary situation, history is nevertheless present as the contemporary workings of the colonial past, and as the personal experiences of becoming a refugee within Danish welfare society.

Policy context

The legal conditions of refugees in Denmark have changed fundamentally and repeatedly during the last 30 years and have in recent years been framed by a form of instrumental, negative nation-branding to hinder the arrival of new refugees (Gammeltoft-Hansen 2021). These changes must be seen in relation to a concurrent shift within Danish domestic policies and labor market reforms that have been characterized as having an "all-encompassing focus on productivity, activation and employability as a shift from welfare to workfare" (Shapiro and Jørgensen 2021, 174). These tendencies have made their mark on the

shifting rights and duties of refugees already granted residence in Denmark. Thus, while the Bosnian refugees arriving at the beginning of
the 1990s owing to special legislation (Jønsson 2018, 69), were given
group-based, temporary protection (asylum and residence permits)
but initially prohibited from taking up any kind of work or schooling, the following tendency within Danish integration policy has been
an increasingly strong focus on employment and self-reliance. These
changes culminated in the revised Integration Acts of 2015 and 2019,
the latter presented as a so-called "paradigm shift," by substantially
limiting the possibilities for permanent residency. Thus, in the last
decade, the regulation and surveillance of refugees has increased along
the lines of a neoliberal logic, casting refugees as immediate assets for
the local needs of the labor market, e.g., in unpaid internships, while
concurrently limiting their prospects for leading stable and equal lives
on their own terms. One example of these symbolic changes is found in
the reduction and renaming of the prior "integration benefit" provision
to the so-called "self-provision and return benefit" (Vedsted-Hansen
2022, 20), which depicts integration as something at once desirable
and impossible for non-Danes to obtain (Rytter 2019). Research has
shown how these negative nation-branding policies, which other
Scandinavian and European countries also apply (Persdotter, Lind,
and Righard 2021, 98), are "designed to make the prospective asylum
country appear as unattractive as possible – and at the very least less
attractive than neighboring states" (Gammeltoft-Hansen 2021, 55).

As the following analysis will show, it is within this ambiguous
landscape that local, well-intentioned integration workers operate and
categorize refugees based on the concrete circumstances and their own
discretion, but the categories they use to do so are socially and historically constructed and, as such, they serve as the object of study in this
chapter.[7]

Processes of refugeedom and its bordering practices

Four key processes are involved in refugee transformation and incorporation into Danish society. Our founding understanding is that refugeedom entails a coming down in the world: the individual arrives in
a new social structure and situation where prior assets, social and professional competencies, and so on are demolished. We understand this

"coming down" as a complex dynamic of four key processes that each activate an evaluative and affective space in which differences between social kinds are drawn. We have named these processes:

1. Becoming part of a new flock
2. Dreaming and becoming rational
3. Work and becoming self-sufficient
4. Rebuilt but kept down.

The processes are interwoven, and each of them illuminates key elements of refugees' and municipal integration workers' accounts. In the following, we describe the four processes by identifying and elucidating each one through central empirical examples that, in relation to the body of empirical material, represent the most characteristic tendencies of the differing narratives; see also the analytical reading strategy. In conclusion, we return to the notion of refugeedom to understand the interior frontiers of what it means to be human within Danish welfare state formation processes.

1: Becoming part of a new flock

The first process we identify relates to the refugee category itself. Becoming "a refugee" entails incorporation into a new flock, being recast in a new social category and reality marked by the loss of recognized individuality, agency, and prior identity and status. At the same time, the refugee category intersects with further subcategories such as "immigrant" and "Muslim." It is attributed with characteristics that work to designate the gradual transformation process. One such characteristic that is present in several of the narratives is that of passivity or nonparticipation. The image of the "passive refugee" strikes a special chord for many Bosnian refugees, who were placed in refugee camps and not allowed to either work or study. For instance, Mehmed recalls the experience of 30 years ago:

> You just sat there, there were no activities, no schooling, no work. There was a TV, a common room, but no one showed any particular interest. We just existed. And so, the kids, they didn't have an awful lot to do, so we just ran around like in a flock; as a bunch. (Mehmed, arrived from Bosnia 1992, 4)

Mehmet says that working and taking care of himself is of great importance for him today as a way of opposing the image inflicted on him
and his family back then.

Other subcategories include the labels "primitive" and "traditional,"
which are directly or indirectly brought into play by several municipal
integration workers. This is for instance the case in situations in which
"the culture" of the refugee is presented as the overall challenge to integration and employment. This is so, for instance, for the job consultant
Ingrid, who explains:

> For the Syrians, it is the cultural. That is where the biggest challenge
> lies. It is in the culture. All this with women also working. (Ingrid, job
> consultant, Z municipality, 19)

In this way, the "culturally different refugee" constitutes a category that
marks out challenges for the municipal integration workers to combat,
for instance when culture seems to stand in the way of gender equality
or when assumptions about culture entail certain assumptions about
knowledge and schooling. Relating to the latter, the language teacher
Gerda explains:

> Depending on which culture we receive, … being in school is very much
> about copying what is written on the blackboard, very much about
> reproduction of knowledge. Where in Denmark … we can be a bit inno-
> vative and think out of the box. (Gerda, language teacher at a center for
> adults, X municipality, 42)

In such understandings the refugee category connotes passivity and
dependency. If "they" are to progress, to transform, something needs
to be added to them. This feeling of being perceived and precast as passive, primitive, and uneducated is stressed by Hamza, who recalls how
he and his family seemed to disappoint the local Red Cross workers
when they arrived in Denmark as refugees in 2001:

> [They] were a bit disappointed that we were wearing nice clothes. And
> … that my mother was not wearing a headscarf. (Hamza, arrived from
> Iraq 2001, 2)

He contrasts this with other refugees, whom he represents as people
who more directly resemble somebody in need of help:

> They lowered their heads more and apologized more, and then it worked out. But if you are proud and you come with nice clothes and say, "I would like to have what is my right"; then you are really met with more "nos". (ibid.)

This example illustrates the need to be attentive to and able to navigate within the conditions offered, but also the cost of experiencing the distinctions implied within a space of inequity, which animate affective responses, including resistance.

Such hierarchizing and bordering practices are experienced in many ways. Some of the integration workers interviewed after the arrival of Ukrainian refugees attest to these practices, albeit in ambivalent ways. Alice, for instance, explains:

> They [the Ukrainians] are from Europe, they look like us, I don't know exactly what is going on, but we do see a greater hospitality towards these children, and that was more difficult years back, when we received the children from Syria. (Alice, head of reception classes, X municipality, 47)

Thus, while Alice is aware of and sympathetic toward the fact that the Syrian refugees encountered less hospitality and help from the authorities than the Ukrainians do, she seems at the same time to explain and justify this difference through the bordering logic that the Ukrainian group "look like us" and therefore they "naturally" activate help from the system more effectively.

2: Dreaming and becoming rational

Dreaming and aspiring for a better future is another key process in the incorporation and transformation of the refugees. Dreams appear as engines of certain actions and shape goals for who to become. And dreams can serve as motivation both for the individual and for municipal integration workers in their drive to "move" or "develop" the refugee toward a better and "higher level." In this way, dreams appear in the material as individual aspirations that, however, can be read in a social context in which common themes of social mobility and of gaining a stable and secure future dominate. This is expressed in dreams such as getting an education, being allowed to stay in Denmark, and being able to marry and to found a family.

In several cases, dreams and hopes for the future are articulated as direct and conscious ambitions for education, thus making long-term investments for a better future as new beginnings become thinkable with the refugee status. This is the case, when for instance Hanan, who has just graduated from Danish high school, envisions herself as a future dermatologist, in order to:

> do research in fibromyalgia, an illness my mother suffers from, that doesn't have a treatment. (Hanan, arrived from Syria 2015, 8)

or when Esin more generally states:

> I had a dream [that] when I came to Denmark, it would be very easy to be here. (Esin, arrived from Afghanistan 2011, 1)

The reality in Denmark, however, turned out differently from how Esin imagined. Like many others, Esin dreamed about independence and getting a good education. But she was discouraged by the municipality and was instead told to work in internships while learning Danish:

> It was very hard for me; sometimes I say it was easier to be in my country. It's not a life, what's going on here. And eh, it was not a job, that uhm, [I was] proud of or [that was] interesting for me. It was like a very shameful job for me because I had a big dream; but I was doing the cleaning of a park. (ibid., 2)

In Esin's mind, the distance between her "big dream" and her actual unpaid internship as a cleaning assistant leads to humiliation, passivity, and lack of self-esteem. She recalls one integration worker:

> She told me: "If you want to live in Denmark, you should forget about that [getting an education]. You should learn Danish, and you should work in Denmark. Don't think about your education and something. It is not important here and you will be, eh, you won't have any value for us if you do like that."

Esin's story thus represents the refugee without agency, and as one who is steered in a direction considered of value for the system. This form of governing dreams in accordance with the needs of society is mirrored in the demands of the current Aliens Act, in which steady employment – as opposed to education – is a precondition for meeting the strict requirements for obtaining a permanent residence permit.

In Awdar's story, dreams play an ambiguous role. For him, dreams are present as continuous nightmares of the brutality of the war he fled from and are thus a strong drive to move forward. Consequently, Awdar keeps "very busy ... so I don't think about it anymore. It is deleted in my life" (Awdar, came from Syria 2014, 2). Awdar does everything possible to create a new life with work, education and Danish friends. In this way, he silences his nightmares with his dreams of social mobility and ambitions for the future:

> I want to become a part of this. In my eyes, as you say, "language is the key to society, right?" If you don't know the language, you cannot do anything. So, if I couldn't speak Danish, how could I meet friends, how could I go to work? (ibid., 9)

Dreams are also present in the municipal integration workers' accounts as points of transformation, in which dreams in several cases serve as a starting point for conversations, but also at times in opposition to what is deemed a realistic future. One integration worker, for instance, explains how she works with people's dreams:

> They are always allowed to talk about their visions. I usually ask what they dream of becoming, if they could be whatever they wanted to. (Kia, employment officer, Y municipality, 3)

She draws a line between what can be dreamt of and what is "realistic":

> It doesn't work out if the citizens say, "I want to be a captain of a ship". They must be realistic. We talk about that with them. What are realistic job tracks? For a lot of them, especially the women, it is really the same job tracks. It is typically kitchen assistant, cleaning assistant, factory worker. (ibid., 3)

Another integration worker likewise tells how she "sketches out their dreams" and tries to make the refugee fit the lower echelons of the employment hierarchy. The well-known tropes of liberalism, the ideological foundation of capitalism, are thus clearly mobilized when such harnessing of passions is activated (see also Stoler 2022, 46–47).

While the dream in this way constitutes a starting point for educational and employment plans, it also appears as something considered utopian or irrelevant to pursue. Rather, while dreaming and aspiring for something better evokes desires for the individual, it is at the same time instrumentalized to illustrate "the realistic" within the social

hierarchy of designated possibilities. In such cases, then, the instrumentalization of dreams becomes a form of racialized governance in
which unarticulated inequalities are amplified and by which dreaming
constitutes an example of an interior frontier in the gray zone between
the personal and political in which some people are allowed to dream
(big) while others are not.

3: Work and becoming self-sufficient

Yet another key process in the incorporation and transformation journey is entering the labor force and becoming able to support oneself.
This is indeed a process whereby the refugee is drawn in and appreciated as an asset to the local labor market and the local community. At
the same time the refugee is placed on certain job tracks, that is, those
in a shortage of manpower. This point presents itself as a truism. Both
refugees and municipal integration workers point to work as what is
needed for the refugee to become self-sufficient and gain independence.

This is shown, for instance, when the head of an integration unit
presents his work with refugees:

> In principle, it is about marketing, i.e. how do you sell a product so that
> you also get the recipient to believe in it? … My perspective is: how
> do we get rid of people again? How do we make sure that they do not
> remain on public benefit? (Marius, head of integration, Y municipal-
> ity, 8)

This suggests that a refugee is considered a commodity to be sold on
the local labor market. This way of thinking is rewarded by the state in
a way that makes the integration unit cost-effective to the municipality:

> You could say that we have a task to solve. The sooner we solve this task,
> the sooner you can get a result grant for the effort. So the more we do to
> get people into jobs, out of integration benefit or self-support/repatria-
> tion benefit, the greater the chance that we can get these 80,000,- and
> 50,000,- in bonus, and this and that. For six or seven years in a row …
> we have earned our salaries through performance subsidies … It's not
> something my employees experience. I never talk about it. (ibid., 12)

This cost-effective mechanism is thus a hidden condition energizing the focus on work. A business consultant within an integration unit confirms the strength of the work imperative:

> If it was someone who was "ready for work",[8] and if they say no [to a job offer], then we said: you will be sanctioned. (Mikkel, business consultant, X municipality, 2)

He continues:

> We often took people in and told them: "listen, we have two jobs, there's a cleaning job or a kitchen job" for example, "and you have to take one of them. And you may want to be a bus driver, but that must be in the long run." (ibid., 3)

This pressure to work "no matter what" also presents itself for many of the refugees, who tell about having been assigned to random work, or being forced to choose between two equally unattractive job functions. Throughout our data, the refugee category has made it possible for the municipalities to retain refugees in consecutive unpaid internships and thus serve local businesses in accumulating profit. However, most of the refugees talk passionately about how they want to work and *are* self-sufficient, asserting themselves as liberal independent and able individuals, highly reluctant to receive public benefits. This is for instance the case for Mehmed, who was denied education and work during his and his family's first years in Denmark:

> I'm not one of those guys thinking "uh, I have an education, so I'm too big for my boots to take any kind of job" … It's also because I don't want some paper to appear saying that I received some benefits at some point … Because one of the things that is often said, is that "we" are all receiving social security benefits. And it breaks me so much, because I have a work ethic, which I think is just top of the line. (Mehmed, arrived from Bosnia 1992, 11)

Likewise, Awdar confirms his will to work and its link to how he envisions himself as a human being in the world:

> I am a grown man. I have two legs; I have two hands. I have a healthy body so I can work. It has always [been] like that. It's a mindset I had from before. Until now, I'm not going to approach the municipality announcing: "I'm sorry, I can't work, you must give me money." …

> We come from a family where we want to ... we always work. (Awdar, arrived from Syria 2014, 13)

The tale of being an individual with a great work ethic is mirrored in how an integration consultant observes the incorporation and transformation processes as well:

> We've had several Eritreans who have been employed in agriculture, for example, and who had a huge success there. And some who were employed in some fish factories, who were very happy with their work and the tasks they performed. This meant that the companies also spoke positively about those population groups. They came to get a new narrative. (Lisa, integration consultant, Y municipality, 20)

This led to Eritreans being a group of workers in demand to such an extent that the municipality now monitors how many of this kind of work force "it has" in stock:

> I'm not quite up with the numbers, but we have very few, if any, Eritrean men "ready for work" [jobparat] left on our books. And very few Eritrean women who are "ready for work" [jobparat]. (ibid., 21)

According to Lisa, the "successes" of Eritreans sets an affective circulation in motion in which normative and economical value are accumulated and joy and satisfaction are diffused within the municipality.

Interventions are also used to channel the refugee into the available jobs by trying to bend the refugees' inclinations:

> Not many Muslims wanted to work at the bacon factory. They did not want to look at pigs. But in this area, something happened. We made a course together with the factory ... And now they discovered that it is possible to do butchery and still be a good Muslim. (Mikkel, business consultant, X municipality, 7–8)

In this municipality, situated in an isolated rural area, there has been a political discussion about the intake of refugees between the Social Democrats, who were in favor and wanted to integrate refugees, and the Danish Peoples Party, who wanted to stop the intake completely. The integration unit explicitly asked for more refugees because "we are convinced that the labor market can absorb them" (ibid., 2).

As our analysis shows, refugees are considered a commodity, and refugees are forced to take random work assigned by the municipality, often within a frame of unpaid internships. Thus, human beings cast as refugees are considered as people to tamper with economically within a capitalist cycle. The overall political goal within the municipalities is more growth, and the availability of refugees' cheap or free labor enables this goal.

4: Rebuilt but kept down

The last key process in the transformation concerns the rebuilding and development of the refugee. A ladder or a staircase is a widely used metaphor around which this appears and takes shape in an evaluative and affective space that separates between social kinds. Such metaphors place the refugee at the lower stages in a hierarchy of "up and down" from where they are expected to move and develop or be moved, improved, or developed. Involved in this process is a search for a position in "the hierarchy" and this also implies that "the hierarchy" is defined implicitly. For example, it may take the shape of a civilizational ladder, which appears in the integration worker Cille's somewhat ambivalent, belittling yet indulgent, account:

> So, let's listen to what and where they are coming from. Because if I'm going to be able to move them, I want to find them at the level where they were. If I expect too much from them in advance, they don't understand what I mean. (Cille, integration worker, Y municipality, 32)

This implies an immersion at "their level" from where they should be "picked up."

Several of the refugees indeed express experiences of being placed on the lower stages of a civilizational ladder related to observations of feelings. For instance, Hamza recalls the encounter with a municipality:

> I sensed that they saw it [our behavior] as if we were barbaric because we were loud. And they said: "Why are you so angry, is it because you come from a hot country?" … Implying: "This is how refugees are; they're from where you have to yell and scream to get things done." (Hamza, arrived from Iraq 2001, 2, 5)

This sense of being placed on a ladder is evidenced also when integration workers describe the differences between refugee groups, implying their ability to differentiate between those who slowly climb the steps and those who jump up the steps:

> I would say there is a difference between how they work and how they develop. Those from Eritrea, they are pretty much ready to go out to work tomorrow. They take anything. They are not hesitant, but they will not settle for a longer period of practice either. They want to be sure that there is work. For example, someone from Syria will too, but they are more receptive to what is being said to them in terms of their development and how they should move … Those from Eritrea, they jump up the steps faster. The Syrians ascend slowly. (Mathias, job consultant, Z municipality, 32–33)

Thus, the hierarchy is often also formed as a ladder of employment opportunities. In one municipality, through a special method called "the goal staircase" (*Måltrappen*), a space opens to draw out the refugees' aspirations in an effort to reform these aspirations from below. After listening to "their visions," which are often deemed "too high," the process usually results in firmly establishing "their position" at the bottom and occluding the potential conflict:

> Then we have some tools we use, including "the goal staircase" and then we say: "We think you're here at the bottom of the stairs now. If you were to be a doctor, what would it take for you to achieve that goal?" Then we write down the milestones. Some Danish education is needed. There must be some higher secondary education, some further adult education or something. Once we've done that, it might be much easier to say: "Where are you and what can you do now?" Then there won't be that conflict, because they can see that they can't just become captain of a ship, right now. The question is also whether they can in the future. They usually come down and gain understanding. (Kia, employment officer, Y municipality, 4–5)

Another job consultant also uses "the ladder" to direct his work, which is based on an understanding of the refugee as someone who "needs" to be developed and slowly "built up" by the consultant's activity. This consultant explains how he is intrigued by the fact that "you could develop them" (Mathias, job consultant, Z municipality, 24). Thus, you can *add* something to "them" by *giving* them something they did not have in advance, so they can take *a step up* the ladder:

> I can help them integrate into society, by giving them some understand-
> ing of work; how to behave in a workplace, and by giving them a job
> opportunity in the long run. (ibid., 24)

The ability to recover perpetually, including the will to work, is however, as mentioned, part of several of the refugees' accounts. In the narrative of Sahra, personal will and buoyancy are manifested and inter-
twined with being degraded during her education, as well as in her
working life as a social and healthcare assistant:

> I remember one day, doing an internship and accompanying one of my
> colleagues. Uh, then I went to an older couple's house where you had to
> change a catheter, and I had to learn how to do it. So, when I entered the
> home: "You there" the wife said to me: "Don't come in." (Sahra, arrived
> from Somaliland 1992, 3)

Through an "inner battle," Sahra fought her way up and back, insisting
on her right to live and work: "Yes, this thing about school, my education, etc., if I experienced something, then my goal was: I live here; I
have to live" (ibid., 2). She continues:

> I'm Sahra, I can do whatever I want, and I'm happy with who I am, but
> I want to be here … I continue to be a social and healthcare worker. I
> will continue to work in the hospital, and at some point, I want to get my
> master's degree, if I get the time to do so. (ibid., 3)

Sahra manifests herself as an individual able to restore her life despite
her long-term experience of being cast as a refugee and incorporated
within interior frontiers of inequality, including racism and hostility.

Renarrating Danish histories of refugeedom and its bordering practices

In this chapter we have linked the experiences and affective realities of refugee lives in Denmark with tensions, double standards and
hidden narratives within Danish integration practices. Our analysis
shows how global human flows are subjected to classifying and racializing processes that push refugees into useful occupational slots while
ensuring that they are managed socially and economically to adapt to
a nonthreatening image of a good worker and acceptable foreigner.
Throughout the analysis, we have focused on the incorporation and

transformation processes that forced migration involve, but we have retained notions of agency and power through the concepts of *refugeedom* and *interior frontiers*, making it possible to show how a global order of inequality with its complex racial and colonial trajectories continues to shape refugee lives through multiple sensibilities. In this way, our analysis nuances the literature on racial capitalism, in which the role of racism can be understood as "enabling key moments of capitalist development" (Bhattacharyya 2018, ix) without being engineered by a master plan. As our analysis shows, the quest for productivity involves multiple forms of coercion and mobilization of desire and aspiration to participate in capitalist relations that promise inclusion as a subject on the margin of society, but that also depend on technologies of othering, including racial divisions that keep the hierarchy intact. This quest is paradoxical and illustrates the double bind and difficult navigation for many refugees, aspiring toward social progress through work.

Becoming part of a new flock is thus the process where the refugee category paves the way for new group-forming processes in which multiple and hierarchized subcategories are in play. It relates to historically shifting arrangements, stressing protection, care and/or employment. Such processes function both as a take-off power for refugees' aspirations toward a better future and as a way to make it possible for municipalities to administer the refugee, enabling exploitation.

Dreaming and becoming rational is a process that testifies to a hidden narrative that racializes the space in which some are authorized to pursue their aspiration to be educated and others are not. It takes place through a channeling and exploitation of refugees' passions and ambitions via instrumentalizing their dreams. The division and interior frontier between acceptable "labor from the outside" and "taking good care of Danish employees" as the minister of immigration and integration puts it, is also in play here.

The key process of *Work and becoming self-sufficient* is not surprisingly a dominant focus in our analysis. Following the main theme of Danish welfare since the 1990s (Jønsson 2018), the refugee is indeed increasingly cast as an unemployed person in need of work and to be kept "active and ready for work" so that whenever labor shortages appear productivity can be pursued. Therefore, local communities and integration workers, as opposed to the government, may passionately ask for "more refugees" and lead them into positions at the bottom of a stratified, postindustrial labor market, while cherishing them as fellow citizens and taxpayers. This testifies to the fact that local integration workers and authorities are inclusive in complex ways while at the same time maneuvering in a nexus of immigration, integration, and labor market policy, bordering wanted and unwanted migrants, as also observed in other Nordic countries (Persdotter, Lind, and Righard 2021, 97–98). As our analysis shows, in the Danish case this system is sanctioned by administrative regulations that the state economically rewards municipalities for following, and the law thus sanctions the ambiguous but ever-toughening borders of a racial capitalism, based on the very categorization of the refugee that reduces the refugee to a potential worker to be subordinated and managed. But it also points to how refugeedom as a social category in relation to the category of humanity, as Gatrell (2016, 178) phrases it, is effectively inscribed within the multiple economic and sociopolitical workings of capitalism, including an affective economy dividing and potentializing humanity for productivity. This means that the concept of refugeedom, understood as a complex and capacious social category, is stuffed with passions, openings, and incentives, as well as resistance and struggle for benefits and visibility in a global world of human flows.

Rebuilt but kept down is the final key process we depict in our analysis of Danish integration practices. It summarizes how this progressive and liberal kind of developmental thinking works through metaphors of a ladder or a staircase that the refugee is invited to ascend. Meanwhile, the ladder or the staircase seems to be perpetually sinking, legitimized by racist stereotypes that seem to be steeped in historical European Orientalist logics of othering that also entail a differentiating, bordering and hierarchizing logic that divides humanity within Danish integration. We see this in the stereotypes used to label different groups, for example Ukrainians who "look like us," and Eritreans who performed well as low-paid workers but in jobs with almost no prospect for social mobility. Hence, even when Eritreans are positively stereotyped, the ascending figure effectively gets nowhere. As our analysis also shows, former refugees do, however, ascend, respond, resist, and negotiate the divisions and positions assigned to them, and they do play a role through these assignments, albeit in different ways.

We argue that the analysis of the incorporation and transformation of refugees' life aspirations and willpower within Danish society, and the analysis of the affective lives of individuals who fled to Denmark, can contribute to renarrating Danish histories. Such renarration reveals the tensions and double-edged prospects of Danish integration practices and recognizes other forms of being human than the ascribed division of humanity by Western Man, thus challenging the normalization of racism that seems to be part of the welfare state's foundational liberal and capitalist logic.

Notes

1 We would like to thank members of the international reference group of the research project RESTORE and members of the "History and Sociology of Welfare Work" research group, University of Copenhagen, for valuable comments on an earlier draft of the chapter.
2 This has for instance included the depiction of Denmark as historically profiting from trade, exploitation, and enslavement of people, as engaged in (post) colonial modernization projects and development aid as well as Western military interventions from the Arctic to the tropics (Keskinen 2022, 17–24; Jensen 2012; Padovan-Özdemir and Øland 2022, 44–47).
3 "Refugees' Stories and Stories about Refugees: Crafting New Narratives of the Danish Welfare State" (RESTORE, https://komm.ku.dk/forskning/paedagogik/velfaerd/restore) is funded by a grant from the Independent Research Fund Denmark, case number: 0132-00093B.
4 The full material consists of six municipalities. The data collection for the RESTORE project is approved by the Unit for Data Management, Research & Impact, Faculty of Humanities, University of Copenhagen, file number: 514-0085/21-4000.
5 Our contact with the individuals of refugee background was diverse as none of them was longer a part of any municipal integration arrangement. Therefore, our contact was initiated through posts on social media, and through different networks.
6 A big thank-you to the student research assistants Ditte Margrethe Hermann Hauge, Kathinka Klarskov Nielsen, and Julie Stokholm Daugaard, who conscientiously transcribed the interviews. Additional thanks to Julie Stokholm Daugaard, who conducted 11 of the interviews with municipal integration workers.
7 In general, the integration workers struggle to make sense of the complex and unpredictable working space given to them, and the maneuvering between social rights and disciplinary measures it demands. Although some ambivalent statements appear in the analysis, this "sense-making" is not the focus here.
8 According to the local bureaucracy, the refugee is either placed as "ready for activity" (*aktivitetsparat*), which for instance triggers language internships to qualify the refugee, or "ready for work" (*jobparat*), where the goal is to find work for the refugee as soon as possible, for example four weeks of internship and then ordinary employment or employment with wage subsidies for a period.

Bibliography

Benjamin, Walter. 1998. "Om Historiebegrebet". In *Kulturkritiske Essays*, 159–71. Moderne Tænkere. Copenhagen: Gyldendal.

Bhattacharyya, Gargi. 2018. *Rethinking Racial Capitalism: Questions of Reproduction and Survival*. London: Rowman & Littlefield.

Brøndum, Tine. 2023. "'The Curse of the Refugee': Narratives of Slow Violence, Marginalization and Non-Belonging in the Danish Welfare State". *Kvinder, Køn & Forskning* 2 (November): 96–112. https://doi.org/10.7146/kkf.v36i2.141131.

El-Tayeb, Fatima. 2020. "The Universal Museum: How the New Germany Built Its Future on Colonial Amnesia". *NKA (Brooklyn, N.Y.)* 46: 72–82. https://doi.org/10.1215/10757163-8308198.

Gammeltoft-Hansen, Thomas. 2021. "The Do-Gooders' Dilemma: Scandinavian Asylum and Migration Policies in the Aftermath of 2015". In *Do-Gooders at the End of Aid: Scandinavian Humanitarianism in the Twenty-First Century*, edited by Antoine de Bengy Puyvallée and Kristian Bjørkdahl, 38–59. Cambridge: Cambridge University Press. https://doi.org/10.1017/9781108772129.003.

Gatrell, Peter. 2016. "Refugees—What's Wrong with History?" *Journal of Refugee Studies* 30 (2): 170–89. https://doi.org/10.1093/jrs/few013.

Jackson, Michael. 2002. *The Politics of Storytelling – Violence, Transgression, and Intersubjectivity*. Copenhagen: Museum Tusculanum Press.

Jensen, Lars. 2012. *Danmark: Rigsfællesskab, Tropekolonier Og Den Postkoloniale Arv*. 1. udgave. Nummer Fem i Serien Samfund i Forandring. Copenhagen: Hans Reitzels Forlag.

Jønsson, Heidi Vad. 2018. *Indvandring i velfærdsstaten*. 100 danmarkshistorier. Aarhus: Aarhus Universitetsforlag.

Keskinen, Suvi. 2022. *Mobilising the Racialised "Others": Postethnic Activism, Neoliberalisation and Racial Politics*. First edition. London: Routledge. https://doi.org/10.4324/9781003002031.

Lowe, Lisa. 2015. *The Intimacies of Four Continents*. Durham, NC: Duke University Press.

Øland, Trine. 2019. *Welfare Work with Immigrants and Refugees in a Social Democratic Welfare State*. Abingdon and New York: Routledge, Taylor and Francis.

Øland, Trine. 2024. "'Maybe We Should Start Paying the Hours Properly': State Violence and Ambivalent Moments of Enforced Emancipation of Refugee Women". *Social Politics: International Studies in Gender, State & Society* 31 (3): 586–609. https://doi.org/10.1093/sp/jxae009.

Padovan-Özdemir, Marta and Trine Øland. 2022. *Racism in Danish Welfare Work with Refugees: Troubled by Difference, Docility and Dignity*. Routledge Research in Race and Ethnicity. Abingdon and New York: Routledge.

Persdotter, Maria, Jacob Lind, and Erica Righard. 2021. "Introduction to Special Issue: Bordering Practices in the Social Service Sector – Experiences from Norway and Sweden". *Nordic Social Work Research* 11 (2): 95–102. https://doi.org/10.1080/2156857X.2020.1861895.

Phillips, Nelson. 1995. "Telling Organizational Tales: On the Role of Narrative Fiction in the Study of Organizations". *Organization Studies* 16 (4): 625–49. https://doi.org/10.1177/017084069501600408.

Rytter, Mikkel. 2019. "Writing Against Integration: Danish Imaginaries of Culture, Race and Belonging". *Ethnos* 84 (4): 678–97. https://doi.org/10.1080/00141844 .2018.1458745.

Shapiro, Ditte and Rikke Egaa Jørgensen. 2021. "'ARE WE GOING TO STAY REF- UGEES?' Hyper-Precarious Processes in and Beyond the Danish Integration Programme" 11 (2): 172–87. https://doi.org/10.33134/njmr.151.

Stoler, Ann Laura. 2022. *Interior Frontiers: Essays on the Entrails of Inequality*. New York: Oxford University Press.

Toivanen, Mari, Unnur Dis Skaptadottir, and Suvi Keskinen. 2019. *Undoing Homogeneity in the Nordic Region: Migration, Difference, and the Politics of Solidarity*. First edition. Studies in Migration and Diaspora. London, New York: Routledge. https://doi.org/10.4324/9781315122328.

Udlændinge- & Integrationsministeriet. 2023. "Stor stigning i arbejdstilladelser til udlændinge i 2022". http://uim.dk/nyhedsarkiv/2023/januar/stor-stigning-i- arbejdstilladelser-til-udlaendinge-i-2022/.

Vedsted-Hansen, Jens. 2022. "Refugees as Future Returnees? Anatomy of the 'Paradigm Shift' towards Temporary Protection in Denmark". *CMI Report* 2022:6. https://www.cmi.no/publications/8567-refugees-as-future-returnees-anatomy- of-the-paradigm-shift-towards-temporary-protection-in-denmark.

Zembylas, Michalinos. 2022. "Sylvia Wynter, Racialized Affects, and Minor Feelings: Unsettling the Coloniality of the Affects in Curriculum and Pedagogy". *Journal of Curriculum Studies* 54 (3): 336–50. https://doi.org/10.1080/0022027 2.2021.1946718.

PART III

Forced migrants in public discourses

"The Parasites"

Danish underground discourses and German refugees 1945

Henrik Lundtofte

Archives of Danish Occupation History, Museum Vest

Abstract

The aim of this chapter is to give insight into public discourses on forced migrants in a special era in refugee history. Thus, the chapter analyses discourses in Danish underground papers related to German refugees – in 1945, the Nazi regime evacuated 200,000 refugees from Prussia and Pomerania to occupied Denmark.

The chapter analyses a selection of 14 underground publications to discuss how the Danish resistance movement tried to influence public opinion on the refugees. Second, it discusses the political and social purposes of the anticompassion campaign that the underground press began against the refugees. Finally, the chapter focuses on discussing the question of why the underground agitation was radicalized.

Here the chapter demonstrates not only that the harsh refugee discourses were related to German politics and terror in Denmark but

How to cite this book chapter:
Lundtofte, Henrik. 2025. "'The Parasites': Danish underground discourses and German refugees 1945." In *Forced Migrants in Nordic Histories*, edited by Johanna Leinonen, Miika Tervonen, Hans Otto Frøland, Christhard Hoffmann, Seija Jalagin, Heidi Vad Jønsson and Malin Thor Tureby, 181–201. Helsinki: Helsinki University Press. https://doi.org/10.33134/HUP-32-8.

also that they must be interpreted as a final showdown with the Danish state's collaboration with Hitler's regime and as an attempt to signal Denmark's belonging to the Allied side.

Introduction

During winter and spring 1945, the Nazi regime evacuated more than 200,000 German refugees to occupied Denmark. The refugees were mainly women, elderly men, and children, among them many seriously ill infants, from Eastern Prussia and Pomerania fleeing the advancing Soviet armies.

The Danish resistance movement responded by an underground media campaign against any kind of aid to the refugees – weakened infants included – were described as "parasites." At the same time, the resistance considered itself humane and a participant in the Allied struggle against Nazi barbarism. The way the underground media dealt with the clash between humanity and anticompassion *or* even conceived of it as a dilemma is a thought-provoking dimension of the greatest influx of refugees in Danish history. There are two facts to consider here. First, the resistance movement still constitutes an important part of a national narrative of democratic Danes fighting Nazi persecution and racism (Bundgaard Christensen et al. 2015). Second, since the 1990s Danish historiography has challenged the postwar narrative (by Havrehed 1987) of a humane refugee treatment, and a crucial result is the documentation by the historian and senior physician Kirsten Lylloff of the deaths of 13,000 refugees – 7,000 of them children under the age of five – in 1945 (Lylloff 1999, 58). While the excess child mortality remains a fact, the political and social background is disputed. Most historians (Hansen Nielsen 2013; Jensen 2020; Harder 2020) explain high mortality in the light of the terrible condition of many refugees and the occupational regime's inability to handle infectious diseases; Lylloff (1999, 2003), however, emphasizes the refusal of Danish doctors to treat German refugees.

Despite the conflicting interpretations there is a consensus that anti-German sentiment if not hatred was widespread in 1945. Thus, the reactions to the refugees through the underground resistance media are important to analyze in order to explain the rejective attitude. This has partially been done in works on the refugees (Lylloff 1999, 2003; Schultheiss 2009; Harder 2020; Jensen 2020), as well as in studies of the illegal press (Trommer 2001; Lundtofte 2009; Søby Pedersen 2021; Jensen and Andersen 2015 (most thorough)) and of Danish public opinion (Roslyng-Jensen 2007).

This contribution concentrates on the underground press coverage of the German refugees. Thus, it gives insight into public discourses on refugees and political instrumentalization of forced migrants in a rather special era in refugee history, when a totalitarian state at war evacuated civilians and when underground media bypassed censorship.

Methodically, the article is based on a qualitative analysis of illegal papers to discuss refugee discourses in the resistance underground media – refugee discourses and public discourse are understood as how language was used to communicate and influence the public – that is, the Danish people – in their political views regarding German refugees.

Thus, the chapter asks and analyzes three key questions: How did illegal papers try to influence public opinion on the refugees, what was the political and social purposes of the anticompassion campaign, and why was it so hateful?

Most historians agree that the merciless character of the illegal campaign was a consequence of Nazi occupation and terror (Lylloff 1999, 2003; Jensen 2020; Harder 2020). Their interpretation will be supported by this analysis. But, in addition, it is the hypothesis in this contribution that the refugee discourses in the underground media also must be interpreted as part of a final showdown with the Danish state collaboration with Hitler's regime and as an attempt to signal Denmark's belonging to the Allied side. The validity of this hypothesis is demonstrated by research literature (Lidegaard 2006) and by the overall political arguments in the illegal media (Lundtofte 2009; elaborated below).

The underground press

In occupied Denmark, the resistance publications along with Danish broadcasts on the BBC and Swedish radio formed alternative news channels presenting uncensored political views designed to influence public opinion. From the tenuous beginning in 1941, the illegal press had two enemies: national socialism/the German occupation power and the Danish government policy of adaptation and cooperation

185

184   Forced Migrants in Nordic Histories

with the occupation power (Trommer 2001, 69). In late August 1943, declining popular support, strikes, sabotage, and harsh German demands caused the Danish government's demission. From that point, the resistance concentrated on raising popular sympathy for the fight against the Nazi occupation power as well as the Danish collaborators and emphasized that Denmark was a part of the Allied struggle. By 1945, several hundred underground papers were published in their thousands all over the country (Lundtofte 2009, 84).

A wide selection of 14 underground periodicals have been researched to this study, with special focus on authoritative printed nationwide publications as the cross-party *Frit Danmark* (Free Denmark). The largest underground periodical in 1945 was *Land og Folk* (Land and People). This was the pioneer paper of the forbidden Danish Communist Party (DKP), printed in monthly editions of over 100,000 copies. Another pioneer paper was the national conservative *De Frie Danske* (The Free Danes). Also, the chapter focuses on the important illegal news agency *Information*, where all proclamations by the Danish underground leadership, Frihedsrådet (the Freedom Council), were printed. In addition, papers like *Morgenbladet* (The Morning Post), distributed by the Christian national party Dansk Samling, has been analyzed, as well as *Ungdommens Røst* (Voice of the Youth), directed at the working-class youth. The social democratic *Det Politiske* (The Political, published by the underground organization Ringen) was influential, and so were *Den Danske Parole* (The Danish Slogan) and *Danske Tidende* (Danish News), both written by prominent Conservative and Social Democratic politicians under pseudonyms. *Folk og Frihed* (People and Freedom) was an intellectual underground periodical with articles by writers and poets, while *Kirkens Front* (The Church's Front) was published by people connected to the Christian Church. *Landboen* (The Country Dweller) appealed directly to Danish farmers. Finally, the analysis includes two of the small papers that were distributed in local communities: the communist *Vestjyden* (The West Jutlander) and the cross-party *Sydvestjylland* (Southwest Jutland), both published in Esbjerg and in Southwest Jutland.

The underground publications differed in layout quality (not all of them had a publication date) and in terms of political agenda and agitational form. While references to the German refugees are scarce in some papers, other periodicals contain many articles. Typically, underground articles about refugees were not only informative but tried to influence public opinion against the German occupation. While especially the communist illegal press long remained sympathetic to the German working class, this changed in the last phases of the war. Still, differences remained between the illegal papers. But in general the rhetoric was radicalized, and became hateful against everything German when during winter 1945 there were brutal Nazi reprisals in Denmark (Lundtofte 2009). This happened at the same time as Hitler's regime began to evacuate millions of civilians from East Prussia, Danzig, and Pomerania, along with thousands of wounded soldiers (not included in this analysis) to the West (Jensen 2020).

What was known?

Right from the great Soviet offensive on January 12, 1945, the underground media had reported on chaos and desperation among the population in the eastern parts of Germany: "Panic everywhere, Hundreds freezing to death or perishing from exhaustion. Of a refugee column of 600 people, 100 died in the course of a day" (*Information*, February 22, 1945). This was part of a narrative in which the Nazi regime was portrayed as corrupt and collapsing, and where an Allied victory was soon expected. In this way the flow of refugees became part of a general narrative to create optimism among the Danes.

The appalling loss of human life during the evacuee transports in the Baltic Sea was no secret. *Kirkens Front* (*Nyhedstjeneste*, February 14, 1945), *Information*, and *Morgenbladet* (February 15 and 19, 1945) reported on torpedoes and shipwrecks on the cold seas, including the sinking of the *Wilhelm Gustloff* on January 30. This catastrophe at sea brought the highest death toll in maritime history; approximately 8,000 evacuees, primarily refugees, drowned (Jensen 2020, 8).

On February 8 and 10, it appeared from *Information* and *Morgenbladet* that refugees from the east were approaching Denmark. The German authorities seized homes for accommodation in Southern Jutland. The following days, the first refugee group reached Southern Jutland by train. From the beginning, the illegal press informed the readers that many evacuees were women and children in a poor condition. The frontpage of *Sydvestjylland* (February 25, 1945) brought a report:

These days, the flow of refugees is pouring over our borders. While these lines are being written, a train with 15 carriages filled with women and children stops at Esbjerg railway station … Ladies in elegant furs sit in the compartments with ragged children and women wearing men's clothes … ragged, filled with vermin and dirt.

In Copenhagen, ships transporting wounded soldiers had begun to arrive in February, and on the night of March 10 the first refugee vessel reached Copenhagen (*Information*, March 12, 1945).

Danish officials protested the arrival of German refugees and claimed it was a violation of the promises Germany had made on April 9, 1940, not to encroach on Denmark's territorial integrity and political independence (Havrehed 1987; Harder 2020; Jensen 2020).

The mortality rate among refugees was high, and infants died in disproportionate numbers. This was no secret. Without compassion, *Information* (March 19, 1945) wrote about the many coffins transported to a graveyard in Copenhagen:

The mortality rate among the German refugees is very significant. Thus, in the course of Thursday, no less than 70 coffins were brought out to Vestre Kirkegaard's south chapel from various places in Copenhagen, and in several of these coffins were four to six children. Friday morning, new coffins arrived, crudely assembled wooden boxes. On board a refugee ship that had just run into Frihavnen, 46 people had died during the crossing, and these bodies were also brought to Vestre Kirkegaard.

There was a fairly comprehensive level of knowledge about the horrifying circumstances for the escape and the terrible condition of the refugees.

Resistance reactions

In March 1945, three leading underground publications printed proclamations regarding the German refugees. *Frit Danmark* (March 1, 1945) brought a justification of the merciless attitude this illegal paper now propagated: The Germans terrorized the country, and while the refugee trains arrived, the deportations of Danes to the concentration camps left for Germany. The refugees carried diseases, and the feelings, which the Gestapo terror had created, would affect the refugees irrespective of the many tragic destinies.

Figure 7.1: Coarse drawing comparing German refugees 1945 with invading German forces 1940. Source: Underground Communist paper *Vestjyden,* April 1945. Courtesy of Historisk Samling fra Besættelsestiden.

This was underground agitation of a kind that could be read in dozens of illegal papers (the argument that refugees were carrying disease will be further discussed below). In particular, the underground media emphasized the juxtaposition of German refugees being evacuated to Denmark with the news on deportations of Danish citizens to Germany (see Figure 7.1). There were many lists and articles about Danish prisoners dying in the concentration camps and about new deportations to Dachau (February 22 and March 2, 1945) and Neuengamme (March 13, 1945). At the same time, the German security police directed terrorist reprisal actions, most notably against a civilian passenger train, where ten innocent people were killed, and then again in Aarhus and in Odense, where an SS terror unit on February 20 ravaged and murdered four doctors from the city's hospital in revenge for resistance liquidations. The reprisals created intense anger and condemnation throughout the underground press and contributed to the verbal radicalization regarding the attitude to Germans and to German refugees (Jensen 2020; Jensen and Andersen 2015; Lundtofte 2009). *Land og Folk* (no. 61, March 25, 1945) interpreted the stream of refugees as a Nazi attempt to prolong the war instead of taking the consequences of the defeat and sparing the German people and the world more suffering. This bit of sympathy, however, did not include the refugees, who were regarded as dedicated Nazis with the task of relieving housing shortages in Germany. The view that evacuations and refugee aid would prolong the war, lead to the arrival of more refugees, and fundamentally help the Nazis was widespread in the underground media. Consequently, *Land og Folk* included the treatment of the refugees in the war and the resistance fight: "Do nothing voluntarily for the refugees and continue to sabotage all German arrangements – the refugees as well."

At the same time, *De Frie Danske* (no. 5, March 1945) let the readers know: "Now, the refugees are pouring across our borders, lousy, tattered, hungry, sick … BUT WE CANNOT PITY FOR THAT IS – as the situation has developed – TO BETRAY OUR OWN COUNTRY." Obviously, *De Frie Danske* in capital letters presented a much more brutal rhetoric – this was the tabloid underground media in action. Nonetheless, the conservative *De Frie Danske* and the communist *Land og Folk* were united in the allegation that any refugee aid would prolong the war. So, essentially, the attitude to the German refugees was made a part of the war.

The rejective and contemptuous attitude in these leading underground media were along with proclamations by the Freedom Council (see below) and speeches in the Danish broadcasts in Swedish radio and the BBC influential on public opinion. The moderate underground voices shared the position. There was no reason to be "sentimental" as long as Germany was led by criminals and Danes suffered in concentration camps, *Morgenbladet* concluded in an editorial comment (February 28, 1945). In fact, the view was shared by all underground media analyzed – Christian, Communist, Conservative, Social Democratic or cross-political (Jensen 2020; Harder, Jensen, and Andersen 2015; Lundtofte 2009). Therefore, the total illegal output can be characterized as an anticompassion campaign.

Views like the ones presented in *Frit Danmark*, *De Frie Danske* and *Land og Folk* influenced discussions about medical aid during March 1945. But the debate also contained another crucial dimension.

Quid pro quo rejection

During March 1945, thousands more refugees arrived by train to Jutland and by ship to Copenhagen. By the end of the month there were 100,000 German refugees in the country. The many and often weakened and sick people made the question of medical assistance urgent. The German health institutions and hospitals in Denmark were completely inadequate. The Danish authorities refused to help unless the Nazi regime repatriated Danish prisoners or improved their conditions in the concentration camps. On March 12, the chairman of the Danish Medical Association, Mogens Fenger, took the initiative for a quid pro quo deal with the German occupying power: The doctors would treat refugees for a number of illnesses if conditions for Danish prisoners in Germany were improved and some of them were sent home. While the German authorities fulfilled the requirements, for ten to 14 days the Danish doctors would take care of births, epidemic diseases, and certain acute cases of illness (Lylloff 2003, 209). The resistance movement was aware of this plan, and parts of the underground press expressed their support for the negotiations (*Information*, March 19, 1945).

But many doctors refused any help because of the German terrorist reprisals and the underground news. And, not least, the resistance leadership, the Freedom Council, now took a dismissive position toward help for German refugees. On March 16, a member of the Freedom Council, Professor Erik Husfeldt, contacted Mogens Fenger and pointed out that, after the position Denmark had obtained among the Allies, it was necessary to follow Allied guidelines, and thus it was not right to do business with the Germans (Lylloff 2003, 210–11).

Fenger, however, continued his negotiations. This prompted a proclamation from the Freedom Council, dated March 21 and presumably written by Husfeldt (Harder 2020, 106, printed in *Information*, March 22, 1945). This "Proclamation from Denmark's Freedom Council Regarding Aid to German Refugees" began by pointing out that refugees, including terminally ill infants, had been treated in Danish hospitals despite the German inhumane treatment of Danish citizens. Then the proclamation said: "but it is not a task for the Danish people, who in practice are recognized as an Allied nation, through their authorities and organizations to establish medical services for the Germans and thereby facilitate their warfare." That was a matter for the German authorities. Finally, the Freedom Council unmistakably rejected quid pro quo negotiations.

Since the general strike in Copenhagen in the summer of 1944, the Freedom Council had won great authority, and along with the underground agitation the proclamation had an effect. Thus, on March 25 a majority among doctors and physicians decided to deny German refugees aid and treatment. Several of them referred to the rejective position in the illegal papers and to the Freedom Council's proclamation (Lylloff 2003, 213–14). From that time on, only epidemic diseases that could threaten the *Danish* population were treated by the doctors.

It is not only the process leading to an almost complete rejection that matters here. The statement by the Freedom Council that the Danish people were "in practice" recognized as an Allied nation reveals the obvious point that Denmark was *not* a real member of the Allied alliance. A similar statement appeared, for example, in an article on the refugees in *Det Politiske* (March 24, 1945), presumably written by Erik Husfeldt: "The Danish people considers itself (and is regarded by the United Nations) as an Allied [nation] and cannot organize medical services for the enemy."

These statements were related to Danish political wishes. The resistance movement tried to convince the population that Denmark in fact was an Allied nation at war with Germany. For the US, Great Britain, and the USSR, the matter was more complicated. Denmark was, as President Roosevelt declared at the Yalta conference, a strange case (Bundgaard Christensen et al. 2015, 608). There was no Danish government in exile in London and no official Danish declaration of war against Germany. Given this, the resistance allowed nothing to endanger the Danish position as a kind of "Allied prospect." Here it is crucial to understand that the refugee rejection took place at a time when both politicians and leading members of the resistance were working to convince leaders in London, Washington, and Moscow to declare Denmark an Allied nation (Lidegaard 2006). Therefore, it was decisive to emphasize that the government policy of state collaboration with the German occupation power was history. Thus, even a negotiated solution that might help Danish prisoners and give aid to German refugees was neither possible nor desirable seen form the resistance point of view. Right before the end of the war in Europe, there was no room for doubt regarding the Danish position.

The interpretation that the evacuees from the east were hit by the final resistance showdown with the Danish government's cooperation policy in 1940–1943 makes the treatment of them part of a broader pattern. There are clear parallels to the increased activities of the resistance movement at the end of the war. The growing number of sabotage actions had much greater significance as a political signal than they had for German supplies and economy. In the same way, the purges of Danish Nazis and collaborators that had begun months before the German capitulation in May had political and symbolic dimensions (Lundtofte 2022).

The political considerations had grave implications for the refugees – and at that time the great influx of evacuees had not even begun. From late March through April to the German capitulation in May tens of thousands of Germans were evacuated to Denmark (Lylloff 2003, 217).

Refugee treatment as a patriot test

In spring 1945, daily life in Danish society became more polarized than ever during the occupation. The underground press wanted to rally the Danes behind the resistance and to commit the population to the Allied cause. So the illegal papers raged against "lukewarmness" and opportunism. In the light of this political and social development, the German refugees represented a possibility for the resistance members at the typewriters to demand that Danes demonstrate everyday rejection and enmity toward Germans. This also made the treatment of the refugees related to the war.

The refugees, however, were not always met by ice-cold shoulders, which led to many underground descriptions of wrong behavior. A typical and well-known example is the scorn in *De Frie Danske* (April 15, 1945) for the kindness some hungry refugees had been shown on a railway station on Zealand, where railway personnel had given them Danish pastry. *De Frie Danske* reacted by describing the railway personnel as the "soft-spoken and nationally crooked individuals." *De Frie Danske* was keen on ostracizing, but similar articles can be found in many illegal papers (*Information*, February 24, 1945).

Wrong and unpatriotic behavior served to ostracize Danes. The refugees were an opportunity to behavioral regulation. This had a wider perspective. Many underground writers wanted the occupation experience to be an end to the phenomenon they characterized as typical Danish "porridge," meaning indifference and opportunism. Instead, they dreamt about a new patriotic spirit with the will to defend the nation.

Every German an enemy, a threat, and a perpetrator

The political and social purpose decisively shaped the illegal images of the evacuated Germans. It is hardly surprising that the images were full of stereotypes. But in its essence it was not about the Germans but rather about the Danes – stereotyping was an element in the underground writers work to convince the population that every German was an enemy. This is somewhat surprising in view of traditional Danish resentment and fears of the big southern neighbor and after almost five years of world war and occupation. Nevertheless, the illegal press thought it had to establish who the enemy of all decent patriotic Danes was and considered it necessary to apply resources to create anti-German sentiments (Lundtofte 2009).

This helps to explain the stereotypes, where a typical one claimed that every German was a Nazi. *Landboen* (no. 3, 1945) wrote that the German children behaved like "small Gestapo hooligans." *De Frie Danske* (no. 5, March 25, 1945) claimed that the behavior of the refugees was scandalous and that even children acted like small Hitlers. Thus, some underground media turned German children into agents of Hitler's regime, which meant that the ordinary Dane had to treat them as enemies.

The same way German women were often portrayed as Nazis and accomplices in the regime's crimes (*Ungdommens Røst*, no. 23, April 1945). This depiction of Germans made national socialism a deeply rooted *German* or Prussian feature.

But the refugees were also often portrayed as devoid of any kind of gratitude or moderation. Instead, illegal news described how refugees demanded clothes and food and behaved with arrogance and *Herrenvolk* mentality and constituted a threat to Danish food supply (*Information*, March 5, 8, and 26, 1945).

Finally, another way of impressing the population the necessity to keep a cold distance to the refugees was the frequent references to the infectious diseases. Many refugees had been evacuated under horrible

power deliberately transported the most weakened refugees through the streets to make the Copenhageners feel sorry for them.

Humanity vs barbarism?

Some illegal papers went to the extremes, and sometimes underground rhetoric became Nazi-like, when for example *Landboen* (no. 3, 1945) wrote: "in their thousands the refugees tumble over the border like rats from a sinking ship, ragged, lousy, hungry and ill."

De Frie Danske (no. 4, February 26, 1945) also used harsh rhetoric and made every German responsible for the Nazi crimes, claiming that "[a]fter this war the German will be a pariah in Denmark." Nothing would "soften the hatred." The article caused a direct opposition from another illegal paper, the *Kirkens Front* (no. 17, April 1945), in which the writer described *De Frie Danske*'s spirit as Nazi. *Kirkens Front* distinguished between national socialism and the German people. As previously mentioned, such a distinction had been quite widespread in the underground media, but this changed along with the brutalization of German antiresistance measures and the bulletins of the concentration camp horrors. Thus, *De Frie Danske* represented the typical illegal position. Even the communist underground like *Vestjyden* in Esbjerg now tabooed any kind of humanity or compassion (March 1945) – earlier, in 1943, *Vestjyden* had written about the Nazi regime and its suppression of the German people (no. 5, February 1943). That was all over now as it was in the leading communist publication, *Land og Folk* (no. 61, March 25, 1945).

Almost all resistance underground media no longer differed between the Nazi regime and the German population. The refugee discourse demonstrated that ideological beliefs no longer affected the way the illegal papers presented ordinary Germans.

On the other hand, some underground writers felt forced to legitimize the relentless attitude to the refugees. To some degree, their articles dealt with the clash between the resistance movement as a defender of humanity against Nazi barbarism *and* the resistance campaign against vital aid to German children and adults. In *Information* an author asserted (March 10, 1945):

> The Danish people – and for that matter many other peoples in the world – against whose nature all brutality conflicts, and whose ideals

revolve around humanity and charity, allow themselves to be easily caught in the Goebbels net ... We are inclined to sympathize with the individual innocently suffering German and to forget that he is alone in an all-destroying crowd ... We must cultivate hatred – not as a negative release of our emotions, but as a positive defensive measure for our mind. We must be prepared to meet the German Compassion campaign that has already been unleashed.

The article was another answer to the alleged Goebbels campaign.

Another writer in *Information* presented similar reflections (March 27, 1945) in a comment on German appeals to Danish doctors and authorities to help wounded soldiers and refugees:

It is not in accordance with the Danish way of thinking to wage war against women and children, but the Nazis themselves have started such a form of warfare ... The anger and hatred that the murders and executions of the last few months have raised in the Danish people demands its release.

In *Folk og Frihed* (April 16, 1945), the well-known author (under pseudonym) Martin A. Hansen in a rare comment on the refugee situation wrote: "The door is closed ... If you want to enter, you must kick the door in. We can't open." This was said in a context where Hansen had written about deportations and terror – the Nazis had destroyed compassion.

De Frie Danske (no. 5, March 25, 1945) indirectly commented the cognitive dissonance: "Under normal circumstances our hearts would bleed. For children are children, though they belong to our enemies." But now pity was the same as betraying the country. Also the Christian *Morgenbladet* (April 5, 1945) seemed to try to solve a cognitive dissonance when a writer claimed that Christian love was not the same as weak mercy.

The Danish self-image constitutes another dimension of the anti-German illegal agitation: the German became the negation to the non-militarist, antiauthoritarian, tolerant, humoristic, and humane Dane (Lundtofte 2009). The self-image was frequently reproduced by the underground media. Obviously, it was contradicted by the resistance campaign against refugees and humanity. This cognitive dissonance was reinforced by the genuine underground *Schadenfreude* in not only articles but also in satirical drawings, which was induced by the bombing of Germany, destruction, defeat, and the sight of refugee masses.

Conclusion

This chapter has concentrated on underground material to give insight into public discourses on forced migrants in a special era in refugee history, with illegal media bypassing censorship and using brutalized rhetoric.

In 1945, the illegal papers tried to influence public opinion as well as the way ordinary Danes behaved in their daily encounter with the German refugees. Therefore, the underground writers applied varied methods: they exposed Danes who had helped German refuges to public contempt and they stereotyped refugees, including the children, as incorrigible Nazis; at the same time, they depicted the refugees as a serious threat to public health in Denmark; finally, they seem to have invented a Goebbels compassion campaign, which the underground writers used as a straw man argument to strengthen their agitation.

In this way it is not an exaggeration to claim that the resistance media launched an anticompassion campaign. The political and social purposes of this campaign was to prevent any kind of Danish aid to the refugees. But why did the campaign become so hateful?

Essentially, the resistance refugee discourses, and the underground verbal radicalization was related to mechanisms that did not have much to do with desperate families fleeing cold, starvation, and war.

One obvious reason to the radicalization was the rage over concentration camps, escalating Nazi terror killings and suppression in hitherto rather peaceful Denmark. In that sense, the underground media became a mouthpiece for sentiments widespread in the population that tended no longer to distinguish between soldiers and civilians, between Nazis and Germans, or between adults and children.

Second, in 1945 there were many unknown factors: when would the Nazi regime capitulate/collapse, and how many of several million German refugees would be evacuated to Denmark? It is often neglected in the literature that no one in February and March or even in April 1945 could know, exactly when and how the war would end – except for the fact that the Nazi German breakdown for everyone seemed imminent, which, clearly, just made the resistance work even harder to establish the Danish position on the Allied side. When a hated regime in this precarious situation evacuated thousands of civilians to an occupied country, a cold and rejective reception was hardly surprising.

Third, this analysis has demonstrated that the underground refugee discourses played a role in the resistance effort to signal the final and complete showdown with the Danish policies of adaptation to Nazi Germany. Suddenly, a dismissive attitude to the German evacuation operation and hence to the refugees seemed like a chance to contribute to the war with Nazi Germany.

Seen in the larger context, the hateful underground response to the refugees was also related to political maneuvering regarding postwar politics, which left no room for compassion. For those who wanted to gain influence on the future Danish society and democracy it was tantamount to political suicide to plea for a humane treatment of German refugees. For example, *Den Danske Parole* (The Danish Slogan), written by prominent Conservative and Social Democratic politicians, urged the population to behave with dignity but not to show any compassion (no. 5, 1945). This seems to be an important dimension of the illegal discourses and is comparable to the attitude among leading politicians and resistance members to the purge of Danish collaborators; in spring 1945, no one with political postwar aspirations dared to argue for a mild treatment of collaborators (Lundtofte 2009, 2022).

It seems obvious that the verbal radicalization and the strict demands not to help had implications for the German refugees (Lylloff 1999) – but based on an analysis of the underground discourses it is of course not possible to assess the exact consequences for the refugees and for mortality among them.

Finally, the implications of the resistance views on German refugees are worth considering in relation to a future postwar Germany. In the light of the radicalized underground discourses one might ask whether the perceptions of Germans left them any chance to develop into future democratic neighbors? This was not only a question of the underground portrayal of Germans as suffering of an ineradicable Nazism and *Herrenvolk* mentality. No doubt, the shock of the underground media news and articles about Nazi Germany's huge and incomprehensible crimes against humanity in Europe in combination with the terror reprisals in Denmark also influenced the way the resistance and, presumably, the population perceived Germany and German refugees in postwar Europe.

During the war, in late autumn 1943, Arne Sørensen, leader of the Christian national party Dansk Samling (Danish Unity), published an underground book carrying the title *What Shall We Do with the Germans Afterwards*. It rejected harsh treatment: "But if we only have our burning hatred of the Germans to make peace with, then we form an image of the German that is just as perverted and inhumane as the one the Nazi has made of the Jew" (see also Lammers 2021). *Kirkens Front* shared the ambition to create room for both humanity and Germans in postwar Europe. In March 1944 (no. 8), it declared that not every single German was a Nazi. *Kirkens Front* had confidence in German Christians and workers (nos. 12 and 13, 1944). The same year, *Land og Folk* had published a comment by the famous author Martin Andersen Nexø on "The German People and the Future" (no. 37, February 1944). Andersen Nexø developed the distinction between Hitler's regime and the German population and claimed: "As regards the poisoning of the German youth, I do not think it goes deep."

In spring 1945, there was little room for these ideas and very few thoughts about the refugees after the war. *Folk og Frihed* was one of the exceptions (May 1, 1945). This underground paper directly dealt with the situation of the refugees after a German capitulation and warned against the tendency in some illegal papers to dehumanize the Germans. "All hatred is a denial of humanity. And where humanity is denied, demonry takes power." The demon, of course, was Nazism. Regarding the German refugees the article said: "So it turns out that the problem is not solved by saying that we must show them our contempt, and they are accomplices. They are, but they are still fellow human beings and must be treated as international law requires."

However, in 1945, the majority of the illegal publications would never emphasize that the Germans were fellow human beings. And the implications of the dominating underground refugee discourses did not ever leave Germans any chances to become democrats in a peaceful neighbor state.

But this was the last phases of the war, a special era in modern Danish history. Still, in the first period after the liberation there were many vehement anti-German voices and harsh antirefugee rhetoric – with an obvious continuity to the underground media (Havrehed 1987, 63–64, 72–73). Gradually, the general attitude changed. Ironically, the German refugees probably played a role in the change. During the summer of 1945, the British instructed the Danish authorities that the

CHAPTER 8

An eternally grateful refugee?

Silences in Swedish public discourse and the (De)historicization of Polish-Swedish activist Ludwika Broel-Plater

Victoria Van Orden Martínez

Lund University

Abstract

This chapter examines how the history and legacy of Polish-Swedish activist Ludwika Broel-Plater have been obscured in Swedish public discourse, in which she is recognized mainly as a passive and grateful recipient of Swedish humanitarianism. The first part of the chapter examines silences that have entered narrative constructions in Swedish public discourse about survivors who came to Sweden as repatriates in 1945 and how these have contributed to creating embedded narratives about Broel-Plater and refugees of the early postwar period more generally. Second, it begins to construct an alternative narrative that recognizes Broel-Plater's historical significance by using her own and other neglected source material. In doing so, the chapter counters

How to cite this book chapter:
Martínez, Victoria Van Orden. 2025. "An eternally grateful refugee? Silences in Swedish public discourse and the (de)historicization of Polish-Swedish activist Ludwika Broel-Plater." In *Forced Migrants in Nordic Histories*, edited by Johanna Leinonen, Miika Tervonen, Hans Otto Frøland, Christhard Hoffmann, Seija Jalagin, Heidi Vad Jønsson and Malin Thor Tureby, 203–223. Helsinki: Helsinki University Press. https://doi.org/10.33134/HUP-32-9.

conventional narratives of survivors of Nazi persecution in Sweden as refugees and thus enhances the possibilities of understanding forced migration of the period in transnational contexts.

Introduction

What makes someone or something historical? Surely it is enough to be a part of the social processes of history – how past events unfolded in particular contexts – to be a part of history. Not exactly. Many people and events of the past have been effectively erased from history – dehistoricized (Malkki 1996, 385) owing to their gender, race, religion, geographical location, social or political status, and so on – in narrative constructions of the social processes of history. Anthropologist Michel-Rolph Trouillot (2015) calls this the dual nature of historicity: It is not enough for people and events to be a part of the social process of history because it is only through narrative constructions that "history reveals itself" (25). When silences enter narrative constructions, whether consciously or otherwise, people and events are dehistoricized or made ahistorical. History is an inherent and explicit part of public discourse (Trouillot 1999, 452), which is composed of written, spoken, and other communications that engage the public at various levels and through a variety of media, including books, magazine and newspaper articles, blogs and websites, museum exhibitions and their descriptions, and so forth. If we acknowledge that discourses are social systems and/or processes that have the power to produce and exclude knowledge and meaning (Foucault [1969] 2002), then public discourse can be understood as having an authority that gives it the power to shape who, what, and how people and events are historicized through what it communicates and/or dehistoricized through silences in the narratives it constructs. In other words, public discourse constructs narratives that contribute to shaping if, how, and the extent to which the people and events of the past are visible.

This power is illustrated with the help of an April 1966 Swedish newspaper article about the opening of an exhibition at Kulturen, a museum in Lund, Sweden, titled "Att överleva" (To Survive), which featured objects that had belonged to liberated prisoners of Nazi concentration camps who were evacuated to Sweden in 1945. Prominently placed just below the headline of the article is a photograph of a woman identified as one of these former prisoners, Polish countess Ludwika

Polska grevinnan Ludwiga Broël-Plater, 80, höll den sista flämtade livs-lågan uppe hos många landsmän i flyktingkontingenten till Sverige 3 maj 1945

Figure 8.1: The picture of Ludwika Broel-Plater as it appeared in the 1966 *Sydsvenska Dagbladet Snällposten* (SDS) article titled "Lunda-polacker kände pust från koncentrationslägren." Reproduced with permission from *Sydsvenskan*. All rights reserved.

Broel-Plater (see Figure 8.1). The article portrays her as "a curved little lady," age 80, who after gazing at the objects on display "had to take support from her friend's arm." The reader is told how during her visit to the exhibition Broel-Plater came face to face not only with objects that reminded her of her time as a prisoner of the Nazis but also with "some of the Swedes who perhaps first saw her on arrival in Malmö" (SDS 1966).[1] The article makes no mention of how Broel-Plater and other survivors of Nazi persecution who came to Sweden as "repatriates" – refugees welcome in the country for a maximum of six months or until well enough to leave[2] – in the spring and summer of 1945 substantially contributed to the collection of this material and were active agents in documenting the Nazis' crimes for history and justice as part of the Polish Research Institute in Lund (PIZ).[3] Instead of being highlighted for how she contributed to collecting the objects in the exhibition, Broel-Plater is notable in the article only as an embodiment of the traumatized former prisoners who received refuge in Sweden and whose belongings were on display.

Although it was published 21 years after Broel-Plater arrived in Sweden as a repatriate, the article's depiction of her is little different from how she and other repatriates were described in Swedish public discourse soon after they arrived in 1945: as vulnerable and passive "objects of care" (Wagrell 2020, 363) who were graciously helped by "a good, democratic country and a well-organized refugee relief pro-gramme" (Thor Tureby 2013, 158). The durability of this narrative, expressed through public discourse, and the silences it has contributed to creating reflect how forced migrants are stripped of a "post-refugee narrative" and discursively frozen as traumatized and passive victims long after the "act of flight" (Mahendran et al. 2019). It also begins to demonstrate how silences can and do enter narrative constructions of history through public discourse irrespective of the people and events of the past and available knowledge about them. While this often involves deliberation, it can also be due to ignorance. The journalist who wrote the article may not have known that Broel-Plater and other Polish survivors who came to Sweden as repatriates not only contrib-uted the items on display but also contributed to collecting them as part of PIZ, a transnational endeavor that existed in various forms from 1940 to 1972 but is best known for its collection of documents, evidence, and witness testimonies gathered from Polish survivors of Nazi persecution in Sweden in 1945 and 1946 (see, e.g., Dahl 2021; Kruszewski 2001; Martínez 2023; Rudny 2007). Other newspaper arti-cles about the exhibition likewise mention nothing about this part of the history (*Arbetet* 1966; *Dagens Nyheter* 1966). But, whether it was deliberate or not, the result is that Broel-Plater is erased as an active agent of her own history, the PIZ documentation initiative, and the material on display at the exhibition.

This example does not reflect an obsolete narrative. Nor is it an isolated case. Rather, it is indicative of how Broel-Plater and other Pol-ish repatriates associated with PIZ, especially women, continue to be represented in Swedish public discourse to this day, with the result that they are effectively erased from significant transnational histori-cal contexts. Although they were integral to processes in events of the early postwar period that involve Sweden but also stretch beyond it and create a multitude of transnational and transhistorical entanglements, their contributions, their voices, and their experiences remain, as Philip Marfleet writes in this volume, "unheard."

This chapter addresses questions raised by Marfleet in his chapter, such as how historians and other scholars can retrieve refugees' experiences and make them a part of the historical record. It also begins to reverse the dehistoricization of Ludwika Broel-Plater – particularly in terms of her work with PIZ and as an activist – and contributes to research that recognizes forced migrants as purposeful agents in their own lives and histories, as well as in history more generally (e.g., Banko, Nowak, and Gatrell 2021; Gatrell 2017; Kushner and Knox 1999; Malkki 1996; Marfleet 2013). Anthropologist Liisa Malkki (1996) argues for a reversal of the dehistoricization of refugees in part by "acknowledging not only human suffering but also narrative authority, historical agency, and political memory" (398). The analysis aims to achieve this, first, by examining silences that have entered narrative constructions in Swedish public discourse about survivors who came to Sweden as repatriates in 1945 and how these have contributed to creating embedded narratives about Broel-Plater and refugees of the early postwar period more generally. Second, it begins to construct an alternative narrative that recognizes Broel-Plater's historical significance by using her own and other source material. In doing so, the chapter counters conventional narratives of survivors of Nazi persecution in Sweden and thus enhances the possibilities of understanding forced migration of the period in transnational contexts.

In the context of this chapter, "Swedish public discourse" primarily involves narratives written in Swedish, by Swedish scholars/authors, from the Swedish perspective, and/or about the context of Sweden. However, because Broel-Plater and the other repatriates were originally from Poland and PIZ was a transnational endeavor, it also includes narratives written in Polish and/or by Poles that were published in Sweden or another Nordic country.

Dehistoricizing narratives in Swedish public discourse

Ludwika Broel-Plater was nearly 60 when she arrived in Sweden in the spring of 1945 as a repatriate. She had survived torture by the Gestapo in Nazi-occupied Poland's notorious Pawiak Prison, sustaining spinal injuries that required her to wear an orthopedic corset for the rest of her life, and more than three years as a non-Jewish political prisoner in Ravensbrück concentration camp. As soon as she was physically able, she became part of PIZ. She began her work with the institute in an informal capacity while still in a Swedish refugee camp and then became one of the nine Polish survivors employed to collect this material in the immediate postwar period. But, rather than leave Sweden as was expected of repatriates, she remained in the country and dedicated the rest of her life to PIZ and supporting Poles and Polish causes in exile. She became a Swedish citizen in 1957 and served as the driving force of PIZ until she died in 1972, at age 86. Her commitment to political and social work, Polish causes, documenting the Nazis' crimes against the Polish people, and commemorating the Nazis' victims can be seen in many of the artifacts and materials now held in Swedish archives and museum collections, as well as in a monument dedicated to Polish victims of Nazi persecution that she led the effort to establish.

Despite a relative abundance of archival documentation and other source material, Broel-Plater has received little attention from scholars and has existed in most Swedish public discourse related to PIZ as a subordinate figure to Dr. Zygmunt Łakociński, one of the founders of PIZ. More generally, she has been constructed in much the same way as other survivors who came to Sweden as repatriates in 1945: frozen in time as a passive, grateful, and vulnerable recipient of Swedish benevolence. This characterization stands in stark contrast to the way she perceived herself and was understood by others: as a lifelong political and social activist and a sworn soldier who devoted the last 25 years of her life to continuing the work of PIZ.

This part of the chapter explores how narratives about repatriates in Sweden that have been constructed in and through public discourse have dehistoricized Broel-Plater in a way that, despite evidence to the contrary, has not only been durable but also appears almost impervious to change. The analysis draws upon Trouillot's (2015) conception of how silences enter the production of history at four "moments": when sources are created and thus establish "facts"; when facts are assembled, such as in the making of archives; when facts are retrieved, as in when narratives are created and communicated through public discourses; and, finally, when the past becomes "history" through the establishment of retrospective significance (26). This process is not necessarily linear. As anyone who has ever followed a "breaking news" cycle knows, narratives can be and often are created before facts are established. Thus, this part of the chapter considers how silences have entered into the production of histories pertaining to Broel-Plater at the four crucial moments described by Trouillot, but it does so by zigzagging through them, illustrating how the two sides of historicity are both distinctive and overlapping. As Trouillot argues, it is through examining this overlap that it is possible to understand the power public discourse has had to not only establish historical narratives but also establish silences within them (25). This chapter shows how this process has constructed a specific narrative that has not only silenced other narratives about Broel-Plater but has also made it difficult for other narratives to emerge, despite available archival material.

As the introduction began to demonstrate, among the most resounding silences in Swedish public discourse are that Broel-Plater and other Polish repatriates made substantial contributions to the PIZ initiative and were active agents in documenting and collecting valuable evidence about Nazi atrocities for history and justice. When these silences entered into the 1966 newspaper article about the "Att överleva" exhibition at Kulturen, Swedish public discourse had long since firmly established the survivors who came to Sweden in 1945 as silent, passive, and grateful recipients of Swedish humanitarian aid. Yet, at approximately the same time, facts that could reveal the silences and contribute to more nuanced narratives were both available and still being actively created. In November 1966, just a few months after the opening of the exhibition, Zygmunt Łakociński wrote the following in a memorandum marked "strictly confidential":

> The [PIZ] collections were stored for many years in a private apartment, under the personal care of Countess Plater ... Two years ago, the library and archives were transferred on permanent deposit to the University Library in Lund, where they are stored in a shelter, available for research. In the spring of 1966, in connection with the commemorative exhibition of a selected part of the collection, museum items were also deposited on a permanent basis ... in the Museum of Cultural History [Kulturen] in Lund. (PIZ n.d., 44:3 q)

This statement reveals that parts of what is now recognized as the PIZ archive had been available for research at Lund University's library for two years before the "Att överleva" exhibition.[4] Had the journalists writing about the exhibition (or anyone else for that matter) consulted this material, they would have seen ample evidence that Broel-Plater did far more than contribute the artifacts on display. Moreover, they would have learned that, until only recently, they had been in her care. Other sources in the archives confirm that Broel-Plater had carefully stored and safeguarded much of the PIZ collection in her apartment in Lund from at least 1949 (PIZ n.d., 48).[5] Yet, one of the other spring 1966 newspaper articles about the exhibition, which featured a large photo of Łakociński, stated that *he* had stored the material, including the objects in the exhibition, in *his* home "for a long time" before depositing them at the Lund University Library (*Dagens nyheter* 1966). The reason for this discrepancy is not clear, nor is it the purpose of this chapter to investigate it. What is important to this analysis is understanding how silences entered the spring 1966 narratives at roughly the same moment facts were being created (the making of sources) *and* the moment of fact retrieval (the making of narratives) in distinct but interrelated ways. Even as Łakociński was creating a source containing facts about Broel-Plater's role in the social process of history, he was obscuring that source by making it confidential and by implicitly (or perhaps explicitly) enabling a contradictory narrative in the newspaper article. Moreover, the silences entered the narrative *after* other facts had already been assembled in an archive.

The juxtaposition of the narratives and the source, both from 1966, begins to illustrate the intertwining of the two sides of historicity in this particular context, and how this enabled some narratives and silenced others. Moreover, when this part of the construction of narratives about the history of PIZ is understood in relation to the construction of narratives in public discourse about repatriates in Sweden, a clearer picture emerges of how silences that had entered into these processes long before 1966 had already determined who and what did and did not gain retrospective significance. "Silences are inherent in history because any single event enters history with some of its constituting parts missing," Trouillot (2015) argues. "Something is always left out while something else is recorded" (49). Retrospective significance – the making of history in the final instance – is always made at the expense of something else (58–60). From the beginning, Swedish narratives about survivors of Nazi persecution who came to Sweden as repatriates in 1945 were not about the repatriates so much as they were about the heroic actions of the Swedish state and Swedish actors (Östling 2011). The repatriates were necessary to these narratives mainly or only as passive objects of care to enable the national narrative of Swedish rescue and relief (Chapter 1, this volume; Trouillot 2015, 129; Wagrell 2020).

Since the history of PIZ is about these same people, it followed suit. The narrative that the exhibit and the larger PIZ collection were *Łakociński's* and that *he* had safeguarded the material fit the embedded narratives of passive and helpless repatriates on the one hand and rescuers and helpers on the other, making it difficult to draw other conclusions even two decades later. What specifically was left out of the 1966 newspaper narratives was that Broel-Plater was always more than just a grateful refugee and traumatized survivor of Nazi persecution. But, at the moment of establishing retrospective significance, the silences that had already entered the narrative constructions of history ensured that she had little chance of being granted that significance in any other way.

Such narratives and the silences perpetuated by them continue to endure. For example, fundraising material for the Lund University Foundation's Ravensbrück campaign, which was established to raise money for the digitization of the archival material in the PIZ collection, is noticeably silent about the role of the repatriates in assembling the collection (e.g., LUF n.d.). This is in line with the way the campaign's chair, Robert D. Resnick (2018, 273), wrote in 2018 that Łakociński personally conducted interviews with survivors and handwrote the hundreds of survivor witness testimonies in the PIZ collection. As in the 1966 narratives, the collection is Łakociński's. However, at the time Resnick wrote this narrative, the sources that point to a completely different narrative were not only available in the PIZ and Zygmunt Łakociński archives but were also the very same archives that he explicitly and implicitly refers to and for which funds are being raised to digitalize.

The sources in these archives demonstrate not only that the survivors conducted all the interviews but also that Łakociński himself emphasized that *only survivors* could conduct the interviews (PIZ n.d., 44:1 c). Thus, the silences entered the fundraising and Resnick narratives even though they do not exist in readily available sources and archives. Granted, Resnick is not a scholar, so perhaps he did not consult the testimonies or other sources in the archives before making this incorrect assertion. However, scholars who would ostensibly consult the sources in the archives before making such a claim have similarly asserted that Łakociński alone was responsible for collecting the PIZ witness testimonies (e.g., Gerner 2011, 95).

It is now possible to further see how silences enter narrative constructions of a particular history not only irrespective of the social process of history but also irrespective of available sources and archives. The PIZ and Łakociński archives, which together are composed of more than 100 volumes that occupy approximately 18 shelf meters of space,[6] have been fully or partly available to researchers for decades, since long before more recent narratives perpetuated the silences of earlier narratives.[7] The silences have therefore entered narrative constructions of the history of PIZ not only before but also during and after the making of sources and archives, independently and regardless of them. It might even appear that the sources and the archives do not matter in public discourse about the history of PIZ since narratives of this history have been constructed irrespective of them for so long. Except that narratives do exist that have countered the silences.

A notable example is the description of the PIZ archive (Rudny 2003) that can be found on the Lund University Library's "Witnessing Genocide" web page (LUB n.d.), where the digitalized material from the PIZ collection is indexed and can be accessed. This comprehensive and competent history of PIZ and its archive dates to 2003 and was written by historian Paul Rudny, who worked extensively with the PIZ archive and contributed to its cataloging, description, and digitization. Not only does Rudny describe how survivors collected evidence from and conducted the interviews with other survivors but he also describes how it was Broel-Plater, not Łakociński, who carried out most of the work at PIZ between 1949 and 1972 (Rudny 2003, 13; see also Rudny 2007, 193). Yet even the easy availability of this information, which summarizes the sources in the archive, has ostensibly done little to change the dominant narratives.

According to Trouillot (2015, 48), the reason the availability of the sources in the archives and an accessible official summary of the facts contained within them has not demonstrably changed the narratives is that the enlargement of an empirical base and the availability of facts are not a solution in and of themselves. "New facts," Trouillot argues, "cannot emerge in a vacuum." Rather, he continues, "[t]hey will have to gain their right to existence in light of the field constituted by previously created facts. They may dethrone some of these facts, erase or qualify others. The point remains that sources occupy competing positions in the historical landscape" (48–49). Although the facts in the PIZ and Łakociński archives are not "new," they nonetheless emerged after the Swedish narratives about survivors in Sweden as refugees and PIZ were already firmly embedded, after retrospective significance was already established. And, as Trouillot indicates, altering that paradigm is not easy. One way this can be seen is in how narratives written in Polish and/or by Poles that circulate in Swedish public discourse differ from Swedish narratives but have rarely influenced or altered them.

An important distinction between what shall be called the "Polish" and "Swedish" narratives of PIZ and the repatriates in Sweden is that the Polish narratives recognize Polish repatriates, particularly those who remained in Sweden, not as passive and helpless recipients of Swedish humanitarian care but as activist-exiles working for and against national and transnational cultural and political forces (Dahl 2013; Kłonczyński 2016; Kruszewski 2001; Nowakowski 1992; Uggla 1997). The most comprehensive history of PIZ, written by Polish historian Eugeniusz S. Kruszewski (2001) and published in Denmark, draws extensively on the PIZ and Łakociński archives. Kruszewski presents a balanced narrative of the contributions made to PIZ by Łakociński and Polish repatriates, including Broel-Plater. Because it is in Polish, this work has been utilized by a limited number of non-Polish scholars.[8] However, considering how much this scholarship contributes to a more complete understanding of how transnational social and political processes were unfolding in Sweden in the immediate postwar period, it is difficult to understand why the monograph has never been translated into Swedish or English. But, to be fair, other Polish narratives about repatriates in Sweden and/or PIZ, even when translated (e.g., Uggla 1997),[9] have seemingly had relatively little impact on the corresponding Swedish narratives.

Of course, silences have entered Polish narratives as well. Perhaps the most relevant to this chapter is how the activist roles of female Polish repatriates in general and of Broel-Plater specifically have been neglected or minimized. Kruszewski's (2001) history of PIZ stands as a notable exception, although he does not give insight into Broel-Plater's long-term importance in relation to PIZ beyond citing in full Łakociński's written eulogy of her (114–16). In other works, such as Polish-Swedish scholar Andrzej Nils Uggla's (1997) monograph on Poles in Sweden during and after the Second World War, which includes an examination of PIZ, Broel-Plater is barely mentioned. And, in an article about the thousand-year history of Polish women in Sweden and how they "fought for the Polish cause" in exile, Polish-Swedish journalist Tadeusz Nowakowski (2004) does not mention Broel-Plater even though she is included in a biographical dictionary of Poles in Sweden that he compiled (Nowakowski 1992, 37–38). The reason for this may be that Nowakowski's focus is not so much on Polish women's activism in Sweden as it is on the *wives* of Polish activists whose actions, he suggests, were merely an extension of their husbands' activism. For instance, referring to the activities of Polish women who came to Sweden as repatriates, some of whom were associated with PIZ, he remarks: "It is characteristic that they were mostly the wives of the main activists of the Polish emigration in Sweden, which at the same time testified to the extremely patriotic attitudes of these Polish families" (Nowakowski 2004, 4). Broel-Plater's husband died in the Dachau concentration camp, apparently precluding her and her activism for Polish causes in Sweden from this narrative.

So far, the analysis has focused mainly on some of the ways silences have entered the making of sources, narratives, and history, and little on how they have entered into the making of archives. This has been reserved for the last since it ties together this part of the chapter and the next. When Broel-Plater died in 1972, her personal documents, letters, literary works, and so on – what effectively constituted her personal archive – were left to the person she was closest to in Sweden: Łakociński.[10] Following Łakociński's death in 1987, his personal papers were donated to the Lund University Library, and this material became "Zygmunt Łakociński's Archive" (Rudny 2003, 15). Except that among Łakociński's papers were Broel-Plater's papers, and the latter were not indexed as a separate archive but instead became categorized within the Łakociński archive as "*Handlingar rörande Ludwika Broel Plater*" (Documents concerning Ludwika Broel Plater).[11] There is little to indicate in the index of the Łakociński archive (Alvin n.d.), or anywhere else that this is not just material "concerning" her but is *her archive*.[12]

Once again, this silence did not necessarily entail deliberation. Nonetheless, insofar as archives "convey authority and set the rules for credibility and interdependence" and "help select the stories that matter" (Trouillot 2015, 52), this particular silence has, arguably, significantly contributed to the perpetuation of the other silences by inadvertently reinforcing the notion that Broel-Plater was not an agent in her own history. The purpose of the next part of the chapter is to begin to rectify this by drawing on some of her own and other sources to construct a new narrative that recognizes her historical agency and significance, uncovers her powerful voice, and provides a perspective currently missing from history.

An alternative narrative

The introduction to this chapter presented the principle that public discourse has the power to shape if, how, and the extent to which the people and events of the past are visible, while the previous section demonstrated that the material available to construct a narrative about Ludwika Broel-Plater that is different to those already embedded is readily available. Having unearthed silences in the existing narratives, this part of the chapter utilizes previously neglected sources that endow Broel-Plater with retrospective significance (Trouillot 2015, 58).

In May 1957, just a few months before she was granted Swedish citizenship,[13] Ludwika Broel-Plater described her lifelong commitment to Poland and social work in a letter to Reverend Czesław Chmielewski, rector of the Polish Catholic Mission in Sweden. She characterized this letter as her "political testament" and explained that she started what she described as her social and political activity in 1905, when she was just 20 years old (ZL n.d., 41). By her own and other accounts, this included but was not limited to working as an educator, a social reformer, and a political activist, not to mention a playwright (ZL n.d., 41; SUK n.d.). Some 35 years later, on August 25, 1940, she swore a military oath that she described as committing her to "Serving the Polish cause to the last drop of blood, to the last breath" (ZL n.d., 41). This oath was clearly a watershed moment in her life. But, aside from being an overtly political commitment that made her a soldier in the Polish Home Army[14] and ultimately led to her arrest, torture, and imprisonment by the Nazis, the way she carried out her oath was consistent with how she had previously conducted her life. According to Łakociński, her house in Warsaw served as a transfer point for aid to the Jewish ghetto, and this activity was what led to her arrest in 1941 (ZL n.d., 41).

In Ravensbrück concentration camp, she continued her work as an educator by teaching clandestine courses (ZL n.d., 41). She was also a supportive and motherly figure to both Jewish and non-Jewish prisoners, something attested to in the archival sources. For instance, the non-Jewish French survivor of Ravensbrück Germaine Tillion – who, unlike Broel-Plater, is today well-known as a member of the French Resistance and for her postwar activism – wrote to Broel-Plater in 1949, "You may not remember me in Ravensbrück, but I knew you and have the fondest memories of you" (ZL n.d., 41). Surviving objects now in public collections also demonstrate her importance to other prisoners, such as the remarkably fine and delicate autograph album given to her by her fellow prisoners in Pawiak Prison in 1941 (ZL n.d., 42) and the small handmade tokens of appreciation gifted to her in Ravensbrück (e.g., Kringla Riksantikvarieämbetet n.d.; see Figures 8.2 and 8.3).[15]

Liberation from Ravensbrück and refuge in Sweden saw her continuing along a similar trajectory despite severe damage to her physical health and a precarious existence as a refugee in an unfamiliar country. Before joining PIZ in February 1946, she became actively involved in the Polish organization Towarzystwo Przyjaciół Szwecji (Friends of Sweden), founding and serving as the chairperson for the branch in the Doverstorp refugee camp for Polish women (ZL n.d., 43 t). She also began her work with PIZ before she was officially employed, conducting interviews in the refugee camp.[16] When government funding for PIZ ended in late 1946, she remained in Lund to continue the institute's work without remuneration.

Although Łakociński wrote after her death that of all her many activities she was most strongly associated with PIZ (ZL n.d., 41), Broel-Plater's work with PIZ was just one of the ways she continued her commitment to social work and fulfilled her soldier's oath in Sweden. In Lund, the apartment where she safeguarded the PIZ collection became, in Łakociński's words, "a center of Polishness known in the wide world, mainly in Sweden and Poland" (ZL n.d., 41). Her letters tend to characterize her apartment as a Polish cultural, literary, and political salon (PIZ n.d., 48), but hints of how she used it as a base to fulfill her commitment to social work can be seen in documents like a 1947 police report (required for refugees in Sweden), which notes that her landlord observed her making and serving soup to Poles in need the previous winter (SUK n.d.). She also continued to pursue her literary work, in which she appears to have found catharsis. "I've taken revenge on the Nazis in my Ravensbrück comedy," she wrote in a letter to Łakociński (PIZ n.d., 48).

Contrary to the portrayal of Broel-Plater as a fragile old woman, she did all of this while supporting herself financially by working as

Figure 8.2: An autograph book given to Ludwika Broel-Plater from her fellow inmates in Pawiak Prison in Warsaw in 1941. This is among her documents contained in the Zygmunt Łakociński Archive at Lund University Library. Author's personal photo.

Figure 8.3: A green cross made of a toothbrush handle in the Ravensbrück concentration camp and presented to Ludwika Broel-Plater by a Jewish prisoner in February 1944. In the collection of *Kulturen*, Lund, Sweden. Image courtesy of the Carlotta Database, https://carl.kulturen.com/web/object/186626.

a so-called archive worker, first with PIZ and then for many years as a literary translator at Lund University (SUK n.d.; ZL n.d., 41).[17] She also contributed to the financial considerations of PIZ by renting out rooms in her apartment (PIZ n.d., 48). Her satisfaction with the circumstances of her paid work was low, however, at least in 1954, when she complained in a letter about the "fate of the great number of Polish intellectuals in Sweden," including herself and Łakociński. The position of archive worker, she explained, was "basically an intellectual worker created against the background of local emigration conditions" who, in her view, was rarely given work appropriate to his or her intellect and skills and did not receive sufficient recognition (ZL n.d., 41). This assessment was made even as her employer and co-workers wrote glowing letters of recommendation that supported her application to become a Swedish citizen (JD n.d.).

The conditions she described were shared by others and caused many Polish intellectuals to leave Sweden (Kłonczyński 2013, 40–41). But, although her adult daughter was in Poland, Broel-Plater made it clear from an early date that she "did not want to return to Poland as long as the country was controlled by the Russians because she feared for her safety" (SUK n.d.). The undercurrent in much of her archival material is that she believed she could do much to serve Polish independence and other causes in exile. While Sweden had become the site of that exile by chance, her decision to remain in the country appears to have been at least partly driven by her deliberate decision to make PIZ a central conduit for her commitment to Polish causes in exile. Evidence of this can be found in a 1949 letter she wrote to Łakociński:

> So as for the Institute [PIZ], remaining here as its only member active in the area of Lund, I undertake with all goodwill the work which will be required of me to maintain and continue to operate this institution. Understanding, however, my responsibility towards Polish society for continuing work in such difficult conditions as we have here today, as well as the enormity of this work … I now wish to do everything in my power to help you in this work and to maintain this institute in such a form as will be required to preserve its integrity. (PIZ n.d., 48)

She fulfilled this oath as she had sworn to do in 1940, to the last drop of blood and last breath. During what Łakociński described following her death as "[t]he last stage of her extremely active life, covering almost a quarter of a century" (ZL n.d., 41), she remained, as ever, an activist, educator, and soldier. She acknowledged the continuity of her commitments in the 1957 letter to Reverend Chmielewski by referring to what she had accomplished during what amounted at that point to 70 years of life and 50 years of social work activity: "If my words and social work in exile contribute to the erection of a common front for the defense of Polish interests and a dignified representation of our country abroad, I will consider my soldier's oath kept" (ZL n.d., 41).

In closing the letter, she expressed her hope "that at the moment when my soul will give its report to God, my earthly grave will be decorated with a well-worn soldier's cap" (ibid.). In figurative terms at least, this ambition was fulfilled. Following her death on February 28, 1972, Ludwika Broel-Plater was buried in the Northern Cemetery in Lund, close to the memorial monument to the victims of Nazi concentration camps that she had initiated and led the effort to erect in 1963. Around her are buried many of the compatriots whom she swore to help and support.

Conclusion: Unearthing silences, nuancing history

Starting with the question of what makes someone or something historical, this chapter has shown how Ludwika Broel-Plater and other Polish survivors of Nazi persecution involved with PIZ have been dehistoricized by Swedish public discourse since they arrived in Sweden as repatriates in 1945. Although Broel-Plater and other repatriates like her were active agents in transnationally significant events unfolding in the early postwar period and there is ample material evidence to demonstrate this, narrative constructions in Swedish public discourse have rarely historicized them as anything other than passive recipients of Swedish humanitarian relief. Broel-Plater and other repatriates have thus bolstered Swedish national narratives of the Second World War and the Holocaust but have themselves remained "unheard" in these histories (see Chapter 1, this volume). But this chapter has gone beyond merely proving this point. Rather, it has illustrated through Broel-Plater how historians and other scholars can retrieve refugees' experiences and make them a part of the historical record (ibid.) by returning to archival sources, which exist in relative abundance, and constructing alternative narratives that recognize the previously unheard voices and allow them to speak for themselves. At the same time, it has neither negated the Swedish national context nor contested Sweden's humanitarian work of the early postwar period. Instead, by unearthing some of the silences in the existing narratives and incorporating the hitherto neglected history of Ludwika Broel-Plater, it has placed these important aspects of the events of Swedish history into a more nuanced transnational context.

Notes

1 Unless otherwise noted, all translations are by the author.
2 The term used in Sweden was *repatriandi*.
3 In Polish, Polski Instytut Źródłowy, abbreviated to PIŹ; in Swedish, Polska Källinstitutet i Lund, abbreviated to PIZ. I have adopted the English usage of the Lund University Library, which holds the PIZ collection. On the repatriates' contributions to PIZ, see Victoria Van Orden Martínez, *Afterlives: Jewish and Non-Jewish Polish Survivors of Nazi Persecution in Sweden Documenting Nazi Atrocities, 1945–1946*, PhD dissertation, Linköping University, 2023.
4 To my knowledge, other researchers have not acknowledged this information and have used the date of the official contract between Łakociński and Lund University Library (1974) as the date researchers first had access to PIZ archival material. My thanks to Tomasz Lesniak, library assistant at Lund University Library's Department of Special Collections, for sharing my enthusiasm over this finding.
5 This did not include, for example, the witness testimonies and prisoner transport lists, which had been sent to the US for safekeeping.
6 My thanks to Tomasz Lesniak for providing me with the dimensions of the archival volumes.
7 As Zygmunt Łakociński noted in the cited memorandum, the PIZ collection was available at the Lund University Library starting around 1964, although this did not include the complete collection. For example, the witness testimonies did not enter the collection until the early 1970s and were not available to researchers until the mid-1990s. The PIZ archive is increasingly available in a digitalized form online. Zygmunt Łakociński's archive has been available to researchers in the university library since the early 2000s. See, e.g., Rudny (2003, 15).
8 Some of the exceptions have been cited.
9 This monograph was originally published in Polish and subsequently translated into Swedish.
10 My thanks again to Tomasz Lesniak for confirming my hypothesis about this.
11 This material comprises five volumes (41–45) in the Łakociński archive.
12 In addition to her material, one of the volumes (41) also includes material related to her death, including tributes written by Zygmunt Łakociński.
13 She was granted Swedish citizenship on July 12, 1957 (SUK n.d.).
14 In Polish, Armia Krajowa (AK); this was a branch of the Polish underground resistance movement during the Nazi occupation of Poland.

15 A cross made of a toothbrush handle given to Ludwika Broel-Plater in 1944, held by Kulturen, with an image available at Kringla. Of relevance to this chapter is that the online descriptions of this and other objects provide substantially more information about Łakociński than about Broel-Plater.

16 She was officially employed with PIZ starting February 11, 1946, but several testimonies in the PIZ collection that she was responsible for are dated January 1946.

17 Her literary works can be found in the Łakociński archive, volumes 43–45.

Bibliography

Alvin. n.d. "ŁAKOCIŃSKI, Zygmunt Otto Roman (1905–1987)". Accessed December 8, 2022. https://www.alvin-portal.org/alvin/attachment/document/alvin-record:64405/ATTACHMENT-0006.pdf.

Arbetet. 1966. "Nazistoffers handarbeten till Kulturen". April 1.

Banko, Lauren, Katarzyna Nowak, and Peter Gatrell. 2021. "What Is Refugee History, Now?" Journal of Global History Journal of Global History 17 (1):1–19. https://doi.org/10.1017/S1740022821000243.

Dagens Nyheter. 1966. "Nazifångers handarbeten på utställning i Lund". April 5.

Dahl, Izabela A. 2013. "Ausschluss und Zugehörigkeit polnische jüdische Zwangsmigration in Schweden nach dem Zweiten Weltkrieg". PhD thesis, Metropol.

Dahl, Izabela A. 2021. "Witnessing the Holocaust: Jewish Experiences and the Collection of the Polish Source Institute in Lund". In Early Holocaust Memory in Sweden: Archives, Testimonies and Reflections, edited by Johannes Heuman and Pontus Rudberg, 67–91. Basingstoke and New York: Palgrave Macmillan.

Foucault, Michel. (1969) 2002. The Archaeology of Knowledge. Translated by A. M. Sheridan Smith. Routledge Classics. London: Routledge.

Gatrell, Peter. 2017. "Refugees—What's Wrong with History?" Journal of Refugee Studies 30 (2): 170–89. https://doi.org/10.1093/jrs/few013.

Gerner, Kristian. 2011. "The Holocaust and Memory Culture: The Case of Sweden". In Historicizing the Uses of the Past, edited by Helle Bjerg, Claudia Lenz, and Erik Thorstensen, 91–106. Bielefeld: Transcript Verlag.

JD (Justitiedepartementet). n.d. "1957-07-12 M21 Broel Plater". Riksarkivet, Stockholm, Sweden.

Kłonczyński, Arnold. 2013. "Sweden as a Temporary State of the Polish Emigration to America". In East Central Europe in Exile Volume 1: Transatlantic Migrations, edited by Anna Mazurkiewicz, 35–47. Newcastle-upon-Tyne: Cambridge Scholars Publishing.

Kłonczyński, Arnold. 2016. "Nationally and Religiously: Commemorations in the Life of the Polish Diaspora in Sweden in 1945–1989". Polish American Studies 73 (2): 83–97. https://doi.org/10.5406/poliamerstud.73.2.0083.

Kringla Riksantikvarieämbetet. n.d. "Kors". Accessed December 10, 2022. https://www.kringla.nu/kringla/objekt?referens=Kulturen/objekt/186626.

Kruszewski, Eugeniusz Stanisław. 2001. Polski Instytut Źródłowy w Lund (1939-1972): Zarys historii i dorobek. London and Copenhagen: Polski Uniwersytet na Obczyźnie; Instytut Polsko-Skandynawski.

Kushner, Tony and Katharine Knox. 1999. *Refugees in an Age of Genocide: Global, National and Local Perspectives during the Twentieth Century*. London and Portland, Oregon: Frank Cass.

LUF (Lund University Foundation). n.d. "Ravensbrück Archive – Witnesses of the Holocaust". Accessed December 6, 2022. https://lunduniversityfoundation.org/ravensbruck-archive-fundraising-project/.

LUB (Lund University Library). n.d. "Witnessing Genocide". Accessed 7 December 2022. https://www.ub.lu.se/hitta/digitala-samlingar/witnessing-genocide.

Mahendran, Kesi, Nicola Magnusson, Caroline Howarth, and Sarah Scuzzarello. 2019. "Reification and the Refugee: Using a Counterposing Dialogical Analysis to Unlock a Frozen Category". *Journal of Social and Political Psychology* 7 (1): 577–97. https://doi.org/10.5964/jspp.v7i1.656.

Malkki, Liisa. 1996. "Speechless Emissaries: Refugees, Humanitarianism, and Dehistoricization". *Cultural Anthropology* 11 (3): 377–404. https://doi.org/10.1525/can.1996.11.3.02a00050.

Marfleet, Philip. 2013. "Explorations in a Foreign Land: States, Refugees, and the Problem of History". *Refugee Survey Quarterly* 32 (2): 14–34. https://doi.org/10.1093/rsq/hdt006.

Martínez, Victoria Van Orden. 2023. "Afterlives: Jewish and Non-Jewish Polish Survivors of Nazi Persecution in Sweden Documenting Nazi Atrocities, 1945–1946". PhD diss., Linköping University.

Nowakowski, Tadeusz. 1992. *Polacy w Szwecji: Słownik biograficzny emigracji Polskiej w Szwecji*. Tullinge, Sweden: Polonica.

Nowakowski, Tadeusz. 2004. "Polski w Szwecji – historia tysiąca lat". *Nowa Gazeta Polska* 7.

Östling, Johan. 2011. "The Rise and Fall of Small-State Realism: Sweden and the Second World War". In *Nordic Narratives of the Second World War: National Historiographies Revisited*, edited by Henrik Stenius, Mirja Österberg, and Johan Östling, 127–47. Lund: Nordic Academic Press.

PIZ (The Polish Research Institute in Lund). n.d. Archive, Lund University Library, Lund, Sweden.

Resnick, Robert D. 2018. "Voices from the Holocaust: The Story of the Ravensbrück Archive". *Svensk Teologisk Kvartalskrift* 4: 267–80.

Rudny, Paul. 2003. "Polski Instytut Źródłowy w Lund (The Polish Research Institute in Lund): A Presentation of the Archives". Lund University Library.

Rudny, Paul. 2007. "Zygmunt Lakocinski och polska källinstitutets arkiv i Lund 1939–87". In *Skandinavien och Polen. Möten, relationer och ömsesidig påverkan*, edited by Barbara Törnquist-Plewa. Lund: Lund University.

SUK (*Statens utlänningskommission*). n.d. *Kanslibyrån*, "F 1 B-5698 Broel Plater Ludwika Ida". *Riksarkivet*, Stockholm, Sweden.

SDS (*Sydsvenska Dagbladet Snällposten*). n.d. 1966. "Lunda-polacker kände pust från koncentrationslägren". April 5.

Thor Tureby, Malin. 2013. "Swedish Jews and the Jewish Survivors". In *Reaching a State of Hope: Refugees, Immigrants and the Swedish Welfare State, 1930–2000*, edited by Mikael Byström and Pär Frohnert, 145–64. Nordic Academic Press.

Trouillot, Michel-Rolph. 1999. "Historiography of Haiti". In *General History of the Caribbean*. Vol 6., *Methodology and Historiography of the Caribbean*, edited by Barry W. Higman, 451–77. London: UNESCO.

Trouillot, Michel-Rolph. 2015. *Silencing the Past (20th Anniversary Edition): Power and the Production of History*. Boston, MA: Beacon Press.

Uggla, Andrzej Nils. 1997. *I Nordlig Hamn: Polacker i Sverige under Andra Världskriget*. Translated by Lennart Ilke. Uppsala multiethnic papers: 40. Uppsala: Centrum för multietnisk forskning, Uppsala Universitet.

Wagrell, Kristin. 2020. "Chorus of the Saved. Constructing the Holocaust Survivor in Swedish Public Discourse, 1943–1966". PhD thesis, Linköping University Press.

ZL (*Zygmunt Łakociński Arkiv*). n.d. Lund University Library, Lund, Sweden.

CHAPTER 9

Narratives on refugeeness in Sweden

Shifting representations over time

Dalia Abdelhady
Lund University
Minja Mårtensson
Independent researcher

Abstract

This study examines shifts in Swedish media representations of
refugees over three decades by analyzing coverage of refugees from
Yugoslavia (1992), Syria (2015), and Ukraine (2022) in the newspaper *Dagens Nyheter*. Through frame analysis, the research reveals how
media narratives reconcile Sweden's humanitarian self-image with
increasingly restrictive refugee policies. While institutional responsibility remains the dominant frame across all periods, representing
65 percent of coverage, significant variations emerge in the portrayal
of different refugee groups. Coverage of Yugoslav refugees focused on
bureaucratic management and deservingness, Syrian refugee coverage emphasized both humanitarian concerns and security threats, and
Ukrainian refugee coverage highlighted institutional barriers to integration while portraying them as culturally compatible and deserving.

How to cite this book chapter:
Abdelhady, Dalia and Minja Mårtensson. 2025. "Narratives on refugeeness in Sweden:
shifting representations over time." In *Forced Migrants in Nordic Histories*, edited
by Johanna Leinonen, Miika Tervonen, Hans Otto Frøland, Christhard Hoffmann,
Seija Jalagin, Heidi Vad Jønsson and Malin Thor Tureby, 225–251. Helsinki:
Helsinki University Press. https://doi.org/10.33134/HUP-32-10.

The study introduces the concept of "inclusive othering" to describe the subtle mechanisms of differentiation in Ukrainian refugee coverage. These findings demonstrate how media framing contributes to the politicization of refugees while maintaining Sweden's self-perception as a humanitarian nation, even as policies become more restrictive.

Introduction

Since the end of the Second World War, Sweden has been a net immigration country. In addition to the international recruitment of foreign labor to meet the needs of the expanding industries, the number of asylum seekers (despite being modest) steadily increased up until the early 1990s. One important consequence of increased immigration is the self-image of Sweden as a humanitarian superpower and a safe haven for refugees (for example, Abiri 2000; Idevall Hagren 2022; Valenta and Bunar 2010). A humanitarian self-image notwithstanding, recent policies and analyses document restrictive tendencies governed by concerns about national security, identity, and resources (Krzyżanowski 2018). Since the 1990s, neoliberal welfare reforms in Sweden have increasingly framed refugees as potential economic burdens, strategically constructing their presence as a threat to the social security system (Mulinari and Neergaard 2022). Our analysis contributes to such understandings through investigating the forms of representation in mainstream media over time. This chapter examines how mainstream media representations of refugees reflect and reconcile Sweden's humanitarian self-image with restrictive policy approaches. As we focus on mainstream media discussions of refugees from former Yugoslavia, Syria, and Ukraine, we provide an analysis of representations in various historical and sociopolitical contexts that contribute to a more comprehensive inquiry into media representation of refugees in general.

Constructions of refugees and refugee crises play out in the public sphere, of which media is a significant component. The general agreement among researchers is that media's portrayals of refugees hold great power in shaping public perceptions, influencing societal attitudes, and contributing to the construction of the "other" (for example Georgiou and Zaborowski 2017; Krzyżanowski 2018). An important example is that the concept of a "refugee crisis" in 2015 was to a large extent constructed by the media and led to the increased politization of refugees (Krzyżanowski, Triandafyllidou, and Wodak 2018). Throughout this study, we critically examine the politicization of refugees in the media and its implications for the construction of otherness. The politicization of refugees refers to the instrumentalization of their plights for political purposes, often leading to the reinforcement of stereotypes and marginalization of refugee populations. By analyzing media narratives, we shed light on the ways political agendas and public discourses shape the perception of otherness, impacting both refugees and the broader society. The mediatization and politicization of refugees in the media needs to be historicized, however, in order to account for the ways these processes emerge and change over time. This chapter investigates the representation of refugees in Sweden over the last three decades.

Our analysis highlights the ways the representation of refugees is a product of ideas about nationality and ethnic difference that intertwine and intersect in various ways to inform our understandings of self and refugee other. Specifically, our analysis highlights the institutional logic of media representation that is common to all three time periods. That institutional logic provides a foundation for calls for restricting borders for the first two groups. Importantly, the institutional logic allows for a construction of an understanding of the self (Swedes/Sweden) as humanitarian and benevolent while also problematizing refugees as fraudulent, threatening, and oftentimes undeserving. By unpacking the complexities and ambiguities of media portrayals, we can uncover the complex interplay of power dynamics, societal attitudes, and political agendas that contribute to the construction of otherness. Furthermore, focusing on Yugoslav, Syrian, and Ukrainian refugees allows us to explore the nuanced variations in these constructions across different contexts over time.

In the next section, we review key arguments on the role of media in the social construction of refugees, including a discussion of othering as an element in the representation of refugees in general and in Sweden in specific. We then move to describe the methodological strategies followed in data collection and analysis, including a discussion of framing as an analytical tool. The following section presents key findings from our data, which are presented separately by group. These key findings are discussed in the conclusion section in light of their similarities and differences. The chapter concludes by stressing that, in the Swedish context, the focus on institutions in media discourses on refugees was key in reconciling an understanding of Sweden as benevolent with a restrictive policy environment that works to exclude refugees.

The role of the media in othering refugees

The mainstream media plays an important role in shaping perceptions, attitudes, and actions toward the issues they represent, and the representation of refugees is no exception. Studying how refugees and refugee-related events are represented in mainstream media is therefore necessary to understanding how society makes sense of what refugees are and what to do about them. With regard to migration in general, negative media coverage was found to correlate with negative public attitudes toward immigration (Crawley 2005; Jacobs, Meeusen, and d'Haenens 2016). It is an over-simplification to assume that media coverage of migration, refugees, or any topic for that matter, can be straight-forwardly negative or positive (Binder and Allen 2015; Clare and Abdelhady 2016). Instead, media coverage of any topic, but especially those related to migration and refugees, is found to point toward contestations and contradictions (Clare and Abdelhady 2016, see also Abdelhady 2019).

Contested narratives notwithstanding, negative portrayals of refugees are well documented in the research field. While generally constructed as a "flood" or "tide" that would "engulf" the host country (Pickering 2001; Pruitt 2019), they also pose an eminent threat to the nation-state (Esses, Medianu, and Lawson 2013) or as victims or both at once (Don and Lee 2014). However, there is also a tendency in the media to occasionally provide a more nuanced and humanizing representation of refugees (Abdelhady and Delioğlu 2022; Abdelhady and Malmberg 2018; Steimel 2010). Despite attempts toward a more humanized representation, however, there continues a strong focus on the othering of refugees in news media. Regardless of whether refugees are depicted as a threat or as victims, they are in both cases assigned traits that are different from members of the host society. The notion of otherness, as it pertains to refugees, encompasses the process through which certain groups are portrayed as different, foreign, or culturally distinct.

Othering refugees is also a strategy observed by analysts of Swedish media's representation of refugees (Brune 2000; Burns, Machado, and Hellgren 2007; Hultén 2007; Nohrstedt 2006; Tigervall 2007). While othering is analyzed in relation to various groups of refugees, media representation of Islam and Muslims reflects an even stronger negative trend. A report on Swedish news from 2015 by the Equality Ombudsman, a Swedish government agency for safeguarding against discrimination, concluded that "almost all articles with a representation of Muslims relates either directly or indirectly to violence, threats or tension in society" (Axner 2015, 8). Abdelhady and Malmberg (2018) show that the othering of refugees in 2015 relied on a specific understanding of Islam as incompatible with Swedish values and as a threat to security and national cohesion. Additionally, they observe that, when simultaneously referring to refugees and Islam, newspaper articles focus more on conflict and security threats as opposed to an observed tendency toward humanization when referring to refugees more generally.

Analyzing the othering of refugees in media representation has important relevance to understanding the self-constructions of nation and national identity. Swedish identity is based on a specific historical conceptualization of the other, even though who the other is and what traits are ascribed to otherness changes over time (Idevall Hagren 2022). The idea of a Swedish national identity therefore relies on a binary construction where some traits are considered "Swedish" whereas some other traits are viewed as going against the concept of Swedishness (ibid.; Hultén 2007). Importantly, media representation of refugees underscores the self-representation of Sweden as a "good, just and safe country populated by benevolent and righteous people" (Hultén 2007, 31). Swedish diligence and good behavior are also often emphasized as qualities lacking among refugees (ibid., 49–50). It is important to note that the othering of refugees can follow different strategies, but a number of researchers emphasize that benevolence, compassion, and a sense of responsibility toward refugees do not preclude victimization and securitization.

Methodology

We focus on three case studies, which reflect important time points in Sweden's contemporary history. While the number of annual asylum applications in Sweden has generally stayed below 30,000, two specific instances stand out from that general pattern. According to the Swedish Migration Agency, there were over 80,000 asylum applica-tions made in 1992, but in 1993 the number dropped to less than half that number. The number of applications rose again in 2015, this time reaching 160,000, only to drastically drop to less than 30,000 in 2016. In 1992, the large majority of applicants were from former Yugoslavia, and in 2015 from Syria and the representation of these two groups con-stitute two of our case studies. Our third case study focuses on refugees from Ukraine, as the most recent refugee group arriving in Sweden.

We investigate the representation of refugees in one major main-stream newspaper, *Dagens Nyheter* (thereafter DN). DN describes itself politically as "independent liberal." While newspapers in Sweden may still reflect original political affiliations, the media landscape in the country is increasingly driven by market interest and newsworthiness rather than political motivations (Strömbäck and Nord 2008). Previ-ous research on how Syrian refugees are represented in three Swed-ish newspapers, each with distinct political leanings, shows how these newspapers, driven by market considerations, ultimately converged on similar framing approaches (Abdelhady 2019). A such, similar results can be expected in other major daily newspapers in Sweden. Mean-while, focusing on the coverage of refugees in one newspaper allows for a comparison of how narratives have changed over time in rela-tion to different refugee groups. Articles were selected through the online archive Retriever by combining simple search words such as "Ukraine" and "refugees." The search was restricted to the most intense time period in terms of refugee reception in each of the three cases. Some articles were later discarded as they were not deemed relevant, for instance if the focus was only on war or if they mainly addressed refugees outside of Sweden. Our sample includes 66 articles on Yugo-slavs, 140 on Syrians, and 155 on Ukrainians that were published in DN during 1992, 2015, and 2022, respectively. The observed increased number of articles over time reflects the mediatization of refugees in Sweden.

Framing as a theoretical lens

We use "framing" to explain and understand how media shape and construct public discourses around refugees, and how this has changed over time within the Swedish context. According to Entman (1993, 52), framing is a process by which communicators "select some aspects of perceived reality and make them more salient in a communicating text, in such a way as to promote a particular problem definition, causal interpretation, moral evaluation, and/or treatment recommendation." In other words, the way that the media frames issues related to refugees can affect how audiences understand and respond to the issue at hand. Previous research shows that media frames, pertaining to various issues, can roughly be divided into five categories (Semetko and Valkenburg 2000). These are conflict, human interest, morality, economic consequences, and responsibility. We utilize the same frames in coding the collected news articles as a first stage in analyzing the content.

The conflict frame portrays refugees as potential threats to host communities, emphasizing the need for stricter immigration controls. This frame presents refugees as strains on national resources, competitors for jobs, and threats to security, social cohesion, and welfare systems. Such narratives often criminalize refugees and can promote xenophobic attitudes. The human-interest frame focuses on refugee suffering and appeals for compassion through personal stories and emotional narratives. While effective at humanizing refugees, this approach can inadvertently reinforce stereotypes and create a paradoxical perception of refugees as both abstract and tangible. It may also oversimplify complex experiences and neglect broader structural factors. The morality frame differs from human interest by emphasizing universal values like justice, fairness, and social responsibility rather than individual perspectives. This frame sometimes overlaps with responsibility/institutional framing and examines ethical implications of refugee-related policies. The responsibility/institutional frame attributes accountability and proposes solutions by identifying actors – whether institutions, individuals, or groups – responsible for refugee-related issues. Our research aligns with previous studies of the Swedish media (Abdelhady 2020), showing this combined institutional-responsibility frame as the dominant narrative across all analyzed groups. The economic frame evaluates refugee-related financial impacts, addressing both costs and benefits. While economic considerations typically carry significant weight in public discourse, our analysis shows limited use of this frame in Swedish media coverage.

Table 9.1 presents the distribution of articles by group and frame. While articles often incorporate multiple frames, categorization reflects the most salient frame as determined by the authors.[1]

Table 9.1: Distribution of newspaper articles by frame and group

	Conflict	Human interest	Economic consequences	Institutional responsibility	Morality	Total
From former Yugoslavia	9 (14%)	2 (3%)	4 (6%)	47 (71%)	4 (6 %)	66
From Syria	22 (16%)	25 (18%)	—	93 (66%)	—	140
From Ukraine	8 (5%)	29 (19%)	5 (3%)	95 (61%)	18 (12%)	155
Total	39 (10%)	56 (16%)	9 (2%)	235 (65%)	22 (6%)	361

The distribution reveals several key media framing patterns across refugee coverage. The most prevalent frame discusses institutional responsibilities toward refugees. Morality and economic consequences are rarely central themes. The human interest frame dramatically increased in Syrian and Ukrainian refugee coverage compared to Yugoslav refugee reporting, reflecting efforts to humanize refugees. Syrian refugees were frequently associated with both human-interest and conflict narratives, which suggests a more complex and potentially polarized narrative. Contrastingly, Ukrainian refugees were predominantly portrayed through human-interest perspectives with minimal conflict framing, providing a more consistent narrative about their deservedness as refugees. Notably, the morality frame, almost absent in Syrian and Yugoslav refugee coverage, emerged significantly in Ukrainian refugee reporting. This shift can potentially influence public empathy and policy responses, suggesting a more sympathetic narrative approach toward Ukrainian refugees.

Swedish media representations of refugees over time

Refugees from former Yugoslavia

The conflict in former Yugoslavia resulted in a series of wars and ethnic hostilities that took place in the 1990s following the breakup of the Socialist Federal Republic of Yugoslavia. The conflicts were primarily driven by ethnic and nationalist tensions among various groups within the region, including Serbs, Croats, Bosnians, Albanians, and others. Following the declaration of independence by Croatia and Slovenia in 1991, the Yugoslav government deployed armed forces and denounced these declarations as unconstitutional. Conflict spread and escalated when Bosnia and Herzegovina also declared independence in 1992. While the conflict continued to escalate and spread throughout the 1990s, 1992 marks significant population displacement, with millions of people being forced to leave their homes due to violence, ethnic cleansing, and other war-related factors. Many became refugees within the region, while others sought refuge in neighboring countries and farther afield in Western Europe. As with other forms of forced displacement, the experiences were marked by stories of suffering, loss, and human rights abuses. By the end of 1992, 80,000 refugees had arrived in Sweden. Most of those arriving at the time were ethnic Albanians from Kosovo, a region that in the eyes of Swedish media had so far been relatively spared from violence. Sweden was under a new rightist government for the first time in decades, and economic problems such as unemployment and inflation were widespread.

As media attention to refugees arriving from former Yugoslavia increased, the stories were dominated by a perception of institutional incapability to handle the unprecedented numbers. A large portion of the articles discuss the need for legal, political, and institutional reform to manage refugees and prevent a disruption of order. The "problem" with the refugees from Yugoslavia is conceptualized as a "bureaucratic dilemma" that has the potential to overwhelm institutions (Hellberg 1992a). As many from former Yugoslavia did not need visas to enter Sweden, news articles stressed that they arrive and live with relatives without going through any institutional process leading to a situation where Sweden has "no clue" how many there are (Flores 1992). The Immigration Office (Invandrarverket), which was the office responsible for receiving the refugees, was the focus of many articles, and its general director, Christina Rogestam, was frequently featured and quoted. In May 1992, as refugee arrivals increased, Rogestam warned of diminishing resources (Hellberg 1992b) and advocated for temporary residence permits to provide "breathing space" for asylum-seeking countries (DN 1992b). In June, she complained that the government had not responded to her office's request to announce a peace time crisis that would have given them the right to use schools and sport facilities for refugee housing (Hellberg 1992c). While Rogestam stressed that Invandrarverket was reaching the limit of what it could handle, a representative for the minister of migration asserted that "there is no need to panic" (Hellberg 1992c). An ambiguous portrayal of the situation was communicated as several articles stressed the seriousness of the situation and simultaneously Sweden's ability to deal with it.

Opinion pieces criticized the bureaucratic refugee response, arguing "it is not a question of being able, it is a question of wanting to" (DN 1992a) and questioning whether creating "panic sentiments" amid growing refugee influx and rising xenophobia was advisable (Narti 1992). The focus, however, remained on how institutions were to handle the number of refugees and the lack of control over regulating those numbers. A rapid state response in the form of visa requirements and temporary residency permits became the focus of the debate.

The bureaucratic dilemma posed by refugees from former Yugoslavia was established not only in light of institutional capacity to provide them with services but, more importantly, institutional desire to differentiate deserving and undeserving refugees. Newspaper articles debated refugee "deservedness," emphasizing the need to demonstrate that "the right people" were permitted to stay in Sweden (DN 1992g). The discussion of refugee deservedness differentiated ethnic groups from former Yugoslavia based on perceived asylum needs. Bosnian war refugees were seen as deserving protection, while young Macedonian men seeking employment were not. Kosovo Albanians occupied an intermediate position, facing potential discrimination and war risks but still lacking sufficiently strong grounds for asylum (DN 1992h). Media coverage drew distinctions between Bosnian and Kosovo refugees, highlighting varying perceptions of asylum eligibility. Bosnian refugees, predominantly Muslim and requiring visas, were viewed as legitimate due to ongoing conflicts. In contrast, Kosovo Albanians (both Muslim and Christian) were portrayed as economic migrants, with media calling for differential visa policies that would restrict their entry while easing access for Bosnian refugees, often critiquing arbitrary bureaucratic rules.

Kosovo Albanians became scapegoats for restrictive policies, portrayed as economic migrants causing a "mass exodus" (DN 1992e). Journalists argued for clear borders to deter residency hopes (DN 1992e), with media depicting young Albanian men as criminals prone to stealing and wandering streets (Granestrand and Ånnerud 1992). Despite refugees' desire to work, coverage focused on potential criminality and the need to combat it through employment (Engman 1992), ultimately calling for legal changes allowing deportation of those exhibiting "deviant behavior" (Brattberg and Sjöblom 1992).

Besides criminality, the lines of difference between Swedes and refugees from former Yugoslavia were also established along moral values that are used to accentuate Swedish reflexivity, rationality and benevolence. While refugees were presented as grateful and willing to "pay back," benevolence was stressed as an important aspect of Swedishness (Engman 1992). Readers were urged to forgo blanket assumptions about refugees, noting it was "unreflecting" to view all from former Yugoslavia as religious fundamentalists (DN 1992d). The Discrimination Ombudsman suggested that Swedes who "have the opportunity to think things through are both decent and understanding" (Vinterhed 1992). While critiquing bureaucratic processes as potentially going "against the spirit of Swedish refugee policy" (DN 1992c), the coverage simultaneously justified asylum policies through a framework of rationality and benevolence. This included arguments that early rejection of applications, limiting refugee numbers, and helping refugees near their homes could prevent ethnic cleansing and reduce trauma (Sjöblom 1992; DN 1992f).

The framing of refugee coverage reveals a complex narrative that attempts to reconcile racist or exclusionary attitudes with a self-image of moral rectitude. This dynamic is particularly evident in the case of reporting on Yugoslav refugees in Sweden. The analysis suggests that the institutional focus and language of "formal rationality" provided a convenient cover for denying asylum rights without overtly challenging Sweden's reputation as a humanitarian, welcoming state. The closing of an unoccupied refugee camp, as described in one article, exemplifies this dynamic. Neighboring residents objected to the camp on the grounds of environmental and safety concerns, rather than directly voicing opposition to having refugees in their community. The municipal authorities, in turn, invoked institutional rationales about the camp's unsanitary conditions and "unsafe" nature to justify its demolition. Notably, the article references the "tones of the national anthem" echoing over the empty camp after the decision, evoking a sense of patriotic pride and righteousness (Kihlberg 1992). This symbolic gesture suggests the underlying nationalist and exclusionary sentiments that motivated the residents' actions, despite the ostensibly neutral, institutional framing. By cloaking antirefugee attitudes in the language of formal procedure and environmental protection, the narrative upholds Sweden's image as a compassionate, rule-of-law society – while effectively denying asylum to the very individuals it is meant to protect. This dynamic points to the power of media framing to obscure the more pernicious undercurrents of xenophobia and racism, even as it maintains a veneer of objectivity and morality.

Refugees from Syria

In Syria, protests against President Bashar al-Assad erupted in 2011, resulting in military crackdowns on civilians. The conflict quickly escalated as various factions, sometimes supported by foreign powers, joined the fighting. The war has been characterized by extreme violence carried out against civilians, displacing millions from their homes and into neighboring countries. The protracted nature of the conflict and the worsening conditions in neighboring countries led many Syrians to seek asylum outside the region, particularly in Europe. In 2014, Sweden became the first country in Europe to grant immediate permanent residence to all Syrians within its territory. In what has been coined the long summer of migration in 2015, a total of 160,000 people applied for asylum, of whom 51,000 came from Syria. The sentiment in the public sphere quickly escalated from a mood of relative calm to the announcement of a crisis and the need for a "breathing space" on the border. Eventually this resulted in tightening border control between Sweden and Denmark and increased restrictions on asylum.

The media's portrayal of Syrian refugees in 2015 primarily focused on institutional responsibility, highlighting the pressure on the Migration Agency. Articles debated the institutional emergency, with one questioning: "Do we want to live in a society where human life has such small value?" (Egnell 2015). A letter to the editor passionately urged Sweden to maintain its humanitarian values and "welcome those who need protection" (DN 2015b). However, the sense of crisis was more acute compared to 1992, with attempts to justify the "crisis" interpretation. An editorial described the situation as a "painful reality" of overwhelmed institutions (Wolodarski 2015) "rather than a negative attitude towards strangers" (DN 2015d). This crisis narrative was directly used to justify asylum restrictions, framed as a rational response rather than xenophobia. While some blamed government agencies for unpreparedness (DN 2015f), the decision to restrict asylum was defended as "painful but necessary" (DN 2015e). Rationality and necessity were thus used to justify restrictions in asylum policy allowing a perception of the Swedish self to remain unaltered. DN simultaneously sought to affirm Sweden's antiracist character, noting that "Racism and xenophobia are concepts and ideas that Swedes are worried about and fear" (Sahlin 2015).

Eventually, the debate shifted to problematizing integration, warning that "[i]f integration does not work, the Swedish model will collapse" (DN 2015d). Syrian refugees were portrayed as needing to demonstrate gratitude and eagerness to integrate, with a psychologist suggesting that gratitude facilitates learning and "successful integration" (Helmersson 2015). Simultaneously Syrian refugees frequently failed to demonstrate this trait, as they were portrayed as complaining – about the cold weather or having to relocate – and unsympathetic toward Swedish rules (Holmberg 2015).

Despite minimal refugee representation in these debates, human-interest stories increased from 3 percent in 1992 to 18 percent in 2015, emphasizing refugees' individual experiences of "why people flee" (Orrenius 2015). These narratives often described Syrian refugees' journeys as reaching "pure heaven" in Sweden (By 2015). However, humanization did not preclude othering. As a number of articles report of unfathomable events leading Syrians to flee their country, the illegibility of their trauma was also stressed and linked to violence. Articles portrayed refugees as both victims and potential threats, with one highlighting their trauma's potential for violence. A Migration Agency security chief warned that traumatized asylum seekers "may become threatening towards public servants or other residents" (Lund 2015), creating a narrative of uncertainty similar to earlier descriptions of Yugoslav refugees. This framing constructed refugees as mentally unstable, inserting an element of suspicion about whether they were victims or potential perpetrators, echoing previous refugee representations that linked perceived boredom or frustration with institutional systems to potential deviance.

As elsewhere in Europe following the rise of the Islamic State and especially after the terror attacks in Paris in November 2015, there was anxiety in Sweden about terror attacks and connections were made between refugees and terrorists. The increased securitization shifted the media focus to control rather than reception. For example, terror experts were provided space claiming that Sweden's generous refugee policy might be exploited by terrorists hiding "within the refugee flow" (Holmgren 2015). This idea was repeated to increase suspicion about "people who are dishonest about their identity and who do not want to account for their past in their home country" (Engberg 2015). Within a narrative that blurred the lines between terror suspects and asylum seekers, asylum seekers were portrayed as potentially deceptive (see also DN 2015c). While refugees were portrayed as victims of terrorism, there was a risk that they would join terrorist organizations if not integrated into Swedish society (Engberg 2015; Eriksson 2015).

Previous research notes that media representations of Muslim refugees contained elements of subtle Islamophobia (Abdelhady and Malmberg 2018). Subtle Islamophobia (Moosavi 2015) does not openly display violence or outright hostility, which can sometimes make it harder to detect. Instead, it relies on coded stereotypes about Islam and Muslims that may result in harassment or discrimination. However, Islamophobia as a discourse results in both inclusionary and exclusionary practices (Wodak 2008). For example, one reporter, writing on refugees arriving, criticized right-wing warnings of a "Muslim invasion" in Europe and explained that "[t]hey're not the bearded mullah types at all" but included families and professionals who could afford staying in a hotel (Nevéus 2015). The article seeks to downplay the perceived threat refugees pose by portraying them as stereotypical victims of women and children in need of saving, and commenting on their material status. The result is an inclusion of the "good Muslim" or "good refugee," simultaneously entailing the silent exclusion of its opposite, the "bad" Muslim or refugee. That Sweden only welcomes good refugees was asserted: "Sweden must be able to set certain fundamental requirements for people who want to establish their residence here. For example, that they respect and adhere to Swedish legislation concerning the rights for Christians, Jews, women, and LGBTQ individuals to be free from harassment" (DN 2015a).

Ultimately, DN's coverage reflects Sweden's struggle to reconcile its self-image as a humanitarian, welcoming state with the political and social anxieties generated by the refugee influx. The frames employed – emphasizing institutional strain, selective humanization, and the specter of cultural threats – suggest an emerging narrative that seeks to uphold a veneer of benevolence, while subtly reinforcing exclusionary impulses and hierarchies of deservedness. This analysis underscores the media's pivotal role in shaping public discourse and policy responses to complex issues of immigration and belonging.

Refugees from Ukraine

Following the Russian invasion of Ukraine in February 2022, Ukrainian refugees started arriving in the EU, sparking debate about their reception. Shortly afterwards, the EU activated the Temporary Protection Directive (TPD), allowing Ukrainians the right of protection for one year without having to apply for asylum. Ukrainians could travel freely to Sweden and apply digitally for TPD. TPD minimized the pressure on the Migration Agency and other institutions dealing with the immediate reception, and Ukrainians did not have to wait for a decision to be granted (temporary) protection. The directive also allowed Ukrainians to benefit from the same (limited) rights and services available to asylum seekers in Sweden, including a daily subsidy and access to urgent health care.

Similar to the two other case studies, the majority of articles analyzed in the context of Ukrainian refugees also fall within the frame of institutional responsibility. At the beginning of the period examined, there is, similar to the other periods, a focus on the number of people expected to come to Sweden and the institutions' ability to receive them. DN reports, after the implementation of the TPD, that the government warned that the reception could become chaotic and characterized by disorder (DN 2022a). As an EU directive, the TPD eliminated debates about asylum policies that ensued at the beginning of the other two case studies. Nonetheless, in the initial period of uncertainty, an atmosphere of a looming crisis dominated the news in DN. Several articles stated that Sweden would not go back to what the situation was like in 2015 and there was an emphasis that Swedish institutions and civil society had learned from the previous crisis. Some of these articles convey that a crisis could be avoided through different measures, such as the equal distribution of refugees across the municipalities. A new law on equal distribution was enforced on July 1, 2022, after which the general director of the Migration Agency announced in DN that "order is significantly better" than in 2015 (Ribbenvik 2022). This shows that, although the situation was initially framed as a case of potential institutional exhaustion and crisis, those fears were quickly eradicated.

Instead, the focus turned to other issues, such as integration and identifying institutional obstacles that prevented the integration of Ukrainians. Stressing the need to "give the Ukrainian refugees an honest chance to establish themselves" (DN 2022b), journalists called for an increased daily subsidy to combat inflation. This is a stark contrast to the ways inflation was used to justify restrictive policies in 1992, and the rhetorical choice "between a poor retiree or a refugee in Malmö" that politicians had to make in 2015 (Orrenius 2015). Sympathy to the plight of Ukrainian refugees was encouraged in the readers by describing the refugees' inability to buy new clothes, meat and vegetables, or their favorite type of cheese (Fyrk 2022a). While utilizing a human-interest frame by interviewing refugees, the focus remained on the failure of bureaucracies to adapt to the current reality lived by Ukrainians in Sweden. The institutional logic was echoed when relying on the Swedish Consumer Agency's calculations to stress the insufficiency of the allowance (DN 2022c). In these examples, the deteriorating economic situation was used as an argument to increase the allowance to Ukrainians rather than restricting it. Consequently, Ukrainians were not seen as an economic burden putting a strain on welfare.

Language was also identified as "key to integration" (Lindeberg 2022). The exclusion of Ukrainians from Swedish for Immigrants (SFI) courses was criticized, stressing that Swedish language knowledge is a requirement for most jobs in Sweden (Fyrk 2022d; DN 2022b; DN 2022c). Even in cases where a Ukrainian refugee successfully found a job, other institutional barriers such as having a bank account might still be present (Fyrk 2022c). Similar to the stories criticizing economic allowances, this group of articles provides numerous personal narratives of Ukrainians who managed to find jobs. Using human-interest strategies to criticize institutional obstacles that hinder integration is a novel pattern, especially when compared to debates about integration taking place in 2015.

Overall, DN painted a picture of Ukrainians as ideal for Swedish society, but Swedish institutions failed them: "they are well educated" (Sundbeck 2022) and, despite not having access to SFI, they learn the language but "without getting their language skills documented" (Lindeberg 2022). And, when some might leave Sweden to another country, "it feels like Sweden has not prepared for receiving this kind of refugees" (Fyrk 2022e). As institutions failed Ukrainian refugees, their vulnerability to human trafficking (DN 2022c), labor exploitation (Fyrk 2022b), and prostitution (DN 2022b; Sokolnicki 2022) increased. Nonetheless, their cultural capital was emphasized as "many are incredibly driven, they seek employment and find their way to activities that are offered" (By 2022c).

Media coverage of Ukrainian refugees predominantly focused on women and children, highlighting personal narratives rarely seen in previous refugee reporting. Despite 40 percent of refugees being men, many stories emphasized women as mothers, entrepreneurs, and artists (Lindholm 2022; Nyman 2022; Torén Björling 2022). Many of these contain interviews with children, and some are completely focused on children (By 2022b; Schück 2023). Unique aspects of media coverage, especially when compared to the two previous cases, include detailed personal backstories, emphasis on young single women (By 2022b; Fyrk 2022e), incorporation of pet narratives (Nyman 2022; Ritzén 2022), and emotional accounts of separation from family members (Kulneff 2022; Sundbeck 2022; Lindholm 2022; Näslund 2022; Torén Björling 2022).

Articles frequently explored refugees' premigration lives (Adin Fares 2022; Samuelsson 2022), showcasing their strong homeland connections and desire to return (Adin Fares 2022; Näslund 2022). Men are notably present through heroic absence, depicted as fathers kissing children goodbye before fighting (By 2022a) or helping others escape (Adin Fares 2022; Kulneff 2022; Lindholm 2022; Näslund 2022; Sundbeck 2022; Torén Björling 2022). The different stories consistently illustrate refugees' complex identities beyond victimhood, presenting them as multifaceted individuals with agency and cultural depth.

Their agency is most pronounced in their expression of gratitude toward Sweden. For example, a "struggling mother" who was "incredibly grateful for everything" explained that the insufficient allowance provided a motivation to seek employment (Lindholm 2022). Another Ukrainian woman described Swedish generosity as "almost like a dream" (By 2022b). Different from the two other groups, Ukrainians were unambiguously portrayed as grateful and noncomplaining. For example, one article narrates a story of a young refugee: "Complaining isn't in his nature. Shortly after he and his mother, Olga, arrived, he started distributing flyers and newspapers on weekends to afford bus and gym passes" (Näslund 2022). Thus, the voices of refugees were welcomed especially as they established Swedish generosity that never seems to be in danger of exploitation by the grateful refugee.

As news articles emphasize vulnerability and benevolence, attempts to humanize refugees can still work to set them apart from the receiving community. Lighthearted accounts of appreciation of Scandinavian design and nature (Nyman 2022), pouring the right amount of wine (By 2022b), and knowing about the Swedish ritual of the coffee break (*fika*) despite not being fans of licorice (Fyrk 2022e) showed that Ukrainian refugees needed to adjust to Swedish society but that they were willing to do so and manage to navigate Swedish customs with ease. The affinities between Swedes and Ukrainians are not total, however, as traditional gender roles continue to set them apart (Hörmark 2022). The portrayal of similarities and differences points to the attempt to be inclusive of the other (for similar patterns elsewhere, see Abdelhady and Delioğlu 2022).

Inclusive othering also facilitates upholding the distinction between deserving and undeserving refugees. Compared to other groups, whose deservedness was questioned, Ukrainians were repeatedly portrayed as real refugees who long to return to their homeland (Adin Fares 2022) but were unable to do so as "their hometowns are occupied by Russians and their homes are leveled to the ground" (By 2022c). A particular debate about deservedness took place in the case of a municipality (Staffanstorp) refusing to receive quota refugees (who happened to be from Syria) as the local government expressed that they wished to prioritize refugees from Ukraine instead. The debate took place over the course of a few weeks (Nyström 2022; Rankinen 2022a, 2022b; Ärlemyr 2022) and showcased existing tensions in Swedish society over the treatment of refugees from different nationalities. The debate also reflects similar arguments that surfaced during the previous time periods we analyzed earlier.

Discussion

The analysis of media framing around the coverage of refugees in Sweden reveals a complex and at times contradictory narrative that attempts to reconcile restrictive and exclusionary policies with the country's self-image as a humanitarian, welcoming state. This dynamic is evident in the treatment of both Syrian and Yugoslavian refugee populations, as well as the more recent case of Ukrainian refugees.

The coverage of refugees from former Yugoslavia centered on the perceived "bureaucratic dilemma" of controlling and differentiating between "deserving" and "undeserving" asylum seekers. The media emphasized the institutional capacity and desire to manage refugee flows, drawing stark distinctions between groups like Bosnian Muslims and Kosovan Albanians. This allowed for the implementation of increasingly restrictive policies under the guise of rational, benevolent governance. In the case of Syrian refugees, the media discourse was dominated by a "responsibility" frame focused on the institutional and bureaucratic challenges of managing the arrivals. While there were efforts to uphold Sweden's reputation for compassion, the "crisis" framing was ultimately used to justify asylum restrictions, couched in the language of pragmatic necessity rather than overt xenophobia. Refugee voices were largely absent, with the media relying on "human-interest" stories that gave an ambiguous portrayal of Syrians as simultaneously grateful and ungrateful, traumatized victims in need of saving and a potential threat – a framing that subtly reinforced hierarchies of deservedness. The analysis of Ukrainian refugees in Sweden presents Ukrainian refugees unambiguously as deserving. While there were initial concerns about institutional capacity, these fears were quickly alleviated as the government enacted measures to better manage the arrivals. The media coverage then shifted to critiquing institutional obstacles that hindered the integration of Ukrainians, such as access to language courses and other bureaucratic barriers. Ukrainian refugees were generally portrayed in a positive light – as highly educated, motivated, and culturally compatible with Swedish society. While the obstacles facing Ukrainians were also encountered by the two other groups of refugees, they went unaccounted for when the focus was on institutional crises.

Researchers have found that organizational efficiency and pragmatic approaches to problems are held in high regard in Sweden (Graham 2003). As such, it comes as no surprise that the institutional frame is the most commonly utilized in Swedish newspapers. Underlying all of these narratives was a complex dynamic of upholding Sweden's self-image as a moral, welcoming society while accommodating exclusionary impulses and subtle forms of xenophobia. The media accomplished this by framing refugee issues primarily through an institutional and bureaucratic lens, invoking the language of formal rationality to deny asylum rights without overtly challenging the national self-image. Since bureaucratic institutions are perceived to be neutral (politically and otherwise), the focus on institutional response and responsibility politicizes the topic in such a way that makes political decisions seem apolitical and neutral.

Research on media representation of refugees emphasizes their othering through various mechanisms in diverse national contexts. In Sweden, as elsewhere, othering refugees also includes reflections on the self – the national self-image of Sweden and Swedes. Throughout the examined time periods, Swedish generosity and concerns about its potential exploitation by refugees has been a recurrent theme in the media discourse. This theme has been particularly pronounced in the cases of Syrian and Yugoslav refugees, in comparison to Ukrainians. In both instances, a dominant narrative revolved around distinguishing between "legitimate" and "fraudulent" and between "deserving" and "undeserving" asylum seekers. In the Yugoslav case, the media differentiated economic migrants from people fleeing from war, clearly identifying a specific group, the Albanians from Kosovo, as the nondeserving refugees. This group of refugees were also portrayed more often in articles related to conflict and criminality. In the case of portrayals of Syrians, fraudulence was also stressed, but in relation to terrorism and security threats, eventually justifying (at least implicitly) more extreme restrictions on movement. While DN stressed that Swedish generosity risked being exploited by refugees from Yugoslavia and Syria, in the case of Ukrainians the narrative of exploitation has been reversed, and a large number of articles instead depict how Ukrainian refugees are exploited in different ways by Swedish society. In the case of Ukrainians, questions of deservedness do not surface in media coverage. All put together, DN's representation of Ukrainians positions them as worthy of protection.

Despite the increase in using human interest as a frame when covering Syrians, refugee voices were largely absent from these debates, with the media instead relying on stories that portrayed Syrians as grateful, traumatized victims in need of saving. This framing, while ostensibly sympathetic, also served to reinforce a hierarchy of deservedness – where "good" refugees who demonstrate gratitude and eagerness to integrate are contrasted against the potential threats posed by the "bad" or "dishonest" refugee. Underlying this dynamic was a subtle form of Islamophobia, where Syrian refugees were viewed with suspicion, particularly in the wake of terror attacks in Europe. The media engaged in a delicate balancing act, at times critiquing overt anti-Muslim rhetoric, while nevertheless propagating stereotypes and implicit biases that cast refugees as potentially dangerous or culturally incompatible.

Othering refugees from Ukraine takes place through more subtle mechanisms, which we describe as "inclusive othering." On the one hand, similarities between Swedes and Ukrainians are stressed: they are well-educated, easily integrated, good dads, and hard-working women who possess agency. On the other hand, they are treated as an institutional problem and subjects of labor and sexual exploitation. More importantly, through repeated accounts of Ukrainian gratefulness and Swedish benevolence (which are mentioned in 1992 and 2015 but are more pronounced in 2022), victimization and othering continue to set the boundary between the two groups. As such, inclusive othering stresses the appearances of inclusion while concealing deeper issues of exclusion and marginalization, such as the exclusions of Ukrainians from SFI, healthcare and the uncertainty of their situation with residency permits that are only valid for a year.

While our analysis supports the observation of the mediatization of refugees over time (the increased media coverage being a strong indicator), we focus on media's politicization of the topic. Newspapers in Sweden are understood as free from political affiliations, but this does not preclude politicizing refugee reception through media's focus on institutional mechanisms. Given the seeming neutrality of the institutional focus, need to debate the reception of refugees from moral positions is diminished. At the same time, it is used to justify a perception of crisis, questioning deservedness, and securitization in the case of refugees from Yugoslavia and Syria. The same focus, however, draws attention to the ways institutions exclude refugees from Ukraine and hampers integration instead of facilitating it. It is important to stress that the institutional focus supports arguments on politicization within the particular Swedish context.

Notes

1 Salience here refers to the primary or dominant frame that shapes an article's message. Though articles may contain multiple frames, they are categorized according to their most prominent perspective – the one that most significantly influences the article's overall narrative and impact.

Bibliography

Abdelhady, Dalia. 2019. "Framing the Syrian Refugee: Divergent Discourses in Three National Contexts". In *The Oxford Handbook of Migration Crises*, edited by Cecilia Menjivar, Marie Ruiz, and Emmanuel Ness. New York: Oxford University Press. https://doi.org/10.1093/oxfordhb/9780190856908.013.16

Abdelhady, Dalia. 2020. "Media Constructions of the Refugee Crisis in Sweden: Institutions and the Challenges of Refugee Governance". In *Refugees and the Violence of Welfare Bureaucracies in Northern Europe*, edited by Dalia Abdelhady, Nina Gren, and Martin Joormann, 122–43. Manchester: Manchester University Press.

Abdelhady, Dalia and Fatmanur Delioğlu. 2022. "Human Interest Stories in the Coverage of Syrian Refugees: A Case Study from Turkey". *Mashriq & Mahjar: Journal of Middle East and North African Migration Studies* 9 (1): 93–120. https://doi.org/10.24847/v9i12022.310

Abdelhady, Dalia and Gina Frisetedt Malmberg 2018. "Swedish Media Representation of the Refugee Crisis: Islam, Conflict and Self-Reflection". In *Antisemitism, Islamophobia, and Interreligious Hermeneutics*, edited by Emma O'Donnell Polyakov, 107–36. Leiden: Brill. https://doi.org/10.1163/9789004381674_008

Abiri, Elisabeth. 2000. "The Changing Praxis of 'Generosity': Swedish Refugee Policy during the 1990s". *Journal of Refugee Studies* 13 (1): 11–28. https://doi.org/10.1093/jrs/13.1.11

Adin Fares, Nora. 2022. "Jana fick skydd i Tumba-nu vill hon återvända till Kiev". *Dagens Nyheter*, April 26.

Ärlemyr, Hilda. 2022. "Staffanstorp vägrade ta emot: kvotflyktingarna placeras i Vellinge". *Dagens Nyheter*, May 13.

Axner, Marta. 2015. "Representationer, sterotyper och nyhetsvärdering: Rapport från medieanalys om representationer av muslimer i svenska nyheter". *Diskrimineringsombudsmannen*. Report 9.1 2015.

Binder, Scott and William L. Allen. 2015. "Constructing Immigrants: Portrayals of Migrant Groups in British National Newspapers". *International Migration Review* 50 (1): 1– 38. https://doi.org/10.1111/imre.12206

Brattberg, Lisbeth and Anita Sjöblom. 1992. "Snatteri kan ge utvisning". *Dagens Nyheter*, October 13.

Brune, Ylva. 2000. *Stereotyper i förvandling: svensk nyhetsjournalistik om invandrare och flyktingar*. Stockholm: Regeringskansliet.

Burns, Tom R., Nora Machado, and Zenia Hellgren. 2007. Avslutande reflektioner. In *Makt, kultur och kontroll över invandrares livsvillkor. Multidimensionella aspekter på strukturell diskriminering i Sverige*, Tom R. Burns, Nora Machado,

Zenia Hellgren and Göran Brodin, 535–43. Uppsala: Acta Universitatis Upsaliensis.

By, Ulrika. 2015. "Från Damaskus till Märsta på tre dagar". *Dagens Nyheter*, September 15.

By, Ulrika 2022a. "Leken lindrar sorgen efter flykten från Ukraina". *Dagens Nyheter*, April 15.

By, Ulrika. 2022b. "Intensivkurs i service ska ge ukrainska flyktingar jobb snabbt". *Dagens Nyheter*, May 26.

By, Ulrika. 2022c. "Efter två månader i sovsal: 'nu undrar alla vad som händer 1 juli'" *Dagens Nyheter*, June 13.

Clare, Matthew and Dalia Abdelhady. 2016. "No Longer a Waltz Between Red Wine and Mint Tea: The Portrayal of the Children of Immigrants in French Newspapers". *International Journal of Intercultural Relations* 50: 13–28. https://doi. org/10.1016/j.ijintrel.2015.10.003

Crawley, Heaven. 2005. "Evidence on Attitudes to Asylum and Immigration: What We Know, Don't Know and Need to Know". Working Paper Series 23. Oxford: COMPAS, University of Oxford.

Dagens Nyheter. 1992a. "Stäng inte Sveriges gränser". June 30.

Dagens Nyheter. 1992b. "Inget flyktingpolitiskt klipp". July 1.

Dagens Nyheter. 1992c. "Europas förlegade flyktingpolitik". July 3.

Dagens Nyheter. 1992d. "Regeringen kan inte fly den kritiska flyktingopinionen". July 5.

Dagens Nyheter. 1992e. "Kosovoalbaner under luppen. Det är rätt att nu börja pröva". July 10.

Dagens Nyheter. 1992f. "Sverige tur och retur". October 16.

Dagens Nyheter. 1992g. "Behovet av skydd är avgörande. Flyktingpolitiken måste bli tydligare". October 18.

Dagens Nyheter. 1992h. "Vår omoderna flyktingpolitik". December 30.

Dagens Nyheter. 2015a. "Kampen går vidare". August 1.

Dagens Nyheter. 2015b. "Kära Sverige". September 13.

Dagens Nyheter. 2015c. "Säpo letar spioner bland nyanlända". October 5.

Dagens Nyheter. 2015d. "LO står i vägen för jobben". November 7.

Dagens Nyheter. 2015e. "Sverige anpassar migrationspolitiken till EU's lägstanivå". November 24.

Dagens Nyheter. 2015f. "Svenska Beredskapen höll in när krisen kom". December 17.

Dagens Nyheter. 2022a. "DN Tänk er för innan ni öppnar era hjärtan hälsar S". May 19.

Dagens Nyheter. 2022b. "Ge de ukrainska flyktingarna en ärlig chans att etablera sig". July 30.

Dagens Nyheter. 2022c. "Nu kommer andra vågen med flyktingar". December 18.

Don, Zuraidah Mohd and Charity Lee. 2014. "Representing Immigrants as Illegals, Threats and Victims in Malaysia: Elite Voices in the Media". *Discourse & Society* 25 (6): 687–705. https://doi.org/10.1177/0957926514536837

Egnell, Robert. 2015. "Vi måste öppna gränserna-också för vår egen skull". *Dagens Nyheter*, September 5.

Engberg, Hannah. 2015. "Fler misstänkta terrorister har upptäckts". *Dagens Nyheter*, July 15.

Engman, Thorsten. 1992. "Flykting i kassan minskade stölder". *Dagens Nyheter*, September 14.

Entman, Robert M. 1993. "Framing: Toward Clarification of a Fractured Paradigm". *Journal of Communication* 43 (4): 51. https://doi.org/10.1111/j.1460-2466.1993.tb01304.x

Eriksson, Karin. 2015. "Höstens kriser fick flyktingdebatten att tvärvända". *Dagens Nyheter*, November 25.

Esses, Victoria M., Stelian Medianu and Andrea S. Lawson. 2013. "Uncertainty, Threat, and the Role of the Media in Promoting the Dehumanization of Immigrants and Refugees". *Journal of Social Issues* 69 (3): 518–36. https://doi.org/10.1111/josi.12027

Flores, Juan. 1992. "Varannan asylsökande från Jugoslavien". *Dagens Nyheter*, December 2.

Fyrk, Johan. 2022a. "Ukrainska flyktingar får 61 kronor om dagen". *Dagens Nyheter*, June 5.

Fyrk, Johan. 2022b. "Ukrainiare jagar lagligt arbete-men erbjuds svartjobb". *Dagens Nyheter*, June 24.

Fyrk, Johan. 2022c. "Flyktingen Victoria fick anställning: får inte börja jobba". *Dagens Nyheter*, June 27.

Fyrk, Johan. 2022d. "Ukrainare på flykt i fem månader-fortfarande ingen SFI". *Dagens Nyheter*, August 22.

Fyrk, Johan. 2022e. "Ukrainska uttrycken om Sverige du inte visste fanns". *Dagens Nyheter*, September 2.

Georgiou, Myria and Rafal Zaborowski. 2017. *Media Coverage of the "Refugee Crisis": A Cross-European Perspective*. Council of Europe.

Graham, Mark. 2003. "Emotional Bureaucracies: Emotions, Civil Servants, and Immigrants in the Swedish Welfare State". *Ethos* 30 (3): 199–226. https://doi.org/10.1525/eth.2002.30.3.199

Granestrand, Lasse and Annika Ånnerud. 1992. "Attentat mot flyktingar. Kosovoalbaner skyddas av patrullerande vakter". *Dagens Nyheter*, August 21.

Hellberg, Anders. 1992a. "Flyktingström ökade kraftigt: 'Vi kan snart inte ta emot fler'". *Dagens Nyheter*, June 5.

Hellberg, Anders. 1992b. "Fler flyktingar till Ystad". *Dagens Nyheter*, May 12.

Hellberg, Anders. 1992c. "'Visumtvång kan behövas' Sverige klarar inte ensamt hela flyktingvågen". *Dagens Nyheter*, May 14.

Helmersson, Erik. 2015. "Sverige måste också integreras". *Dagens Nyheter*, December 10.

Holmberg, Kalle. 2015. "Flyktingar vägrade gå av bussen". *Dagens Nyheter*, January 1.

Holmgren, Mia. 2015. "Svenskar kan göra karriär i IS". *Dagens Nyheter*, April 18.

Hörmark, Andreas. 2022. "Ukrainska Larysa Denysenkos barnbok ges ut i Sverige: vi måste tala med barn om". *Dagens Nyheter*, April 9.

Hultén, Gunilla. 2007. "Främlingar i nationens spegel". In *Makt, kultur och kontroll över invandrares livsvillkor. Multidimensionella aspekter på strukturell diskriminering i Sverige*, edited by Tom R. Burns, Nora Machado, Zenia Hellgrena and Göran Brodin, 23–54. Uppsala: Acta Universitatis Upsaliensis.

Idevall Hagren, Karin. 2022. "Othering in Discursive Constructions of Swedish National Identity, 1870–1940". *Critical Discourse Studies* 19 (4): 384–400. https://doi.org/10.1080/17405904.2021.1918195

Jacobs, Laura, Cecil Meeusen, and Leen d'Haenens. 2016. "News Coverage and Attitudes on Immigration: Public and Commercial Television News Compared". *European Journal of Communication* 31 (6): 642–60. https://doi.org/10.1177/0267323116669456

Kihlberg, Jannike. 1992. "Tältläger ska rivas. Oro för flyktingar i Upplands Väsby". *Dagens Nyheter*, July 4.

Krzyżanowski, Michał. 2018. "'We Are a Small Country that Has Done Enormously Lot': The 'Refugee Crisis' and the Hybrid Discourse of Politicizing Immigration in Sweden". *Journal of Immigrant & Refugee Studies* 16 (1–2): 97–117. https://doi.org/10.1080/15562948.2017.1317895

Krzyżanowski, Michał, Anna Triandafyllidou, and Ruth Wodak. 2018. "The Mediatization and the Politicization of the 'Refugee Crisis' in Europe". *Journal of Immigrant & Refugee Studies* 16 (1–2): 1–14. https://doi.org/10.1080/1556294 8.2017.1353189

Kulneff, Ebba. 2022. "Här fortsätter flyktinghjälpen: handlar mycket om värdighet". *Dagens Nyheter*, July 29.

Lindeberg, Daniel. 2022. "Ge alla ukrainska flyktingar undervisning i svenska". *Dagens Nyheter*, April 19.

Lindholm, Amanda. 2022. "Mariana är rädd att behöva starta om igen". *Dagens Nyheter*, August 25.

Lund, Lina. 2015. "Trångboddhet och väntan ökar våld på boenden". *Dagens Nyheter*, August 1.

Moosavi, Leon. 2015. "The Racialization of Muslim Converts in Britain and Their Experiences of Islamophobia". *Critical Sociology* 41 (1): 41–56. https://doi.org/10.1177/0896920513504601

Mulinari, Diana and Anders Neergaard. 2022. "The Swedish Racial Welfare Regime in Transition". In *Racism in and for the Welfare State*, edited by Fabio Perocco, 91–116. Cham: Springer International Publishing.

Narti, Ana Maria. 1992. "Manipulerade massmedier mobbning". *Dagens Nyheter*, August 21.

Näslund, Lars. 2022. "Mamma Olga drömmer om att åka hem-Sonen Oleg vill bli polis i Sverige". *Dagens Nyheter*, December 26.

Nevéus, Ingmar. 2015. "Det är en flaskhals av guds nåde". *Dagens Nyheter*, September 12.

Nohrstedt, Stig Arne. 2006. "Krigsjournalistiken och den strukturella diskrimineringen". In *Mediernas vi och dom. Mediernas betydelse för den strukturella diskrimineringen*, edited by Leonor Camauër and Stig Arne Nohrstedt, 257–308. Stockholm: Fritzes.

Nyman, Jenny. 2022. "Kateryna flydde Ukraina – gör blodig konst i Sörmland". *Dagens Nyheter*, June 7.

Nyström, Susanne. 2022. "Hur kan en kommunledning få för sig att det är valfritt att följa lagen". *Dagens Nyheter*, May 16.

Orrenius, Niklas. 2015. "Nationalismen krymper världen". *Dagens Nyheter*, December 6.

Pickering, Sharon. 2001. "Common Sense and Original Deviancy: News Discourses and Asylum Seekers in Australia". *Journal of Refugee Studies* 14 (2): 169–86. https://doi.org/10.1093/jrs/14.2.169

Pruitt, Lesley J. 2019. "Closed Due to 'Flooding'? UK Media Representations of Refugees and Migrants in 2015–2016–Creating a Crisis of Borders". *The British Journal of Politics and International Relations* 21 (2): 383–402. https://doi.org/10.1177/1369148119830592

Rankinen, Matias. 2022a. "Staffanstorp ändrar sig-kvotfyktingar välkomna". *Dagens Nyheter*, June 13.

Rankinen, Matias. 2022b. "Jo kräver svar om Staffanstorps flyktingstopp". *Dagens Nyheter*, July 13.

Ribbenvik, Matias. 2022. "DN-debatt: Replik". *Dagens Nyheter*, May 9.

Ritzén, Jessica. 2022. "Jag skulle aldrig lämna Fenji – han är ju en familjemedlem". *Dagens Nyheter*, April 2.

Sahlin, John Alexander 2015. "Många svenskar välkomnar flyktingarna". *Dagens Nyheter*, January 28.

Samuelsson, Fredrik. 2022. "Alona flydde från kriget – vill nu starta hembageri i Sverige". *Dagens Nyheter*, December 25.

Schück Katarina 2023. "Jag saknar mina vänner i Ukraina". *Dagens Nyheter*, March 12.

Semetko, Holli A. and Patti M. Valkenburg. 2000. "Framing European Politics: A Content Analysis of Press and Television News". *The Journal of Communication* 50: 93–109. https://doi.org/10.1111/j.1460-2466.2000.tb02843.x

Sjöblom, Anita. 1992. "Idé om tillfälligt skydd får stöd". *Dagens Nyheter*, July 30.

Sokolnicki, Amanda 2022. "Ni säger att ni stödjer Ukraina – Så varför tvingas kvinnor in i prostitution?" *Dagens Nyheter*, November 26.

Steimel, Sarah. J. 2010. "Refugees as People: The Portrayal of Refugees in American Human Interest Stories". *Journal of Refugee Studies* 23 (2): 219–37. https://doi.org/10.1093/jrs/feq019

Strömbäck, Jesper and Lars W. Nord. 2008. "Media and Politics in Sweden". In *Communicating Politics: Political Communications in the Nordic Countries*, edited by Jesper Strömback, Mark Örsten, and Toril Aalberg, 103–25. Nordicom.

Sundbeck, Johanna. 2022. "Så ska ukrainska flyktingar få jobb: 'det är svårare än de sager'". *Dagens Nyheter*, April 16.

Tigervall, Carina. 2007. "Svenska invandringsfilmer—antirasistiska motbilder i samtidsdebatten?" In *Makt, kultur och kontroll över invandrares livsvillkor. Multidimensionella aspekter på strukturell diskriminering i Sverige*, edited by Tom R. Burns, Nora Machado, Zenia Hellgren and Göran Brodin, 55–70. Uppsala: Acta Universitatis Upsaliensis.

Torén Björling, Sanna. 2022. "Poeten Halyna Kruk: 'Kriget i Ukraina är ett långdistanslopp'". *Dagens Nyheter*, December 31.

Valenta, Marko and Nihad Bunar. 2010. "State Assisted Integration: Refugee Integration Policies in Scandinavian Welfare States: The Swedish and Norwegian Experience". *Journal of Refugee Studies* 23 (4): 463–83. https://doi.org/10.1093/jrs/feq028

Vinterhed, Kerstin. 1992. "Sverige måste vara generöst". *Dagens Nyheter*, July 6.

Wodak, Ruth. 2008. "'Us' and 'Them': Inclusion and Exclusion–Discrimination via Discourse". In *Identity, Belonging and Migration*, edited by Gereard Delanty, Ruth Wodak, and Paul Jones, 54–77. Liverpool: Liverpool University Press.

Wolodarski, Peter. 2015. "Tydligare signaler". *Dagens Nyheter*, November 6.

CHAPTER 10

From protecting rights to questioning them

Shifts in the depiction of forced migration in Finnish editorials between 1981 and 2004

Päivi Pirkkalainen

University of Jyväskylä

Saara Pellander

Migration Institute of Finland

Abstract

In this chapter, we focus on public debates on forced migrants in Finland by analyzing editorials of the largest Finnish national newspaper, *Helsingin Sanomat*, that were published between 1981 and 2004. During these years Finland implemented the first Aliens Act (1983), amended it and replaced it with a new law in 1991 and 2004 as a result of the rapid internationalization of Finland. We analyze the editorials with the public justifications analysis method. We argue that identifying public claims and justifications related to forced migration can deepen our understanding on dynamics of contestation around the

How to cite this book chapter:
Pirkkalainen, Päivi and Saara Pellander. 2025. "From protecting rights to questioning them: shifts in the depiction of forced migration in Finnish editorials between 1981 and 2004." In *Forced Migrants in Nordic Histories*, edited by Johanna Leinonen, Miika Tervonen, Hans Otto Frøland, Christhard Hoffmann, Seija Jalagin, Heidi Vad Jønsson and Malin Thor Tureby, 253–275. Helsinki: Helsinki University Press. https://doi.org/10.33134/HUP-32-11.

topic in Finnish public discourse. We show in the chapter that the politization and securitization of the issues related to forced migration did not arrive in Finland with the larger amount of asylum seekers after 2015 but can be traced back historically.

Introduction

This chapter[1] focuses on public discourses and debates involving forced migrants by analyzing editorials in the largest Finnish national newspaper, *Helsingin Sanomat*, about issues relating to forced migration. We analyze editorials published between 1981 and 2004 that were collected using the following keywords: refugees, migrants, deportation, Aliens Act, asylum, and foreigners. We chose this time period and type of media data as we wanted to understand public claims related to forced migration in line with the political framework around the topic, and to see which topics related to forced migration have been so heated that they were considered central enough to be dealt with in editorials.

The era considered, 1980 to 2004, proves particularly interesting. From a country that was neighboring the Soviet Union and had little regulation of alien affairs, Finland was aligning more closely with its Nordic and other European neighbors. Its reception and treatment of asylum seekers, coupled with the associated discourse, would be no exception. Where once the largest relevant flow had been expatriate Finns' return migration, Finland welcomed its first larger groups of postwar refugees in the early 1990s and ultimately would treat refuge-seeking new arrivals with heightened suspicion. After the 9/11 watershed, Finland demonstrated a clear break from earlier stances: securitization of migration in its legislation and parliamentary discourse intensified (see Palander and Pellander 2019). Emphasis on fulfilling international human rights standards waned in priority. This is the setting we examine.

Our aim is to analyze, in response to the Aliens Act (Ulkomaalaislaki) amendments, (public) claims on forced migration issues in editorials. We are particularly interested in who has made these claims and how they are justified. In order to do this, we will apply the methodology and theory of public justifications analysis, originally developed by Luc Boltanski and Laurent Thévenot (2006) and further elaborated, for the purposes of media analysis, by Eeva Luhtakallio and Tuomas Ylä-Anttila (2011). This theory identifies six different "worlds of justification": civic, market, industrial, domestic, inspiration, and fame (Boltanski and Thévenot 2006).

By pinpointing public claims and justifications related to forced migration, we can deepen the understanding of the dynamics of contestation in Finnish public discourse, and in doing so reveal changes in these patterns over time. Alongside these key contributions to addressing the "forced migrants in public discourses" theme of the book, our analysis provides a fuller picture of the justifications of claims as various legal regimes shifted, specifically in the years around the legal regime changes of 1983, 1991, and 2004. In summary, our analysis shows that early forced migration debates were centered on migrants' rights, reflecting the perceived need for Finland, as a small country at the periphery of Europe, to gain a good international reputation, but after the second regime change the debate framing forced migration veered toward threat-oriented discourse. The politicization and securitization of Finland's migration discourse then intensified in the early 2000s, manifesting a parallel with public debate in other European countries near the 2004 crux point. The trajectory uncovered clearly demonstrates that the large influx of asylum seekers after 2015 did not usher in this threat-oriented discourse. Its ties were merely rewoven at that time.

Delving into the politics of editorials enabled us to examine how the main national newspaper both reflected the tone of national debate and, through gatekeeping, helped shape that arena by creating discourses. Public justification analysis allowed us to longitudinally focus on three key cross-cutting themes of this book: temporality, transnational/international influence on national debate, and critical consideration of forced migrant-related categories in public debate.

By analyzing editorials, we apply a filter to current issues: unlike news articles, editorials only address topics that have risen to a broader public consciousness. Most often, they tackle issues already known to the reader, whether through news reports or via other sources. Newspaper editorials both reflect the ideological views and agendas of the newspapers (and their owners) and those of the public. Editorials are not only opinion pieces of individual writers but give insight into the broader ideological views of the paper (Dijk 1998). Thus for example, where the editorials addressed deportation, the editors regarded it as a central topic at the time. This factor points to another matter vital for our work: the politics of editorials. News does not appear out of a vacuum, and no items are inherently interesting or relevant. They are forged and shaped through numerous interests. Capitalist media houses' financial motivation to sell papers is just one factor, albeit an important one: they may maximize profits via topics that potentially attract a large readership. Simultaneously, other interests of owners and stakeholders can influence editorial decisions, from legal compliance to the apparent traction of various political views. Even for outlets asserting independence from party politics, as *Helsingin Sanomat* does, some views gain a greater foothold than others. Moreover editorials, by their very nature, are intended to comment and take a stand. Even though they do not often bear a sole author's name, they represent the paper itself, yet are far from neutral. Editorials are also geared toward political and economic elites in society, and can influence the opinions of these elites (Henry and Tator 2002, 94). Editorials thus have a special place in setting an agenda and an opinion (Pimentel and Marques 2021; Mont'Alverne and Marques 2022).

The fact that media narratives influence public opinion has been shown in comparative studies for several countries (McCann, Sienkiewicz, and Zard 2023), but we find one facet of our data particularly noteworthy in the Finnish context, namely the relative dominance of *Helsingin Sanomat*. Though not the country's only news source, it is the biggest daily paper with nationwide readership and influence. Whereas readers in many other countries choose papers that somewhat correspond to their political perspective, Finnish audiences regard *Helsingin Sanomat* as *the* newspaper, even though the landscape features smaller and regional papers. We posit that its editorials, hence, function much more strongly in gatekeeping and in establishing discourses for national political debate than other news outlets do. We understand discourse in a Foucauldian manner, referring to a historically social system of knowledge production (Foucault 1981). With discourse being an institutionalized way of thinking and speaking, mainstream media entities hold discursive power by shaping what gets thought, said, and discussed about certain topics. Importantly, however vital discourse is to the context we examined, we did not resort to discourse analysis – rather, a focus on "worlds of justification" seemed more suitable for a rich exploration of the phenomena connected with forced migration. We believe that justification analysis allows us to better grasp the nuances of public debates in different decades when moral values are at the core of analysis (see for example Luhtakallio and Ylä-Anttila 2023, 10). Nevertheless, the various distinct worlds and justifications that we identify here approach the Foucauldian understanding of problematizations. By how one makes and situates claims as solutions, one casts specific matters – particular aspects of migration in the case at hand – as problems and, hence, are in need of solving (Foucault 1998).

Most media coverage of forced migration falls into one of two general categories: victim or threat. Those seeking refuge are depicted either as helpless and in need of rescue or as potential criminals, as would-be abusers of immigration regulations (not "real" refugees), and/or as a financial threat and a burden on public resources (Chouliaraki and Stolic 2017; Georgiou and Zaborowski 2017; Szczepanik 2016). Scholars have focused on the latter category of Finnish reporting on migration, criticizing it for exaggerating immigrational risks, expected threats, and a tendency to stress putative effects on crime rates, expenses, and national security (Hellman and Lerkkanen 2017; Niemi and Perälä 2018; Vehmas 2012).

Previous scholarship on deportation and the media has approached the phenomenon by focusing on antideportation protests, especially the "impossible activism" (see Nyers 2003) of noncitizens within these protests (Haavisto 2020; Patler and Gonzales 2015; Pellander and Horsti 2018). For instance, Haavisto (2020) finds that Finnish media have framed antideportation demonstrations predominantly as a threat to order/security, and Pellander and Horsti (2018) show that journalists have depoliticized related hunger strikes by medicalizing the protests rather than considering hunger strikers' political assertions.

A recent analysis of gender dynamics in deportation representation in Finnish news points to an apparently new element in the aftermath of the 2015 refugee reception crisis: depictions of suffering and despair, which had previously been reserved for reporting on "women and children," now portray the struggles of males (Pellander 2022). Furthermore, we find studies showing that media portrayals depicting the Roma people in a manner evoking disgust and dehumanization increase support for deportation (Dalsklev and Rønningsdalen Kunst 2015). Prior literature exhibits a tendency to treat deportations as a rather new phenomenon, which is why we attempt to extend the perspective beyond the present day.

When we look back at news coverage of forced migration even from the days when immigration to Finland was a rather marginal phenomenon numerically, the data reveal attempts to securitize migration. While such findings support arguments by Palander and Pellander (2019) and dovetail with contributions from a Finnish-language edited volume tracing the country's history of deportation and of its contestation thereof (Pirkkalainen, Lyytinen, and Pellander 2022), our central contribution lies in analyzing public claims pertaining to the contentious topic of migration, alongside the moral justifications for them, particularly in light of proposed amendments to the Aliens Act. With the aid of the methodology and theory of public justifications analysis by Boltanski and Thévenot (2006), more recently refined for media analysis by Luhtakallio and Ylä-Anttila (2011, 2023), we examine the differences between decades (the 1980s, 1990s, and early 2000s) in claims concerning migrants and refugees. Thus, we tackle two crucial research questions: (a) Are we able to see discrete "waves" of justifications in certain years and decades? And (b) how do the justifications in *Helsingin Sanomat* editorials tie in with contemporaneous wider debates in both the public and the legal sphere?

Our analysis method applied the notion of "worlds" of justification, as found in public justification theory, through which "worth" gets defined (ultimately from philosophical underpinnings; see Boltanski and Thévenot 2006): civic, market, industrial, domestic, inspiration, and fame spheres. The method is built on content analysis and various forms of frame analysis (Luhtakallio and Ylä-Anttila 2023; see Table 10.1). This lens advances the understanding of, on the one hand, the shared reference points for everyone involved in the public debate while, on the other, also highlighting disparities in anchors for the legitimization of claims. While certain views tend to dominate public debates, it is essential to analyze their political and moral dimensions, as through the doctrine of justification analysis, the "analysis of what is going on in a public debate becomes more nuanced when (also the dominating) arguments are analyzed as subject to tests between different moral values" (Luhtakallio and Ylä-Anttila 2023, 10). While frame analysis is often criticized for neglecting questions of power (Luhtakallio and Ylä-Anttila 2023; see also Carragee and Roefs 2004), justification analysis does not present dominating discourses or frames as "neutral" but as being embedded in power dynamics.

Our method of instrumentalizing this theory identified the claim made, the claimer, the justification cited (in which we consider the theoretical concept of the world of justification as an ideal type in which

Table 10.1: Theory and method – public justification analysis (per Boltanski and Thévenot 2006; Luhtakallio and Ylä-Anttila 2011)

World of justification in the ideal type	Philosophical under-pinnings	Worth/utility logic
Civic	Jean-Jacques Rousseau	Equality, solidarity
Market	Adam Smith	Money, productivity
Industrial	Henri de Saint-Simon	Efficiency, regulation
Domestic	Jacques Bénigne Bossuet	Tradition, hierarchy
Inspiration	St Augustine	Spirituality, religion
Fame	Thomas Hobbes	Attention, recognition from others

worth is considered and repackaged as a utility logic), and the target at whom this claim was directed. We categorized the editorials accordingly in an Excel spreadsheet. Applying subcategories, we grouped the texts into those including direct claims and those not featuring any definite claim. Most editorials, 131 out of 173, contained a claim, while the rest presented certain refugee-related circumstances or political situations in foreign countries. Centering our analysis on those editorials featuring a claim, we grouped the claims by theme and by the world(s) of justification involved. This enabled distinguishing among debates by their boundaries – debates within a single world of justification, debates between distinct worlds of justification, and debates displaying hybrid forms of justification by drawing from different worlds (see Luhtakallio and Ylä-Anttila 2011).

Below, we argue, furthermore, that the "historical sediments," or *Zeitschichten* in the language of Koselleck and Gadamer (2000), of the present and their multiple temporalities inform and influence today's understandings of forced migration. We agree with Koselleck, who, while renowned for his contributions to conceptual history, points out that history can and should be studied not merely through language: histories become possible through tensions of the inside/outside, borders, and boundaries. When looking at confluence between how forced migration is addressed legally (in the Aliens Act etc.) and commented on in the media, we uncover sediments of dealing with forced migration. Even though some worlds of justification are bound up with specific geopolitical and historical contexts, even when the legal and political context is different, certain justifications reappear. With this awareness, we can sensitize ourselves to flows and accretions rather than search for linear development and see legal regimes that cleanly progress from one era to the next. As Hoffman and Franzel (2018) state, there are "multiple historical times present at the same moment, layer upon layer pressed together, some still volatile, others already hardened – this is what the metaphor of sedimented layers or strata of time attempts to capture."

Temporal distribution of the ideal types

We found 173 editorials in the 1980–2004 data using the following keywords in Finnish: asylum seeker, refugee, deportation, Aliens Act, foreigner, and forced return.[2] The composition of the editorial corpus (encompassing in-house and guest editorials) reflects developments in the number of immigrants moving to and living in Finland. In 1980, when there were very few immigrants, *Helsingin Sanomat* printed only two editorials on immigration-related themes (Figure 10.1). That pattern held for the whole decade, with just one to eight relevant editorials per year, for, all told, 38 editorials about migration in the 1980s. Net immigration to Finland between 1981 and 1989 totaled 34,182 people, with 85 percent being return migrants from Sweden (which had been a target of mass emigration prompted by structural changes in Finland and a peak in unemployment between 1967 and 1968). As for nonreturnees, while Finland had received its first groups of post–Second World War refugees, from Chile and Vietnam, between 1973 and 1978, most foreigners moving to Finland on a permanent basis in the 1980s did so for marital reasons (Korkiasaari and Söderling 2003; World Bank Group 2022).

As the number of arrivals began to rise, 87 immigration-related editorials were published in the 1990s. In this decade, the total number of immigrants to Finland increased fivefold, the most coming from the former Soviet Union. This represented a striking change, although the proportion of foreign residents has always been among Europe's lowest (Eurostat 2016). Alongside the collapse of the Soviet Union, a facilitated immigration status granted to Ingrian Finns contributed to growth in immigration from the East. Between 1990 and

Figure 10.1: A collage of scanned articles and headings from the 1980s about Finnish migration policy that were published in the *Helsingin Sanomat* newspaper.

1997, roughly 20,000 Ingrian Finns claimed returnee status. Furthermore, the beginning of the 1990s is when the first asylum seekers from Somalia arrived in Finland. As the decade unfolded, the prevailing understanding wherein Finland's legal responsibilities were restricted to its own citizens started being challenged (see Lepola 2000, 44–48; Pyrhönen 2015, 45). With Finland having become a European Council member in 1989 and signed the European Convention on Human Rights (ECHR), its legislators had to reconsider the treatment of foreigners. The country's rapid internationalization, in terms of both people's mobility and the engagement of international human rights, was a major motivating factor for overhauling Finland's Aliens Act.

As the 2000s dawned, 44 editorials during the years 2000–2004 dealt with immigration issues. The number of asylum seekers from Eastern Europe was on the rise, and the Aliens Act would be rewritten once again, with many of the changes being related to the ratification of international and EU regulations (Lepola 2000, 77–78; Pyrhönen 2015). As debate on immigration intensified, the Ministry of the Interior took five years to prepare the new act. According to Pyrhönen (2015, 64), the fact that developing the Aliens Act of 2004 required more than one term of government shows that immigration policy constituted a divisive issue.

Most of the editorials contained one specific claim but a few made two claims, often directed simultaneously at Finland and either the EU or another country (seven targeted a foreign nation, such as Sweden, Denmark, or Israel, and 12 targeted the EU). Our analysis homes in on the claims directed at Finland claims, most of which were aimed at national authorities – for example, the Office for Alien Affairs (Ulkomaalaisvirasto), the Ministry of the Interior (Sisäministeriö), the government, and parliament – and at citizens at large. On some occasions, editorials directed their claims at some combination of several "actors," such as politicians, the media, Finland's citizenry, and governmental/other authorities. A few editorials targeted claims at the refugee reception centers, social as well as health services, courts, the police, and activists.

What themes were raised? Throughout the 25-year span, the following main themes were evident in those editorials featuring a claim: improving refugee rights (including seeing this as a global issue) (20 claims), strengthening the rights of foreigners in Finland (14), attitudes toward foreigners (including refugees) and a need for more tolerance (10), criticism of the authorities' handling of deportations or deportation decisions (11), better asylum decisions to protect human rights (9), fraudulent asylum seekers/needing to keep would-be abusers of the system from entering or deport them quickly (7), the need for an EU-wide asylum/migration policy (7), the rising number of refugees Finland accepts (6), a need for swifter processing of asylum applications (6), required revisions/updates to the Aliens Act or policies regarding foreigners (5), the need to improve migration-related administration/for amending the Asylum Act from an administrative efficiency standpoint (6), refugees needing to be employed or active contributors to society (2), and either criticism about excessive internationalization or defense of Finland's national interests (6).

Most claims focused on improving and strengthening the rights of foreigners, especially forced migrants. However, when we delve into the justifications of the claims, the picture gets a somewhat blurrier, especially as the analysis approaches the 2000s, when harsher lines on immigration appeared, constructing hierarchies of migrants. With the general scene set, we can now consider such specifics of the public justifications. Below, we delve into those articulated in each decade's editorials.

The 1980s: concerns over the legal rights of foreigners and Finland's international image

The government proposal for Finland's Aliens Act (HE 186/1981), designed to replace a 1958 regulation, was submitted to parliament in late 1981 and approved in 1983, its initial form being enacted in April 1984. The editorials published prior to 1983 especially embrace the idea of Finland taking the necessary legislative and administrative steps to ensure the equal and fair treatment of foreigners. The most frequent claims of editorials in the 1980s were that Finland should take greater responsibility for refugees in accordance with international principles and that it should be more open and tolerant. This is consistent with findings from an analysis of the era's parliamentary debates, wherein the overwhelming tone was critical of Finland for having insufficient protection of the legal rights of foreigners (Palander and Pellander 2019, 179).

Most claims dealt specifically with forced migrants. In the ones from the 1980s, the world of justification appearing most often was civic (seen in 14 distinct claims), followed by a combination of civic and fame (5). Appearing the least often, but still present, were fame (2), industrial (1), civic+market (1), market+fame (1), and market (1). When it was used, market justification was featured in individual editorials demanding stronger legal rights for foreigners in Finland. These three editorials stressed the importance of productivity and trade, with comments such as this, from 1980: "Legal protection for foreigners is weak and needs to be supported by law" (all extracts are presented in translation from Finnish but available in their original form upon request). This editorial stressed the need for legal protection particularly in deportation cases, using Finland's needs for better functioning international trade, tourism, and other international activities as justification. Editorials from this decade commonly combined civic justifications with fame and market ones. A 1982 "guest editorial" entitled "The Proposed New Aliens Act Is Inadequate in Many Ways" demanded improvements to the rights of refugees, for humanitarian (civic) reasons, in conjunction with a comparison to laws in neighboring countries, which allegedly safeguarded human rights more fully.

Such comparison might fall into the fame category, in questioning Finland's international reputation and its conception of itself relative to other countries in civic terms.

In 1983, the year of the Aliens Act's approval, only one editorial mentioned immigration, and it lacked specific claims. The legislation started receiving editorial criticism some years later. Meanwhile, editorials continued combining civic and fame-based justifications; for example, 1985's "We Should Also Have a Responsibility for Refugees" stated that humanitarian factors justify taking greater responsibility for the world's refugee problem. The claim was supported by the fact that very few refugees were arriving in Finland as compared to its neighbors and that the presence of refugees would expand the citizens' rather narrow views on foreign people.

Then, editorials directly criticizing the Aliens Act emerged, demanding changes to improve circumstances for foreigners. For instance, a 1987 editorial stated that the new act had merely "polished our xenophobic facade by correcting only the worst beauty flaws." It continued by arguing that, given the remoteness of any large migration waves, efforts to frighten people with the specter of a "foreign invasion" or of bureaucracy growing overly burdensome were disingenuous. This editorial made the specific claim that foreigners in Finland should be able to resubmit an application for a visa and residence permit while staying in Finland, without having to leave the country. Again, the justification was civic, involving the rights of foreigners.

The idea of Finland's civic nature, both in its national understanding and in the eyes of other countries, shows well in justifications combining the civic and fame worlds. One example can be seen in an editorial from 1986 bearing the title "Finland Can Repay Its Debt to Refugees," which demanded better treatment and stronger rights of refugees because "it's the duty of a civilized country to help refugees." Attention to how Finland appears to other nations is best understood in light of increasing internationalization. Finland would soon join the European Council and sign the ECHR. Signatories had to reconsider their treatment of foreigners in the context of immigration control.

Hence, editorials from the late 1980s started focusing explicitly on internationalization. For example, "Lines of Policies for Foreigners" supported its claim that council membership requires revisions to the Aliens Act via the civics-oriented idea that foreigners should be granted equal rights in Finland. This editorial articulated the criticism that "our reality is still marked by a rejecting attitude, inflexible bureau-cracy, and an unwillingness to grant full and equal rights in any of life's spheres."

The 1990s: realigning Finland's geopolitical position from East to West – internationalization and human rights issues in Finland and abroad

With approval of Bill HE 47/1990 (submitted to Parliament in May 1990 and enacted the following year), the Aliens Act now covered the right to appeal decisions by the immigration authorities and codi-fied a right to legal assistance. Moreover, the principle of nonrefoule-ment, articulated in international treaties, started dictating aspects of Finnish immigration policy (Välimäki 2022, 122). Another defining phenomenon in the early 1990s was a sudden spike in the number of asylum seekers: from 179 applicants in 1989, the number rose to 2,743 in 1990 (Välimäki 2022, 110), with the largest group fleeing the Soma-lia Civil War. This constellation of developments precipitated changes to media discourse. Especially from 1991 onward, laws connected with foreigners, forced migration, and deportation were often framed in the editorials from a human rights perspective. In the decade's first few years, most claims were centered on improving refugee rights, demanding rapid asylum processes, and amending laws and policy. It is worth noting at this juncture that these editorials did not mirror societal sentiments at large: Somalis were not met with open arms in Finland, and not everyone was concerned about their human rights. In an environment plunged into economic recession, this was far from the best time for public acceptance of foreign arrivals, and it brought regrettable racist mobilization and often quite serious attacks leveled at foreigners (see, for example, Aallas 1991).

Some similarities to the previous decade's treatment remained: the claims most often received civic justification (used 28 times), with a focus on the human rights of foreigners, especially the right of refugees' protection. Combining the civic and fame worlds was still second most common (with 10 instances), followed by the indus-trial (5), civic+industrial (2), civic+market (2), market (2), fame (1), market+industrial (1), fame+industrial (1), and domestic (1) worlds. The 1990 editorial "Granting Asylum Mustn't Be Arbitrary" illustrated the civic focus. It criticized the bill for the new Aliens Act, stating that it should not be accepted as is, because of "many flaws ... vague word-ings, the regulations related to the non-refoulement principle are not sufficient, asylum granting would still be arbitrary, and an asylum decision would not be appealable." The claim was supported in terms of civic worth, with reference to equality for all and solidarity with asylum seekers. Also, justifications still combined the civic and fame worlds, as seen in the case of another editorial from 1990 demand-ing urgent amendment. Since the law enacted seven years prior was "embarrassingly intolerable," amending it was deemed crucial from a human rights angle, with Finland's reputation being at stake. The edi-torial stated that, "after amendments, the Aliens Act takes Finland to the forefront in Europe."

Another part of the picture is that the collapse of the Soviet Union brought an end to the "special treatment" of asylum seekers coming from the eastern border (Ervasti and Tiitinen 2018, 155–57). With 1991 came further changes to Finnish asylum processing policies too; for example, the role of foreign and security policy factors in the handling of asylum cases decreased (Palander and Pellander 2019; Välimäki 2022, 122). One topic, at that time, that became prominent in the editorials was the 1990 Finnish–Russian agreement on prevent-ing civil airplane hijacking. One editorial claims that the agreement is too categorical as it forces Finland to deport airplane hijackers to the Soviet Union no matter what motives they had. The claim made in this editorial was based on human rights, which should have been more prevalent in the abovementioned agreement, because Finland had joined the European human rights treaty. Here, Finland's politically and geographically ambivalent position between the East and the West received focus and the editorial stated: "Finland is simultaneously tied to Moscow and Strasbourg."

Claims addressing the human rights of refugees and asylum seekers from a civic angle retained prominence, as with 1991's "Asylum Seek-ers without Safety" calling for a more rapid processing of asylum appli-cations and a cease to some citizens' racist and xenophobic treatment of refugees. Likewise, accentuating human rights and civic justifica-tions, editorials from the following year spotlighted the plight of forced migrants. For instance, "New Challenges for Refugee Policies" asked Parliament to pay special attention to how the Aliens Act responds to refugee policy challenges, in that "Europe is now different from the time when the Aliens Act was last amended, but the biggest pressures in the refugee situation might still be there in the future [and] we will not survive these challenges if country after country makes laws very restrictive and makes deporting people as easy as possible." This was not the decade's only editorial addressing increasing internationalization: quite a few directed claims toward foreign countries or dealt with Finland signing the Schengen Agreement. A 1998 guest editorial ("Credibility Crisis for Guarding the EU's External Border") demanded that the new members' borders be opened only after a transitional period, citing law-and-order concerns, anchored in the domestic world of justification. The world with the strongest ascendancy in the 1990s, though, was the industrial one, with only the civic and civic+fame world behind. These justifications pertained to administrative efficacy in the Finnish bureaucratic system. For example, the 1990 editorial "Minister Rantanen and the Aliens Act" demanded rapid amendments to the Aliens Act for the sake of a well-functioning legal system, and 1994's "Commotion about Alien Affairs" claimed that administrative issues related to foreigners should be under central control (with appeals to a single institution) for bureaucratic efficiency reasons. In a similar vein, 1997's bluntly titled "Administration Is a Mess" castigated the slow processing of asylum applications.

This reflected a shift in the claims themselves. In 1993, a general debate, especially with regard to forced migrants, started gaining additional attention, and the editorials were no longer firmly centered on refugee rights from a civic perspective. Alongside the rights of refugees and asylum seekers, some brought up issues of misusing the asylum system via the notions of asylum gambling (*turvapaikkakeinottelu*), fraudulent asylum applications (*vilpilliset turvapaikkahakemukset*), and unfounded applications (*perusteettomat turvapaikkahakemukset*). One editorial from 1993, for instance, criticized processing times from a perspective quite different from human rights – "it seems that, with various appeals by asylum seekers, processing times can be exceeded unduly," which "irritates taxpayers and authorities involved in processing the cases."

By 1999, there were direct claims that the Aliens Act should be amended so that unfounded asylum applications by people from "safe" countries could be processed quickly, as was needed, but without human rights violations. These were justified in terms of law and order, bureaucratic efficiency being to "everyone's advantage." Still, the editorials advocated balance. While the minister of the interior was demanding amendments such that people with unfounded asylum cases could be sent back more quickly, the editorials noted that the matter is not so straightforward, as doing so may be against the law: everyone has the right to be heard and to a well-justified decision that can be appealed. An intriguing aspect of the treatment of "unfounded asylum cases" is that it started arranging people – especially asylum seekers – into hierarchies. This reflects the domestic world of justification, which ended up prevailing in the editorials as the 2000s began unfolding.

Attesting to the diversification of worlds present, three editorials from 1996 discussed the deportation of forced migrants from markedly different perspectives. The civic world-oriented guest editorial "Deportation Cases Are about Fortune" cited a claim by public law researchers that "deportation orders should not be done too easily," in connection with efforts to secure the rights of foreigners. Second, "More Humanity to Deportations" directed a claim to the Finnish police, stating that, because "authorities under civic state policy should even be able to deal with difficult deportations, in a manner respecting human rights," this part of police expertise should receive greater emphasis in police training. Then, in the following month's guest editorial, "Police and Deportations of Foreigners," the police's head of alien affairs made a claim to the media and Finnish citizens that "deportation issues should be dealt with without passion and we need to discuss on what basis the state grants residence permits." The editorial continued by claiming that "pressuring against deportation of certain people is not equal treatment of all deportable people" and that the public might end up with a very one-sided view.

The 2000s: Heightened worries about "economic refugees" – negotiating deservingness and administrative effectiveness

While the 2000s began with most claims still overtly cohering around ensuring and improving the rights of refugees, other claims often accompanying them were that people who try to misuse the asylum system by applying for economic reasons must not remain in the system. In fact, most claims, especially in 2000, pertained to reforming the laws so there would be support for deporting "economic refugees" (*elintasopakolaiset*) or people who submit fraudulent applications. Criticism of legal amendments or immigration bureaucracy (e.g. of lengthy processing times) were prominent during these years, and, as in previous decades, justifications were largely civic in orientation ("pure" civic justification being used 13 times). For example, two editorials printed in 2001 justified calls for expedited processing from a rights angle – waiting as long as two years for a final decision is neither humane nor good for an asylum seeker's well-being – and several guest editorials between 2000 and 2004 cited rights-related comments by experts, saying that Finland, in line with the aims of the EU, should do its part to "create a common asylum system and to develop and actively implement a humane asylum policy."

The question of "real refugees" vs. "economic migrants" in the 2000s started becoming central to the debate. Many editorials cited foreigners who misuse the asylum system as a key problem. A large number of editorials from 2000 to 2004 feature domestic world justifications that articulate hierarchies of worth, with several drawing a distinction between people who try to misuse the system and those worthy of protection. "Pure" domestic justification was used seven times during these years, and sometimes the claims' backing involved a combination of civic and domestic justification (with four instances) in that they stressed a call for protecting "real refugees": the human rights of those foreigners who really need protection should be respected. For example, "Getting Rid of Asylum Tourism," a 2004 editorial, stated that groundless applications are burdensome for the system, such that "the help is directed not to real asylum seekers but to asylum tourists."

Some of the domestic world-anchored claims involved direct appeals for changing the system/law. As the decade dawned, the Ministry of the Interior had been preparing amendments to permit fast-track processing of asylum applications from "safe" countries (ultimately passed in June 2000), a matter highlighted by the February 2000 guest editorial "Manufacturing of Applications Requires Fast Asylum Processing," in which the Ombudsman for Aliens demanded amendments whereby asylum bureaucracy could deal with unfounded applications quickly and with more resources. The sense of a hierarchy was clear from early on. For example, the very first *Helsingin Sanomat* editorial in 2000 claimed that the Asylum Act "must be amended quickly," in that "the current law and its obvious loopholes do not serve anyone's interests, least of all those people in danger and in real need of protection and asylum" and that, furthermore, by allowing "economic asylum," the current law encourages xenophobia. While the industrial world of justification featured in such efficiency-focused claims, the text noted that Finland was not (yet) deporting people to Afghanistan, Somalia, and Iraq. Such comments recognized the civic angle, in that bureaucratic efficiency still respects human rights at least insofar as it respects the principle of nonrefoulement.

Often in these editorials, "asylum tourists" is a gloss for ethnic minorities, such as the Roma people from Eastern European countries, and several claims were targeted at the EU and/or new EU countries: they should take better care of their minorities, so that people do not need to flee for economic reasons. Again, a hierarchy is evident. These distinctions between "good"/deserving and "bad"/nondeserving migrants further reproduce inequalities in migration debates (on similar categorizations of deservingness and undeservingness, see Hinger 2020; Kotilainen and Pellander 2022; Sales 2002).

In parallel with such a focus, the editorials still stressed human rights and the humane treatment of the Roma people and other foreign citizens from "safe" countries, especially in deportation circumstances. For example, the editorial "In a Low Mood," centered on the deportation of Roma individuals, was highly critical of the Finnish police – "the way 53 Roma people were deported to Romania was disgusting," and "oversized deportation arrangements [by] the Finnish police showed that the Roma people are not only outcasts in Romania." Similar criticism focused on the human rights and dignity of deportees was presented in the editorial titled "Even a Deported Person Is a Human Being," from 2003, which quoted another Finnish newspaper, the left-leaning *Kansan uutiset*, in connection with the deportation of a Ukrainian family that had been drugged during removal. The editorial demanded a thorough investigation of what had happened and, in light of it, proper instructions for how authorities should handle asylum cases.

Conclusions and implications

Our technique and materials illuminated both gradual and rapid change over the time span considered. At the beginning of the 1980s, immigration in Finland was not represented as a prominent phenomenon but as an opportunity for showcasing adherence to international principles and demonstrating responsibility for openness and tolerance. Especially prior to the first Aliens Act, enacted in 1984, the majority of editorials focused on defining regulations, and most claims specifically dealt with forced migrants, with civic justifications employed accordingly in calls for the legislative and administrative steps required to ensure their equal, fair treatment. The world of fame was prominent too – our data indicate that this decade's editorials addressed Finland's international reputation primarily: treating foreigners poorly or not honoring civic obligations to comply with international law would harm this reputation. While the early 1990s retained the civic and partly fame angle, coupled with a human rights framing, other threads started emerging.

While most claims in 1990s editorials, as the previous decade had, demanded stronger rights for refugees, rapid processing, and legal and policy amendments, the debate from 1993 onward diversified increasingly from a civic approach to refugee rights: notions such as unfounded asylum applications and asylum gambling started to emerge, and with these the domestic world of justification arose. This world ushered in hierarchies of immigrants – who is worthy of protection and who is not – with more critical stances clearly prevalent by the decade's end.

While domestic justification for the heightened suspicion of asylum seekers was definitely growing as the 2000s dawned, the most common justification was still civic. Tellingly, references to Finland's reputation were now absent, with only one editorial using the fame world of justification. Considering the writings in light of Finnish political history reveals why: the rather "closed" Finland of the 1980s, which occupied a fairly peripheral position on the European stage, had been concerned with shifting its political orientation westward and internationalizing itself to become "fit for" the European Union. That era's editorials, hence, addressed a key part of the country's reputation (how the human rights of refugees were recognized and treated) and the phenomena of the day (e.g., receiving larger groups of postwar asylum seekers and return migrants, although still in small numbers by international standards).

In its developments between 1980 and 2004, *Helsingin Sanomat* discourse paralleled public debate in other European countries, even those that, while experiencing larger numbers of immigrants, characterized humanitarian migration especially from a rather critical perspective, as a "burden" to national economic welfare. One could argue that Finland wanted to be "like the others" in this regard too (see Keskinen 2009 for argumentation along these lines in relation to honor-related violence). Nevertheless, the commonality of such discriminatory expressions as "asylum tourist" in these editorials attests to how strong this language adopted by the far right is. Importantly, as Horsti and Pellander (2015) show though comparison between parliamentary debates and *Helsingin Sanomat* editorials, these expressions often creep in within quotation marks or with the prefix "so-called" until ultimately becoming everyday, matter-of-fact language that is no longer questioned.

Although civic justification involving the human rights of (forced) migrants received emphasis throughout the decades analyzed, this underpinning also functions to create room for something more: hybrid forms of justification, drawing from multiple worlds. By paying closer attention to how these worlds blend together such discourse, one could argue that criticism of immigration control is not so evident after all. While the editorials rather frequently took issue with deportation processes, justifying these claims in civic, human rights terms, the criticism often lay with the deportation arrangements and took an industrial tone, especially in more recent years. We found no fundamental critique of the larger immigration control and deportation apparatus. Overall, the editorials seem to give public debate a reminder of the human rights of forced migrants but, at the same time, promoted a critical perspective on forced migration flow and partly encouraged discriminatory views among readers.

Notes

1 This research has been conducted within and funded by the Research Council of Finland project titled "Deportation in a Mediated Society," decision number 320323, as well as Mobile Futures, a project funded by the Strategic Research Council established within the Research Council of Finland, decision number 364422.
2 We are grateful to Pirja Hyyryläinen and Heidi Latvala-White for compiling the corpus and to Maria Niemiharju and Inna Sinersaari for the initial analysis of some of the data. We owe a special thanks to Marika Saarinen for continuing the analysis and offering insightful comments on the data, and to Ella Nybäck for her help in compiling parts of the literature.

Bibliography

Aallas, Esa. 1991. *Somalishokki* [Somali Shock]. Helsinki: Suomen pakolaisapu.

Boltanski, Luc and Laurent Thévenot. 2006. *On Justification: Economies of Worth*. Princeton, NJ: Princeton University Press.

Carragee, Kevin and Wim Roefs. 2004. "The Neglect of Power in Recent Framing Research". *Journal of Communication* 54 (2): 214–33. https://doi.org/10.1111/j.1460-2466.2004.tb02625.x

Chouliaraki, Lillie and Tijana Stolic. 2017. "Rethinking Media Responsibility in the Refugee 'Crisis': A Visual Typology of European News". *Media, Culture & Society* 39 (8): 1162–77. https://doi.org/10.1177/0163443717726163

Dalsklev, Madeleine and Jonas Rønningsdalen Kunst. 2015. "The Effect of Disgust-Eliciting Media Portrayals on Outgroup Dehumanization and Support of Deportation in a Norwegian Sample". *International Journal of Intercultural Relations* 47: 28–40. https://doi.org/10.1016/j.ijintrel.2015.03.028

Dijk, Teun A van. 1998. *Ideology: A Multidisciplinary Approach*. London and Thousand Oaks, CA: Sage Publications.

Ervasti, Pekka and Seppo Tiitinen. 2018. *Tiitinen: vakoilijoita ja veijareita* [Tiitinen: Spies and Cons]. Helsinki: Otava.

Foucault, Michel. 1981. "The Order of Discourse". In *Untying the Text: A Post-Structuralist Reader*, edited by Robert Young. Boston, London, and Henley: Routledge & Kegan Paul.

Foucault, Michel. 1998, "Polemics, Politics and Problematizations". Interview by Paul Rabinow, May 1984. In *Essential Works of Foucault* Vol. 1. The New Press.

Georgiou, Myria and Rafal Zaborowski. 2017. *Media Coverage of the "Refugee Crisis": A Cross-European Perspective*. Council of Europe.

Haavisto, Camilla. 2020. "'Impossible' Activism and the Right to Be Understood: The Emergent Refugee Rights Movement in Finland". In *Nostalgia and Hope: Intersections between Politics of Culture, Welfare, and Migration in Europe*, edited by Ov Cristian Norocel, Anders Hellström, and Martin Bak Jørgensen, 169–84. Cham: Springer Open.

Hellman, Matilda and Tuulia Lerkkanen. 2017. "Kuka on riittävän hyvä pakolainen?" [Who Is a Good Enough Refugee?]. Alusta! New Social Research at Tampere University. https://alusta.uta.fi/2017/10/23/kuka-on-riittavan-hyva-pakolainen.

Henry, Frances and Carol Tator. 2002. *Discourses of domination: Racial bias in the Canadian English-language press*. Toronto: University of Toronto Press.

Hinger, Sophie. 2020. "Integration through Disintegration? The Distinction between Deserving and Undeserving Refugees in National and Local Integration Policies in Germany". In *Politics of (Dis)Integration*, edited by Sophie Hinger and Reinhard Schweitzer, 19–39. Cham: Springer.

Hoffmann, Stefan-Ludwig and Sean Franzel. 2018. "Introduction: Translating Koselleck". In *Sediments of Time. On Possible Histories*, by Reinhart Koselleck (translated and edited by Sean Franzel and Stefan-Ludwig Hoffmann), ix–xxxi. Stanford, CA: Stanford University Press.

Horsti, Karina and Saara Pellander. 2015. "Conditions of Cultural Citizenship: Intersections of Gender, Race and Age in Public Debates on Family Migration".

Citizenship Studies 19 (6–7): 751–67. https://doi.org/10.1080/13621025.2015.1 008998

Keskinen, Suvi. 2009. "'Honour-Related Violence' and Nordic Nation-Building". In *Complying with Colonialism: Gender, Race and Ethnicity in the Nordic Region*, edited by Suvi Keskinen, Salla Tuori, Sari Irni, and Diana Mulinari. Farnham: Ashgate. https://doi.org/10.4324/9781315573212

Korkiasaari, Jouni and Ismo Söderling. 2003. *Finnish Emigration and Immigration after World War II*. Turku: Siirtolaisuusinstituutti – Migrationsinstitutet.

Koselleck, Reinhart and Hans-Georg Gadamer. 2000. *Zeitschichten: Studien zur Historik* [Layers of Time: Studies in History]. Berlin: Suhrkamp.

Kotilainen, Noora and Saara Pellander. 2022. "(Not) Looking Like a Refugee: Symbolic Borders of Habitus in Media Representations of Refugees". *Media History* 28 (2): 278–93. https://doi.org/10.1080/13688804.2021.1932445

Lepola, Outi. 2000. "Ulkomaalaisesta suomenmaalaiseksi: Monikulttuurisuus, kansalaisuus ja suomalaisuus 1990-luvun maahanmuuttopoliittisessa keskustelussa". [From Foreigner to Finn: Multiculturalism, Citizenship and Finnishness in Immigration Debates of the 1990s] PhD thesis, Suomalaisen Kirjallisuuden Seura.

Luhtakallio, Eeva and Tuomas Ylä-Anttila. 2011. "Julkisen oikeuttamisen analyysi sosiologisena tutkimusmenetelmänä" [Public Justification Analysis as a Sociological Research Method]. *Sosiologia* 48 (1): 34–51.

Luhtakallio, Eeva and Tuomas Ylä-Anttila. 2023. "Justifications Analysis". In *Handbook of Economics and Sociology of Conventions*, edited by Rainer Diaz-Bone and Guillemette de Larquier, 1–20. Cham: Springer. https://doi.org/10.1007/978-3-030-52130-1_72-1.

McCann, Katherine, Megan Sienkiewicz, and Monette Zard. 2023. *The Role of Media Narratives in Shaping Public Opinion toward Refugees: A Comparative Analysis*. Geneva: International Organization for Migration.

Mont'Alverne, Camila and Francisco Paulo Jamil Marques. 2022. "What Makes an Issue Relevant to Newspaper Editorials? An Empirical Approach to Criteria of Editorial-Worthiness". *Bracilian Journalism Research* 18 (1). https://doi.org/10.25200/BJR.v18n1.2022.1475.

Niemi, Mari and Anna Perälä. 2018. "Keiden ääni kuuluu, keiden 'kriisistä' puhuttiin? Ylen journalistiset valinnat turvapaikanhakijoita käsittelevissä ohjelmissa" [Whose Voice Was Heard, Whose "Crisis" Discussed? YLE's Journalistic Choices in Programs Dealing with AsylumSeekers]. In *Media & Populismi. Työkaluja kriittiseen journalismiin*, edited by Mari Niemi and Topi Houni. Tampere: Vastapaino.

Nyers, Peter. 2003. "Abject Cosmopolitanism: The Politics of Protection in the AntiDeportation Movement". *Third World Quarterly* 24 (6): 1069–93.

Palander, Jaana and Saara Pellander. 2019. "Mobility and the Security Paradigm: How Immigration Became Securitized in Finnish Law and Policy". *Journal of Finnish Studies* 22 (1–2): 173–93.

Patler, Caitlin and Roberto G. Gonzales. 2015. "Framing Citizenship: Media Coverage of Anti-Deportation Cases Led by Undocumented Immigrant Youth Organisations". *Journal of Ethnic and Migration Studies* 41 (9): 1453–74. https://doi.org/10.1080/1369183X.2015.1021587

Pellander, Saara. 2022. "Karkotukset mediassa pakolaisten vastaanottokriisin jälki-mainingeissa" [Mediated Responses to Deportations in the Aftermath of the Refugee Reception Crisis]. In *Suomesta poistetut: Näkökulmia karkotuksiin ja käännytyksiin* [Deported from Finland: Perspectives on Deportations], edited by Päivi Pirkkalainen, Eveliina Lyytinen, and Saara Pellander, 201–18. Tampere: Vastapaino.

Pellander, Saara and Karina Horsti. 2018. "Visibility in Mediated Borderscapes: The Hunger Strike of Asylum Seekers As an Embodiment of Border Violence". *Political Geography* 66: 161–70. https://doi.org/10.1016/j.polgeo.2017.01.005.

Pimentel, Pablo Silva and Francisco Paulo Jamil Marques. 2021. "The Structure, Production Routines, and Political Functions of Editorials in Contemporary Journalism". *Atlantic Journal of Communication* 30 (4): 365–78. https://doi.org/10.1080/15456870.2021.1931218.

Pirkkalainen, Päivi, Eveliina Lyytinen, and Saara Pellander, eds. 2022. *Suomesta poistetut: Näkökulmia karkotuksiin ja käännytyksiin* [Deported from Finland: Perspectives on Deportations]. Tampere: Vastapaino.

Pyrhönen, Niko. 2015. "The True Colors of Finnish Welfare Nationalism: Consolidation of Neo-Populist Advocacy as a Resonant Collective Identity through Mobilization of Exclusionary Narratives of Blue-and-White Solidarity". PhD thesis, Helsingin yliopisto.

Sales, Rosemary. 2002. "The Deserving and the Undeserving? Refugees, Asylum Seekers and Welfare in Britain". *Critical Social Policy* 22 (3): 456–78. https://doi.org/10.1177/026101830202200305

Szczepanik, Marta. 2016. "The 'Good' and 'Bad' Refugees? Imagined Refugeehood(s) in the Media Coverage of the Migration Crisis". *Journal of Identity and Migration Studies* 10 (2): 23–33.

Välimäki, Matti. 2022. "Kylmän sodan maastapoistamisen käytäntöjen murros ja nykyperiaatteiden synty" [The Breakdown of Cold-War Deportation Practices and Emergence of Current Principles]. In *Suomesta poistetut: Näkökulmia karkotuksiin ja käännytyksiin*, edited by Päivi Pirkkalainen, Eveliina Lyytinen, and Saara Pellander, 101–25. Tampere: Vastapaino.

Vehmas, Susanna. 2012. "Maahanmuuttokirjoittelu sanomalehdissä" [Immigration Writing in Newspapers]. In *Maahanmuutto, media ja eduskuntavaalit*, edited by Mari Maasilta, 116–35. Tampere: Tampere University Press.

World Bank Group. 2022: United Nations Population Division. World Population Prospects. Revision. https://data.worldbank.org/indicator/SM.POP.NETM?end=1989&locations=FI&most_recent_value_desc=false&start=1981.

PART IV

Memories of forced migration

CHAPTER 11

Forced labor displacement during the Second World War

Czechs in Norway and their postwar memorialization

Hans Otto Frøland
Norwegian University of Science and Technology

Vendula V. Hingarová
Charles University

Abstract

Nazi Germany conscripted some 2,000 young men from the occupied Protectorate of Bohemia and Moravia for forced labor in Norway (and Finland) during the Second World War. Their experiences as forced labor migrants in a distant polar habitat, as well as their commemoration during the Cold War, have been largely neglected in Norway and deliberately ignored in Czechoslovakia. Based on documents from the German bureaucracy, ego-documents from individual workers, and interviews with their descendants, this chapter explores the cohort's collective experiences, memories, and memorialization from a

How to cite this book chapter:
Frøland, Hans Otto and Vendula V. Hingarová. 2025. "Forced labor displacement during the Second World War: Czechs in Norway and their postwar memorialization." In *Forced Migrants in Nordic Histories*, edited by Johanna Leinonen, Miika Tervonen, Hans Otto Frøland, Christhard Hoffmann, Seija Jalagin, Heidi Vad Jønsson and Malin Thor Tureby, 279–301. Helsinki: Helsinki University Press. https://doi.org/10.33134/HUP-32-12.

prosopographic perspective. By first examining their experience from conscription in 1942 to repatriation in 1945, the chapter observes an inherent ambiguity between misery and tourist mode. In the second part of the chapter, it is argued that the ambiguity prevailed as memories persisted in close social networks in Czechoslovakia. Only in the Czech Republic was it possible to commemorate the cohort in public, when the compensation discourse tipped the balance of ambiguity in favor of misery.

Introduction

Josef Lébl (1921–1991) was subjected to Nazi Germany's transnational forced labor program during the Second World War. He was one of nearly 2,000 Czech citizens who were forced to work under harsh conditions in Norway. When Lébl's daughter, Jarmila, was recently asked how her father had spoken about his displacement, she claimed that he had eagerly recounted the experience: "When I was a child, my father would read from his Norway diaries before I went to bed. His reading was always like chocolate on the tongue. He talked about the fjords and showed postcards. In my childhood I felt that Norway belonged to us together with the Czech lands" (Hingarová, Maršálek, and Vlk 2021, 35). Lébl obviously talked about his experience as a forced labor migrant in rather lively and almost touristic tropes. A careful reading of his ego-documents confirms that he did not conceptualize his experience in terms of decay and misery, although he never ignored the elements of coercion and constraint.

The massive Nazi forced labor program in Europe was transnational and may have involved 20 million people, the majority from Eastern and Central Europe (Wagner 2011). Repatriation was part of the equally massive "unmixing of peoples" that occurred in Europe as Germany capitulated (Brubaker 1995). During the Cold War, the Kremlin tended to limit memory of the program in order to avoid embarrassing attention to its own use of forced labor displacement (Polian 2004). We agree with Gatrell (2007) that it was only with the collapse of communist rule in Eastern and Central Europe that a more profound debate on the history of forced displacement became possible. Even in the West, research on the Nazi forced labor program was hesitant well into the 1980s (Herbert 1985; Jacobmeyer 1985). It was the German compensation scheme for former forced laborers in 2000 that triggered the wave of historical research on this program (Borg-gräfe 2014). The same is true for the Norwegian program (Hatlehol 2020). Norwegian studies have shown that it involved about 130,000 foreigners, of whom more than 100,000 were Soviet and Polish prisoners of war (POWs), and Yugoslav and German prisoners. The rest were conscripted civilian workers from 21 countries. This scholarship has focused on the organizational machinery that affected living and working conditions and showed that, even with a high demand for labor, Nazi racial ideology played a role in shaping working conditions (Soleim 2009; Hatlehol 2015; Stokke 2024). In contrast to local memories and memorials to foreign forced laborers, there was no national act of remembrance. Norway's policy of limiting commemoration of Soviet POWs during the Cold War is well documented (Soleim 2018). While a formal bilateral friendship group was created to honor Yugoslavia's suffering, marked by immense casualties, the Czech forced labor contribution was not memorialized in Norway until the 2020s.

This study aims to understand how the forced labor displacement in Norway was experienced, remembered, and memorialized by focusing on the Czech group. Former studies show that communist Czechoslovakian governments stifled public discussion about forced labor memory, while Czech conscripts who had worked in the German Reich found practical ways to come to terms with their past individually (Jarská 2010; Thonfeld 2011). While we agree, we also argue that experiences in Norway influenced memories and that postwar remembrance continued. The prevailing view is that the Czechs in Norway had relatively extensive rights, were treated comparatively well, and exercised some agency (Hatlehol 2015; Frøland et al. 2021). We inquire about the collective experience that emerged during the war and its subsequent remembrance and memorialization. We will refer to the group as *Noráci*, which in the Czech colloquial language means the Norwegians, although this phrase was applied by the group itself only from 1985. We indeed acknowledge the bias of memory studies towards "cultural homogeneity, consistency and predictability" (Kantsteiner 2000) but believe that using the historical prosopography approach (Verboven, Carlier, and Dumolyn 2007) weakens this bias. The data we use originate in our research project, which works up historical knowledge on the conditions of the Czech group and how it preserved memory about its Norwegian experience based on ego-documents (https://noraci.cz/en/front-page/). The corpus consists of

12 wartime diaries, 600 wartime letters, and 4,000 photographs, along-side 15 retrospective postwar memories written mostly in the 1990s. In addition, we have conducted 20 oral interviews and 200 email communications with descendants.

The first part follows the *Noráci* cohort from the first day of drafting in the Protectorate of Bohemia and Moravia in September 1942 until their repatriation to Czechoslovakia by August 1945. We argue that the *Noráci* indeed acknowledged being victims of forced labor displacement, but, although working conditions were hard and provisions insufficient, and despite the constant risk of punishment, their collective experience also emphasized pleasant tourist impressions: natural scenery and social encounters with a friendly local population. This ambiguity was most succinctly expressed in retrospect by Jan Šefl (2009): "Beautiful islands and fjords all around, but hunger didn't allow me to take care of them." While emphasizing the shared meaning of community within the group, we explore this ambiguity between victimhood and tourist mood. Inspired by literary analysis, we view the two moods as narrative memory tropes (Mellard 1987), implying that they served as dominant and persistent rhetorical figures that bound memory to the narrated group experience.

In the second part, we show how the ambiguous experience of the *Noráci* cohort evolved into an enduring memory after the war. Although our approach is genuinely historical, we take into account Jan Assmann's (1988) simple and robust conceptual distinction between communicative memory and cultural memory. While the former is socially negotiated in an everyday manner in small groups such as family, neighborhood, or friendship networks through everyday oral exchanges with eyewitness(es) in the midst, the latter implies that memory has reached the public sphere and tends to be negotiated by larger social groups, formal organizations, and experts – and, not least, influenced by the state. Museums and memorials, commemorative rituals and speeches, written documents, and media coverage tend to shape and sustain cultural memory. We argue that an enduring communicative memory soon took hold, and that the communist government rejected its potential transformation into a cultural memory. The transformation to cultural memory did not occur until after the Velvet Revolution of 1989. We further argue that the ambiguity between victimhood and tourist sentiment prevailed and was passed on to the next generation but suggest that the discourse of forced labor compensation in the 1990s reoriented commemoration in favor of victimhood.

Drafted and displaced: the experience of Czech forced labor in Norway

It is not entirely clear how many *Noráci* worked in Norway. In total, 1,366 people were registered in the index file of the Einsatzgruppe Wiking, the task force of the Organization Todt (OT) that was sent to Norway in the spring of 1942 to build infrastructure, but about 400 unregistered people were observed in other records (Hingarová and Maršálek 2022, 247). In addition, Czechs were brought to Finnish Lapland for the same purpose and transported across the Norwegian–Finnish state border. In August 1944, only 86 Czechs remained in Finland (Lundemo 2020, 86). From this we can estimate that between 1,800 and 2,000 Czechs were deported to Norway as forced laborers. The majority were between 18 and 22 years old, but about 20 percent were older. The total duration of their displacement is not yet known, but most were conscripted between September and November 1942 and arrived in Norway between November 1942 and January 1943. From the spring of 1943 the number remained stable until the fall of 1944, when several hundred were transferred to Germany.

Most *Noráci* followed a standardized itinerary, as illustrated by the first group of 313 people. Nineteen-year-old Jan Jansa (1923–unknown), a resident of Cizkrajov in southern Moravia, had been ordered by letter to report to the local labor office one week after receiving his blacksmith's certificate in August 1942. To avoid being drafted, he immediately signed a short-term contract with a German company operating in his area. When it expired in October, the labor office called him to work for OT. Joseph Lébl, a 20-year-old resident of Černolice near Prague, was drafted by the local labor office on November 2. From their various congregations, Jansa and Lébl met at Prague railway station, from where they arrived at the OT transit camp at Schlachtensee, south of Berlin, on November 7. The group remained in the camp for a week, undergoing medical examinations and receiving identification marks, before being transported to another transit camp near Szczecin. After waiting there for 16 days and receiving individual equipment, the batch left by ship and arrived in Oslo on December 3. On December 6, they were sent by train to Trondheim, where they arrived the following day (Frøland et al. 2021).

While acknowledging conscription, the ego-documents indicate uncertainty and curiosity during the voyage. Though the journey to Norway and along its coast was dangerous, the tourist trope was already in operation. Oldřich Svoboda (1921–1996), from the town of Třebíč in Moravia, took part in this first group and vividly described in his diary the ambiguity between fear and touristic excitement on board the ship bound for Oslo:

> Our escort consists of 7 ships. A searchlight is flashing in the distance, illuminating the sea. It's a great spectacle. But then a cannon shot rang out, a second and a third, and the air shook with the distant cannonade. There was alarm and panic on our ship. Everyone puts on life jackets. In a moment, all is quiet. Half an hour later, it is again. Then a thunderclap, the whole sea was flooded with the glow of a rocket, a second, a third, a fourth. – Alert, everyone below decks. We're waiting. For what? – We're going to sink. With God.

The ship did not sink, and the days that followed were filled with joy:

> I'm walking on deck, it's a beautiful sunny day … The beautiful sunset, low over the horizon, the golden glow in the sea, the snow-covered Danish islands, the black forests, the coastal rocks, but most of all the sea – the sea, so much praised, painted, the most beautiful thing I've ever seen. (Svoboda 1988)

Trondheim was the main hub for further redistribution. The vast majority were sent to work in northern Norway. The three largest concentrations were in the cities of Mo i Rana, Narvik, and Trondheim, but many were also used in the province of Finnmark. They were assigned to companies from the Reich that had signed contracts with the OT. Some companies also brought in workers from abroad. The company Funke & Co. from Saxony built railroads for the OT in Austria and Russia. When it began work on a railroad in Norway, it transferred some of its Czech workers north. The Czechs' construction work consisted mainly of fortifications and bunkers, but also airfields, roads, and railroads. All of these tasks involved hard work in polar conditions. A small but unknown number worked in OT camps. Josef Hofman (1921–2000), from Černice in northern Bohemia, worked with compatriots repairing clothing and shoes for the OT in Skippagurri on the Finnish border (Hingarová and Maršálek 2022, 6).

The Czechs were often skilled workers (Hingarová and Maršálek 2022, 113–35). OT regulations treated them as if the Protectorate had been incorporated into the German Reich. Material provisions, wages, and social benefits were supposed to be at the level of German workers. Outside of working hours, they could leave their camps and move about fairly freely. Ego-documents reveal a lot of socializing with the local population. The (limited) freedom to take photographs has left thousands of images representing the unity of the group and testimony to their touristic behavior. Many written and photographic testimonies reveal numerous love affairs with Norwegian women. Jaromír Šimr (1923–) reported in an interview in 2022 that his local girlfriend eagerly pursued the love relationship and pointed out that this was typical in remote areas (Šimr 2022). Numerous pictures show their fascination toward the exotic Sámi population (Hingarová, Hætta, and Lindi 2024).

Nevertheless, discontent prevailed. The Czechs accused the OT of not treating them equally with German workers and wrote to the Nazi authorities about the matter. The food was unsatisfactory and often referred to as pig food. Jan Šefl (1922–2014) mentioned that he begged the local population for food, while Josef Lébl reported that he would work longer hours to obtain larger supplies (Frøland et al. 2021, 142). After arriving in Narvik in January 1943, Oldřich Svoboda wrote in his diary: "What annoys me most is that the Germans here get double rations, cigarettes, wine, liquor, you name it. A complete mess." After a few months he received none of these goods (Svoboda 1988). In retrospect, Karel Jirgl (1920–2007) painted a grim picture: "The camps were hungry, cold, infested with disease, lice, bedbugs, and the food was mostly stew made of half-rotten cabbage or carrots" (Jirgl 1990–2000). The uninsulated barracks were often cold and lacked space, making individual life and simple practical matters such as drying clothes difficult. Many became injured or ill from the working and living conditions (Opl 1953).

Unfulfilled expectations fed the experience of victimhood. Oldřich Svoboda reported in June 1943 that no cars appeared to bring his work crew back to the camp after 12 hours of hard labor on a faraway mountain construction site. His diary reads: "With the memory of home and loved ones, we fell asleep on the slightly cold ground under an

Figure 11.1: Unprepared for the Arctic workplace in northern Norway. Czechs building ground infrastructure around Kirkenes in 1943. Courtesy of the Noráci photo collection, Charles University. All rights reserved.

overcoat." (See Figure 11.1.)They did not sleep long because it rained all night. His reaction reads: "What would my mother say if she saw me here? Or my friend Anna. Sleepless, dirty, ragged, this is the office job I was promised. Bastards!" (Svoboda 1988). Discontent led Czechs to desert as early as 1942, but mostly in 1944–1945. We have registered 57 people who successfully fled to Sweden and several hundred who resisted returning to Norway after a vacation in the Protectorate. Many of them failed and were imprisoned before being sent back to even harsher forced labor. This was the case of Rostislav Holub (1923–1995), from Skalka in Moravia, who went into hiding in the Protectorate in 1943 but was arrested after an informer betrayed him. He was returned to Norway, where he worked until the end of the war. When individuals deserted, the OT withdrew leave for other Czechs. Such collective punishments increased discontent among the workers (Hingarová and Maršálek 2022, 128).

Conditions deteriorated throughout 1944 as resources became increasingly scarce but improved when Norway came under the authority of the British-led Allied Land Forces Norway (ALFN) in

1945. Josef Hofman was still in the northernmost region with a Czech group when Germany surrendered. After reaching the boat that would take him south, he enjoyed the abundance of food on board. He arrived at a camp that had been reorganized to facilitate repatriation. Czechoslovaks who had served in the Wehrmacht were brought together with Czechs who had done forced labor for the OT. Hofman stayed in the camp until July 1945 with about 100 compatriots and found the food satisfactory. Karel Jirgl reported that the Czechs spent much of their time in sports, dances, socializing with the locals, and hiking in the northern midsummer. Those who gathered in cities like Trondheim and Narvik took part in the Norwegians' freedom celebrations. Forty Czechs married Norwegian women while awaiting repatriation. Rostislav Holub did not. He had fallen in love with a local girl but, although she wanted to go to Czechoslovakia with him, he decided to end the relationship. He could not, he later said, imagine her on a farm in Moravia (Hingarová and Maršálek 2022).

The repatriation went smoothly. The ALFN worked with the Norwegian Ministry of Social Affairs, but as early as May 1945 the Czechoslovak exile government sent officials to help organize the process. The Czechs were gathered in six camps around the country before being brought together at the main repatriation center in Oslo. The move to Czechoslovakia took place in two waves. The first included 280 people who had been gathered in the three southern camps. They left Oslo in July in almost daily batches on American planes to Brussels and were then transported by truck to a former concentration camp near Verdun. They then left Verdun by train via Munich to reach the Czechoslovakian repatriation center in Pilsen on August 2. There they received a modest transportation allowance to reach their homes. The 700 or so Czechs gathered in the three northern camps left Oslo on August 27. Together with Red Cross representatives and Czechoslovak repatriation officers, they boarded a ship bound for Bremen. From Bremen they went by train to Pilsen. A group of 14 people, who had been impatiently awaiting repatriation during the long wait in Oslo, had accepted a Soviet offer to travel via Finland and Moscow together with 1,600 Soviet POWs. According to Jan Pták (1921–2008), they spent a month in a guarded prison camp 800 km east of Moscow in deplorable conditions. They arrived in Prague on August 16 via Minsk and Warsaw (Hingarová and Maršálek 2022, 195).

Unlike many Polish forced laborers and prisoners of war who refused to return to Soviet-controlled Poland, no Czechs refused repatriation to a still free Czechoslovakia. A few Norwegian wives arrived in Czechoslovakia with a last repatriation group in November, but most arrived in the following years after having given birth in Norway.

The Czechoslovak government began informing families about the return of former forced laborers in July. The families had prepared for the return of their sons, and many had maintained some form of contact after their sons' conscription (Hingarová and Maršálek 2022, 190–93). Miroslav F. (1922– unknown) reported that he was well received:

> On returning home, after dinner, a toast is made to a happy reunion and good health. Then there is a photo and stories about Norway. The next day the neighbours invited me for lunch, where they again asked me about the experiences of the last 3 years. But I turn on the radio instead. The memories are some happy, but also some bad. (Miroslav F. 2001)

In conclusion, we suggest that narrative tropes formed a group identity among the Czech cohort even during their displacement in Norway. It consisted of young men who were forced into new conditions and new impressions. They shared common experiences since conscription, while insecurity and fear brought them together during travel and displacement. For many it was their first experience outside Czechoslovakia, for some even outside their village region. Sailing at sea for the first time was a common experience. They had been transported together in groups, and they worked and lived together in groups during their deployments. Spread over the northern half of Norway, they shared space with their compatriots, but those who were stationed near the largest cities had their own Czech barracks. A few of them, such as Jaroslav Malý (1922–1971), who had graduated from a business school in Prague and spoke German, were assigned to report from several construction sites and served as liaison informant among the Czech accumulations (Hingarová et al. 2023, 35). Obviously, group identity and shared narratives took shape through oral communication.

Although dissatisfied with working conditions and provisions, they used their freedom to enjoy the tourist aspect of the expulsion. They bought postcards and souvenirs, which were also sent home by the military post, suggesting that they wanted the landscape of their locations to be the image that would take root at home. The field post system was indeed subject to censorship, which obviously influenced

Figure 11.2: Czechs having fun in a forced labor camp in Trondheim. The relaxed atmosphere helped them to cope with hardships and homesickness. Private collection, Czech Republic. All rights reserved.

their expressions and phrasing, but countless accounts, photographs, and artifacts suggest that the touristic mode was genuine. The ambiguity between the tropes of victimhood and hardship on the one hand and the enthusiastic tourist mode on the other, which was already in operation during the journey to Norway, prevailed. We assume there was a psychological link between the tourist tropes and homesickness experienced. We also suggest that the joyful and expectant three months between the German surrender and repatriation must have had a significant impact on memory. (See Figure 11.2.)

Postwar memory and memorialization

Although 500,000 Czechs were subjected to transnational forced labor, public memory in Czechoslovakia ignored their collective experience for decades after the war. From 1948, the communist regime deliberately silenced their memory, but not even the preceding Nuremberg trials prompted the media to draw public attention to their experience.

The victims themselves rarely spoke publicly about their experiences. For a long time, even the tiny *Noráci* group had no interest in bringing their common experience into public memory.

Why did the *Noráci* not engage in public remembrance even before the communist coup? We agree with Reissman (1993) that people tend to find it difficult to express traumatic experiences in language because of a lack of words. We suggest, however, that the absence of words was related to the fact that this cohort of young people was moving on. The vast majority had returned to their homes, families, and workplaces to pursue family life, work, and education. Some had found their homes and villages destroyed, and some, like Miroslav Marek from Vraný nad Vltavou near Prague, had found new opportunities with their forced labor wages. His return was not a happy one, as his mother and sister had reported him missing and claimed his inherited property. He therefore decided to start a new life in the Sudetenland (from where ethnic Germans had been expelled) and used his savings to buy a small farm in the border region of Karlovy Vary (Marek 2021). In agreement with Jarská (2010), we assume that Marek and others simply did not have much time to engage in memorialization, even if they had the vocabulary to express it publicly.

Even the sharing of memories between generations within the family seems to have been moderate. Josef Lébl's eager and vivid narration to his daughter, described in the introduction, was not so common. Unlike Lébl, Zdeněk Opl (1922–1987) was reluctant to share his experiences with his family. According to his two sons, he "never told us about his stay in Norway. Apparently, he did not want to ruin our childhood with memories of the war and experiences of forced labour." Jaroslav Buchtík's son (1920–1997) claimed: "My father remembered the time in Norway with pleasure, he never mentioned anything negative … In fact, he did not talk much about that time." Only a limited number of memories were passed on, leaving out the hardships. Although the limited generational sharing of memories could be understood in traumatic terms, descendants tend to interpret it as highly rational: their fathers wanted to protect them from unpleasant feelings (Hingarová, Maršálek, and Vlk 2021). Nevertheless, the ambiguous experience revolving around the narrative tropes of hardship and tourism persisted. This is best expressed by Jan Benc, the son of Jiří Benc (1922–1995), who reported on his father's memoirs: "It was remarkable that the unpleasant experiences of hard winter months

Figure 11.3: Czechs socialising with local women in Skibotn. Private collection, Czech Republic. All rights reserved.

and hard work were overshadowed by pleasant experiences such as the midnight sun and almost four months in Norway before his return" (Hingarová et al. 2023, 87).

Importantly, the public silence did not end the wartime narrative networks among the Noráci. Those who lived in the neighborhoods met regularly, and many others corresponded by letter about their shared experiences. Jaromir Šimr recalled in 2022 that he had met some 20 or 30 *Noráci* compatriots in Prague, probably in 1947 (Šimr 2022). However ambiguous their shared experience, it was engraved in their memories and provided a solid foundation for the maintenance of personal ties. Love affairs and the touristic imaginary were a recurring narrative trope in their early exchanges (see Figure 11.3). Emil Mynář (1922–1986) wrote to a former fellow forced laborer:

I too am more in Norway than here at home. Believe me, I have received several letters from the boys and almost all of them write the same thing. None of them can get used to it here. Everyone is drawn back to the Scandinavian country or to a Norwegian girl. (Mynář 1945)

Many hundreds of love relationships were formed during the expulsion, and about 70 children were born after the war. The early exchanges, whether oral or written, told of a shared memory that preferred the tourist trope to the victim trope. They even seem to have fueled a desire to return voluntarily to Norway to maintain old friendships. Several corresponded with Norwegian friends as they built new lives in Czechoslovakia.

This networked commemoration before the communist takeover in 1948 clearly falls under Assmann's notion of communicative memory. A potential for public discourse did exist, however, as the Czechoslovak government began to record individual citizens' claims against Germany prior to the Paris Reparations Conference in late 1945. Zdeněk Kunštátský (1921–2005) and 60 compatriots filed a claim for unpaid wages in September 1945. They had been recruited to work for a German company and had not been paid for five months (Kunštátský 1945). The government received a quota of reparations, but the outstanding wages were never paid before the communist government abruptly ended the compensation schemes started by the previous government.

The communist takeover in 1948 had several inhibiting effects on the commemoration of the *Noráci* experience. First, the government maintained a public silence on Nazi forced labor expulsions because it did not want to challenge the privileged victimhood of the communist resistance (Thonfeld 2011). The Union of Anti-Fascist Fighters, founded in 1953, did not include forced laborers, unlike resistance fighters, political prisoners, and soldiers who had served in the Czechoslovak exile army. Although its press occasionally allowed forced laborers to recall their experiences, it is illustrative that after Zdenek Opl (1922–1987) filed a 30-page account of his experiences in Norway in the municipal archives in 1952; it was later destroyed by the local authorities (Hingarová et al. 2023, 19). The academic publications by the historians Zdeněk Konečný (1967) and František Mainuš (1970), which elaborated on Czech forced labor in Germany and the Protectorate, did not challenge the prevailing silence either.

Second, the government cut off the possibility of maintaining close ties with friends and relatives in Norway. Jaroslav Malý met his future wife Ellen Romsloe in Narvik in 1943. They married shortly after liberation and moved to Czechoslovakia before the coup in 1948 after a few years in Sweden. Their hopes of visiting relatives in Scandinavia were soon dashed. After Jaroslav's death in 1971, Ellen wanted to return to Norway, but her children were not allowed to join her. She never visited Norway before her death in 2013 (Hingarová and Maršálek 2022). Before the communist coup in 1948, however, several Norwegian women had returned to Norway after divorce or the death of their husbands, and several more were actually allowed to return during communism. We also observed a dozen people visiting former Norwegian friends during the political thaw in the mid-1960s, when the government issued travel permits in exceptional cases. Jaroslav Buchtík visited a former Norwegian friend with his wife in 1965, while Vladimír Herec (1921–unknown) was allowed a ten-day visit with his wife and son in 1966. Soviet intervention in 1968 ended the thaw and the visits.

Statements by *Noráci* descendants suggest that communist constraints allowed the ambiguity of tropes between victimhood and tourism to prevail. It is not entirely clear how the generational shift affected the balance between the dominant memory tropes, but there is much evidence that the descendants' affinity with Norway was strengthened. Rostislav Holub's son Antonín vividly recounted an experience with his father at an international cycling race in Czechoslovakia:

> In Bukovec, there's a long, steep hill that the cyclists had to ride up. Dad and I were waiting halfway up the hill. When we saw the cross in the Norwegian colours and the words "Norway" on the riders' jerseys, I shouted as I ran up the hill alongside the riders. Dad kept his dignity, stood calmly and waved. We shouted "Long live Norway" in Norwegian and the Norwegian riders waved back. I could see the tears running down my father's cheeks. (Hingarová et al. 2023, 39)

Holub's daughter Milada Svozilová recalled:

> As children we knew that daddy had been in Norway. For a long time we even bragged about it. We thought he was there on holiday. It was only after he had a stroke that he occasionally shouted. "Don't hang him," he said. He had experienced something there with the Russians. The memories kept coming back. Sometimes he jumped out of bed and shouted that he wanted to go home. (Hingarová et al. 2023, 31)

Her father had witnessed the brutal killing of a Soviet POW and apparently suppressed the trauma, which could indicate that Rostislav Holub had long suppressed his victimhood while narrating the tourist trope. The political thaw saw another innovation in 1965, when Adolf Šutera (1922–1999), who had been stationed in the Narvik area, organized a first informal reunion as part of the official twentieth anniversary of the victory over fascism. One hundred and ten people attended in the small Moravian village of Lysice. Šutera's motivation is not entirely clear. He had made no previous efforts to commemorate but it seems that he had no political ambitions. We therefore see this meeting as a spontaneous gathering of a loose network of acquaintances, constrained by the communist discourse of remembrance. Nevertheless, this network compiled a first short list of former forced laborers used in Norway and, not least, established a common consciousness to maintain and expand the network of remembrance.

It was not until May 1985, on the fortieth anniversary of the liberation, that the *Noráci* met again, in two sessions. This was initiated by two short newspaper appeals by non-*Noráci* organizers, inviting former forced laborers who had been at the OT transit camp at Schlachtensee. Because the camp also housed people who had been used elsewhere than Norway, Adolf Šutera therefore decided to hold a separate meeting for the *Noráci* in the small Moravian town of Svitavy. Around 100 people attended each of these meetings, but many more joined by correspondence, bringing the *Noráci* list up to 700 names. After the meetings, more members of the group apparently tended to engage more actively in collective remembrance, including in public. This coincided with the retirement of the cohort, giving them more time. However, although censorship at both meetings forced them to conform to communist rituals and rhetoric, a close reading of the transcripts suggests that speakers attempted to weave their own contradictory experiences into the dominant communist discourse. One semi-veiled message was that forced laborers were victims of fascism, and that many were also involved in workplace sabotage. Another was that the similarities between Czechoslovakia and Norway were stronger than official communist foreign policy rhetoric claimed (Šutera 1985). This suggests some agency in breaking constraints to make room for their own narratives.

Although more informal gatherings were organized in the late 1980s, the shared memory of the Norwegian forced labor experience

Figure 11.4: Noráci gathering in Czechoslovakia in 1990 to commemorate their experiences of forced labor in Norway. Noráci picture collection, Charles University. All rights reserved.

never transcended the character of communicative memory before the Velvet Revolution of 1989 destroyed the dominance of the communist memory regime. It is symptomatic of the situation under communism that the organizers of the 1985 *Noráci* meetings completely failed to attract the interest of the regional and national media.

It was only in the 1990s that memorialization gradually developed into cultural memory. The fall of communism and its regime of remembrance was the basic prerequisite, but several forces beyond the narrative network of the Noráci cohort contributed to this change. The establishment of the Czech Union of Forced Labourers of World War II as a nationwide interest group in 1990 was important (Figure 11.4). Its aim was to raise public awareness of the victims of forced labor and to improve health care for its members. It played a key role in the Czech Republic before the German government and industry formally established a compensation fund for victims of the Nazi forced labor program in 2000. It maintained liaison with the Czech–German Fund for the Future, which was set up in 1998 to register compensation claims and transfer individual payments. The scheme paid out 38,000

Czech claims in 2003. Only a fraction of the victims was still alive, and next of kin were not allowed to file claims if their husband or father had died before February 1999 (Zloch 2017), which explains the low number of claims. Nevertheless, the compensation scheme brought the experience of forced labor to the attention of the Czech public, and formal agencies and institutions were established to commemorate and remember the victims. Eyewitness accounts were submitted, and historians began to research the Czech experience of forced labor from new perspectives and evidence (Pažout 2004; Kokošková, Pažout, and Sedláková 2011).

The *Noráci* network played an active role in this overall transformation, although we do not know how many of them were involved in the Association of Second World War Forced Labourers. The network assisted claimants, although the compensation fund received only 239 claims from claimants who had been deployed in Norway or Finland (Hingarová and Maršálek 2022, 222). It also honored deceased friends by providing evidence of their forced labor deportation. Adolf Šutera organized another Noráci meeting in 1990. By 2005 there had been 12 more meetings, usually attended by around 50 people. A Noráci secretariat with an archive was established in 1992. Members of the group, most of them retired, encouraged each other to write down their memories and share them with the public. Some wrote short articles in newspapers (Jirgl 1990–2000) and others in regional historical magazines (Pátek 1993), while some published their stories in books (Mejzlík 1997; Šefl 2007). Oldřich Svoboda wrote a 25-page narrative about his experiences in northeastern Norway, but never managed to get it published. His grandson later told an interviewer that Svoboda "talked a lot about his experiences as a forced labourer at the end of his life and was eager to have it published" (Hingarová at al. 2021, 31). Jan Šefl also gave an interview about his experiences for the public collection Memory of the Nation. Indeed, the Noráci archive, the archive of the Union of Forced Labourers of World War II and the archive of the Czech–German Future Fund contain numerous written memoirs and newspaper cuttings. Paradoxically, the *Noráci* strengthened its memorialization when most of its members had died. Since the 1990s, their descendants have increasingly taken over memorialization, another feature of cultural memory (Assmann 1988).

During the period of cultural memory, in the context of the public discourse on compensation, the victim trope seems to have become somewhat more prominent in memory narratives. Karel Jirgl's news-paper story, presumably from 1995, illustrates this. He emphasized that the Czechs had had to sacrifice much of their youth, and many even their health and lives. They "shed blood and sweat for German interests … It was a piece of a ruined life, a lost youth living in mis-erable conditions far from home" (Jirgl 1990–2000). Unsurprisingly, trauma, health problems, and misery were highlighted in the compen-sation claims. The electrician JS (b. 1923, anonymized) described his experience as three years of slavery in harsh polar conditions, from which "I got a permanent inflammation of my stomach and duode-num. To this day I am on a diet" (JS 2001). The carpenter AK (b. 1922, anonymized) had suffered a spinal cord injury with brain damage dur-ing his Norwegian deportation. His modest statement reads: "I am not going to write any more, I just want to say that it was said that those who suffered serious bodily injury with permanent disability as forced labourers might have their compensation increased." He had lived on a modest Czechoslovak disability pension and a modest income beyond that: "I could not work as a carpenter and did not earn much working in the factory. My pension was calculated on that basis" (AK 2001). Not surprisingly, the tourist mode was not a constitutive part of the claims. The compensation discourse of the mid-1990s seems to have tipped the balance of the dominant memory tropes in favor of victim-hood.

Conclusion

In contrast to Jarská 2010 and Thonfeld 2011, who studied the large number of Czech forced laborers who worked in the German war economy, this chapter has examined the much smaller group who were brought to Norway. A first finding is that their shared experience of forced labor displacement was transformed into a shared mem-ory even before repatriation. In Czechoslovakia, a postwar collective memory settled as enduring communicative memory (Assmann 1988) within families and informal networks. The communist memoriali-zation regime disallowed this communicative memory to transcend into cultural memory until its fall in 1989. We have observed moderate agency among the group to create space for their collective memory in communist public discourse, but this largely failed. Although reunions of the cohort have taken place at irregular intervals since 1990, and indeed strengthened group identity, it was the German compensation program for Nazi forced laborers at the turn of the millennium that brought *Noráci*'s memory into the public sphere and transformed it into cultural memory (Assmann 1988) in the Czech Republic. By this time, most of the *Noráci* cohort had passed away and the commemoration taken over by their descendants.

Searching for narrative tropes in the ego-documents of the forced laborers and their descendants, we found that even during their time as forced laborers they did not perceive their situation only in terms of misery and victimhood. The *Noráci* also perceived themselves as tourists. Victimhood and tourism formed the core narrative tropes, thus creating an ambiguity in the group's collective memory even before repatriation. This ambiguity between the tropes of victimhood and tourism persisted in Czechoslovakia during the period of communist communicative memory. Nevertheless, within families the descendants were fed more with the joyful tropes of the tourist mood than the traumatic trope of misery and hardship. Not surprisingly, however, we observed a shift in favor of victimhood as the German compensation scheme for former forced laborers from Central and Eastern Europe was established. The German compensation scheme also had an impact on the character of memory.

The ambiguity between the tropes of victimhood and tourism testifies to Gatrell's (2007) point that "historians of war and population displacement need to look beyond the mountain of misery on the balance sheet ... It is simplistic to accept the tragedy of displacement at face value." We accept that there may be other groups with parallel experiences during the forced labor program. We do, however, acknowledge the horrors produced by the Nazi racial machinery in general and suspect that they would not be easy to find. Memory studies of forced displacement during other wars or deep conflicts may reveal parallel, if not equivalent, memory tropes.

Bibliography

Assmann, Jan. 1988. "Kollektives Gedächtnis und kulturelle Identität". In *Kultur und Gedächtnis*, edited by Jan Assmann and Tonio Hölscher, 9–19. Frankfurt a.M.: Suhrkamp.
Borggräfe, Henning. 2014. *Zwangsarbeiterentschädigung: Vom Streit um „vergessene Opfer" zur Selbstaussöhnung der Deutschen*. Göttingen: Wallstein Verlag.

Brubaker, Rogers. 1995. "Aftermaths of Empire and the Unmixing of Peoples: Historical and Comparative Perspectives". *Ethnic and Racial Studies* 18 (2): 148–78. https://doi.org/10.1080/01419870.1995.9993861

Frøland, Hans Otto, Gunnar D. Hatlehol, Vendula Hingarová, and Zdenko Maršálek. 2021. "De tsjekkiske tvangsarbeiderne i Oberbauleitung Drontheim". In *Midtnorske historier*, edited by Magne B. Rabben et al., 147–85. Oslo: Novus Forlag.

Gatrell, Peter. 2007. "Introduction: World Wars and Population Displacement in Europe in the Twentieth Century". *Contemporary European History*, 16 (4): 415–26. https://doi.org/10.1017/S0960777307004092

Hatlehol, Gunnar D. 2015. "'Norwegeneinsatz' 1940–1945. Organisation Todts arbeidere og gradene av tvang". Unpublished PhD diss., NTNU.

Hatlehol, Gunnar D. 2020. "Fangenskap og tvangsarbeid i det tyskokkuperte Norge 1940-1945". *Arbeiderhistorie* 34 (1): 61–83. https://doi.org/10.18261/issn.2387-5879-2020-01-05

Herbert, Ulrich. 1985. *Fremdarbeiter, Politik und Praxis des „Ausländer-Einsatzes" in der Kriegswirtschaft des Dritten Reiches*. Bonn: J. H. W. Dietz.

Hingarová, Vendula., J. A. Hætta, and Gudrun E E. Lindi. 2024. *Sámi-Čehkkalaš oktavuodat. Česko-sámské kontakty*. Prague/Karašjohka: FHS UK– RiddoDuottarmuseat.

Hingarová, Vendula and Zdenko Maršálek. 2022. *Posláni na sever. Češi nucené práci v Norsku*. Červený Kostelec: Nakladatelství Pavel Mervart.

Hingarová, Vendula, Zdenko Maršálek, Lars Busterud, and Vojtěch Vlk. 2023. *Posláni na sever: 20 příběhů/Sendt til nord:20 historier*. Prague: Univerzita Karlova, Filozoficka fakulta.

Hingarová, Vendula, Zdenko Maršálek, and Vojtěch Vlk. 2021. *Posláni na sever:15 příběhů/Sendt til nord:15 historier*. Prague: Univerzita Karlova, Filozoficka fakulta.

Jacobmeyer, Wolfgang. 1985. *Vom Zwangsarbeiter zum Heimatlosen Ausländer. Die Displaced Persons in Westdeutschland 1945-1951*. Göttingen: Vandenhoeck & Ruprecht.

Jarská, Šárka. 2010. "Czechs as Forced and Slave Labourers during the Second World War". In *Hitler's slaves. Life Stories of Forced Labourers in Nazi-Occupied Europe*, edited by Alexander von Plato, Almut Leh, and Christoph Tonfeld, 47–58. New York: Berghahn Books. https://doi.org/10.3167/9781845456986

Kantsteiner, Wulf. 2000. "Finding Meaning in Memory. A Methodological Critique of Collective Memory Studies". *History and Theory* 41 (2): 179–97. https://doi.org/10.1111/0018-2656.00198

Kokošková, Zdeňka, Jaroslav Pažout, and Monika Sedláková, eds. 2011. *Pracovali pro Třetí říši: nucené pracovní nasazení českého obyvatelstva Protektorátu Čechy a Morava pro válečné hospodářství Třetí říše (1939-1945)*. Prague: Scriptorium.

Konečný, Zdeněk. 1967. *Pracovní nasazení válečných zajatců a obyvatel Evropy v ČSR (1939-1945)*. Brno: Univerzita J. E. Purkyně. Konečný.

Lundemo, Mari O. 2020. "Engineering, Resources and Nature: Organisation Todt in Finland, 1941-1944". Unpublished PhD thesis, European University Institute.

Mainuš, František. 1970. *Totální nasazení: Češi na pracích v Německu 1939-1945*. Brno: Universita J. E. Purkyně.

Mellard, James M. 1987. *Doing Tropology. Analysis of Narrative Discourse.* Champaign, IL: University of Illinois Press.

Pažout, Jaroslav, Stanislav Kokoška, and Zdeňka Kokošková, eds. 2004. *Museli pracovat pro Říši: nucené pracovní nasazení českého obyvatelstva v letech 2. světové války: sborník ze semináře konaného ve Státním ústředním archivu v Praze dne 2. dubna 2004.* Prague: Státní ústřední archiv.

Polian, Pavel. 2004. "Soviet and Russian Historiography on the Issues of Forced Labour during World War II". In *Revisiting the National Socialist Legacy. Coming to Terms with Forced Labour, Expropriation, Compensation, and Restitution*, edited by Oliver Rathkolb, 100–112. New York: Routledge.

Riessmann, Catherine K. 1993. *Narrative Analysis.* London: Sage.

Soleim, Marianne Neerland. 2009. *Sovjetiske krigsfanger i Norge 1941–1945: Antall, organisering og repatriering.* Oslo: Spartacus.

Soleim, Marianne Neerland. 2018. *Operasjon Asfalt – kald krig om krigsgraver.* Stamsund: Orkana Forlag.

Stokke, Michael. 2024. "Jugoslaviske fanger i Norge 1942-1945. Fra SS' dødsleirer til Wehrmachts krigsfangeleirer". Unpublished PhD diss., University of Tromsø.

Thonfeld, Christoph. 2011. "Memories of Former World War Two Forced Labourers – An International Comparison". *Oral History* 39 (2): 33–48.

Verboven, Konrad, Myrian Carlier, and Jan Dumolyn. 2007. "A Short Manual to the Art of Prosopography". In *Prosopography Approaches and Applications. A Handbook*, edited by K. S. B. Keats-Rohan, 35–70. Oxford Oxford University Prosopographica et Genealogica.

Wagner, Jens-Christian. 2011. "Zwangsarbeiter im Nationalsozialismus – ein Überblick". In *Zwangsarbeit. Die Deutschen, die Zwangsarbeiter und der Krieg.* Begleitband zur Ausstellung, herausgegeben von Volkhard Knigge, Rikola-Gunnar Lüttgenau und Jens-Christian Wagner im Auftrag der Stiftung Gedenkstätten Buchenwald und Mittelbau-Dora. (3. Auflage), 180–193. Weimar.

Zloch, Stephanie. 2017. "Compensation for Forced Labourers in the Czech Republik". In *Compensation in Practice. The Foundation "Remembrance, Responsibility and Future" and the Legacy of Forced Labour during the Third Reich*, edited by Constantin Goschler, 156–81. New York: Berghahn Books.

Cited or referenced ego-documents and interviews

AK (anonymized). 2001. Letter of 8.5.2021 to Czech–German Future Fund (CGFF). Applicant's file CGFF archive, Prague.

F. Miroslav. 2000. Bylo to v roce 1942. Unpublished manuscript. Applicant's file CGFF archive, Prague.

Jirgl, Karel. 1990–2000. Letters and newspaper clips. Archive of the Noráci organization, Charles University, Prague.

JS (anonymized). 2001. Letter from 2.7.2021 to Czech–German Future Fund. Applicant's file, CGFF archive, Prague.

K. Josef (anonymized). 2000. Testimony filed in the CGFF archive, Prague.

Marek, Antonín. 2021. Interview by V. Hingarová 24.5. 2021. Archive collection of the Noráci research project, Charles University, Prague.

Mejzlík, Jaroslav. 1997. Naši krajané v boji za svobodu. In Mejzlík, Jaroslav. Naši krajané v boji za svobodu: občané Třebíčska v zahraničním odboji 1937–1945. Třebíč: Český svaz bojovníků za svobodu, 31–32.

Mynář, Emil. Letters 1945–1946. Archive collection of the Noráci research project, Charles University, Prague.

Opl, Zdeněk. 1952. Vzpomínky na Norsko. Archive collection of the Noráci research project, Charles University, Prague.

Pátek, Jiří. 1993. Osudy Čechů na nucených pracech v Norsku 1942–45. In: Ročenka vlastivědné muzejní společnosti v Jeseníku. Jeseník: samizdat: 7–9. Archive collection of the Noráci research project, Charles University, Prague.

Poledna, Milan. 2003. Moje severská anabáze v rámci totálního nasazení v letech 1942–1945. Archive collection of the Norácresearch project, Charles University, Prague.

Svoboda, Oldřich. 1988. Vzpomínky 1942. Archive collection of the Noráci research project, Charles University, Prague.

Svozilová, Milada. 2021. Interview by V. Hingarová, 26.5.2021. Archive collection of the Noráci research project, Charles University, Prague.

Šefl. Jan. 2009. Za války v Norsku. Vyprávění z totálního nasazení. Rožmitál pod Třemšínem: Own publisher.

Šimr, Jaromír. 2022. Interview by V. Hingarová, 11.1.2022. Archive collection of the Noráci research project, Charles University, Prague.

Šutera, Adolf. 1985. Correspondence with organizers of Noráci meeting. Archive collection of the Noráci research project, Charles University, Prague.

CHAPTER 12

Children and the Lapland War

Experiences of forced displacement

Outi Autti

University of Oulu

Abstract

This article analyzes a previously understudied refugee case that connects two Nordic countries by exploring the experiences of children and young people evacuated from Finnish Lapland to Finnish Ostrobothnia and Sweden during the Lapland War (1944–1945). The study focuses on children's experiences of leaving home, the evacuation journey, and either remaining in Ostrobothnia or crossing the border into Sweden. The article is based on qualitative interview material and three written narratives. By exploring the experiences of children, the study aims to reveal new interpretations of the past. Children's key experiences of the evacuation period were related to refugee status, a sense of adventure and threats to home and family. Feelings of fear and insecurity were ever-present. The war and flight meant violence, losses, and uncertainty, but the events were not unilaterally negative for the children involved. The Lapland War and the resulting evacuation were also portrayed as a great adventure.

How to cite this book chapter:
Autti, Outi. 2025. "Children and the Lapland War: experiences of forced displacement." In *Forced Migrants in Nordic Histories*, edited by Johanna Leinonen, Miika Tervonen, Hans Otto Frøland, Christhard Hoffmann, Seija Jalagin, Heidi Vad Jønsson and Malin Thor Tureby, 303–326. Helsinki: Helsinki University Press. https://doi.org/10.33134/HUP-32-13.

304 Forced Migrants in Nordic Histories

Introduction

This chapter[1] explores the experiences and memories of children and young people evacuated from Finnish Lapland to Finnish Ostrobothnia and Sweden during the Lapland War (1944–1945). It analyses a previously understudied refugee case that connects two Nordic countries. When the Continuation War ended on September 5, 1944, the terms of the Armistice required Finland to deport all German troops, an army of about 215,000 men, from Finnish territory within two weeks. To protect the civilian population from the anticipated conflict, the entire Province of Lapland was to be evacuated. Around 56,500 people were evacuated to Sweden, and 47,500 were evacuated to the remainder of Finland, mainly Ostrobothnia. Hostilities between the Finnish and German armies erupted into war on September 15 (Tuominen 2015; Ursin 1980).

The Lapland War has remained relatively invisible in national histories, scientific research, and national memory. Research has mainly consisted of traditional war history studies, with evacuation being a secondary theme. Local memory cultures, however, suggest that the experiences of the war and evacuation have been very significant. These memories have mostly been dealt with privately, within families and local communities. Researchers have only recently begun to take an interest in the Lapland War, and the war has also become the subject of several cultural performances and works of fiction.

Recent analytical interest in the histories of experiences has shed light on the role and perspective of civilians in war. This view has given us a better understanding of the total, all-encompassing nature of war. Research on experiences of the Lapland War has previously focused on memories of German soldiers, Soviet prisoners of war, the evacuation of the Saami, and the reconstruction of a destroyed Lapland (Autti and Laitala 2019; Junila 2000; Lehtola 2004, 2018; Tuominen 2015; Tuominen, Ashplant, and Harjumaa 2020). The perspective of children has been marginal. Merja Paksuniemi (2014) has studied the experiences of Finnish refugee children in Swedish refugee camps based on six interviews. Her findings show that daily routines and the presence of reliable adults helped children through exceptional circumstances. Sari Näre, Jenni Kirves, and Juha Siltala (2010) explore the emotional memories of children and young people during the Winter War and Continuation War and how the traces of war are still visible in children and young people today. Eerika Koskinen-Koivisto and Oula Seitsonen (2019) have studied Saami childhood memories of the Second World War. They write about how traumatic experiences have been neglected and suppressed in public debate and studied only recently by academics. Ulla Savolainen (2015) explores the experiences of Karelian evacuees, and Hanna-Leena Määttä (forthcoming) investigates how the refugee experiences of children are portrayed in refugee literature.

My study focuses on children who fled the Lapland War: their experiences of leaving home, the evacuation journey, and either remaining in Ostrobothnia or crossing the border into Sweden. The chapter is based on qualitative interview material (n = 14) collected almost 70 years after the end of the Lapland War. My data also include three written narratives that were originally published on the internet pages of a village association. By exploring the experiences of children, I aim to expand the prevailing narratives and reveal new interpretations of the past. What were the key experiences of the children who were forcibly moved to Sweden or Ostrobothnia? How did childhood and adolescence frame these experiences?

My study is linked with historical social science, cultural studies, and cultural sociology. I assume the experiences of refugee children during the Second World War have much in common with those of children experiencing war and forced migration today. Ilesanmi, Haynes, and Ogundimu (2024), leaning on UN statistics, state that children make up over 40 percent of the world's refugee and internally displaced population. UN reports indicate that over 47 million children had been forcibly displaced as of the end of 2023, and between 2018 and 2023 about two million children were born as refugees. Ilesanmi, Haynes, and Ogundimu (ibid.) write that forced displacement exposes children to a high amount of traumatic material that impacts the child's development and health outcomes. The authors suggest these impacts should be understood from the lived experiences of the forcibly displaced children. Resent research has mostly focused on studying the physical and mental health consequences of refugee children and young adults (e.g., Rizkalla et al. 2020), how refugee-background young adults manage their psychosocial well-being (Gitau, Arop, and Lenette 2023), and young people's experiences of coping in the context of unaccompanied forced migration (see e.g., Kauhanen, Kaukko, and Lanas 2022; Scott, Mason, and Kelly 2024). The approaches of many studies are normative and aim to create better practices, but there is also a need for more descriptive research.

Materials and methods

My research material consists of memoirs written by three men evacuated to Sweden when they were children and 14 qualitative interviews conducted between 2013 and 2018. Of those interviewed, nine were women and five were men. They were all elderly, having been born in the 1920s or 1930s. During the war, they had been children or young people and been evacuated to Sweden, Ostrobothnia, or relatives in southern Finland. The interviews lasted an average of one hour and were recorded and transcribed verbatim. The interviewees were asked for permission to use their names in the transcription of the material, archiving and reporting, and 12 gave their permission. For the two who wished to remain anonymous, pseudonyms are used. The three memoirs were collected as part of a project by a local history study group, "Yläkemijoen historia" (2014–), in which the Lapland War and evacuation were among the project themes. The memoirs are published on the web pages of the group (https://ylakemijoenhistoria.wordpress.com). Therefore, they are referred to by the names of the writers.

Methodologically, I draw from sociological interview research (in-depth interviews), which I pair with oral history research. The methodological tool used in the analysis is qualitative content analysis, specifically several readings and the thematization of the data, using the research questions as reference points (see, e.g., Denzin 2006; Finger-roos, Haanpää, and Heimo 2006; Neuendorf 2017).

As my methodological base is sociological research, I use the words "interviewer," "interviewee," and "data." However, I understand that the narratives of the war are cocreated, selective, changing, and fragmented. They are pathways into both the personal past of the narrator and the experiences of other people (see, e.g., Koskinen-Koivisto and Seitsonen 2019, 27). The struggle between remembering and forgetting has social and cultural significance, as the community determines what is worth remembering and retelling. Interviewees told of situations that had occurred some 70 years earlier. Such a long temporal distance shapes memories and narratives. Collective memories, written memoirs, and public discussion of the Lapland War have built up a particular way of remembering the evacuation period. The interviewees support and maintain the evacuation narrative, and they had to decide which memories were suitable for the collective narrative and which were not. Memories are also socially constructed. It is easier to express unpleasant personal experiences as part of the experiences of the refugee group (see also Autti and Intonen 2022).

My family background is firmly rooted in the refugee experience. Both my parents and their families were evacuated, one to Sweden and the other to Ostrobothnia. I have brought this to the fore in the interviews I conducted and have seen how these experiences build a bridge between interviewer and interviewee. Sharing my family's experiences has also given the interviewees confidence that the interviewer understands what they are saying. Despite this trust, many things were also left unsaid. These were related to painful memories, such as deaths of loved ones, abuse, or exploitation. The number of refusals to be interviewed was higher than in my interviews on other subjects. The reason given for refusal was not wanting to remember unpleasant times.

The importance of animals

The fate of pets

The children's first experiences of displacement at the time of their departure were strongly linked to animals. When it was time to leave home, it became clear that only cows and horses could be brought along. Teenage girls and boys with milking skills were often the first to leave so as to transport cows to Sweden and Ostrobothnia.

The evacuation was successfully completed in Lapland within two weeks. Instructions for evacuation were mainly provided via radio, newspapers, and notices on walls. People were only allowed to take what they could carry in their hands. All other possessions had to be left behind. Transport was organized based on trains, lorries, and boats. Travel conditions were cramped and cold, and many people went hungry. Some used their personal contacts and sought refuge with relatives or friends in southern Finland. Others defied the evacuation order and remained hidden in the forests (Autti and Intonen 2022).

All interviewees were used to having animals, both as pets and as farm animals. Small farms in Lapland at the time had horses, cows, domestic reindeer, pigs, sheep, chickens, dogs, and cats. The children spent time with the animals and were often responsible for caring for them. Through taking care of the animals, they developed warm attachments to them.

The miserable fate of small livestock and other animals soon became clear. They were either slaughtered or set free. Sometimes, this liquidation occurred in a brutal way. Veikko Kerätär (2023) wrote that people in his village were waiting for further transport to the evacuation center: "All the people and all the village dogs had gathered there. A soldier on leave started shooting the dogs, but he was such a bad shot that the dogs ran along the woods in their blood."

Many adults attempted to spare children the unpleasant experience of losing an animal. Martti Karjalainen's (2023) father had left with his horse and Pipsa, the dog.

> Pipsa was very important to us children. The cats and dogs were to be killed. Father said he would take the dog with him. It calmed us down. When we then met our father in Sweden several months later and asked about Pipsa, he told us that Pipsa's string had apparently rubbed against the cartwheel and that she had run away. Later, I realised that Dad had probably killed the dog on his way to Sweden.

Some cats and dogs attempted to follow the evacuees, and the memories of the animals being rushed back home were very saddening. Määttä (forthcoming) states that the refugee children's departure is strongly linked to sadness and trauma over animals left at home or killed. Both children and animals were at the mercy of the adult world.

Cows as companions

Two municipality councillors came to ask 14-year-old Aino Hepola if she could milk. Thus began Aino's journey toward Haparanda and the Swedish border as a cattle driver. Aino and her cousin Maire were responsible also for the neighbor's cows, 20 in all. The work became a chore, as the responsibility for the animals passed entirely to the young cow-carers. It was difficult to convince the cows to obey and remain in line. Cows strayed, and they had to be searched for in the woods. The cattle drivers also had to carry all the equipment needed to milk and care for the cows.

> On 13 September, we left at dawn, and it was raining. At first, the cattle were all over the meadows and woods. We decided that if two of us held

the cows, they would soon get used to walking in line … We went off to go and walked the cows, and the others ran around and kept them together. (Eila Tapio)

Taking care of the cows was seen as an important task, and the work of transporting them structured the course of the day. Despite the company of other cow-carers, driving cattle felt lonely and unsafe without the support of one's family. The young cattle carers had been the first to leave home and had no knowledge of the fate of their family members. Gradually, the cows became significant as they formed an important link to home and family. Cows were also a source of shelter. Aino Hepola stated, "Well, it got cold there. We went to sleep under the cow's armpit, and it was warm."

Cattle transport was mostly on foot and by rail in cattle wagons. The distances involved were several hundred kilometers, so it took weeks to complete the distance. The feet of both drivers and cows became sore before they became used to the strain of the journey. Cows were transported beside small roads to avoid blocking the main roads. These roads were in bad condition. The daily distance traveled on foot was 20 to 30 kilometers.

The hardship of the journey was exacerbated by the poor nutrition available for both drivers and cows. Helge Kuosmanen drove the cows from Eastern Lapland to Ostrobothnia. The drivers were fed twice a day, and the cows were given hay at night. Helge recalled that the quality of the food was poor and, sometimes, the drivers had to argue about the hay: "The state had asked locals to reserve hay for the cows, but there were often quarrels about it because the old men and women would not give their hay."

After crossing the Swedish border, the burden of taking responsibility for the cows was increased by the fact that the drivers were now in a foreign country, one with a language they did not understand. The cow and its driver were now in a very similar position, at the mercy of the Swedish authorities. They had to do what they were told and go where they were told.

In Ostrobothnia, Lappish families were mostly settled on farms, where they kept their cows in their hosts' barns. In Sweden, cows were transported to farms with completely empty barns or room for extra cows. The cattle carers settled either on Swedish farms or in temporary accommodation in public buildings, such as schools or courthouses, from which they went to look after their cows nearby.

The animals in the receiving areas could also become significant for children and young people. Some children evacuated to Sweden helped on farms, and those evacuated to Ostrobothnia could also work on host farms or in their neighborhoods. Helge Kuosmanen, who transported the cattle of his home village to Sievi, Ostrobothnia, recalled how, at the age of 14, he had worked on farms in the neighborhood of his evacuation site. The work paid little but Helge's main motivation was to keep busy and be able to look after animals. "I remember that it paid very little, but I was so keen because there were two horses," he said.

New blood for Lappish livestock farming and hunting

After the war ended at the end of April 1945, as demining progressed, most refugees were able to return home. This did not apply to the inhabitants of the areas of Petsamo, Salla, and Kuusamo, ceded to the Soviet Union, whose refugee status might continue for years before final settlement. Upon the return of the inhabitants, new animals were also brought in, such as calves born during the evacuation or puppies received from Swedes or Ostrobothnians. All the animals could not always be taken back home. Olavi Ahola recalled that a foal born to their horse had to be left as payment for the upkeep of their evacuee family.

Toivo Saunavaara (2023) wrote that during the winter in Sweden their family had four new calves. The calves were transported to Finland in boxes made of boards. Because the bulls at home were often slaughtered, the family exchanged one of the cow calves for a Swedish bull calf.

This black-and-white bull, called Mikko, grew up to be an unusually large and tame breeding bull, who held his post for many years after the evacuation. At the same time, it mixed the pure white northern Finnish cow breed so that, by the end of the 1950s, black patches could be seen on the flanks of white cows in the pastures.

Saunavaara described his return to Finland vividly. He sat in the train's passenger carriage with his mother and brother. Cows, horses, and their drivers traveled in open wagons. The carriages were full, and Toivo held in his arms a puppy he had brought from Sweden. The puppy became hot and started to cry and a police patrol ordered Toivo and the puppy into the cattle car. "It got cold in the open carriage, and I did not have warm clothes. However, we managed quite well by digging into the straw, the cows protected us from the wind, and the puppy in my arms kept us nice and warm," he said.

The cows and their drivers faced another long journey, but this time the atmosphere was completely different. Peace had come after five long years of war. Although they were shocked to see Lapland in ruins, the refugees were glad they could return home. The journey home was easily delayed, by both tired drivers and exhausted cows. As the refugees approached home, they noticed that the animals were also happy to return. Old, tired horses cheered up when they realized they would soon be home. Even the cows, exhausted and sometimes just lying down because of their aching legs, were cheered up. Toini Inkeröinen recalled how the cows identified the familiar landscape. She described the cows' joy: "When … those cows saw the home shore, they ran straight to the summer barn and to their own pens! Yes! How is that possible? [laughs] They didn't need to be guided. It was so strange."

The fact that dogs and cats were not allowed on the evacuation journey almost destroyed the reindeer-herding dog population (the Lapponian herder and Finnish Lapphund). However, some reindeer owners remained in Lapland for the winter evacuation. Their dogs were instrumental in saving the reindeer-herding breeds. The Lappish dog population, on the other hand, was enlivened by animals brought from Sweden. Toivo Saunavaara (2023), who traveled home with a puppy on his lap, wrote about the later life of the dog:

We brought a puppy from Sweden when our former dog was shot by the Germans. The puppy was called Stella. I wonder what breed it was, bigger and sturdier than a Finnish spitz, with a black back, brown legs and belly and floppy ears. Stella had lots of puppies. She had eight the first time. There were only a few dogs in the village at the time, so the puppies went like hot cakes. Not all of them looked like great dogs. They were long haired and floppy eared, but there were a few that looked like Finnish spitzes. They made good bird- and squirrel-hunting dogs.

Fear and insecurity

Broken families

One of the biggest causes of insecurity for children was family break-ups. The children were afraid of losing their parents and siblings during the evacuation (see also Paksuniemi 2014). Family members may have been separated from one other at departure. Young people left to drive cattle, some children were sent to stay with relatives in southern Finland and some people remained in hiding in the woods. Sometimes, the departure was very quick. Vilma Autio described her family's sudden escape from Salla after the outbreak of the Winter War. The enemy was already on the other side of the village. Vilma's brother, at the time aged 11, had come running home from the village, shouting "Mummy, the school is already in fire!" Her mother quickly put the children in the sledge. She did not have time to dress and left without a proper jacket. When they arrived at the meeting place, she had discovered that her five-year-old son was not with her. A desperate search was made for the boy, and he finally arrived at the meeting place, hanging on the heels of another sledge.

Even if the family set off together, it was easy to get lost. Many people were on the move at the same time. Children were given name tags to wear around their necks in case they got lost, and sometimes they were also tied to their relatives with strings. Olavi Ahola, aged seven during Lapland War, recalled how he was curious about the places in the city of Oulu, where the evacuees stayed on their way to Ostrobothnia. He became lost and was frightened, but luckily his mother found him: "How did I slip in there? On the outside of the fence, I did not know where I was. It started raining, and I went and stood under a birch tree. Then, my mother noticed that one was missing."

Vilma Autio was also frightened after being accidentally separated from her family:

> We went to the station, and there were a bunch of people leaving, and I was walking next to my mother … and we started going up the stairs. Then, I realized that this wasn't my mother who I was with. My mother panicked and sent my eldest brother to find me, and I saw him running there back and forth, and that's how they found me.

Some children went missing during health checks and vaccinations at the Swedish border. Toini Inkeröinen talked about her four-year-old sister, who had a sore leg. The child had been taken to a doctor. She had not been returned, and at the doctor's office no one knew whose child she was. Eventually, the family got the child back, although she had not been able to say anything about her family other than that her mother was wearing a red dress.

Those lost in crowds were usually found, but not always. Toivo Saunavaara (2023) wrote about his cousin's three-year-old son, who disappeared soon after the evacuees reached Sweden. Soldiers had been searching for the boy in a line, but with no result. Later, in the autumn, the boy was found dead.

Diseases also separated family members. Contagious diseases, such as diphtheria, tuberculosis, whooping cough, and polio, were common. The sick were taken to hospitals, and often family members were not allowed to visit. Martti Karjalainen (2023) wrote that his mother became seriously ill during the evacuation and was hospitalized. Martti's eldest brother was 11 at the time and was then responsible for his younger siblings. Children and elderly people, in particular, died of illnesses, both on the journey and during the evacuation. Vilma Autio noted that there are still memorials in Ostrobothnian cemeteries to the evacuees who died there. Such memorials can also be found in Sweden.

Children who were separated from their families attempted to find their family members, for example by meeting trains containing evacuees or asking Swedish officials to help locate their relatives. Eino Piipponen was informed of his family's whereabouts two months after he had been evacuated: "In December, I was told where my parents were. They were in different places, and my youngest brother was with my mother, and my eldest brother with my father … Getting information like this was not very well organized."

Some of the interviewees reflected on the effects of being separated from their families. Kaija Kähkönen described how "[i]t was a difficult time for my little brother because he missed our mother so much. He was so little then … The time of evacuation was no time to be happy."

Families could even break up when it was time to return home. Some left children to host families in Sweden for a better standard of living. Veikko Kerätär (2023) recalled that a Swedish family he had become close to asked him to stay as their adopted son. He would have liked to stay, but his mother refused.

"We were refugees of that time"

The children witnessed the distress and plight of their community. They saw their family and community being subjected to control measures and losing their autonomy. This was particularly pronounced for those evacuated to Sweden. The loss of autonomy was reflected in passive expressions, such as "We were picked up," "We were taken away," and "We were loaded" (Autti and Intonen 2022). Those who crossed the border to Sweden went through health control measures without any explanation. Unexpected lice saunas, vaccinations, and health checks were organized in a humiliating way. The interviewees recalled unpleasant visions of tired and sick corefugees. Veikko Kerätär (2023) remembered seeing disabled and mentally ill people for the first time and being frightened by the shouting of a delusional old woman. Toivo Saunavaara (2023) remembered the unpleasant sight of a tired mother of many children.

> There was a young mother with many small children, the oldest maybe seven or eight years old, dragging a bag and carrying the smallest one. The mother with a small child in her arms was so tired that she didn't react even though pee was dripping on the ground.

Children in vaccination queues began crying when they saw other children being injected. Younger children were less bothered by the shame of being naked in the lice sauna, but many children noticed the distress of their mothers and other adult women. Aino Hepola and Eila Tapio described the humiliation of the lice saunas. The worst part was to be stripped naked in front of the Swedish soldiers:

> In the sauna, there were men and women mixed up … just get naked, and the clothes were put on a kind of iron ring, and they were taken to a hot steam that would kill all the lice … It was so disgusting when you had to walk naked and the soldiers were there. Awful!

The children discovered that not everyone's attitude toward the Lappish refugees was friendly. Social segregation and bullying were experienced at the hands of both host adults and children. For example, the refugees were called beggars and "second-class gypsies." Helmi Ahola described how their hosts were friendly toward the refugees, but the neighbors had a different attitude. "There were people who said, 'refugee stinks', and they kept their doors and windows closed. We were not allowed to go to their house at all." Veikko Kerätär (2023) recalled that the Swedish hostess gave her own children apple pieces when peeling fruit and only the peels to the refugee children. Some found that they were regarded as inferior and, at worst, uncivilized carriers of diseases and vermin (see also Autti and Intonen 2022). The spread of diseases and lice was easily blamed on the refugees. The refugees were offended by such accusations and made sarcastic jokes about it. Toini Inkeröinen remembered how the refugees were amazed at the Swedish milk trucks that collected milk from even the most remote farms. The refugees had heard that lice had been found further afield, and they laughed, saying, "Did the milk truck take the lice there?"

While one of the key experiences was the condescending attitude of some people, another very important one was the sincere humanity and kindness of others. Sometimes, strong friendships were formed between refugees and local families, which continued for generations to come. Kindness was important to the refugee children, especially when they were in the position of being helped.

Exposure to danger and violence

On the refugee journey, children were exposed to danger and violence. Fears and insecurity were compounded by the children's previous experiences of wartime bombings and their consequences. Hanna-Leena Määttä (forthcoming) states that the essence of memories and traumatic and embodied affective experiences have gained attention in memory studies and war history research only recently. Based on her data, Määttä writes about how the sense of horror caused by the threat of war emerges as a bodily experience, even later in life. Kirves et al. (2010) state that things that cannot be shared in words are expressed in action. Such embodied memories were also abundant in my interview data. Experiences of bombings, especially, had left still-visible traces on the interviewees. Vilma Autio reported reacting to planes flying overhead with fear even today. Pirkko Moisala lost her aunt in the bombing of Rovaniemi hospital, and she described how she still suffers from the fear this caused: "When the hornet-planes come,

I always get crouched down. Yes, it feels like they are coming down on my neck—it is the war—it left quite a lot of traumas."

Kaija Kähkönen was in a bomb shelter when Rovaniemi was bombed during the Continuation War. She was afraid of the alarms, and memories of them haunted her for a long time. The smell of a cellar could still make her vomit because it reminded her of the smell of a bomb shelter.

> There was a bang in our bomb shelter. You could hear it came close. Everyone's ears were hurting. Then, someone came to the door, shouting "Are there people here who are capable of providing medical care?" They said that there were many wounded, and nurses were needed. We children grabbed mum and said, "Mum, don't go!"

Children worried about the well-being of their loved ones (see also Kirves et al. 2010). Olavi Ahola was concerned about his mother's health and the fate of his entire family. When the air-raid alarm sounded, everyone had to go to the bomb shelter, but Olavi's mother had been too tired. She had said that she was no longer able to take her children to the shelter and that, if a bomb hit them, it would hit them. The others had then helped the family to the shelter.

The children were also exposed to dangers and violence. There was a constant danger of becoming lost in the crowd and falling off crowded trains or lorries. Interviewees recalled seeing many prisoners of war transported by the Germans and witnessing how they were treated violently. It also became clear that the previously friendly Germans now had to be feared. They had destroyed the infrastructure, and this made traveling difficult. Helge Kuosmanen was in a group driving cattle toward Ostrobothnia. Near Oulu, they heard sounds of explosions and soon found the Germans had just blown up a bridge they had been about to cross.

Interviewees recalled how they listened carefully to adults talking about war, violence, disappearances, and destroyed homes (see Kirves et al. 2010). Rumors were common. The cattle drivers were frightened by rumors that retreating Germans were grabbing women by the hair and dragging them into cars. Thus, the cattle drivers avoided going out alone. Another cause of insecurity was the uncertainty of returning home. There were rumors that the Soviets would invade Lapland. Aino Hepola told of a man she met on a lorry ride in Sweden. The man had intimidated the young people into thinking they would never get home. An older woman comforted the frightened girls.

> He said, "There will be Russians, and Russians will take all. You will never get back home! It's useless for you to hope!" But one of the older women said, "Don't you poor girls believe him. No, he is talking nonsense." We were already crying terribly, thinking that we wouldn't see our parents anymore. The man said, "You won't see your siblings, your mother or anyone." But it was such a comfort when the woman said, "Don't believe that. It's not true."

The interviewees talked about how their parents attempted to protect children from unnecessary worry. Some adults tried not to show their feelings and focused on funny incidents. Worries and fears were not discussed in front of the children. Vilma Autio, whose family lived in Eastern Lapland, recalled her mother walking from window to window on summer nights during the Continuation War, constantly checking for movement in the village. It was only later that Vilma realized that her mother had been keeping watch because of her fear of partisans.

Evacuation as an adventure

Getting on the road

Unlike the adults, the children knew how to make the most of their experience. Only some of the children had been able to travel before, and many had never been on a lorry, train, or ferry, for example. Evacuation was an exciting adventure, and a chance to see new things. Helmi Ahola summed up the positives: "It was a lorry and an adventure! We got to go on a trip, and think of all the things we will do there!"

There was also a sense of adventure and exuberance among those driving cattle. Eila Tapio was part of a group of cattle drivers heading toward Sweden. They were met by a group of German soldiers heading north: "Some young German soldier asked Inkeri, 'Where are you going?' And Inkeri answered, 'to Berlin!' [laughs]."

Traveling by train was a great adventure, but it was overshadowed by long waits, air alerts, and cramped conditions. Trains carrying civilians had to make room for both German and Finnish military trains. The waiting was tedious. For example, Vilma Autio noted that the train journey from Eastern Lapland to Ostrobothnia took two weeks. Toivo Saunavaara (2023) traveled to Sweden on a net shelf in a train:

> The carriage had wooden benches and wide shelves, where all the children aged around ten were pushed. At first, it was fine, but as the trolley filled up and we kept trying to push more bags in, it became cramped, the heat rose and the air started to run out, so it got very stuffy. It got easier when the train started moving and the windows were opened.

For the children going to Sweden, it was particularly exciting to be in a foreign country. However, there was also enthusiasm among those evacuated to Ostrobothnia. For Esko Kähkönen, the urban status of the host place was impressive. He said, "It was a small town by the sea, and this made the journey so joyful. It felt like a competition between homesickness and getting to the *city* [emphasis added] from this kind of a small village."

Cities seemed miraculous in Sweden, too. Toivo Saunavaara (2023) and his family exited the train at Piteå station. It was already evening, and many people had arrived at the station to receive the first evacuation trains. The refugees were amazed at how brightly lit the town was. There was still no electricity in Toivo's home village, and during the war years the blackout curtains had been kept tightly closed. He said, "There we were in the brightly lit the railway yard, the crowds marveling as we huddled together like a herd of cattle seeking refuge from one another."

Children noticed the wealth of the host communities and the better standard of living on the farms in Ostrobothnia. Interviewees recalled marveling at the gardens with flowers and berry bushes. They had never seen anything like them. Vilma Autio's family had been evacuated to a farm with a separate, very beautiful room in the main building. The chamber was so magnificent that it terrified the children. She said:

> It was the height of grandeur, that chamber. It had lace linen on the table and pink artificial roses on the tables. We had to bring wood there to keep it warm, so we very carefully put firewood in front of the stove and quickly left so that we would not mess up the place. That's where they took their guests for coffee.

Evacuees to Sweden could enjoy films. Toivo Saunavaara (2023) recalled that the older boys could buy a ticket with their daily allowance but that the smaller boys had to create ploys. They became masters at this, and many Swedes even helped them. The boys would crawl past the line or hide under the cover of a big coat to bluff the ticket inspector. Aila Sääskilahti went to the cinema with other refugees, and as none of them had been to the cinema before the events on the screen seemed all too real. As powerful rapids roared in the film, an old woman stood up and shouted in fright, "Whoa, whoa, that's going to come right on top of me!"

The St. Lucia celebration organized by the Swedes was particularly well remembered by the children. Aila Sääskilahti stated that the candle-crowned singers were like angels. Aino Hepola also participated St. Lucia's day: "It was beautiful, and we admired those girls, and we sang in Swedish, but that didn't slow us down. I didn't know that such things even existed." Other parties mentioned were the Christmas party and the burning of the Easter bonfire. Martti Karjalainen (2023) recalled that "at Easter, the villagers gathered a large pile of branches and other things to burn in the field. On Easter Eve, the bonfire was lit, and we could watch the event. All the children in the village over the age of five were there, so it was fun. There was no such tradition at home in Finland."

Food memories

In both Ostrobothnia and Sweden, the refugees encountered different food cultures, yielding both good and bad food memories. In Sweden, the food was more varied than the children had been used to in war-torn Finland, and oranges, for example, were an exotic novelty. Aino Hepola had received a little money in Sweden: "I bought Marie-biscuits and oranges! I had never had an orange."

The light and sweet-flavored bread, the heavy use of sugar, and sweet food in general raised some eyebrows, and the refugees wondered whether the Swedes put sugar in all their food (see also Paksuniemi 2014). Toivo Saunavaara recalled that their train stopped at Boden, where the refugees were allowed to eat sandwiches and meat soup in the station canteen. The refugees had expected to be served soup with meat and potatoes, although some wondered whether sugar had been added to that too. The meat soup turned out to be brown water made from cubes of meat broth. These were not yet known in Finland at the time.

Pirkko Moisala remembered many unusual foods from Sweden:

> Something like fat pancake [laughter]. The fat looked so greasy. On the one hand, it was good. Well, they make ham pancakes and pizza and stuff like that now. Then, there was the fish-eye soup, with some potato in it. It was a bit like "Who's watching from over there" [laughter].

The children soon became accustomed to Swedish food culture. Later, it was a shock to many to return to war-torn Lapland because the quality of the food deteriorated greatly. Veikko Kerätär (2023) wrote that, on their return, the refugees had been provided with meals in Tornio:

> It was quite a change of circumstances when we came to Finland. Even the food was different from what it was in Sweden. When we went for a meal in Tornio, the bread was as black as a bogeyman's shit, and the rest of the food was not that good either.

The specialty in terms of local food was a big mouthful for the Lappish refugees in Ostrobothnia as well. Vilma Autio described *klimppisoppa*, lump soup, which she was forced to eat:

> They cooked lump soup for us. It was a kind of flour balls in a broth. They were made into balls in fat and then put into the broth. And I thought it was awful, and it was hard not to eat because the people in the house watched you eat it.

Language differences

The experiences of the refugees in the host areas were strongly determined by their evacuation status. Communication with the local people was not always easy, as there were large differences between refugees and hosts, especially in terms of cultural and social capital. Language differences, dialect differences, and differences in customary cultures complicated these interactions. Moreover, the refugees were unable to present themselves in the best light (see also Lehtola 2004). They were characterized by isolation, broken families and communities, shabbiness and neediness. The hosts, on the other hand, were stationary, with their possessions, family, culture, and history, and had no experience of escaping the ravages of war. The lack of a common experience made it difficult to build relationships (Autti and Intonen 2022).

For children, however, these differences did not matter as much as for adults. Even a different language or a different dialect was an adventure. Vilma Autio recalled some of the dialect words that had stuck in her mind in Ostrobothnia. "The scoop you used for drinking water was called a 'knappo.' A cow was called 'itikka,' a bug." In Sweden, the language barrier slowed down communication but didn't stop it completely. Among the hosts, there were people who could speak Finnish, and gradually many of the refugee children learned Swedish to the degree that they were able to act as interpreters for others.

> Even though we didn't speak Swedish, we soon found that we could somehow understand each other. We had learned some German during the war years, and there are words in Swedish that mean the same thing, and maybe, they had read German at school. At first, it was just asking for names and ages and exchanging money, "vexla pengar," but from there, the language skills gradually improved and we soon got on well. (Toivo Saunavaara 2023)

Childhood activities: out of the shadow of war

During the evacuation, it was possible to experience a normal childhood and adolescence. One was safe and away from the shadows of war, and especially in the refugee camps, the lack of things to do allowed a level of idleness that one was not used to at home. The children played with one another, roamed around, and came to know their new surroundings and the local children, sometimes by playing rough with them. Merja Paksuniemi (2014) states that, at the Swedish refugee camps, playing and toys distracted the children from thinking about the war and their surroundings in exile and that playing allowed them to cope with their refugee experiences. Toivo Saunavaara (2023) writes that the Finnish boys in the quarantine camp were adventurous and keen to see more of their host village.

For young refugees in particular, leisure time was very important because, during the long years of war, normal social life was not possible. It felt good to leave the war and find better conditions, not only materially but also socially. The best situation was for children and young people who had not been separated from their families (see also Kirves et al. 2010; Paksuniemi 2014). Secure family relationships eased homesickness and were an important prerequisite for understanding a new place and the local people. Visits to films, dances, concerts, and other events were memorable for many. Many girls received their first perm, and in their free time they simply hung out:

> I was 15 years old, and we were out, of course, and there were these Swedish boys ... Well, we walked around in the surroundings, and for me, it was a nice time, as back home, during the war, it wasn't so nice to watch and listen to the planes and cover the windows ... It was like you really came to life when you got to Sweden. (Aila Sääskilahti)

The last Germans crossed the border between Finland and Norway on April 27, 1945. The Lappish refugees began to return home as soon as possible, but the return was often delayed by mines and destroyed housing. The German troops had systematically destroyed their military targets, all infrastructure, and any civilian property within their reach. The built environment was destroyed, and more than 24,000 domestic animals and 24,000 reindeer were lost. Most of the evacuees returned in the spring and summer of 1945; some returned later and the inhabitants of areas in Kuusamo, Salla, and Petsamo, which had been lost to the Soviet Union, were never able to return to their homes. The refugees had mixed feelings of sadness and joy: the built environment had been destroyed, but they were able to return home and enjoy peace after long years of war. Life had to start again from scratch (Autti and Intonen 2022; Lehtola 2015; Seitsonen and Koskinen-Koivisto 2018; Tuominen 2015; Ursin 1980).

Discussion

Children's key experiences of the evacuation period were both negative and positive. They were related to refugee status, a sense of adventure and threats to home and family. Feelings of fear and insecurity were ever-present, and for some, they remain active even today. The war and flight meant violence, losses, and uncertainty, but the events were not unilaterally negative for the children involved. The Lapland War and the resulting evacuation were also portrayed as a great adventure. The war was not only destructive but also creative. The evacuation enabled new social relationships and an understanding of new places and new ways of life. The safe circumstances in Sweden and Ostrobothnia allowed the activities of normal childhood. Playing with peers, exploring the surroundings, and simply hanging out were

uplifting experiences. These experiences became particularly important because, after returning to Lapland, there was no time for playing.
The reconstruction period began, which required the children to contribute. The workload was so great that many children were no longer
able to attend school. They had to grow up too quickly.

The key experiences were similar in both Sweden and Ostrobothnia. The differences in the narratives were mostly related to the surrounding culture and its differences from the prior culture in Lapland.
The standard of living in Sweden was clearly higher than in war-torn
Finland. Foreign language and food culture, for example, caused difficulties but also added to the sense of adventure. Accommodation was
also different. In Ostrobothnia, evacuees were mostly accommodated
in the homes of local families, while in Sweden they were accommodated either in camps or public buildings. Especially for those accommodated in camps, contact with locals often remained scarce. In the
host farms in Ostrobothnia, the children did farm work as they used to
do at home, but in Sweden this was often not possible, leaving time for
other things. For some, the idle time felt like a holiday.

Temporal distance inevitably shapes memories, and collective
remembering has created a certain kind of model narrative of the Lapland War, in which my interviewees had to position themselves. Many
fitted their memories to suit the model narrative and left unsuitable
memories aside. For example, the interviewees described the lice saunas as the experience is shared by many others and an essential part
of the model narrative. Many personal hardships, however, were seen
as not worth mentioning. The Lapland War evacuation is widely seen
as a survival story, and this easily causes people to hide unpleasant
memories. Individual expressions draw from collective memory but
also deviate from it to challenge it. Some people contacted me after
their interview to refine their narratives. They described experiencing
sexual harassment or violence that they had been reluctant to mention
earlier. These unpleasant themes did not fit their initial narrative or the
collective evacuation narrative (see also Autti and Intonen 2022, 114).

Given that 70 years passed between the Lapland War and the interviews, it is important to reflect on the temporal aspect of the situation
and how the interviewees understand their positions during the war
and decades later. At the time of the evacuation, the children witnessed
stressful events and adult conversations and only later reflected on them
through their own adult experience. The interviewees noted how, as

children, they had a poor understanding of the backgrounds and contexts of events. However, the interviewees reflected on the wider contexts of their experiences in the interview situation, in which personal memories, family and community memories, and later understanding developed into a coherent narrative presented to the interviewer. The narratives also incorporated the way in which the history of the Lapland War evacuation has been dealt with in the public sphere over the decades. Focusing on the experiences of children reveals different, new, and nuanced descriptions of the experience of war and forced displacement. The findings enrich the previous, shallower expressions of refugee memories that are aligned with the national war narrative. These memories help to diversify and refine our previous, fragmented understanding of Lapland War refugees.

Both in Finland and Sweden, the refugees were seen as a group of outsiders in need of help. The way refugees were treated emerged as an important factor, as these experiences had an impact on the later lives of many. Good experiences and the friendships formed were remembered fondly, but condescending treatment and name-calling were still on the minds of many interviewees. Unpleasant memories do not fade easily, as they wounded the refugees' sense of self-worth and equality. Experiences like these can have a profound impact on self-understanding.

Notes

1 The chapter has been written as part of two research projects: "ReBel–Recognition and Belonging: Forced Migration, Troubled Histories and Memory Cultures 2017–2021" (Research Council of Finland) and "Muistin marginaalista 2022–2026" (Kone Foundation).

Bibliography

Published memoirs

Karjalainen, Martti. 2023. *Evakko*. Yläkemijoen historia. https://ylakemijoenhistoria.wordpress.com/karjalaine-martti-evakko.
Kerätär, Veikko. 2023. *Evakkoreissu*. Yläkemijoen historia. https://ylakemijoenhistoria.wordpress.com/keratar-veikko-evakkoreissu.

Saunavaara, Toivo. 2023. *Muisteluksia evakkomatkasta Ruotsiin vuosina 1944–1945*. Yläkemijoen historia. https://ylakemijoenhistoria.wordpress.com/evakkomatka-ruotsiin-ts/.

Literature

Autti, Outi and Saara Intonen. 2022. "The Recognition of War Refugees: Lapland, Love, and Care". *The Journal of Interdisciplinary History* 53 (1): 89–115. https://doi.org/10.1162/jinh_a_01799.

Autti, Outi and Marjo Laitala. 2019. "Vihollinen saa kasvot. Neuvostosotavangit suomalaisilla maatiloilla". In *Hiljainen vastarinta*, edited by Outi Autti and Veli-Pekka Lehtola, 109–30. Tampere: Tampere University Press. http://urn.fi/URN:NBN:fi:tuni-201903141362.

Denzin, Norman K. 2006. *Sociological Methods: A Sourcebook*. New York: Routledge.

Fingerroos Outi, Haanpää, Riina, and Anne Heimo, eds. 2006. *Muistitietotutkimus: Metodologisia kysymyksiä*. Helsinki: SKS.

Gitau, Lydia Wanja, Arop Achol, and Caroline Lenette. 2023. "'My Dad Was, Is a Soldier': Using Collaborative Poetic Inquiry to Explore Intergenerational Trauma, Resilience, and Wellbeing in the Context of Forced Migration". *Social Sciences* 12: 455. https://doi.org/10.3390/socsci12080455.

Ilesanmi, Itunu O., Jasmine D. Haynes, and Florence O. Ogundimu. 2024. "Returnees' Perspectives of the Adverse Impact of Forced Displacement on Children". *Social Sciences* 13: 484. https://doi.org/10.3390/socsci13090484.

Junila, Marianne. 2000. *Kotirintaman Aseveljeyttä: Suomalaisen Siviiliväestön ja Saksalaisen Sotaväen Rinnakkainelo Pohjois-Suomessa 1941–1944*. Helsinki: SKS.

Kauhanen Iida, Kaukko Mervi, and Maija Lanas. 2022. "Pockets of Love. Unaccompanied Children in Institutional Care in Finland". *Children and Youth Services Review* 10. https://doi.org/10.1016/j.childyouth.2022.106621.

Kirves, Jenni, Ville Kivimäki, Sari Näre, and Juha Siltala. 2010. "Sodassa kasvaneiden tunneperintö". In *Sodan kasvattamat*, edited by Sari Näre, Jenni Kirves, and Juha Siltala, 386–451. Helsinki: WSOY.

Koskinen-Koivisto, Erika and Oula Seitsonen. 2019. "Landscapes of Loss and Destruction: Sámi Elders' Childhood Memories of the Second World War". *Ethnologia Europaea* 49 (1): 24–40. https://doi.org/10.16995/ee.816.

Lehtola, Veli-Pekka. 2004. *Saamelainen evakko*. Inari: Kustannus-Puntsi.

Lehtola, Veli-Pekka. 2015. "Second World War as a Trigger for Transcultural Changes among Sámi People in Finland". *Acta Borealia* 32: 125–47.

Lehtola, Veli-Pekka. 2018. "'Sielun olisi pitänyt ehtiä mukaan…' Jälleenrakennettu Saamenmaa". In *Lappi palaa sodasta. Mielen hiljainen jälleenrakennus*, edited by Marja Tuominen and Mervi Löfgren, 259–82. Tampere: Vastapaino.

Määttä, Hanna-Leena. (forthcoming). "Evakkokirjallisuus pakolaisuuden kuvauksena ja ylirajaisena muistina". In *Kansallisesta ylirajaiseen. Kulttuuri, perinne ja kirjallisuus*, edited by Niina Hämäläinen, Hanna Karhu, and Tuomas Martikainen. Kalevalaseuran vuosikirja 102.

Näre, Sari, Jenni Kirves, and Juha Siltala, eds. 2010. *Sodan kasvattamat*. Helsinki: WSOY.

Neuendorf, Kimberly A. 2017. *The Content Analysis Guidebook*. Los Angeles, CA: Sage.

Paksuniemi, Merja. 2014. "Finnish Refugee Children's Experiences of Swedish Refugee Camps during the Second World War". *Migration Letters* 11 (2): 28–37.

Rizkalla, Niveen, Nour K. Mallat, Rahma Arafa, Suher Adi, Laila Soudi, and Steven P. Segal. 2020. "Children Are Not Children Anymore; They Are a Lost Generation: Adverse Physical and Mental Health Consequences on Syrian Refugee Children". *International Journal of Environmental Research and Public Health* 17: 8378.

Savolainen, Ulla. 2015. *Muisteltu ja kirjoitettu evakkomatka. Tutkimus evakkolapsuuden muistelukerronnan poetiikasta*. Vantaa: SKTS.

Scott, Jacqui, Barbara Mason, and Aisling Kelly. 2024. "'After God, We Give Strength to Each Other': Young Peoples Experiences of Coping in the Context of Unaccompanied Forced Migration". *Journal of Youth Studies*. 27 (2): 178–94.

Seitsonen, Oula and Eerika Koskinen-Koivisto. 2018. "'Where the F … Is Vuotso?' Heritage of Second World War Forced Movement and Destruction in a Sámi Reindeer Herding Community in Finnish Lapland". *International Journal of Heritage Studies* 24: 421–41.

Tuominen, Marja. 2015. "Lapin ajanlasku. Menneisyys, tulevaisuus ja jälleenrakennus historian reunalla". In *Rauhaton rauha. Suomalaiset ja sodan päättyminen 1944–1950*, edited by Ville Kivimäki and Kirsi-Maria Hytönen, 39–70. Tampere: Vastapaino.

Tuominen, Marja, Timothy G. Ashplant, and Tiina Harjumaa, eds. 2020. *Reconstructing Minds and Landscapes: Silent Post-war Memory in the Margins of History*. New York: Routledge.

Ursin, Martti. 1980. *Pohjois-Suomen tuhot ja jälleenrakennus saksalaissodan 1944–1945 jälkeen*. Oulu: Pohjoinen.

CHAPTER 13

The life of Maria

A Swedish Polish Jewish survivor at the center and margins of public history

Martin Englund

Södertörn University

Abstract

The chapter analyses the historical experiences of Maria, a Swedish Polish Jewish Holocaust survivor born in 1926. The analysis focus on two experiences, the first that she survived the Holocaust in the Soviet Union and the second that she migrated to Sweden in 1970 owing to the antisemitic campaign in Poland. The aim is to examine how one person's historical experiences of forced migration, displacement, survival, and integration can be understood in relation to the public historical consciousness in Sweden. The chapter also aims in the opposite direction and displays how this woman's historical experiences can contribute to the historical consciousness. The Holocaust is central in the historical culture. Yet so are the experience of survival in the Soviet Union and the experience of the antisemitic campaign at the margins of public historical consciousness. The chapter argues for a less peripheral role for these experiences.

How to cite this book chapter:
Englund, Martin. 2025. "The life of Maria: a Swedish Polish Jewish survivor at the center and margins of public history." In *Forced Migrants in Nordic Histories*, edited by Johanna Leinonen, Miika Tervonen, Hans Otto Frøland, Christhard Hoffmann, Seija Jalagin, Heidi Vad Jønsson and Malin Thor Tureby, 327–346. Helsinki: Helsinki University Press. https://doi.org/10.33134/HUP-32-14.

Introduction

The most common way for Polish Jews to survive the Holocaust is almost unknown in public memory. Maria, a Polish Jewish woman living in Sweden, survived the Holocaust in that way. The purpose of this text is to understand the historical experiences communicated by Maria in relation to public memory in Sweden. Her life story includes two major events she shares with many of the Polish Jews in Sweden. The first experience is Holocaust survival in the Soviet Union; the second experience is the expulsion of Jews from Poland due to the antisemitic campaign in the late 1960s.[1]

The Holocaust occupies a central place in Sweden's public history. Since 2003 a state institution, the Living History Forum, has been assigned the task of promoting democracy, tolerance, and human rights based on the historical experience of the Holocaust. Since being established, the institution has received the further assignment of promoting knowledge about crimes against humanity under communist regimes. The Living History Forum has thus prioritized two historical experiences in promoting ethical values: first the Holocaust and second the crimes perpetrated by communist regimes ("Levande Historia: Om oss" n.d.).

I call the main character in this chapter Maria, in accordance with her own wishes. While she has lived a life that is completely exceptional, she nonetheless shares many experiences with a greater collective of Polish Jewish survivors. Maria experienced Holocaust survival and life in the Soviet Union during the Stalin era, both of which are central events in Swedish public history. At the same time are her two major experiences marginalized in public memory: the experience of surviving the Holocaust in the Soviet Union and the experience of forced migration from Poland to Sweden because of the antisemitic campaign. Through Maria, I want to exemplify these experiences. In doing so I hope to contribute to highlighting them in the public memory and historical research. Maria, one of the last Polish Jewish Holocaust survivors, is chosen for this text because she shared with me her exceptional yet typical experiences at the end of her life. She was interviewed about them for the first time at the age of 96.

Hermeneutic oral history

My research is based on a theoretical and methodological framework
I call hermeneutic oral history. I have created it to gain an in-depth
understanding of historical experiences in dialogue with people who
carry those experiences. My way of using the concepts of historical
consciousness, historical culture, historical experience, meaning, and
orientation are inspired by the German philosopher of history Jörn
Rüsen.[2] I use the concept of historical experiences both individually
and collectively, within a defined group and in society at large. All historical experiences are processed in the historical consciousness. A historical experience is a memory with a meaning. Meaning is the result
of a narrative analyzing process that takes place both individually and
collectively, an answer to the human need of orienting ourselves in
time. We understand who we are, where we come from, and where we
might go in the future. With the help of this historical analysis, we can
orient ourselves in terms of identity, ethics, and also concrete strategies
about how to act. We look back to understand the present and how we
should act in the future.

The analysis of historical experiences, to which we humans devote
ourselves, is of course nothing that leads to any final destination. We are
never done with understanding our historical experiences. To understand this process, I use Hans-Georg Gadamer's concept of historically effected consciousness, one of the bearing concepts in Gadamer's
Truth and Method (Gadamer 1989). There are several different aspects
of historically effected consciousness operative in our understanding
of historical experiences. We always reach a subjective understanding
of historical experiences based on our own historical positioning, our
horizon of understanding. This position, the horizon of understanding, is influenced by several different aspects. On the one hand, we can
follow the consequences of what happened, for example, when Maria
seems happy to have migrated to Sweden even if it happened under
painful conditions. Also, when she talks about her father's ambitions
to contribute to the creation of socialist societies, first in the Soviet
Union and then in Poland, she knows that her father's good inten-
tions ended in the establishment of dictatorships. In addition to her
own memories of these episodes, her horizon of understanding is also
shaped in relation to the public history culture of which she is a part,
in combination with how historical development is discussed in her

immediate surroundings. This becomes the horizon from which she approaches her experiences. An illustrative example where a historically effected consciousness is evident is given by Maria at the beginning of the interview when she says about her father: "Unfortunately, he was involved in the communist movement" (Interview with Maria, file 1 (IM1)). We get an understanding of what Maria thinks today about her father's involvement. She expresses a view on communism that correlates with the official historical narrative on this ideology in Sweden. That her father was affected by Stalin's purges shows that he suffered early on for his communist commitment.[3] There are several later historical influences that explain Maria's "unfortunately." Maria's consciousness is, we can say, historically effected.

I see no fundamental difference between "academic" and "nonacademic" historical consciousness. Historical writing at universities has a close connection to historical consciousness outside of the university. Museum exhibitions, historical films, novels, and works of art relate to academic history writing, and historians are inspired and influenced by the historical culture of which they are a part. To this end, I want to enter into a direct dialogue with people about their historical experiences, to understand them together. I also hope that such a dialogue can affect both the academic discipline of history and the historical culture in general.

Dialogue is the most central concept in my hermeneutic oral history. My ideal is to create a common ground, where we are both prepared to listen and respond to each other in a way that means we come out of the dialogue as different people from those who entered it. Oral historian Malin Thor Tureby has argued for conducting oral history based on a subject–subject relationship in the spirit of the dialogical philosophy of Martin Buber: to seek the basic dialogic relationship I–Thou as opposed to I–It, that is, a subject–subject and not a subject–object relation (Thor Tureby 2001).

The analysis of Maria's life narrative through a hermeneutic oral history might appear to be an empathic retelling of a fascinating life beyond the critical gaze of historical research. The knowledge interest of the dialogue is not to question the objective facts she brings to the table but rather to understand them *as* historical experiences. As many oral historians have pointed out, historical experience is not fixed. It changes and develops over time, correlated with new individual and collective experiences (Thomson 2015; Portelli 1991). It is not fiction,

nor is it an unreflective retelling of memories; it is historical interpretation on the level of historical consciousness. My hermeneutic dialogue
heads in two different directions, first toward Maria and the formulation of her experiences, and second toward a public historical consciousness about the events she lived through.

Swedish Polish Jewish history and "We, the Expelled"

Poland is one the most prominent countries in Jewish history and
there has been an established community of Polish Jews since the Middle Ages. The country contained a central part of the vast Ashkenazi
Yiddishland that reached over Central and Eastern Europe. Before the
Holocaust over three million Jews lived in Poland, which was approximately 10 percent of the population. Over 90 percent of these Jews
were killed in the Holocaust. It was difficult for the survivors to resettle
in their former home areas owing to antisemitic attacks and because
their homes and properties had been taken over by others. At the same
time the Polish Peoples Republic was established under Soviet control.
Many of the surviving Polish Jews emigrated to other countries such
as the US, Canada, or the emerging Jewish state. Another major Polish
Jewish emigration happened during the destalinization in 1956.

In 1967 only about 30,000 Jews lived in Poland when the last major
emigration of the Polish Jewry began because of a state initiated antisemitic campaign. The antisemitic campaign resulted in a forced migration of about 15,000, which is not the largest of the Polish Jewish emi-
grations. But, considering how few Jews remained in Poland, it is a
remarkable number. Half of the Polish Jews left the country. The campaign was launched in Poland in connection with the Six-Day War in
Israel in 1967, and it reached its crescendo with the student protests of
1968. This period has been described as the final exodus of the Polish
Jewry.[4]

The group that came to Sweden, approximately 3,000, is not one
of the largest migrant groups during the period. For example, 18,000
refugees came from Chile, after the military coup in 1973 (Svanberg
and Tydén 1992, 342). But, in relation to the Swedish Jewish minority,
this Polish Jewish migration was a significant addition that reconfig-
ured the composition of the Swedish Jewry. They also had historical
experiences of the Holocaust, and yet their experiences continue to

be relatively unknown. The contemporary Czechoslovakian diaspora, with their experiences from the Prague Spring, were better known in Sweden then their Polish counterpart.

I encountered Maria through the project "We, the Expelled," which collects and researches the historical experiences of Polish Jewish forced migrants who came to Sweden because of the antisemitic campaign. I am the initiator of this project and have been collaborating with the Nordic Museum (Nordiska museet). I am writing a PhD thesis based on the collected material while I aim to raise general knowledge about the topic. Since this anthology takes as its point of departure that refugees and forced migrants have been neglected in national historiography, both the project "We, the Expelled" and this anthology share the aim of redressing this neglect. The empirical material used in this chapter is Maria's life story, which can be found at the platform Minnen.se ("Vi, de fördrivna" 2021), and about three hours of interview material, which is divided into three files. The entire interview was conducted on August 10, 2022, in her home in Gothenburg. The interview was conducted in Swedish and translated into English by me.

Key events of Maria's life

Maria was born in Vienna in 1926 to Polish Jewish parents. Her father had taken refuge there because he was a communist, which was outlawed in Poland at the time. Her mother took the opportunity to study in Vienna because Jews' access to universities was restricted in Poland by the so-called Numerus Clausus system. When Maria was three years old the family moved to Moscow. In Moscow, her parents divorced, and Maria lived with her mother, though she still spent time with her father and his new wife. Her mother worked as a biologist, while Maria started school in 1934. Then came the decisive turning point in Maria's life. On September 1, 1937, her mother suddenly disappeared. She left a note saying she would be back in a week. Both Maria's mother and father had been arrested.

Maria stated: "I raised myself on my own" (IM1). I have come across similar statements from others who have participated in "We, the Expelled." In part, this can be described as a shift in norms around upbringing. But in Maria's case it also illustrates the exceptional circumstances in which she grew up. Her parents were busy and then they were imprisoned during the purges of the 1930s. She relates her own age – she was only ten years old in 1937 – to the mass arrest of foreigners that were going on at the time.

After the arrest of Maria's parents, she ended up in an orphanage. These deeply personal experiences are part of the larger development in the Soviet Union during the period known as the Great Terror. She recalled that she had an idea of what was happening and how she acted accordingly, but what she could not recall was whether she believed in the treason charges that were made against her parents. While in an orphanage, Maria decided to run away. She and her friend fled and traveled 1,000 kilometers to Moscow but were ultimately separated at the train station. She made her way to one of her mother's friends but in the end she was picked up by the police. She was declared homeless and ended up in a children's prison and was later placed in another orphanage, this time in the remote countryside. Maria tells about a formative experience from this orphanage she carried with her all through her life. She heard for the first time that she was Jewish and not, as she had learned from home, Polish. During the time in orphanage Maria went to school and through all her experiences from the Soviet Union, she received the education she was later able to build on in life.

Germany attacked the Soviet Union on June 22, 1941, a date Maria knew by heart. Since 1937 she had been estranged from her parents. Maria lived in the orphanage and was about to travel to a school in Ukraine, very close to the front. When she arrived, the school was about to close and she had to leave. At this time, Maria had received word that her father had been found. Maria's aunt had moved to the part of Poland that was occupied by the Soviets in 1939 and she finally managed to track down Maria, along with her father and mother, who were both in Soviet camps. Her father was released from the camp but was not allowed to travel from Uchta in the Komi Republic. After a month's journey, Maria was reunited with her father in Uchta, where she went to school while he worked in a pharmacy. Her father was a publicist by trade, but through his knowledge of Latin another Jewish man in the camp employed him to work in the camp's pharmacy. Maria described as the main advantage of the pharmacy job that her father had access to alcohol, an important hard currency. Alcohol gave them, among other things, access to better food.

In Uchta, Maria graduated in 1944 and moved to Molotov for further studies. She lived in a student dormitory on the brink of starvation.

She studied medicine and laid the foundation for a life as a physician. Maria described how entire universities moved east but continued to function during the war. She emphasized that those who were not Russian had more difficulties but nonetheless were still able to cope and even study.

Although Maria was given access to education and therefore had the possibility of studying during the war, she lived in extremely poor conditions. She brought up a series of vivid examples that describe how she and her fellow students coped on the brink of starvation. It is also clear that she was describing her experiences to me and a Swedish public in a wealthier era. She said in the interview:

> I received cod oil from the pharmacy that my father sent. It tasted very good at the time. Also dry egg yolks, powder, I don't know if it is available in Sweden but there it was. (IM1)

Maria told me that she and her father almost never talked about anything that happened, either then or later. She regretted not asking. "And now it is all gone" (IM1).

Maria survived the Holocaust in the Soviet Union and came to Sweden due to the antisemitic campaign. Maria never experienced German occupation or any Nazi camp. She moved eastward into the Soviet Union as the front approached, though at one point she was very close to the front. After the war, Maria and her father traveled together to Poland. During the journey, they took a detour over the father's hometown of Lwow, which before the war belonged to Poland but afterwards became Soviet territory. In Lwow, they understood that Maria's grandparents had been murdered. The only survivor was the father's 15-year-old nephew, Maria's cousin, who had survived in hiding during the German occupation. They took the cousin, who suffered severely both physically and mentally, to Warsaw. Her mother's family had also been murdered, and Maria recounted how she later began to grasp the extent of the destruction.

Maria's mother was still in a Soviet camp on Kamchatka, the easternmost part of the Soviet Union. Imprisonment lasted for almost ten years and it took another year before she was allowed to return to Poland. It was Maria, her father, and the cousin, who had to start their new life in Warsaw. When the mother returned in 1947, she managed to find an apartment next to Maria's father, and Maria moved in with her while maintaining contact with her father and his new wife.

Maria's father was engaged in the creation of the new Poland. Several of those who participated in the "We, the Expelled" project talked about this enthusiasm for building a new and equal society in Poland. Indeed, Maria did not want to travel after the war to Poland, which she understood to be a capitalist state. She remembered herself as being in complete solidarity with the Soviet Union in 1945, telling me also how the war had taken her whole life and that everything from before felt distant and nonexistent.

Another experience that Maria shares with many returning Holocaust survivors is the violence and antisemitism that threatened returning Jews in Poland. Maria showed an understanding for her parents' political commitment, while at the same time from a later horizon she placed that very commitment within a tragic frame, both because the Polish People's Republic soon became a dictatorship and also because those Polish Jews involved in this project were themselves expelled during the antisemitic campaign. Socialism did not defeat antisemitism.

Maria talked about her arrival in Warsaw after the war in a positive way. First, they lived in a hotel but later moved into a villa that was relatively luxurious. She described a steady and undramatic life in Poland during the postwar era until 1967. Maria experienced the antisemitic campaign from the sidelines. In 1967 she received a medical research grant to work in Paris for eight months. When Jews were being attacked in the press, when people paraded against the "Zionists," and demonstrations critical of the regime were suppressed with brutal force, Maria was in Paris, fully occupied with her research. She had missed the entire buildup to the antisemitic media campaign. It was only because of an employee at the embassy, who explained the situation to her in an honest attempt to help, that Maria became aware of the severity of circumstances. Various people wanted to help Maria with work and permission to stay in France, but her husband remained in Poland and was not allowed to visit, so Maria returned to Poland in the middle of the antisemitic campaign. She had a hard time taking it all in – suddenly, the communist government wanted to expel Jews because they were considered disloyal Zionists! Maria developed a strong conviction that she wanted to leave Poland. Her husband was more hesitant: he had a degree in economics and saw no possibility of being able to work within that field in Sweden. The person most strongly against the migration was Maria's father. He believed that those who were truly Zionists should move, and no one else. He was 66 years old and still had his job at a newspaper. He became furious about Maria's decision and it took ten years before the two of them were reconciled. The experience of crisis and the reorientation of identity at that time is common among those Polish Jews who experienced the antisemitic campaign (Ilicki 1988).

They chose Sweden because it was one of few possible options. In comparison to the Danish language, they perceived Swedish as easier to understand. Sweden was also larger and richer, they thought. As for many others who migrated, the process was lengthy: they had to receive permission from the Polish authorities to leave and all belongings had to be categorized and further permission needed to be granted for them to be taken out of the country. Even though the so-called Zionists, with a lack of patriotic sentiment for Poland, were encouraged to leave, they were drawn into a tiresome bureaucratic process. Finally, Maria stepped onto a train that went to Świnoujście and then by ferry to Sweden.

Maria came to Sweden in 1970 and lived almost 53 years in the country. She talked about life after the migration in a generally positive and less dramatic way than her earlier life. It is almost the case that the life narrative takes the form of a straight highway through language education, work, finding an apartment and social contacts. Maria and her husband moved to an apartment in Gothenburg in which she lived for the rest of her life. The apartment is next to the hospital where she worked. "Everything changes around me, the hospital grows, but I remain" (IM3), she remarked. Maria lost her husband and then met someone she called her life partner, who also passed away. With her life partner, she periodically lived in Paris. She did not want to move to a nursing home and with the help of her car she was able to have the life she wanted.

I have experienced on several occasions during my work with the project that many people find their experiences from Sweden uninteresting. They sometimes compare their life in Sweden with experiences related to the Holocaust. Maria had this tendency, even though she was happy to answer my questions about her life in Sweden. First, Maria ended up in a facility on the island of Marstrand outside of Gothenburg, a popular summer resort used for migrant accommodation and language training during the winter. The author Anna Grinzweig Jacobsson, who had come to Marstrand in 1969 as a child, has written a book based on interviews with other Polish Jewish migrants who came during the same period (Grinzweig Jacobsson 2020). There is considerable overlap between what Maria tells me about Marstrand and what Anna Grinzweig Jacobsson has written about. Maria herself referred to Jacobsson's book and added that she still was in contact with someone who appears in it. The historical orientation takes place dialogically between individuals and literature.

The descriptions of coming to Sweden and being integrated in the new country are consistently positive in the descriptions I encountered during the work with "We, the Expelled." I have explored this topic in an article titled "Facing Sweden" (2022). One explanation I find for their positive portrayals is the effect of contrasts, partly the contrast to their treatment in Poland during the antisemitic campaign, and partly the contrast to migrant reception in Sweden in later periods (Englund 2022). On a more general level of the historical culture in Sweden, the period from 1945 to the 1980s is generally viewed as the glory days of the Swedish welfare state. This narrative is evident in the experiences collected in "We, the Expelled. "

It is also significant to emphasize that Maria had a recognized refugee status and thus had permission to come to Sweden. They had already arranged this through the Swedish embassy in Warsaw before beginning their journey. This also meant a well-organized reception once they arrived. Maria even talked about how they were able to use diplomatic courier mail via the Swedish embassy to ensure that important documents such as grades and work certificates made it safely to Sweden.[5]

Historical experiences and identity

Much of what Maria told me about her life has an identity-orienting function. Her experiences have made her who she is, and through her life story and interview she can communicate publicly who she is. In the interview, she described a strong Jewish identity she did not have as a child. Through her life story, I can follow how this identity develops: first as something negative and threatening, then as something positive. At the orphanage in the Soviet Union, she was shown papers stating she was Jewish. In that context, Jews were something negative and she considered herself Polish. In her life story she describes how she experienced being told that she was Jewish:

Here I experienced my first real, personal life shock, disappointment, downfall, loneliness.

It was, namely, when I was told that I was Jewish, but not Polish, which I knew from home and had been convinced of.

The only thing I knew so far about Jews in the then antisemitic Russia was that being a Jew is something very bad, negative, that one should be ashamed of.

The subject was never discussed at home, at least not in my presence.

But here, in the orphanage, there was no one who could enlighten me, who I could ask, talk to. I was left to cope with it by myself.

My world came crashing down. (Maria's life story, minnen.se/tema/vi)

In a similar way, she talked about the incident in the interview. It seems difficult to accommodate a Jewish and a Polish identity at the same time for the young Maria. When she found out she was Jewish, she immediately thought, "No, I'm Polish. There is nothing to discuss" (IM2). Regarding the time after the war when Maria lived in Warsaw, she knew that she was Jewish but she did not feel it. It was forced on her by others.

Her world thus came crashing down when she found out she was Jewish, but by the end of her life story she had developed an increasingly positive identification. The Polish identity that was primary to the young Maria came under attack in the antisemitic campaign when she was finally forced by the authorities to renounce her Polish citizenship. It was at this point that her Jewish identity turned into an opportunity more than a threat. At the end of her life story, she writes:

It is not so simple with my Jewish self.

I didn't get that Jewish upbringing from home, in fact I didn't even know about my Jewish origins until I was twelve.

I was born of Jewish parents, thus I am Jewish in the same way that I was born as a woman. This can neither be questioned nor denied. My Jewish self is weighed down by my upbringing, surroundings, circumstances, which meant that only in adulthood did I come into contact with Jewish life.

Now I know that I am of Jewish origin, that I am Jewish, non-religious, with a strong affinity and solidarity with the Jewish people.

It is the same way I am convinced that I am Jewish because I have inherited my Jewish genes from my parents, both Polish Jews for several generations. It is in the same way that I know that I am human, woman, that I am a Swedish citizen, etc.

My belonging?

I lived in different European countries, "Jew, the eternal wanderer", my motherland is Poland and mother tongue is Polish. Sweden id the country I have adapted to. I experience myself as a Jew, European, Swedish citizen with great sympathy and gratitude for Israel and the Israeli people.

What is my identity?

My mother called me cosmopolitan. (Maria's life story, minnen.se/tema/vi)

Toward the end of the interview, Maria concluded that she had become a Zionist. She was impressed by the fact that it is Jews who created Israel and she felt a sense of pride, although she emphasized that she herself had not contributed to building the country. She was not a Zionist when she was collectively accused in Poland of being one but her experiences eventually made her one. In her life story, however, she comes to the conclusion that her mother called her cosmopolitan, because, like Zionist, it was something used in the antisemitic campaign as a negatively charged word of accusation. Poles of Jewish origin were suspected as unpatriotic cosmopolitans and secret Zionists. In Sweden, Maria lived in a society where the word cosmopolitan had positive connotations for many. The Nazis tried to crush all cosmopolitans; in communist Poland they were perceived as disloyal and harmful to a national socialist project. Maria survived and at the end of her life she could finally be a proud cosmopolitan.

In his thesis about the migration of the antisemitic campaign, *Den föränderliga identiteten* (The Changing Identity), sociologist Julian Ilicki arrives at the conclusion that Jewish identity was strengthened through migration. Ilicki starts from extensive statistical data from the current migration. Maria's identity development can thus be seen as an exemplification of Ilicki's general image (Ilicki 1988). Maria also commented in the interview how the environment she belonged to in Warsaw lacked Jewish elements. She knew there was a Jewish theater, but she had never been there. Later in Sweden, she understood that there was a more developed Jewish life in Poland in some smaller towns.

Something that recurs in several accounts of the arrival in Sweden is the encounter between the arriving Polish Jews and the Swedish Jewish community. In *Flykten till Marstrand*, Anna Grinzweig Jacobsson (2020) addresses this as a central theme. Although these Polish Jews generally developed a stronger Jewish identity, many experienced a clash between them and the Jews they met in Swedish Jewish congregations. Maria writes in her life story that they thought the Polish Jews were communists, which Maria claims was not true, at least not regarding the younger generation. In addition, they had fled a communist regime. The clash was largely about the ignorance of Jewish traditions among the new arrivals and the fact that the in the lives of the Swedish Jewry religious traditions had a central role. Some I have spoken to expressed how they never joined Swedish Jewish congregational life, while they found Jewish community in other contexts, for example through social arrangements within their Polish Jewish migration. Many of the individuals who make up the Swedish Jewish congregational life were Jews from Poland or with close family ties to Poland. Not having migrated before 1968 could appear less Jewish. In several waves of Polish Jewish migration during the postwar period, they had chosen to stay in Poland. Maria described how through contacts with Swedish Jews and the organized Jewish life in Sweden she developed her Jewish identity over time together with a growing knowledge of Judaism.

Maria as a Holocaust survivor

I had prepared to ask her whether she would call herself a Holocaust survivor. My worry was that this was a sensitive topic. Over 90 percent of Poland's Jews had been murdered. The Nazis' intention was to kill everyone – this, after all, was the basic intention behind the Holocaust. Maria was a Polish Jew who had survived this. Her relatives were murdered and the entire social environment to which her parents belonged was systematically destroyed. She came to Poland after the war and had to face this destruction, while trying to reestablish contact with the few that remained. I consider this as experiences of Holocaust survival. When I finally decided to ask the question, she answered without hesitation: "Yes, it is for sure! Absolutely! Sure! I am a survivor and belong to the association of Holocaust survivors [Föreningen för Förintelsens överlevande]. The Jewish survivors, I belong to them" (IM1).

The 1990s have been described as an era of a public memory boom of Holocaust memory (Olick, Vinitzky-Seroussi, and Levy 2011, 29–36). The Swedish example of the Living History Forum is an expression of that boom. The film *Schindler's List* and later Stephen Spielberg's USC Shoah Foundation initiative are widely regarded as two of the most central features of this boom as well. During the early 1990s, several Holocaust deniers had been publicly active, which motivated several survivors to start making school visits and other public appearances. The focus was, unsurprisingly, on those who had survived despite having been in a camp. Their testimonies came from the places where most had been murdered. *Schindler's List* took place in a camp, and it was the camps that became synonymous with the Holocaust in public memory culture. The French-produced exhibition *Holocaust by Bullets* was shown at the Living History Forum in 2009 and completed the picture of the killing that took place in the camps with the mass shootings during the German attack on the Soviet Union ("Levande Historia: Om oss" n.d.). However, narratives about survival in the Soviet Union are rarely raised in public representations of the Holocaust.

Survival on the margins

Maria considered herself lucky to have moved to the Soviet Union. If her family had not, they would most likely be dead. "One could say that we were lucky in our misfortune" (IM1).

Communism plays a significant role in Maria's life story, especially the communist commitment of her father. It had driven them first to Vienna and then to Moscow during a period when many came to the Soviet Union to build the new socialist society. We have already established that Maria viewed her father's communist commitment as "unfortunate." In the sociological historical study *The Generation*, Jaff Schatz describes a generation of Polish Jewish communists born in the early twentieth century. They became communists during the inter-war years and survived the Holocaust while in the Soviet Union. Then they returned to Poland and engaged in the building of the Polish People's Republic until the antisemitic campaign of the late 1960s, when they were forced to migrate. Maria's father, and to some extent Maria herself, follow the life path that Schatz narrates in his book. Schatz shows the experiences of this generation in a way that makes visible the historical situation in which they became communists. Communism was the only political movement – or messianic movement, as Schatz puts it – that attracted young Jews in Poland, together with other ethnic groups in a joint emancipatory project. The other movements that appealed to the Polish Jewry – for example, Bund and different Zionist and Orthodox groups, were exclusively Jewish (Schatz 1991).

There has been a far-reaching conceptual discussion around the Holocaust and its survivors.[6] It can be stated that those who survived in the Soviet Union have ended up at a marginal position in public memory.[7] Holocaust survivors came to Sweden mainly during three periods, first from the camps immediately after the war, then from Hungary during the revolt in 1956, and finally during Maria's migration, which began mainly in 1968. The last of these was dominated by people who survived the Holocaust in the Soviet Union.

Malin Thor Tureby and Kristin Wagrell have compiled a report, *Survivors Recounting the Holocaust: Definitions, Collections and Uses of Holocaust "Testimony" in Sweden, 1939–2020*, over Holocaust testimonies and stories in Sweden and the circumstances surrounding them. In the initial conceptual discussion about the survivors, "the liberated" (*de befriade*) or "the saved" (*de räddade*) were early names for the survivors who came to Sweden from various camps in connection with the end of the war. The more specific "the liberated of year 1945" was also used (Thor Tureby and Wagrell 2020). These ways of defining Holocaust survivors focus on the saving effort and can constitute a discursive asset in a Swedish narrative of national pride.

The group that survived in the Soviet Union were not saved in this way and thus did not fit into the early image of Holocaust survivors in Sweden. But, if we define the survivors as the *she'erit hapletah* (surviving remnant) of the European Jewry, then those who survived in the Soviet Union are included in this definition. But within that definition, for example, Swedish or British Jews can also be defined as part of the *she'erit hapletah*. Here I want to strongly emphasize that Maria and other Polish Jews who survived in the Soviet Union rather belong to a category of survivors in a stricter sense. While she was in the Soviet Union the German invaders committed genocidal acts on her relatives. She also shares the experience of coming to Poland after the war to find that her family and relatives had mostly been murdered and that the Polish Jewish environment from which her parents came had been destroyed.

It is rare in public representations of the Holocaust to mention the Soviet survivors. There are some circumstances that might account for this. After all, these survivors rarely have the same experiences as those who are generally perceived as having had typical experiences of the Holocaust. Those who survived in the Soviet Union were a small minority of Polish Jews in 1939, even if they would constitute the majority after the war. In research on the Holocaust, these survivors have largely not been categorized as Holocaust survivors and their experiences have been treated only to a small extent. A study that focuses on this group to which Maria belongs is Eliyana Adler's *Survival on the Margins*, which provides a historical overview of the experiences of the 200,000 who survived in the Soviet Union. It was published in 2020 as the first academic monograph dealing with this group and their historical experiences. We are dealing with a specific cohort of people who survived at the margins of the Soviet Union but also at the margins of public Holocaust memory. Adler has named a chapter in the book after the sarcastic but still reasonable expression "Jewish Luck," to describe that those who lived through the war under extremely difficult conditions in the Soviet periphery were still the fortunate ones. It is a sentiment that Maria shared. But, still, it remains a strange kind of luck, Jewish luck (Adler 2020). These Polish Jews were also saved by one of the most oppressive and murderous regimes in history. Perhaps it is precisely this complexity that prevents the experience of survival in the Soviet Union from making it into public memory. When Maria concluded her whole life story, she said:

I feel like I've been lucky. (IM3)

The neglect of forced migrants in national history

This anthology focuses on forced migrants in the Nordic histories and historiographies. I regard historiography as part of a larger historical culture. Historiography is the part that is recorded and put into history books. I regard historical culture as a vast and dynamic category where people orient themselves historically in all possible contexts: orally, in writing, in pictures, or just in their own thoughts. The Holocaust has in many contexts been used publicly to promote certain normative goals, for example in the work of the Living History Forum. It may also promote Swedish national pride as with "the saved" of 1945.

Survival in the Soviet Union is not a topic that easily integrates into the normative aims of the public Holocaust memory in Sweden. The theme signals the same complexity as Finland allying with Germany during the Second World War to stop the Soviet aggressions. Or that the war against Germany was largely won by the efforts of the Soviet Union. Perhaps the most important reason why the public historical narratives about the Holocaust has not taken more interest in survival in the Soviet Union is that the perpetrators, their camps, and their killers are not present. Still there is much in Maria's experiences that contributes to our understanding of the Holocaust.

It is possible to categorize the marginal role in historiography of the Soviet survivors and forced migrants of the antisemitic campaign as part of the same silencing of refugee experience that Philip Marfleet (2007) describes – a lack of history in refugee studies and a lack of refugees in historical studies. Maria's family experiences of Holocaust survival in the Soviet Union, return to Poland, and expulsion to Sweden are a transnational history that breaks the boundaries of national historiography. It challenges the memory culture around the Holocaust and the Soviet Union with ethnic and geographical complexity. I end this chapter with a typical appeal for further studies. The Polish Jews that survived in the Soviet Union and the forced migrants of the antisemitic campaign deserve a less peripheral role in the public memory. I find the extraordinary yet typical life of Maria evidence of that.

Notes

1 The latest study to describe the antisemitic campaign is Anat Plocker's *The Expulsion of Jews from Communist Poland* (Plocker 2022). The antisemitic campaign started in 1967 and targeted Jews in Poland as disloyal Zionists. The campaign reached its crescendo at the student protests of March 1968 and it led to the forced migration of approximately half of the Polish Jews.

2 See for example *How to Make Sense of the Past – Salient Issues of Metahistory* for an introduction (Rüsen 2007).

3 For the Soviet purges against foreign communists see for example Robert Conquest's classical *The Great Terror* (Conquest 2018). Many of the foreign communists that had moved to the Soviet Union were prisoned or executed during the 1930s.

4 The latest work to describe the antisemitic campaign is Anat Plocker's *The Expulsion of Jews from Communist Poland* (Plocker 2022).

5 About the legal status of the forced migration Maria belonged to, see *Swedish Refugee Policy Making in Transition?* (Górniok 2016).

6 See Bothe and Nesselrodt (2016) for a conceptual history of the Holocaust survivor.

7 That is one of the main points in Adler's *Survival on the Margins* (Adler 2020).

Sources

Interview with Maria. August 10, 2022. file 1, 2 and 3. Interviewer Martin Englund. Maria's life story. Minnen.se. https://minnen.se/tema/vi. Accessed October 10, 2024.

Bibliography

Adler, Eliyana R. 2020. *Survival on the Margins: Polish Jewish Refugees in the Wartime Soviet Union*. Cambridge, MA: Harvard University Press.

Bothe, Alina and Markus Nesselrodt. 2016. "Survivor: Towards a Conceptual History". *The Leo Baeck Institute Yearbook* 61 (1): 57–82. https://doi.org/10.1093/leobaeck/ybw013.

Conquest, Robert. 2018. *The Great Terror: Stalin's Purge of the Thirties*. London: The Bodley Head.

Englund, Martin. 2022. "Facing Sweden: The Experience of Sweden after the Forced Migration from Poland during the Antisemitic Campaign, 1967–1972". *Studia Scandinavica* 6 (26): 93–106. https://doi.org/10.26881/ss.2022.26.06.

Gadamer, Hans-Georg. 1989. *Truth and Method*. London: Continuum International Publishing Group.

Górniok, Łukasz. 2016. *Swedish Refugee Policymaking in Transition? Czechoslovaks and Polish Jews in Sweden, 1968–1972*. Umeå.

Grinzweig Jacobsson, Anna. 2020. *Flykten till Marstrand*. Gothenburg: Förlaget Korpen.

Ilicki, Julian. 1988. *Den föränderliga identiteten: om identitetsförändringar hos den yngre generationen polska judar som invandrade till Sverige under åren 1968–1972: en rapport från forskningsprojektet "Judisk identitet, förändringar i samband med migration".* Skrifter utgivna av Sällskapet för judaistisk forskning 7. Åbo: Sällskapet för judaistisk forskning.

"Levande historia: Om oss". n.d. Accessed June 26, 2023. https://www.levandehistoria.se/om-oss/20-ar-av-levande-historia.

Marfleet, Philip. 2007. "Refugees and History: Why We Must Address the Past". *Refugee Survey Quarterly* 26 (3): 136–48. https://doi.org/10.1093/rsq/hdi0248.

Olick, Jeffrey K., Vered Vinitzky-Seroussi, and Daniel Levy, eds. 2011. *The Collective Memory Reader.* New York: Oxford University Press.

Plocker, Anat. 2022. *The Expulsion of Jews from Communist Poland: Memory Wars and Homeland Anxieties.* The Modern Jewish Experience. Bloomington: Indiana University Press.

Portelli, Alessandro. 1991. *The Death of Luigi Trastulli, and Other Stories: Form and Meaning in Oral History.* SUNY Series in Oral and Public History. Albany: State University of New York Press.

Rüsen, Jörn. 2007. "How to Make Sense of the Past – Salient Issues of Metahistory". *The Journal for Transdisciplinary Research in Southern Africa* 3 (1). https://doi.org/10.4102/td.v3i1.316.

Schatz, Jaff. 1991. *The Generation: The Rise and Fall of the Jewish Communists of Poland.* Societies and Culture in East-Central Europe 5. Berkeley: University of California Press.

Svanberg, Ingvar, and Mattias Tydén. 1992. *Tusen år av invandring: en svensk kulturhistoria.* Stockholm: Gidlund.

Thomson, Alistair. 2015. "'Anzac Memories' Revisited: Trauma, Memory and Oral History". *The Oral History Review* 42 (1): 1–29.

Thor Tureby, Malin. 2001. "Oral history – mer än en metod". *Historisk Tidskrift* 121, 325–45.

Thor Tureby, Malin and Kristin Wagrell. 2020. *Vittnesmål från Förintelsen och de överlevandes berättelser definitioner, insamlingar och användningar, 1939-2020.* Stockholm: Forum för levande historia.

"Vi, de fördrivna". 2021. December 29, 2021. https://minnen.se/tema/vi.

CHAPTER 14

Re-membering home in space and time from Chilean exile in Gothenburg

Sjamme van de Voort
Vrije Universiteit Amsterdam

Abstract

This chapter examines the cultural memory of Chilean exiles in Gothenburg, Sweden, through oral history interviews conducted with women who arrived in the aftermath of the 1973 military coup. It explores how metanarratives shaped by Chilean political discourse before exile intersect with and diverge from the migrants' lived experiences in Sweden. By comparing oral histories with Chilean political media from the period, the chapter identifies elements of cultural memory that remained anchored in Chile and those transformed by migration. The study applies Niels Kayser Nielsen's model of historical tropes and Gunnar Olsson's concept of cartographic reasoning to analyze how narratives of displacement and activism structured the community's memory. The chapter ultimately argues that the Chilean diaspora's engagement with political and cultural heritage – through solidarity networks, music, and the Hammarkullen Carnival – redefined notions of home and belonging, illustrating the spatial and temporal dimensions of diasporic memory formation.

How to cite this book chapter:
van de Voort, Sjamme. 2025. "Re-membering home in space and time from Chilean exile in Gothenburg." In *Forced Migrants in Nordic Histories*, edited by Johanna Leinonen, Miika Tervonen, Hans Otto Frøland, Christhard Hoffmann, Seija Jalagin, Heidi Vad Jønsson and Malin Thor Tureby, 347–363. Helsinki: Helsinki University Press. https://doi.org/10.33134/HUP-32-15.

Introduction

After a 30-minute northbound ride on the 9-tram from Gothenburg Central Station, you step out on a cold platform, 25 meters underground. As a nonresident, the place feels different from other tram stops in Gothenburg: there are few other underground stations in the city, and the escalator taking you to the surface, with its 58 meters, the longest in the city, feels like an eternity (Andersson and Forsberg 2010, 31). As you exit the station and try to find your bearings, the large concrete buildings serve as reference points. Built as part of the Swedish Million Homes Program, it has been the target of critique before and after being constructed in 1966–1969 (Zintchenko 1993, 37–50). The difference between the tall, concrete high-rise buildings of the area and the lower and older houses in the rest of Gothenburg is palpable. The change in scenery might even increase the anxious sensation of being in a place of danger, which has been promoted by Swedish media from the very conceptualization of the One Million Homes Program to the present day (Ericsson, Molina, and Ristilammi 2002). If you do let yourself grip by this anxiety, you will probably not be aware of what Ove Sernhede has called a special "Hammarkullen-spirit," consisting of social mobilizing, political awareness, and its yearly carnival celebrating the culturally diverse population of the neighborhood (Sernhede 2021). As you walk around the large buildings, you notice the large murals covering their side walls. Inspired by Mexican muralist traditions, they are colorful, and most have a hint of a political message of one kind or the other (Nardelli 2018). What is striking is how the faces of the people painted in the murals reveal facial features, color patterns, and even natural references to plants and birds, characteristic of southern cone Latin America. This, along with the few storefronts on the bottom floors of several buildings with names such as *Chile Lindo* or *Radio Salvador Allende*, gives the impression of a large Chilean community. Curiously, although the neighborhood has indeed been characterized as a Latin American one, Chilean migrants have never comprised more than 5–6 percent of its inhabitants (Sernhede 2021, 137).

This chapter investigates the cultural memory of the Chilean diaspora in Gothenburg, based on a series of oral history interviews, conducted in 2022, as part of my Bernadotte Fellowship at the Royal Gustavus Adolphus Academy for Swedish Folk Culture. Through a cultural institution central to the neighborhood, as well as on-the-ground fieldwork on location, five women decided to take part in this research. We met for a minimum of two sessions, and a maximum of five sessions, for several hours. The interviews took the form of life-story interviews, narrating the story of each individual's life in Chile, during the military coup, escape from Chile, their settlement and subsequent life in Sweden. Besides documenting a group of migrants with a characteristic larger importance than their numbers might seem to merit (Kelly 2013; De Kievid 2013; Christiaens 2014; Christiaens, Rodriguez Garcia, and Goddeeris 2014; Baud 2018), this chapter asks how this diasporic cultural memory came into being. Through a comparison with a similar analysis of historical tropes in Chilean political media that have certainly had an influence on the promotion of cultural memory among the Chilean diaspora at the time when it was forming as a community in Gothenburg, this chapter is able to determine aspects of cultural memory that were specifically formed by the migratory experience. Finally, it is through the framing of diasporic cultural memory as a traveling entity that this chapter demonstrates the methodological advances made possible by the inclusion of the spatial dimension in its theoretical framework.

From Chile to Gothenburg

When the democratically elected president of Chile, Salvador Allende, was overthrown in a military coup on September 11, 1973, a reign of terror began and an estimated 200,000 people left the country in the years following the coup (Wright and Zúniga 2007). The story of how many of these migrants came to Gothenburg is one of such drama that Hollywood movies are made of – quite literally, as one of my interview subjects various times during our interview insisted that she had been the inspiration behind the character that actress Kate del Castillo plays in the 2007 film *The Black Pimpernel* (Faringer and Hultberg 2007). The sudden influx of migration further adds a dramatic character to this story. In 1970, there were 181 Chilean residents registered in Sweden. In 2003 that number was 45,000 (Padilla 2006).

This story cannot be told without mentioning the Swedish ambassador to Chile during the military coup, Harald Edelstam, the man behind the moniker "The Black Pimpernel." Proactively, often leaving his government with little or no knowledge about his activities, he managed to lead into safety hundreds of Chileans, persecuted by the military for their sympathies with the government of Allende, whether perceived or real. There were those to whom Edelstam gave refuge in the Swedish embassy, family members of persecuted people that he secretly managed to transport to the embassy, and then those that he managed to get out of prison (Padilla 2006; Bonnefoy 2016). The latter category can furthermore be divided into those that he liberated from prison with the sanction of the military government, and those he liberated on his own accord.

Of all the prison installations used by the military junta, the national football stadium is, still today, the most notorious. In the aftermath of the coup, as many as 20,000 men and women were detained there. Many were tortured, many were murdered (Hite and Rajevic 2019). One of my interviewees told me how her husband had been taken to the stadium, and how Edelstam saved him. As the ambassador had gotten paperwork to take another prisoner out and bring him to the embassy, he walked through the halls just as this husband came out from yet another session of torture, looking, understandably, terrible. As he passed by, Edelstam grabbed him by the arm and told his escorting officers: "I'm taking this one as well." Unfettered by the protests of the guards or the guns pointed in his direction, Edelstam left the stadium with the two men, waiving his red diplomatic passport in front of him as protection. Several of my interviewees had such a story, of Edelstam being involved in saving them, their family, or their friends. What is interesting is that even those who did not have any direct contact with Edelstam mentioned him in their stories – some by name, others as "the Swedish ambassador."

After arriving in Sweden, some by way of direct refuge in the Swedish embassy, others through other migratory journeys, Chilean refugees were placed in camps administrated by the Swedish National Labor Market Board (Arbetsmarknadsstyrelsen, AMS). Here, they were given basic lessons on the Swedish language, society, and job market (Berg, Andréasson, and Zintchenko 1989, 83). The stories about these camps in the oral history interviews conducted in Gothenburg suggest that the efforts to educate the migrants varied greatly, partly due to the various levels of education in the group but especially given the fact that many had experienced horrific trauma before arriving in Sweden and needed time to recover, mentally as well as physically. Those of the interviewees belonging to the latter group did instead find greater support once settled in Gothenburg. After a brief initial period of arrival, the interviewees reported that they began establishing connections with fellow Chilean migrants, often based on preexisting friendships and neighborhood connections, but also political affiliation to organizations they had belonged to in Chile.

These connections had a wider reach, beyond Gothenburg, not only due to the preexisting networks of international solidarity organizations, such as the Swedish Chile Committee (Chilekommittén; see Padilla 2014), but also due to the distribution of the migrants immediately after leaving the camps. Several of my interviewees reported initially moving to Malmö or Helsingborg, subsequently moving to Gothenburg owing to personal connections moving there, but maintaining connections to their initial locations in the event that friendly relations with other migrants were established there. Later, when the migrant community in Gothenburg was more firmly established, these connections served as conduits for exchanges. This is especially true when events were held in Gothenburg with a cultural personality, who would often visit these other places, but also less formal events, parties and small-scale political events drew people from other parts of the network. At a later point, this dynamic came to serve the growth of an annual carnival in Hammarkullen, as migrants from other parts of Sweden came to participate in celebrations of their cultural memory.

Although these groups initially had a character of support networks in which newly arrived migrants could rely on advice from those who arrived earlier, many quickly developed into organizations of a political character. Previous research has been done on international solidarity organizations, such as Chilekommittén, which was founded in 1972. Although principally made up of Latin American and Spanish members, the primary purpose of the committee was to generate popular international support for Allende's UP government (Padilla 2014). As the influx of Chilean refugees began after the coup of 1973, this network subsequently became instrumental in welcoming them, but also involving them in their solidarity campaigns (Lindholm 2016, 24–25). By 1975, the organization had transformed into a civil society organization promoting human rights and opposition to dictatorship in Chile, with more than 100 local committees around the country, as well as a publication, *Chilebulletinen* (The Chile Bulletin), about 20,000 copies of each edition being printed and distributed around the country (Padilla 2014; 2015, 134). Susan Lindholm has written that:

"As the Chilekommittén worked toward creating a sense of community, it, at the same time, set out to spread an image of Chilean culture both within and outside the organization" (Lindholm 2016, 88). To this quote, one might add that they – naturally – did so with a distinct political agenda, as well as based on previous conceptions of Chilean political and cultural life prevalent on the Swedish left.

As the groups of Chilean refugees in Gothenburg moved beyond their initial period of functioning as support groups, they moved toward political organization. When asked what she meant by her saying that "she began to work politically," one interviewee mentioned that she, with her group of Chilean friends, began baking Chilean empanadas and selling them in the neighborhood, to be able to send the money back to Chile through networks of her previous political organization. Another interviewee mentioned that she sang in a Chilean choir in Swedish elderly homes, mostly performing Chilean songs such as those written by Chilean left-wing icons like Victor Jara and Violeta Parra. The interviews, however, suggest that the migrants accepted and played into preconceived notions of Chilean identity, while they formed their own. Traditional Chilean dances, such as the cueca, were performed in events where Swedes were present, while the preferred music of the private parties was the more easily danceable pumping rhythm of the Colombian cumbia.

In a similar way, cueca, described by the interviewees as "stiff and serious," was quickly abandoned in favor of the colorful polyrhythm of samba in the celebration of the annual carnival in Hammarkullen. Some interviewees insisted that they personally knew the person who suggested this change, while others merely mentioned that samba was more fun than cueca. Today, the carnival is a large celebration, where the many nationalities populating the area parade with dances and music traditions they feel belong to their community. Since 1977, when it began more or less spontaneously, with only a few groups of children participating, it has today made it to the official list of intangible Swedish heritage ("Hammarkullen Carnival" 2020). Although accounts varied as to who came up with the idea behind the carnival, all highlighted how the Chilean community was fundamental in its inception.

Besides the performance of Chilean-ness for a Swedish audience looking for exotic Latin American socialist refugees, the musical performance of the Chilean cause for solidarity was an arena of mutual reinforcement. Several of my interviewees told me how progressive Swedish folk-rock icons of the 1970s and 1980s, such as Mikael Wiehe and Björn Afzelius, were frequent guests at their parties. Swedish scholarship on folkloristic music traditions has emphasized the substantial influence that Chilean musicians such as Victor Jara and Violeta Parra have had on the development of popular rock-music traditions of those decades – either as topics or even in direct translation (Brolinson 2007). What is interesting from the interviews, however, is how the interviewees used their relationship to these musicians and their music to legitimize their position as valid political forces within the community focused on solidarity with Chile. One interviewee even mentioned how she served as inspiration for the politically charged songs written by these musicians. The political influence of Chilean migrant organizations has been investigated in several contexts of international politics (Gradskova and Quirico 2016; Perry 2016; Baud 2018). My interviews, however, suggest that this influence was mutually reinforcing.

Besides the mutual influence between the community and Swedish popular rock musicians, which contributed to the building of the utopian worldview of Swedish progg in solidarity with oppressed people globally, but especially with Chile (van der Lee 1997; Hyltén-Cavallius 2016), the connection to the Swedish Social Democratic Party was also tangible in the interviews – alongside Fidel Castro and Salvador Allende, one of my interviewees even had a large portrait of Olof Palme adorning her kitchen wall. During his first tenure as prime minister, Palme had substantially strengthened relations with Allende's government (Padilla 2014). One of my interviewees even mentioned that, before the military coup, she had mainly known of Sweden because Swedish engineers had come to Chile with Swedish laundry machines for common laundry rooms in the occupied pieces of land, where groups loosely affiliated with the Revolutionary Left Movement (Movimiento Izguierdista Revolucionaria, MIR) organized the informal building neighborhoods for marginalized people (Araya González 2017; a more extensive description of this movement follows below). Owing to the initial contact with Sweden being conditioned by the perceived benevolence of Palme's Social Democratic Party, the involvement in the community-building efforts of Chilekommittén furthermore meant building a network of politically affiliated groups and individuals from the Swedish left, with a spillover effect of Chileans later joining the party (Gradskova and Quirico 2016, 40). One of the interviewees remained an active member until the 2022 Swedish decision to join NATO under the leadership of Social Democratic Prime Minister Magdalena Andersson. The influence between Chilean communities in Sweden and the Swedish left, including the Social Democratic party, went both ways, as during the 1980s the latter "assembled an impressive expertise, over time, about various aspects of politics in Central America and elsewhere in Latin America" (Nilsson 1991, 174) and used the issue to assume an activist position in international politics during the decade. On the national scene, this discourse of perceived support of Chilean exiles was aided by the role that Chile came to play in popular music, which played a significant role in the formation of the identity of the Swedish left during the decades following the military coup (Arvidsson 2010).

Memory from Chile and heritage in Hammarkullen

The paragraphs above tell the story of a group of people, their journey across half a world and half a century, and some of the strategies they adopted to tackle the seemingly unsurmountable challenges along their way. Not only does this story rely on these people remembering and them relaying their stories to me in the form of oral history interviews but this research also reveals how the concept of memory as a phenomenon in the social realm works, which will hopefully inform future research on the cultural dynamics of migrant communities.

In order to allow memory to play this role, a few definitions need to be clear. Whereas collective memory is to be understood as the keeping of memory in the social life of a closed group (Halbwachs 1950; Jelin 2003, 11), cultural memory refers to a dynamic system of meaning-making about the past in a society, which happens when memories are transferred from one closed social group to another in a mediated version, functioning as the vehicle on which memory travels. The correct interpretation of these mediated memories is often assigned to a specialized person assuming the role of an arbiter of truth, as a so-called "high priest of memory" (Erll 2004, 7–11; Assmann 2011, 72). In this system, the term heritage refers to a particular aspect, often in a material form, to which the canon (for more on this concept, see Assmann 2008) has ascribed a particular importance for the culture in which it functions (van de Voort et al. 2021). This distinction requires us to understand the system of cultural memory as a whole, with distinct methodological approaches to the various vehicles that move within it.

An analytical method designed to understand the oral history interviews of forced migrants could base itself on the concept of the historical trope as proposed by Niels Kayser Nielsen, who approaches historical narratives as lines drawn on a piece of paper. A meta-narrative that designates the past as good, the present as bad, and the future as worse forms a trope of decay; the story of a golden age to which we can return forms a U-trope (as the line looks like a capital letter U); a circular emplotment a trope of repetition; and so on (Kayser Nielsen 2010, 53–61). In the context of an analysis of the history of forced migration, the idea of the historical narrative as a line projected by subjective imaginaries from the past through the present into the future takes on a dimension beyond the temporal, as the story of migration is one that takes place across not only history but also geography, effectively creating a map of both time and space. At this point, it is enlightening to consider the role of the line in geographer and philosopher Gunnar Olsson's conception of the map and its role in the human ability to cartographically reason not only across the geographical world but also the social and cultural.

> To have a map, the only traditional map, only three things you need. A set of points, lines between the points and the projection scheme … So, these lines are steeped in power … when I have to baptize the points, the name sort of sticks. But when I baptize the lines, the lines begin to shake, and they want to change form. (Olsson 2018; see also Olsson 2020)

What Olsson is describing here is not a map in its traditional sense but a transposition of this conception of the map to a world of semiotics. In this understanding, each perceived sign causes the human imagination to engage in "cartographic reasoning," meaning the activity of drawing imaginary lines of power between points on a projection scheme, whether that is a scheme that organizes perceptions of a geographical, a social, or a cultural world across space and/or time (Olsson 2007, 109; 2020, 51–53). One of the possible directions of these lines is backward – back to a time and/or place where the world is perceived as better than the present. This phenomenon has been described as nostalgia by scholars such as Laurajane Smith and Gary Campbell, Kate Houlden, and, perhaps most prominently, Svetlana Boym. Nostalgia here relates to a disassociation with teleologies of progress that comes to inform social and political agendas for the future (Boym 2001; Houlden 2010; Smith and Campbell 2017). These arguments reinforce the agency of the U-trope, and in the light of these conceptualizations the political agency of engagement with heritage becomes apparent. In the examination of historical narratives, we find points – in this case, conceived of as heritage – that the tropes form lines through, and which determine their direction.

Tropes of history at the beginning of exile

The challenge of investigating a diasporic space constructed of memories configuring themselves across both time and space, as this space establishes itself in the country receiving the migrants, is one that is touched upon by Alejandra Serpente, as this dynamic is "constituting different mobile and multidirectional relations between different memorial landscapes" (Serpente 2015, 10). One of the landscapes that must be investigated in order to understand the cultural memory of the Chilean migrants in Sweden is, naturally the one in which they grew into political maturity in Chile. Since most of my interviews were conducted with former members of the MIR, the political journal of this organization, as it was published in the years immediately predating the military coup, gives some enlightening insights into the metanarratives that served to frame cultural memory of these migrants before the beginning of their migration.

During the military coup in Chile, the MIR did not support the leftist government coalition Popular Unity (Unidad Popular, UP), because it advocated for a "revolution from below" and focused on extra-parliamentary organization (Gaudichaud 2009). The MIR was formed by a fusion of various smaller organizations comprising former members of established left-wing parties who were discontented with their political direction in the mid-1960s. The organization was inclined toward Marxism–Leninism, which originated from China, and "Guevarism," which was perceived as the doctrine of the Cuban Revolution. In theory, they preferred armed revolution to the parliamentary path taken by the UP's member organizations (Benavente Urbina 1987). The MIR's influence extended beyond political organizing, as the movement was organized horizontally and engaged in other forms of organizing, such as communal councils, particularly free communes that emerged from collective land occupation movements, the so-called *tomas de terreno*. Although most members of these land occupations were MIR members, the organization's relationship with the communal councils of these new neighborhoods was strengthened during the elections of Salvador Allende and the UP in 1970. Prior to the election, the MIR made a pact with the UP coalition parties to refrain from agitating against the democratic process, paving the way for Allende's triumph in September. After the victory, the MIR, members of the occupation movement, and the public housing administration, now under the control of the UP, agreed to formally designate land to the *tomas* movement, resulting in the construction of the neighborhood of Nueva Habana (Araya González 2017).

Not only did the MIR's ideological framing of history influence the cultural memory of some of my interviewees at the time of migration because of their affiliation with the organization; one of them was also an active member of the community of Nueva Habana. The political journal of the organization, *Estrategia: revista teórica del MIR*, reiterated a series of historical tropes that were explicit and clear. The journal drew up a battlefield through a continuous comparison of a traditional Marxist teleology of societal development, starting from primitive communism and proceeding through an ancient mode of production, a feudal mode of production, the contemporary capitalist mode of production, and, finally, a future communist mode of production, with a Leninist notion of imperialism as the main danger to the capitalist revolution. The journal framed this battlefield of historical conceptualization by publishing extracts from Marxist literature and a selection of articles about current and historical events in Latin America that exemplified what the journal referred to as "Yankee imperialism." In addition to presenting these two opposing teleological tropes of revolution versus imperialism, the journal frequently cited theories derived from the life and work of Ernesto "Che" Guevara and the broader Cuban Revolution. The journal repeated two arguments: first, that the revolution from industrial society toward communist society in Latin America was presently occurring and, second, that the reader had the agency to participate in this development through means that were not limited to the traditional communist and socialist parties. Participation in not only the MIR but also its affiliated organizations was depicted as a third way to actively revolutionize society (Ferrer Mir n.d.).

The two tropes prevalent in these documents are the trope of repetition of imperialist, capitalist violation of not only the rights and desires of the historical subject of Chile but of the very purpose of historical development. This trope combines with a trope of revolution, providing a meta-narrative that frames the present as a continuation of the malaise of the past, placing the responsibility for launching historical progress toward a utopia inherent in its teleology in the subject, thereby providing it with a high degree of political agency.

A blank map. New tropes of heritage?

Although the migrants interviewed during the fall of 2022 did settle in different parts of Gothenburg, most of them did reference the neighborhood of Hammarkullen as a frame of reference for their social circle. They would either have friends there or know of the organizations that had formed there, and, of course, Hammarkullekarnavalen played a role in all interviews. In their ethnographic fieldwork for the Swedish State Committee for Construction Research (Statens råd för byggnadsforskning), Berg, Andréasson, and Zintchenko conducted interviews with Chilean migrants over the winter of 1987 and the spring of 1988 and identified the areas of the city housing the largest Chilean population – with Hammarkullen coming far ahead of the other areas (Berg, Andréasson, and Zintchenko 1989, 84). The newly built residential area of Hammarkullen, with its architectural vision to create what the leading architect behind the Million Homes Program called a "new and free man who can shake off the buoys that class, society, convention, and religion imposed on her" (Alfvén 2020), almost intentionally provided a blank slate for the migrants to project their identity onto.

It furthermore has to be noted that in the initial waves of migration Sweden, owing to the very broadly defined refugee policies of the 1970s, primarily received militants of the MIR, which were considered too radically left-wing for other countries that received Chilean refugees (Camacho 2006, 32). Given the status of the MIR in Chile before September 11, 1973 – especially in the land occupation movement that led to the construction of communal neighborhoods such Nueva Habana – as well as its horizontal organizational structure, the vast majority of these migrants had previous organizational skills. As they now found themselves in a place where the formation of and participation in civil society organizations was not only allowed but seemed almost baked into the very understanding of Swedish nationalism (Östberg 2021; Månsson 2021), and a newly built neighborhood offered space to house these organizations, it is no wonder that political, cultural, and social organizations quickly emerged. As these organizations gained stability, in the form of storefronts with names such as *Chile Lindo* and *Radio Salvador Allende*, or through participation in the organization of the Hammarkullen Carnival, memory in the social realm was inscribed in the material that cultural memory is made of. Within this system, the role of the high priest of memory became relegated to those who had experienced repression by the military government, as well as those who had had close contact with the Swedish embassy in Santiago and Ambassador Harald Edelstam. This happened not only because the most skilled organizers and leaders of movements were also the ones that were most brutally repressed and abused by the military regime – which would mean that these people could almost naturally assume a similar authority in diaspora communities – but also due to the attention that was given to stories of oppression in Swedish society. The Swedish journalists, writers, and songwriters affiliated with Chilekommittén by default gravitated toward the stories that could generate the highest impact in Swedish society.

The tropes that form the metanarratives in the interviews are primarily nostalgic for a time of progress. All begin with the story of an underdeveloped Chile that after the election of Allende began moving toward a more modern and just society. Whether the interviewees relate this time of nostalgia in terms of their increased political engagement in an organizational capacity, in terms of betterment of living circumstances or simply in terms of joyful dancing with like-minded young and hopeful people in newly opened nightclubs, the role of the time immediately before the coup is the same: it is described as a time of great promise. After the coup, terror reigned and all these different dreams were extinguished. Some experienced horrendous torture and left the country under dramatic circumstances, others less so, but, either way, the underlying structures remain the same as those carrying the messaging of the political journals of the MIR: a trope of repeated imperialist violations of the natural development of history toward a better society, along with a high degree of political agency inherent in a trope of revolution, in which the subject itself is both able and responsible to work toward a better future. What is remarkable about the community that formed in Gothenburg is that this agency was rooted in a remarkably clear and strong meta-narrative and did not remain a mere range of possible actions. On the contrary, it was actively sought out and enacted through various, more or less activist, approaches. A nostalgic longing for a better past is intimately related to hope for a better future. While some members of the community acted on a local level, others became members of networks of exiled voices that continue to play a role in Chilean politics; these enactments of agency are all rooted in these tropes of nostalgia for an absent better time and place turned into hope for the present – to such a degree that the Chilean migrants became a defining factor in the local cultural landscape reaching from Hammarkullen, Gothenburg, and beyond.

Bibliography

Alfvén, Gösta. 2020. "An Evidence-Based Examination of the Claims of the Modernism Program: The Case of Sweden". *New Design Ideas* 4 (2).

Andersson, Mats and Anders Forsberg. 2010. *Göteborg och dess spårvagnar: bilder från 2000-talets spårvägstrafik*. Stockholm: Trafik-nostalgiska förlaget.

Araya González, Alejandra. 2017. "'No éramos del MIR los pobladores, nosotros estábamos por una necesidad que era la vivienda': los pobladores del campamento Nueva La Habana y el MIR, 1970–1973". *Revista de historia y geografía* 36: 107–39. https://doi.org/10.29344/07194145.36.337.

Arvidsson, Alf. 2010. *Songs with a Message: Common Themes in Swedish 1970s Rock/Folk Songs*. Ann Arbor: Michigan Publishing, University of Michigan Library.

Assmann, Aleida. 2008. "Canon and Archive". In *Cultural Memory Studies: An International and Interdisciplinary Handbook*, edited by Astrid Errl and Ansgar Nünning, 97–107. Berlin and New York: Walter de Gruyter.

Assmann, Jan. 2011. *Cultural Memory and Early Civilization: Writing, Remembrance and Political Imagination*. New York: Cambridge University Press.

Baud, Michiel. 2018. "Between Academia and Civil Society: The Origins of Latin American Studies in the Netherlands". *Latin American Perspectives* 45 (4): 98–114.

Benavente Urbina, Andrés. 1987. "Movimiento de Izquierda Revolucionaria: trayectoria y presente". *Política (Universidad de Chile. Instituto de Ciencia Política)*: 121–55. https://doi.org/10.5354/rp.v0i12.54928.

Berg, Magnus, Håkan Andréasson, and Lennart Zintchenko. 1989. "Två invandrargenerationers svenska boende som det erfarits och värderats av sextio barn till finska, turkiska och chilenska göteborgare". Byggforskningsrådet (gupea.ub.gu.se). https://gupea.ub.gu.se/handle/2077/47129.

Bonnefoy, Pascale. 2016. "Bending the Rules: An Ambassador's Quest to Save Lives". In *Remembering the Rescuers of Victims of Human Rights Crimes in Latin*

America, edited by Marcia Esparza and Carla De Ycaza, 25–56. Lanham, MD, Boulder, CO, New York, and London: Lexington Books.

Boym, Svetlana. 2001. *The Future of Nostalgia*. New York: Basic Books.

Brolinson, Per-Erik. 2007. *Utländska inflytanden på den svenska visan*. Stockholm: Institutionen för musik-och teatervetenskap.

Camacho, Fernando. 2006. "Los asilados de las Embajadas de Europa Occidental en Chile tras el golpe militar y sus consecuencias diplomáticas: El caso de Suecia". *Revista Europea de Estudios Latinoamericanos y del Caribe/European Review of Latin American and Caribbean Studies* 81: 21–41.

Christiaens, Kim. 2014. "Belgium: The Chilean factor & the changing dimensions of solidarity". In *European Solidarity with Chile 1970s–1980s*, edited by Kim Christiaens, Idesbald Goddeeris, and Magaly Rodríguez García, 207–37. Frankfurt am Main: Peter Lang GmbH.

Christiaens, Kim, Magaly Rodriguez Garcia, and Idesbald Goddeeris. 2014. "A Global Perspective on the European Mobilization for Chile (1970s–1980s)". In *European Solidarity with Chile, 1970s–1980s*. Frankfurt am Main: Peter Lang.

De Kievid, Jan. 2013. "Posters of the Dutch Solidarity Movement with Chile (1972–1990)". *European Review of Latin American and Caribbean Studies/Revista Europea de Estudios Latinoamericanos y del Caribe* 95: 109–13.

Ericsson, Urban, Irene Molina, and Per-Markku Ristilammi. 2002. *Miljonprogram och media: föreställningar om människor och förorter*. Trelleborg: Integrationsverket & Riksantikvarieämbetet.

Erll, Astrid. 2004. "Medium des Kollektiven Gedächtnisses: Ein (Erinnerungs-) Kulturwissenschaftlicher Kompaktbegriff". In *Medien des kollektiven Gedächtnisses: Konstruktivität – Historizität – Kulturspezifität*, edited by Astrid Erll and Ansgar Nünning, 3–24. Berlin and New York: Walter de Gruyter.

Faringer, Åsa and Ulf Hultberg. 2007. *The Black Pimpernel*. Sweden: Nordisk Film.

Ferrer Mir, Jaime. n.d. "Memoria Chilena". Biblioteca Nacional de Chile. Accessed January 11, 2023. http://www.memoriachilena.gob.cl.

Gaudichaud, Franck. 2009. "Popular Power, Oral History, and Collective Memory in Contemporary Chile". *Latin American Perspectives* 36 (5): 58–71.

Gradskova, Yulia and Monica Quirico. 2016. *Solidariteten med Chile 1973–1989*. Huddinge: Samtidshistoriska institutet, Södertörns högskola.

Halbwachs, Maurice. 1950. *La mémoire collective*. Paris: Presses universitaires de France.

"Hammarkullen Carnival". 2020. Institutet för språk och folkminnen. https://www.isof.se/other-languages/english/living-traditions/submissions/2020-05-14-hammarkullen-carnival.

Hite, Katherine and Manuela Badilla Rajevic. 2019. "Memorializing in Movement: Chilean Sites of Memory as Spaces of Activism and Imagination". *A Contracorriente: una revista de estudios latinoamericanos* 16 (3): 1–16.

Houlden, Kate. 2010. "Nostalgia for the Past as Guide to the Future: Paule Marshall's The Chosen Place, The Timeless People". *Memory Studies* 3 (3): 253–61.

Hyltén-Cavallius, Sverker. 2016. "Progg: Utopia and Chronotope". In *Made in Sweden*, edited by Alf Björnberg and Thomas Bossius, 64–77. New York: Routledge.

Jelin, Elizabeth. 2003. *State Repression and the Labors of Memory*. Minneapolis: University of Minnesota Press.

Kayser Nielsen, Niels. 2010. *Historiens Forvandlinger: Historiebrug fra Monumenter til Oplevelsesøkonomi.* Aarhus: Aarhus Universitetsforlag.

Kelly, Patrick William. 2013. "The 1973 Chilean coup and the origins of transnational human rights activism". *Journal of Global History* 8 (1): 165–86.

Lindholm, Susan. 2016. *Remembering Chile: An Entangled History of Hip-Hop In-Between Sweden and Chile.* Malmö University, Faculty of Education and Society.

Månsson, Sven-Axel. 2021. *Den politiska generationen: kontinuitet och förändring 1968-2018.* Edited by Svante Lundberg. Lund: Arkiv förlag.

Nardelli, Laura. 2018. "Hammarkullen 365: Bilden av en stadsdels historia". Kultwatch. https://kultwatch.se/hammarkullen-365.

Nilsson, Ann-Sofie. 1991. "Swedish Social Democracy in Central America: The Politics of Small State Solidarity". *Journal of Interamerican Studies and World Affairs* 33 (3): 169–99. https://doi.org/10.2307/165937.

Olsson, Gunnar. 2007. *Abysmal: A Critique of Cartographic Reason.* Chicago, IL: University of Chicago Press.

Olsson, Gunnar. 2018. *Conversation in Uppsala.* Edited by Sjamme van de Voort, Moniek Driesse, and Ingrid Holmberg.

Olsson, Gunnar. 2020. *Arkography: A Grand Tour through the Taken-for-Granted.* University of Nebraska Press.

Östberg, Kjell. 2021. *Folk i rörelse: vår demokratis historia.* Stockholm: Ordfront.

Padilla, Fernando Camacho. 2006. "La diáspora chilena y su confrontación con la Embajada de Chile en Suecia, 1973-1982". In *Exiliados, emigrados y retornados: chilenos en América y Europa, 1973-2004.*

Padilla, Fernando Camacho. 2014. "Las relaciones entre Chile y Suecia durante el primer gobierno de Olof Palme, 1969-1976". *Iberoamericana (Madrid, Spain)* 7 (25): 65–85. https://doi.org/10.18441/ibam.7.2007.25.65-85.

Padilla, Fernando Camacho. 2015. "The Swedish-Chilean Society. Fascist Solidarity with Pinochet's Chile in Sweden". In *Making Sense of the Americas: How Protest Related to America in the 1980s and Beyond,* edited by Jan Hansen, Christian Helm, and Frank Reichherzer. Frankfurt am Main: Campus Verlag.

Perry, Mariana. 2016. "'With a Little Help from My Friends': The Dutch Solidarity Movement and the Chilean Struggle for Democracy". *European Review of Latin American and Caribbean Studies/Revista Europea de Estudios Latinoamericanos y del Caribe* 101: 75–96.

Sernhede, Ove. 2021. "Hammarkullen – Mellan Motstånd och Stigma". *Ord&Bild* 3-4: 135–44.

Serpente, Alejandra. 2015. "Diasporic Constellations: The Chilean Exile Diaspora Space as a Multidirectional Landscape of Memory". *Memory Studies* 8 (1): 49–61.

Smith, Laurajane and Gary Campbell. 2017. "'Nostalgia for the Future': Memory, Nostalgia and the Politics of Class". *International Journal of Heritage Studies* 23 (7): 612–27.

van de Voort, Sjamme, Hannah Smyth, Rebecca Staats, Nicolás Villaroel, and Laurajane Smith. 2021. "Five Scenarios of Placement: Q&A". Memory Studies Association Fifth Annual Conference: "Convergences", Warsaw (online), July 5–9. https://msaconferencewarsaw.dryfta.com/16246275761/program-schedule/program/164/k6-five-scenarios-of-placement-towards-new-conceptualisations-of-place-in-memory-or-memory-in-place.

van der Lee, Pedro. 1997. "Latin American influences in Swedish popular music". *Popular Music and Society* 21 (2): 17–45.

Wright, Thomas C. and Rody Oñate Zúniga. 2007. "Chilean Political Exile". *Latin American Perspectives* 34 (4): 31–49.

Zintchenko, Lennart. 1993. *Nybyggarstadsdelen Hammarkullen i ett föränderligt Sverige*. Gothenburg: Byggforskningsrådet.

Index

Figures are indicated by the use of italic while tables have bold page numbers. Notes have 'n' after the page number.

www.ingramcontent.com/pod-product-compliance
Ingram Content Group UK Ltd.
Pitfield, Milton Keynes, MK11 3LW, UK
UKHW022109170825

461980UK00005B/103

9 789523 691308